whole grain Breads
by machine or hand

200 Delicious, Healthful, Simple Recipes

Beatrice Ojakangas

WILEY

Wiley Publishing, Inc.

Published by Wiley Publishing, Inc., Hoboken, New Jersey

For general information on our other products and services or to obtain technical support please contact our Customer Care Department within the U.S. at 800-762-2974, outside the U.S. at 317-572-3993 or fax 317-572-4002.

Wiley also publishes its books in a variety of electronic formats. Some content that appears in print may not be available in electronic books.

Library of Congress Cataloging-in-Publication Data:

Ojakangas, Beatrice A.
    Whole grain breads by machine or hand : 200 delicious, healthful,
simple recipes / by Beatrice A. Ojakangas. -- 1st ed.
            p. cm.
Includes index.
    ISBN-10 0-7645-3825-X (Paperback : alk. paper)
    ISBN-13 978-0-7645-3825-4 (Paperback : alk. paper)
1. Bread I. Title.
TX769 .O387   1998
641.8'15--dc22   2003023272

Cover photographs: Tom Eckerle

Manufactured in the United States of America

10 9 8 7 6 5

For Isä, my late father, who felt that if there was no bread in the house there was nothing to eat, and my mother, Esther Luoma, who baked the bread.

CONTENTS

FOREWORD

My mother says I was a hungry baby. Like most mothers, she looked forward to the time I would sleep through the night. One day she discovered that a piece of buttered bread set beside my crib was the answer to a night's rest. I would wake up in the middle of the night, hungry; reach for the bread and gnaw on it until I was satisfied; then go back to sleep.

Bread has always been my favorite food. On the small farm in northern Minnesota where I grew up, our kitchen was busy. My mother baked bread at least twice a week to feed the large family, hired men, and anybody who came in the kitchen door. I stood at her elbow when I was tall enough and watched her punch the dough, pinch off big round loaves, fire up the wood stove, and bake the rye loaves. Then, hot out of the oven, they were smeared with butter.

Bread is one of the miracles of life, physically symbolized by the fact that I can carry into the kitchen a sack of flour in one trip, but I cannot carry out of the kitchen in one trip all the loaves that that flour produced. And, as I've kneaded and shaped, measured and weighed, punched high-tech buttons, I've reflected on the miracle.

ACKNOWLEDGMENTS

A warm "thank you" goes to all those who so generously encouraged me with this book. Recipe ideas, enthusiasm, positive and creative comments inspired me to complete *Whole Grain Breads by Machine or Hand.* Just when I was about to run out of steam, another inspiration would come along through an unexpected source: One Sunday I was overwhelmed by the most descriptive, bread-of-life sermon I've ever expected to hear in church, delivered by Michael D. Wucher.

Thanks to Elise Simon Goodman and Arnold Goodman, for taking care of business.

There are many to thank for assistance in this writing and testing project. Among them are: Marilyn Wise at Toastmaster for her expert advice and for assistance with equipment; Ann Parrish and Mary Jo Exley, consultants for Electric Bread; and Cherine Berg at Sanyo Fisher products.

I also wish to thank Fleischman's, SAF, and Red Star yeast for their enthusiastic support and for the yeast supply. And to King Arthur Flour for their enthusiasm, creative input, and grains and flours that provided inspiration.

Without the support of my family, our circle of personal and professional friends, who number too many to name (you know who you are), this book would have never come together. Thanks to you all!

INTRODUCTION

Baking bread from scratch at home is an old idea. It spans generations, centuries, even thousands of years. When old ideas are revived, they usually come back in a new form.

I remember as a child (I'm the oldest of ten children), my mother baking all of our bread. We lived on a farm, and it was just part of the routine to bake twenty to thirty loaves two or three times a week. I took sandwiches made of homemade bread to school. Many of my friends, whose mothers I thought were either "rich or wasteful," brought sandwiches made with bakery bread. Kids wouldn't trade sandwiches with me; and later when I baked all my own family's bread, my kids had the same experience. They wanted bread that "folds." Although we continued to enjoy homemade bread, I realized that homemade bread baking was becoming a rare skill. It was more fashionable and convenient to buy bread.

My mother's bread pan now hangs on my wall as a kind of reminder of my roots. It holds about five gallons, big enough to make a batch of dough based on a gallon of liquid. When the dough had risen until huge and dome shaped, she pinched off loaves and filled round pans, then fired up the wood stove and started baking. To me, there is still nothing quite like bread baked in the oven of a wood stove!

Undaunted by the heckling and teasing, I was fascinated by the process of bread baking; so as a fifteen-year-old girl, I demonstrated the making of Finnish rye bread in a 4-H program and won a national grand championship with my presentation at the Minnesota State

Fair. People were fascinated by the fact that one could actually bake bread from scratch! Seven years later, my cornmeal and molasses-based Chunk-o'-Cheese bread won the second grand prize at the Pillsbury Bake-Off. Why? I was told later that it was the first time anybody dared to tamper with a basic technique. I had kneaded chunks of cheese into the dough before baking. Evidently, it was a creative breakthrough in bread baking. A few years later, in 1962 when I was on the staff of *Sunset Magazine,* I wrote the first, very revolutionary, article on bread baking for the magazine. My idea was that you can create all kinds of breads by varying a simple basic formula: 1 cup of liquid, 3 cups of flour, 1 package of yeast. Even the men on the editorial staff began to bring in wonderful loaves of bread that they had created at home. The article encouraged people to be creative with different flavors, textures, and grains. All this time, we used the basic "by hand" method of mixing, kneading, and baking breads. Baking bread at home was experiencing a renewal.

When food processors became part of the standard American kitchen, the new "machine age" in bread baking had begun. In response to the boom, I developed two hundred recipes for mixing bread dough in the food processor.

Now, the automatic bread machine has become a standard in some six million households (this is a conservative estimate), and I have had many requests to design recipes for whole grain breads to use with the bread machine. As a result, now anybody can get healthy, delicious, whole-grain loaves at home, despite his or her hectic schedule.

Throughout all of these evolutions, the basic ingredients for making wonderful bread dough have remained the same. All that has changed is the method of mixing and baking. Again, bread baking has experienced a renewal.

You can bake delicious, healthy whole grain breads by hand. Or you can use the bread machine to mix, knead, proof, and bake the bread. Or you can use either the food processor or the bread machine to mix and knead the dough, and then shape the dough by hand into any form you desire. In other words, once the dough is mixed, kneaded, and proofed in a machine (the messy part), the final shaping, rising, and baking (the fun part) can be done by hand. All of the recipes in this book include appropriate directions. That is, when a bread can be made from start to finish in the bread machine, the recipe will indicate that. Of course, a braided loaf will never turn out to be a braided loaf when it is baked in a bread machine, so the directions for braiding the dough and baking it conventionally are provided.

Machine mixing and proofing does not preclude creativity. Combining flavors when selecting ingredients is creative. Handling the dough and shaping it is creative. All you miss is the messy part.

The food processor, of course, does not afford the possibility of baking the bread, too. You, the bread baker, will need to proof the dough, shape it, let it rise, and bake it as if you had mixed the dough by hand or in the bread machine.

I have used a heavy-duty mixer with a dough hook for many years for mixing bread doughs. The bowls range from 3 to 5-quart size, which work well for the regular- and large-sized loaves in this book. For the sampler size, I use the flat beater rather than the dough hook because it is such a small amount of dough. The heavy-duty mixer with a dough hook is great for batches of dough that take up to 8 or 9 cups of flour—so it can handle a doubled recipe easily. Neither the food processor nor any of the bread machines can handle as much volume.

Yeast bread recipes today serve a different purpose from those of two generations ago, when recipes were written with ingredients in such massive quantities that the whole operation was a major production. Today, baking a loaf of bread can be as manageable a task as mixing up a batch of cookies. And the results can be even more dramatic and satisfying. Machines have given us flexibility, too. Using the food processor, you can mix up a loaf of bread in seconds. Using the bread machine, you just measure the ingredients and push a button; and you can even delay the mixing and baking so that the bread is ready when you want it. Or you can simply let the machine mix the dough for you—my personal favorite option because I love handling and shaping the dough. I think that the bread actually tastes better when I shape and bake it conventionally.

Breads made with whole grain flours have properties that most white breads do not. They usually have a finer grain and are more compact. Whole grain flours have less gluten than does white wheat flour, and therefore, the dough is stickier to handle. The balance of flour to liquid is critical but not difficult. The recipes in this book have been tested over and over again to ensure that each one makes a perfectly delicious loaf of bread that stays moist and tasty.

THE BREAD BAKER'S ART

Baking wonderful yeast breads is an art as well as a science. The balance of ingredients, particularly when working with a bread machine, is critical; that is what makes the process a science. A machine cannot think any more than a computer can. It just does what you tell it to do. The magic touch remains with the baker, and his or her good judgment is still a factor. A baker can feel when there's enough flour and when the balance is right.

But regardless of the method, bread is made of two basic ingredients: flour and water. (Yeast-risen loaves, obviously, need yeast.) The most important ingredient after flour and water is salt, which controls the growth of the yeast and brings out flavors. All further ingredients—such as sugars, fats, spices, seeds, sourdough starters, other liquids, and varieties of flours—are ingredients that the baker-artist uses to create loaves of many flavors and beauty. Successful creations don't hang around a long time, so part of the art of the baker is to be able to repeat the creation. That is why it is so important to learn basic skills, to know your ingredients, to understand the principles, and to have good recipes to follow.

The Egyptians were the first to perfect bread baking. It's amazing to realize that the proportions of flour to water that the ancient Egyptians used is still the same today, and that it doesn't matter what method you use in mixing the two together. It can be done by hand or food processor or heavy-duty mixer or automatic bread machine. Flour will absorb just so much liquid when you're making a bread dough. Three parts of flour to one part water. That's it. Any more water and you've got a porridge. Any less and you've got moist crumbs. Of course, other ingredients may add liquid or absorbing power to a mixture. That's why recipes for some breads have more or less liquid and flour.

Today, there is great interest in whole grain breads: hearty, handsome, toothsome breads; breads with texture; and breads with character. It may be because we're better traveled, and we've tasted the hefty rye breads of Scandinavia, Germany, and Russia. It may be because we feel that whole grain breads are healthier. In all cases, we know that whole grain breads are delicious and satisfying to eat.

People who have discovered the joy of baking yeast breads will tell you that it is one of the most satisfying experiences in the kitchen. Machines have simply made it easier to do it. From my experiences as a teacher, one of the most frustrating parts of making yeast breads is to get through that initial mixing process. It's fun when you get the dough to a soft and workable stage. Making doughs in the food processor or in the bread machine will give you this. Other pleasures come from allowing the bread machine to mix, knead, and bake. You can wake up in the morning or walk in the door after a busy day to the aroma of freshly baked bread, if you simply push the right buttons.

That's what this book is all about! Here are some fabulous breads for you, your family, and your guests.

ABOUT AUTOMATIC BREAD MACHINES

When bread machines began to be a topic of discussion among bread bakers like me, I thought they were just another expensive gadget. About that time, we had a Finnish student staying with us, a lovely young woman from Helsinki. Her father had fallen in love with bread machines. Her mother ran a cookware wholesale and retail outlet in Finland and was an excellent, creative cook; but it was her father who baked loaves and loaves of bread. I wondered about that. Finnish breads, to my mind, were so good that I thought there wouldn't be any reason to launch into the use of a bread machine. But it was one way to protest the high prices of the Finnish bakeries. This was in the late 1980s, and the price of a decent loaf of bread was well over ten dollars, translated into American money. We were invited to a party at their home; and during the party, Kaappo had baked, and continued to bake, several loaves of wonderfully grainy, tasty bread.

Whether you are a novice or an expert baker, you, too, can have a lot of pleasure baking breads and making yeast doughs using a bread machine. Many of us are pushed for time and sometimes even for counter space! With a bread machine, you can measure all of the ingredients into the machine, push buttons, and either have beautifully baked bread in a few hours or perfect yeast dough, ready for shaping and baking in less than two hours. You can explore all kinds of new taste combinations, and even experiment with various methods of bread baking, such as sourdough and sponge dough.

Selecting a Bread Machine

There are lots of choices of bread machines on the market. Prices range from less than one hundred to more than three hundred dollars, so finding one to suit your budget should not pose a problem. In fact, I've found name-brand bread machines in local discount stores at much less than their list prices. So how do you choose?

Check the Loaf Size and Shape

1. Loaf size commonly ranges from 1 to $2^1/2$ pounds; the $1^1/2$ and 2 pound sizes are the most popular. A machine that bakes a larger loaf will not necessarily be more expensive than one that bakes a small, 1-pound loaf. Remember that you can always bake a smaller loaf in a larger pan, but not vice-versa.

2. Bread machines bake either square, rectangular, or cylindrical loaves. The shape might seem strange at first, but you can adapt the way in which you slice the bread. The traditional loaf shape, however, is also available with some machines.

Look at the Various Features

1. The selection of cycles: *Basic, French Bread, Whole Wheat, Sweet Bread,* and *Fruit and Nut.* (For the latter cycle, a beep tells you when to add ingredients so they remain intact.)

2. Crust color selection: *Light, Medium,* or *Dark*.

3. *Dough* cycle: handy for making doughs for pizza, coffeecakes, rolls, and all shaped breads.

4. *Delay-Start* option (timer): allows you to program when you want the bread (or dough) to be done so that you can wake or come home to fresh bread or dough that's ready to shape and bake yourself.

5. *Keep Warm* feature: has replaced the "cool down" feature on older machines; some newer machines can keep the bread warm for an hour or longer.

6. Additional features: newer machines have cycles for making quick breads, jam, or rice and even a separate bake cycle that can be used for breadsticks or other special breads. One machine will even churn fresh butter!

Look at the Style of the Machine Itself

Your bread machine must be something you like to look at. Most of them are white metal and plastic, but some are have a stainless steel case. Some have large windows, and each model looks a little different.

There are several model and style choices within each brand of machine, so it is impossible to name a brand that's "the best." It depends on the model. But one thing is true—most machines do an excellent job when it comes to mixing, kneading, and baking bread. Every machine I've worked with has done a lot of work, and the problems have been minimal.

Maintenance of a Bread Machine

It is important to keep your machine clean. Each time you mix or bake a loaf of bread, remove the dough paddle and wash the inside of the pan. If you have trouble removing the paddle, pour enough water into the pan to cover the paddle and allow it to soak for a few minutes. Then dump out the water, hold onto the moving part on the underside of the pan with one hand and wiggle the paddle with your other hand. Never immerse the entire pan in dishwater or wash it in the dishwasher.

With the machine unplugged, clean the interior of the oven with a damp cloth to remove flour and crumbs.

Working with a Bread Machine

The thing to remember is that a bread machine is just a machine. It can't think. It's imperative that measurements are accurate (see the section on measuring). It is also important to get to know your own machine. It is helpful if you know what to look for in a perfect yeast dough. Check the dough about halfway through the first kneading cycle. If the dough is very soft and sticky, (a result of inaccurate measurements, or high humidity),

add more flour, a tablespoonful at a time, while the machine is kneading. If the dough is very dry and feels very firm to the touch, add water, a teaspoonful at a time.

If I find that the dough is extremely dry, I remove the dough from the machine, cut it into pieces, put it back into the machine, and then sprinkle additional water over it so it can be worked into the dough more easily. If I notice this near the end of the first kneading cycle, and I am making dough only, I sometimes reprogram the machine to start at the beginning again.

Learning to Mix Whole Grain Breads by Machine

Working with bread machines, I've had to look at bread recipes from a different perspective. While I've always used the old Finnish method of basing a bread recipe on the amount of liquid (Finnish bakers still talk about their "liter" batches of bread), I've had to base bread machine recipes on the amount of flour per recipe.

I've worked out the breads in this book into recipes based on 2, 3, and 4 cups of flour. My family has especially come to love the small "sampler" loaf of bread, based on 2 cups of flour, for a breakfast bread. This makes a loaf that is just about the right amount for breakfast, plus a couple of sandwiches for lunch. It weighs about 1 pound, depending on the variety of ingredients used. The 3-cups-of-flour loaf (the "regular" loaf) is about right for a small family; and the large loaf, based on 4 cups of flour, is great for a party.

Measuring for the Bread Machine

The main difference between the recipes in this book and traditional bread recipes is the amount of flour called for. Recipes for by-hand baking call for a variable amount of flour, for example, 2 to $2^{1}/4$ cups or 3 to $3^{1}/2$ cups. This leads to an important issue: accurate measuring. *I cannot emphasize enough the importance of careful measuring when baking bread in the bread machine.*

Measuring Liquids

Always use a clear measuring cup, the kind with a spout. Place the measure on a level surface and pour in the liquid to the exact mark on the cup. Pour it into the container of the bread machine or set it aside for adding to the food processor. If the measure calls for a tablespoon of something liquid, pour it into a measuring spoon not a tablespoon to be used as flatware.

Measuring Dry Ingredients

Always use measuring cups that come in a nested set. First stir the flour; then spoon (don't scoop) it into the cup. Level it off with a straightedge. I always keep a wooden chopstick in my flour bin to use for leveling. Measure teaspoon and tablespoon amounts with measuring spoons and level them off in the same way.

About Bread Baking and Humidity

The actual measure of flour or water may vary because of climate conditions. When the humidity is high (over 60 percent), flour and other ingredients absorb moisture from the air; therefore, you need to add less liquid to a recipe. When the humidity is very low (less than 40 percent), flour dries out and you need to add more liquid or less flour to the recipe. Whether a baker measures or weighs the ingredients, the amounts will vary according to the humidity. Professional bakers usually weigh their ingredients because they're working with large amounts. For home bakers, it is more practical to measure (be sure to read the measuring information). In each recipe, I have indicated when and how much flour or water to add to correct the dough if it is either too soft and sticky or too stiff and dry. When a dough is too soft and sticky, I say to add 1 tablespoon of flour to the dough at a time until the dough forms a firm, but still slightly tacky ball (it should feel similar to touching almost-dry paint). For dough that is too stiff and feels as firm as the modeling clay that kids play with, add water 1 teaspoon at a time. As I've indicated, water absorbs three times its measure of flour; so to balance 1 tablespoon of excess flour in a dough, you need to add 1 teaspoon of water.

TROUBLESHOOTING BREAD MACHINE BREADS: PROBLEMS AND POSSIBLE CAUSES

Loaf is "short," it did not rise to fill the pan:

1. If you bake a sampler loaf (1 pound) in a larger capacity pan (2- to 2^1/$_2$-pound size) do not expect it to fill the pan.

2. Try another cycle. The one you used didn't allow enough time for rising. Check the charts in the manual that came with your machine, and select another cycle that has a longer rising time.

3. The ingredients may have been too hot or too cold (see "Yeast" in "About Ingredients," below).

4. The yeast was old—check the expiration date.

5. You used active dry yeast instead of quick-rising, fast-rising, or bread machine yeast, which rise more quickly.

6. Too much salt inhibited the yeast action. Did you add it twice?

7. Whole grain breads have a tendency to be shorter than white breads.

Loaf did not rise at all:

1. The blade was not set properly in the pan.

2. The yeast had expired or was mishandled.

3. The yeast was omitted.

Bread was underbaked and gummy at the core:

1. The recipe was too large for the pan.

2. The dough was too rich; it had too much butter, sugar, or eggs, candied fruits, nuts, or grains.

3. You used the wrong cycle—check the machine's manual.

Loaf collapsed:

1. Too much liquid was used.

2. If the salt is omitted, the bread will overrise and then collapse.

3. The dough exceeded the pan's capacity.

4. Warm weather and/or high humidity caused the dough to rise too quickly.

5. There was too much sugar in the recipe.

6. You didn't use enough flour.

7. Too much yeast was added.

Open, coarse or holey texture:

1. Too much liquid was used.

2. You may have used too much yeast. Note that quick-rising yeast and bread machine yeast rise more quickly than regular active dry yeast. Did you use the appropriate yeast?

3. The salt was omitted.

4. Warm weather and/or high humidity caused the dough to rise too quickly.

Bread overflows the machine's pan:

1. Too much yeast was added. Was the recipe developed for regular active dry yeast? If so, using quick-rising yeast will cause loaf to rise too much.

2. There was too much liquid.

3. There was too much sugar.

4. Warm weather and/or high humidity caused the dough to rise too quickly.

5. The recipe was too large for the pan.

6. Either the salt was omitted or not enough was added.

Heavy texture, gnarly looking top:

1. Too little water, sugar, or yeast was added.

2. There was too much flour.

3. Excess whole grains or dried fruits sucked up too much of the liquid.

4. Flour had dried out, as during times of very low humidity.

5. Inaccurate measure of flour. Be sure to stir the flour when measuring, then spoon into the cup and level the top with a straightedge. Scooping the flour into the cup usually packs several extra tablespoonfuls of flour into each cup, which will dramatically affect the final results.

TROUBLESHOOTING TRADITIONAL DOUGH METHODS

I pulled up to a stoplight in Duluth one day. A woman in the car in the next lane was waving her arms wildly trying to get my attention. I thought I might be called on to make a good samaritan rescue, but when I rolled down my window she shouted, "My husband used to make good bread, but now he makes doorstops! What's wrong?" The light changed. I shouted out my window, "He probably killed the yeast!"

Rising problems By far, the most common problem among home bakers has to do with whether or not the dough rises. The secondary problem has to do with temperature. Using ingredients that are too warm will kill the yeast. Trying to speed the rising process, and thereby overheating the dough, is also a common mistake. Using ingredients that are too cool stunts the growth of the yeast (something like pouring ice water onto houseplants); and trying to proof dough in a too-cool environment retards the dough, which then will require more time to double in volume.

Dough problems Dough that is too stiff and dry will not rise well and will produce a dry, tasteless bread, unless more liquid is added to it. To do this, chop the dough into pieces, put it back into the food processor or into a mixer with a dough hook, and add water, 1 tablespoon at a time. You can do this at any time, even if you've already set the dough to rise. Dough that is too wet will rise and become bubbly and impossible to handle. Even after it has been rising for a while, you can add more flour, but be sure to mix in a small amount of flour at a time to avoid adding it too unevenly (which would produce flour streaks in the finished loaf). Be aware that whole grain breads will normally feel stickier than all white breads.

Texture problems Less-than-perfect texture is related to both dough problems and rising problems. Bread that has overrisen will have a crumbly, open texture, but so will a bread made with a dough that is very wet. A tight, dry texture indicates a dough that hasn't risen sufficiently or that was too dry to begin with.

Baking problems An oven that is too hot will brown the bread before the center is cooked. An oven that is not hot enough will produce pale-crusted bread; and because it will need additional baking time, the bread will be dry. Check the oven temperature with a mercury thermometer. Also, be sure not to crowd loaves of bread in the oven; allow for circulation between pans and between the pans and the sides of the oven.

Baking on a stone is most satisfactory with simple breads. Breads that include eggs, milk, sugar and fats are best baked in traditional pans or on a baking sheet.

About Ingredients

Flour

By volume, flour is the primary ingredient in bread. Most of the recipes in this book call for *bread flour* in addition to whole grain flours, because it contains more gluten than all-purpose white flour. Gluten is one of the proteins in flour: it is a tough, elastic, grayish substance that resembles chewing gum when wet. It's the gluten in bread flour that, when the dough is kneaded, helps form the elastic meshwork that traps the gas bubbles formed by yeast and makes the bread rise, creating a light structure.

Gluten flour, sometimes called "vital gluten," is high-protein, hard-wheat flour treated to remove most of the starch, leaving a high gluten content. It can be used as an additive to doughs made with low-gluten flour, such as rye flour. When making and baking multigrain breads in the automatic bread machine, gluten flour, added by the tablespoonful, can make the difference between success and failure. Some of the breads in this book call for gluten to balance the high-gluten bread flour with the low-gluten whole grain flours. When there is less than 50 percent bread flour in a recipe, it is helpful to add gluten. Most bread flour contains 14 grams of protein per cup; whereas gluten flour contains 36 grams of protein (gluten) per cup. So the addition of 1 or 2 tablespoons of gluten will boost the rising power of most whole grain breads.

Yeast

There are basically two different kinds of active dry yeast on the market. Regular active dry yeast has been around for many years. Rapid-rising, quick-rising, fast-rising, instant-acting dry, and bread machine yeast were introduced to the market within the last ten years. The rapid-rising yeasts are a different strain of yeast from the old active dry yeast and cut the rising time considerably.

All of the recipes in this book were tested with rapid-rising, quick-rising, instant-acting or bread machine yeast as opposed to the active dry yeast, unless the recipe specifies otherwise. Breads that are mixed by hand work well with either kind of yeast. If you plan to refrigerate the dough, then be sure to use the regular active dry yeast. Instant- or quick-rising yeasts were not designed for refrigerated doughs.

How much yeast? The rule-of-thumb measurement for yeast is to use 1/2 teaspoon yeast per cup of flour in the recipe. This amount can vary, and some of the recipes in this book call for a slightly different proportion.

Heat and humidity affect yeast action. When the weather is warm and humid, yeast action speeds up; in cold weather it slows down. During hot weather, if your dough rises too much and collapses, reduce the amount of yeast by one-quarter or more. Or try using cold liquids and avoid using the *Delay-Start* feature on your machine.

Store unopened yeast in a cool, dry place. Use a dry spoon to measure yeast, and store opened jars of yeast in the freezer or refrigerator. Yeast should be used within four months after opening the jar or before the date on the label, whichever comes first.

There are several varieties of yeast that you can use to make bread either by hand or by machine.

Regular Active Dry Yeast

Regular active dry yeast has been freeze-dried. It should be stored in the refrigerator or freezer and should be good until the expiration date that is stamped on the package. It is available in $1/4$-ounce packets, containing $2^1/4$ teaspoons yeast, or in 4-ounce jars in most grocery stores. It is available in bulk at whole foods cooperatives where it should be kept refrigerated, and you can buy it in 1-pound packages. I usually empty a bag of yeast into a jar with a tight-fitting cover and keep it in the freezer, removing a small amount at a time as I need it. For bread machine recipes, you may need to use one-quarter to one-half more regular active dry yeast than instant-acting, bread machine, or quick-rising yeast.

Compressed Fresh Yeast

Compressed fresh yeast is the same strain of yeast as regular active dry, only it has not been freeze-dried. Although it can be used in bread machines, the recipes in this book were tested only with dry yeast.

Instant-Acting, Bread Machine, and Rapid-Rising Yeast

Instant-acting yeast is a different strain of yeast from regular active dry yeast and is noticeably finer grained. Use $1/2$ teaspoon of rapid-rising yeast per cup of flour in most recipes. This yeast generally cuts rising time and is recommended for bread machines. For nonwheat breads, you may have better luck using regular active dry yeast, because the gluten structure is more fragile; and if the bread rises too quickly, it may collapse during baking.

Water and Other Liquids

Water rehydrates and activates yeast and blends with the flour to make a dough. You can use milk in place of water, or you can replace the milk called for in a recipe with water. To enrich the dough, add $1/3$ cup instant nonfat dry milk per cup of water to the dry ingredients. Milk gives bread good volume, makes the crust golden, and produces a cream-colored crumb.

For bread machine baking, water should be at approximately room temperature, between 70° and 80°F. When dissolving yeast in water, the water temperature should be between 105° and 115°F. When adding water to dry ingredients that include the dry yeast, as when using the food processor method, the temperature of the water should be between 120° and 130°F.

In bread doughs, other ingredients may add to the liquid balance; and it's not always obvious. Ingredients such as cheeses, sour cream, vegetables, fruits, and applesauce alter the amount of liquid in a recipe. Sourdough starter is another liquid ingredient; and if you made it according to the recipe in this book, it counts for half the liquid in a bread recipe, because it is made with half flour, half liquid.

Eggs count as a liquid in bread recipes. They also add color, richness, and leavening to the bread.

Sugar, honey and molasses add flavor to the bread and give the crust a golden color, because they increase the browning power. A large amount of sugar in a bread can make the bread brown too much. Depending on your bread machine (if you are baking the bread in the machine), you may need to select the "light" crust option. Because sugar feeds the yeast, an excessive amount of sugar may make bread rise too much. Too much sugar can also alter the liquid-to-flour balance in bread.

Fats

Butter, shortening, and oil will lubricate the dough, give breads a longer shelf life, and make the bread more tender and flavorful. Too much fat inhibits rising. When adding butter or solid shortening, cut it up into small pieces so that it will mix in better. Be careful that the fat does not come in contact with the yeast, as it inhibits the dissolving of the yeast.

Salt

Salt controls yeast action and strengthens the gluten structure of the dough. Obviously, it also adds flavor.

ABOUT ORGANIZATION

Many baking problems, especially when working with bread machines, occur because ingredients were left out or added twice. The recipes in this book call for adding the liquid ingredients first, followed by the fat, and then the dry ingredients and ending with the yeast on top.

If your manufacturer calls for a different order, you can follow that order, but be sure that the yeast is kept separate from the liquids, fat, and salt.

When using the *Delay-Start* feature on a bread machine, place the ingredients in the pan so that the yeast is not in contact with the salt, liquid, or fat. I like to dig a small hole in the dry flour and measure the yeast into it.

When you start baking, set all the ingredients on your counter in the order in which you will add them. It helps to check off the ingredients when following a recipe that has many small added items, such as spices, seeds, and herbs.

About Storing Bread

Never store bread in the refrigerator. Refrigerating bread causes it to age and stale quickly. It is much better stored either at room temperature or in a cool place. To keep extra bread fresh for everyday use, slice it and put it into an airtight container or sealable bag and place in the freezer. After that, you can take out just enough bread for immediate use. Bread that is in the process of being cut and sliced is best stored without plastic; simply place the cut side down on a bread board.

Basic Wheat Bread

Blueberry Bread and Butter Pudding

Buttermilk Wheat Bread

Walnut Pesto

Baked Raclette with Croutons

Honey Whole Wheat Bread

One Hundred Percent Whole Wheat Bread

Beautiful Light Wheat Bread

Apple Brown Bread Betty

Green Salad with Spicy Wheat Croutons

Cracked Wheat Bread

English Granary Bread

Light Wheat Brioche

Summer Pudding with Raspberry Sauce

Milk and Honey Wheat Bread

Herbed Wild Mushroom Pâté

Honey Orange Bread Pudding

Norwegian Wheat Bread

Tuscan Bread

Tuscan Bruschetta

Navy Bean Salad

Panzanella (Italian Bread Salad)

Honey Raspberry Toasts

BASIC BREADS

*T*his is a selection of classic whole grain breads from all over the world. These breads depend on the balance of whole wheat flour to bread flour and variations in liquid, shortening, and sweetening ingredients to distinguish them from one another.

Most of these breads have a classic shape in which they are generally baked. In bread machines, they have been tested on the basic cycle, because it is the most consistently available cycle, and the dough cycle.

These are all delicious, simple breads that are ideal for the most basic delights of bread eating, such as simply hot and buttered, toasted and for use in sandwiches. Once they are at least a day old, these breads are perfect for croutons, rusks, bread puddings, and other recipes.

BASIC WHEAT BREAD

You can use this basic recipe to design your own bread. For instance, you can leave out the sugar, butter or shortening, and milk for a fat-free, sugar-free, or dairy-free bread. You can also use all white flour or another whole grain flour in place of the whole wheat or rye flour with little change in the basic loaf. You can include herbs, nuts, or dried fruits. (See the "Introduction" for more information about the balance of liquid to flour, which varies from season to season, depending on humidity!)

Sampler Loaf

2/3 cup water

1 tablespoon sugar

1 tablespoon butter or shortening

3/4 teaspoon salt

1/4 cup nonfat dry milk

3/4 cup whole wheat or rye flour

11/4 cups bread flour

1 teaspoon rapid-rising or active
    dry yeast

Regular Loaf

1 cup water

2 tablespoons sugar

11/2 tablespoons butter
    or shortening

11/2 teaspoons salt

1/2 cup nonfat dry milk

1 cup whole wheat or rye flour

2 cups bread flour

11/2 teaspoons rapid-rising or
    active dry yeast

Large Loaf

11/3 cups water

3 tablespoons sugar

2 tablespoons butter
    or shortening

2 teaspoons salt

3/4 cup nonfat dry milk

11/2 cups whole wheat or
    rye flour

21/2 cups bread flour

2 teaspoons rapid-rising or
    active dry yeast

TO MIX THE DOUGH BY HAND Heat the water until warm, between 105° and 115°F; pour it into a large, warmed bowl, and add the yeast and sugar. Let stand 5 minutes, until the yeast begins to bubble. Stir in the butter, salt, dry milk, and whole wheat flour. Beat well. Cover, and let stand 15 minutes. Slowly add the bread flour, and beat until a soft dough forms. Turn the dough out onto a very lightly floured board, and knead, adding flour if necessary, until smooth and springy, about 5 minutes. Wash the bowl and grease it; place the dough back in the bowl, and turn it over to grease the top. Cover, and let rise until doubled, about 1 hour.

TO MIX THE DOUGH WITH A HEAVY-DUTY MIXER Heat the water until warm, between 105° and 115°F; pour it into the warmed mixing bowl, and add the yeast and sugar. Let stand 5 minutes, until the yeast begins to bubble. Add the butter, salt, dry milk, and whole wheat flour. Beat well. Cover, and let stand 15 minutes. Slowly add the bread flour, and beat until a soft dough forms. Knead the dough in the mixer with the dough hook, on medium to high speed, adding flour as necessary, until the dough pulls away from the sides of the bowl and is smooth and springy but still soft to the touch. Remove the dough hook, cover the bowl, and let the dough rise until doubled, about 1 hour.

TO MIX THE DOUGH IN THE FOOD PROCESSOR Place the plastic dough blade into the work bowl. Heat the water until very warm, between 120° and 130°F; set aside. Place the remaining ingredients into the work bowl. Turn the processor on, and slowly pour the water through the feed tube, processing until the dough is smooth and pulls away from the sides of the bowl. If the dough is wet and sticky, add more flour, 1 tablespoon at a time, until the dough is smooth yet soft to the touch. If the dough is not soft to the touch but is very firm, add 1 tablespoon of water at a time, and process until the dough is smooth yet soft to the touch. Cover the work bowl, and let the dough rise until doubled, about 1 hour. Or remove the dough to a lightly greased bowl, cover, and let rise until doubled, about 1 hour.

TO MIX THE DOUGH IN THE BREAD MACHINE Pour the water (at room temperature) into the pan, and add the remaining ingredients, except the yeast. Make a small indentation in the dry ingredients, and add the yeast. Select *Dough,* and press *Start.* If the dough is wet and sticky, add more flour, 1 tablespoon at a time, until the dough is smooth yet soft to the touch. If the dough is not soft to the touch but is very firm, add 1 teaspoon of water at a time, until the dough is smooth yet soft to the touch. The machine will stop when the dough is ready to shape and bake.

TO MIX AND BAKE THE BREAD IN THE BREAD MACHINE Pour the water (at room temperature) into the pan, and add the remaining ingredients, except the yeast. Make a small indentation in the dry ingredients, and add the yeast. Select the *Basic* or *Whole Wheat* cycle, set the crust on *Medium,* and press *Start.* During the mixing cycle, if the dough is wet and sticky, add more flour, 1 tablespoon at a time, until the dough is smooth yet soft to the touch. If the dough is not soft to the touch but is very firm, add 1 teaspoon of water at a time, until the dough is smooth yet soft to the touch.

TO SHAPE AND BAKE IN THE OVEN Lightly grease a 9 × 5-inch loaf pan or an 8- or 9-inch round cake pan. Turn the dough out onto a lightly floured board or lightly oiled surface. Punch the dough down, and shape it into an oblong or round loaf. Place the loaf, with the smooth side up, into the pan. Cover and let rise in a warm place until almost doubled, 45 to 60 minutes. Preheat the oven to 375°F. Bake 25 to 30 minutes, until the loaf is golden and a wooden skewer inserted into the loaf comes out clean and dry. Brush the top of the loaf while it's still hot with melted butter, if desired. Remove from the pan and cool on a wire rack.

When shaping dough into a loaf, coat a work surface very lightly with nonstick spray or a drop of vegetable oil. Knead the dough so that all the air bubbles are removed, then turn the loaf so that the smooth side is up and all the wrinkles and seams are on the bottom.

Blueberry Bread and Butter Pudding

This is a simple early-American dessert, no doubt a spin-off of the English summer pudding, which is constructed in much the same way but is not baked and is usually made with juicier fruits. Wheat bread slices provide a nutty, whole grain flavor to the dessert.

8 SERVINGS

8 slices (1/4-inch thick) Basic Wheat Bread
1/4 cup (1/2 stick) butter, at room temperature
4 cups fresh or frozen unsugared blueberries

1 cup sugar
1 cup heavy cream, whipped

Preheat the oven to 350°F. Butter a 1-quart glass loaf pan. Trim the crusts from the bread. Butter each slice. Put the blueberries and sugar into a saucepan. Simmer 15 minutes, stirring occasionally until the sugar is dissolved and the berries are soft. Fit 2 slices of the buttered bread in the bottom of the prepared pan. If necessary, cut the slices to fit. Top with about 1 cup of the cooked berry mixture. Repeat layering of the buttered bread and berries, ending with a layer of the bread. Cover and bake 15 minutes, until bubbly around the edges. Chill 4 hours or overnight.

To serve, unmold onto a serving plate. Spread with whipped cream, and cut into slices.

BUTTERMILK WHEAT BREAD

Buttermilk adds a tangy flavor to this bread, which has a tender yet crisp crust. If I don't have fresh buttermilk on hand, I use water instead, and follow the package directions for adding buttermilk powder. Lemon juice enhances not only the flavor of this bread but its texture, too.

Sampler Loaf	Regular Loaf	Large Loaf
2/3 cup buttermilk*	1 cup buttermilk*	1 1/3 cups buttermilk*
1 tablespoon soft butter or oil	2 tablespoons soft butter or oil	3 tablespoons soft butter or oil
1/2 teaspoon freshly squeezed lemon juice	1 teaspoon freshly squeezed lemon juice	1 1/2 teaspoons freshly squeezed lemon juice
1 teaspoon salt	1 1/2 teaspoons salt	2 teaspoons salt
1 tablespoon packed brown sugar	2 tablespoons packed brown sugar	3 tablespoons packed brown sugar
1/2 cup whole wheat flour	3/4 cup whole wheat flour	1 cup whole wheat flour
1 1/2 cup bread flour	2 1/4 cups bread flour	3 cups bread flour
1 teaspoon rapid-rising or active dry yeast	1 1/2 teaspoons rapid-rising or active dry yeast	2 teaspoons rapid-rising or active dry yeast

TO MIX THE DOUGH BY HAND Heat the buttermilk until warm, between 105° and 115°F; pour it into a large warmed bowl, and add the yeast. Let stand 5 minutes, until the yeast begins to bubble. Stir in the butter, lemon juice, salt, brown sugar, and whole wheat flour. Beat well. Cover, and let stand 15 minutes. Slowly add the bread flour, and beat until a smooth dough forms. Turn the dough out onto a very lightly floured board, and knead, adding flour if necessary, until smooth and springy, about 5 minutes. Wash the bowl and grease it; place the dough back in the bowl, and turn it over to grease the top. Cover, and let rise until doubled, about 1 hour.

TO MIX THE DOUGH WITH A HEAVY-DUTY MIXER Heat the buttermilk until warm, between 105° and 115°F; pour it into the warmed mixing bowl, and add the yeast. Let stand 5 minutes, until the yeast begins to bubble. Stir in the butter, lemon juice, salt, brown sugar, and whole wheat flour. Beat well. Cover, and let stand 15 minutes. Slowly add the bread flour and

*Note *Or substitute water and buttermilk powder, according to the package directions.*

beat until a smooth dough forms. Knead the dough in the mixer with the dough hook, on medium to high speed, adding flour as necessary, until the dough pulls away from the sides of the bowl and is smooth and springy but still soft to the touch. Remove the dough hook, cover the bowl, and let the dough rise until doubled, about 1 hour.

TO MIX THE DOUGH IN THE FOOD PROCESSOR   Place the plastic dough blade into the work bowl. Heat the buttermilk until very warm, between 120° and 130°F; set aside. Place the remaining ingredients into the work bowl. Turn the processor on, and slowly pour the buttermilk through the feed tube, processing until the dough is smooth and pulls away from the sides of the bowl. If the dough is wet and sticky, add more flour, 1 tablespoon at a time, until the dough is smooth yet soft to the touch. If the dough is not soft to the touch but is very firm, add 1 teaspoon of water at a time, and process until the dough is smooth yet soft to the touch. Cover the work bowl, and let the dough rise until doubled, about 1 hour. Or remove to a lightly greased bowl, cover, and let rise until doubled, about 1 hour.

TO MIX THE DOUGH IN THE BREAD MACHINE   Pour the liquid ingredients (at room temperature) into the pan, and add the remaining ingredients, except the yeast. Make a small indentation in the dry ingredients, and add the yeast. Select *Dough,* and press *Start.* If the dough is wet and sticky, add more flour, 1 tablespoon at a time, until the dough is smooth yet soft to the touch. If

the dough is not soft to the touch but is very firm, add 1 teaspoon of water at a time, until the dough is smooth yet soft to the touch. The machine will stop when the dough is ready to shape and bake.

TO MIX AND BAKE THE BREAD IN THE BREAD MACHINE   Pour the liquid ingredients (at room temperature) into the pan, and add the remaining ingredients, except the yeast. Make a small indentation in the dry ingredients, and add the yeast. Select *Basic* or *Whole Wheat* cycle, set the crust on *Medium,* and press *Start.* During the mixing cycle, if the dough is wet and sticky, add more flour, 1 tablespoon at a time, until the dough is smooth yet soft to the touch. If the dough is not soft to the touch but is very firm, add 1 teaspoon of water at a time, until the dough is smooth yet soft to the touch.

TO SHAPE AND BAKE IN THE OVEN   Lightly grease an 8- or 9-inch round cake pan. Turn the dough out on a lightly floured board or lightly oiled surface. Punch the dough down, and shape it into a round loaf. Place the loaf with the smooth side up into the pan. Cover and let rise in a warm place until almost doubled, 45 to 60 minutes. Preheat the oven to 375°F. Bake 25 to 30 minutes, until the loaf is golden and a wooden skewer inserted into the loaf comes out clean and dry. Brush the top of the loaf while it's still hot with melted butter, if desired. Remove from the pan and cool on a wire rack.

Walnut Pesto

Whole wheat bread provides the binder in this spread, which is particularly satisfying for fans of nutty, herbal flavors, as I am. It keeps up to 2 weeks in the refrigerator and can also be frozen. Spread it on bread; toss it with hot, cooked pasta; mix it with freshly mashed potatoes; or toss it with steamed broccoli or cauliflower florets, steamed just to crisp-tender.

3 CUPS

2 slices (1/2-inch thick) whole wheat bread
2 cups toasted walnuts
1 cup loosely packed fresh parsley leaves
1/2 cup loosely packed fresh basil leaves
2 garlic cloves

1 teaspoon coarse (kosher) salt
1/2 teaspoon crushed red pepper flakes
2 tablespoons herb or plain white wine vinegar
1 cup walnut or extra-virgin olive oil
1/3 cup freshly grated Parmesan cheese

Fit the food processor with the steel blade. Add the bread to the container and process until crumbed. Add the walnuts, parsley, basil, garlic, salt, pepper, and vinegar. Process until chopped. Add the oil and Parmesan cheese. Process until smooth. Refrigerate, covered.

Baked Raclette with Croutons

Raclette is a national dish in Switzerland, where the cheese is melted in front of a heat source, scraped off onto boiled potatoes, and eaten with gusto. For my simple version, slice the cheese and bake it with cream; then offer it as a spread for toasted bread.

ABOUT 8 SERVINGS

$1/2$ pound aged Raclette, Swiss or Jarlsberg cheese
3 tablespoons whipping cream

Toasted croutons made from One Hundred Percent Whole Wheat Bread (page 12)

Preheat the oven to 400°F. Cut the cheese into slices about $1/3$-inch thick. Place in a small, shallow casserole or an 8-inch pie pan in a single layer, or slightly overlapping. Drizzle with the cream. Bake, uncovered, for 10 to 15 minutes, until the cheese is bubbly and begins to brown around the edges. Serve immediately with crispy croutons for dipping or spreading.

HONEY WHOLE WHEAT BREAD

This is a simple wheat bread. Honey brings out the grainy flavor and helps the bread to brown well.

Sampler Loaf

2/3 cup milk*

1 tablespoon honey

1 tablespoon butter, soft

1 teaspoon salt

1 cup whole wheat flour

1 cup bread flour

1 teaspoon rapid-rising or active
   dry yeast

Regular Loaf

1 cup milk*

2 tablespoons honey

1 1/2 tablespoons butter, soft

1 1/2 teaspoons salt

1 1/2 cups whole wheat flour

1 1/2 cups bread flour

1 1/2 teaspoons rapid-rising or
   active dry yeast

Large Loaf

1 1/3 cups milk*

3 tablespoons honey

2 tablespoons butter, soft

2 teaspoons salt

2 cups whole wheat flour

2 cups bread flour

2 teaspoons rapid-rising or active
   dry yeast

TO MIX THE DOUGH BY HAND Scald and cool the milk until warm, between 105° and 115°F; pour into a large, warmed bowl, and add the yeast and honey. Let stand 5 minutes, until the yeast begins to bubble. Stir in the butter, salt, whole wheat flour, and half of the bread flour. Beat well. Cover, and let stand 15 minutes. Slowly add the remaining bread flour, and beat until a smooth dough forms. Turn the dough out onto a very lightly floured board and knead, adding flour if necessary, until smooth and springy, about 5 minutes. Wash the bowl and grease it; place the dough back in the bowl, and turn it over to grease the top. Cover, and let rise until doubled, about 1 hour.

TO MIX THE DOUGH WITH A HEAVY-DUTY MIXER Heat the milk until warm, between 105° and 115°F; pour it into a large, warmed bowl, and add the yeast and honey. Let stand 5 minutes, until the yeast begins to bubble. Add the butter, salt, whole wheat flour, and half of the bread flour. Beat well. Cover, and let stand 15 minutes. Slowly add the remaining bread flour, and beat until a smooth dough forms. Knead the dough in the mixer with the dough hook, on medium to high speed, adding flour if necessary, until the dough pulls away from the sides of the bowl and is smooth and springy but still soft to the touch. Remove the dough hook, cover the bowl, and let the dough rise until doubled, about 1 hour.

TO MIX THE DOUGH IN THE FOOD PROCESSOR Place the plastic dough blade into the work bowl. Heat the milk until very warm, between 120° and 130°F; set aside. Place the remaining ingredients

Note   *Or substitute water and nonfat dry milk, according to the package directions*

and into the work bowl. Turn the processor on, and slowly add the milk to the dry ingredients through the feed tube, processing until the dough is smooth and pulls away from the sides of the bowl. If the dough is wet and sticky, add more flour, 1 tablespoon at a time, until the dough is smooth yet soft to the touch. If the dough is not soft to the touch but is very firm, add 1 teaspoon of water at a time, and process until the dough is smooth yet soft to the touch. Cover the work bowl and let the dough rise until doubled, about 1 hour. Or remove to a lightly greased bowl, cover, and let rise until doubled, about 1 hour.

TO MIX THE DOUGH IN THE BREAD MACHINE Pour the milk (at room temperature) into the pan, and add the remaining ingredients, except the yeast. Make a small indentation in the dry ingredients and add the yeast. Select *Dough,* and press *Start.* If the dough is wet and sticky, add more flour, 1 tablespoon at a time, until the dough is smooth yet soft to the touch. If the dough is not soft to the touch but is very firm, add 1 teaspoon of water at a time, until the dough is smooth yet soft to the touch. The machine will stop when the dough is ready to shape and bake.

TO MIX AND BAKE THE BREAD IN THE BREAD MACHINE Pour the milk (at room temperature) into the pan, and add the remaining ingredients, except the yeast. Make a small indentation in the dry ingredients and add the yeast. Select *Basic* or *Whole Wheat,* set the crust on *Medium,* and press *Start.* During the mixing cycle, if the dough is wet and sticky, add more flour, 1 tablespoon at a time, until the dough is smooth

yet soft to the touch. If the dough is not soft to the touch but is very firm, add 1 teaspoon of water at a time, until the dough is smooth yet soft to the touch.

TO SHAPE AND BAKE IN THE OVEN Lightly grease a 4 × 8-inch or 5 × 9-inch loaf pan or a baking sheet. Turn the dough out onto a lightly floured board or lightly oiled surface. Punch the dough down, and shape it into an oblong or round loaf. Place the loaf with the smooth side up into the pan. Cover and let rise in a warm place until almost doubled, 45 to 60 minutes. Preheat the oven to 375°F. Bake 25 to 30 minutes, until the loaf is golden and a wooden skewer inserted into the loaf comes out clean and dry. Brush the top of the loaf while it's still hot with melted butter, if desired. Remove from the pan and cool on a wire rack.

ONE HUNDRED PERCENT
WHOLE WHEAT BREAD

The addition of gluten adds protein to the bread dough so that it will make the proper meshwork, allowing the dough rise well. Gluten is often sold as "vital gluten" in supermarkets and whole foods cooperatives, where it's available in bulk.

Sampler Loaf	Regular Loaf	Large Loaf
2/3 cup water	1 cup water	1 1/3 cups water
2 tablespoons honey	3 tablespoons honey	4 tablespoons honey
1 tablespoon butter, soft	1 1/2 tablespoons butter, soft	2 tablespoons butter, soft
1 teaspoon salt	1 1/2 teaspoons salt	2 teaspoons salt
1/4 cup nonfat dry milk	1/2 cup nonfat dry milk	3/4 cup nonfat dry milk
2 cups whole wheat flour	3 cups whole wheat flour	4 cups whole wheat flour
1 tablespoon gluten	1 1/2 tablespoons gluten	2 tablespoons gluten
1 teaspoon rapid-rising or active dry yeast	1 1/2 teaspoons rapid-rising or active dry yeast	2 teaspoons rapid-rising or active dry yeast

TO MIX THE DOUGH BY HAND Heat the water until warm, between 105° and 115°F; pour it into a large, warmed bowl, and add the yeast and honey. Let stand 5 minutes, until the yeast begins to bubble. Stir in the butter, salt, dry milk, and half of the whole wheat flour. Beat well. Cover, and let stand 15 minutes. Slowly add the remaining whole wheat flour and gluten, and mix until a dough forms. Turn the dough out onto a very lightly floured board, and knead, adding flour if necessary, until smooth and springy, about 5 minutes. Wash the bowl and grease it; place the dough back in the bowl, and turn it over to grease the top. Cover, and let rise until doubled, about 1 hour.

TO MIX THE DOUGH WITH A HEAVY-DUTY MIXER Heat the water until warm, between 105° and 115°F; pour it into the warmed mixing bowl, and add the yeast and honey. Let stand 5 minutes, until the yeast begins to bubble. Add the butter, salt, dry milk, and half of the whole wheat flour. Beat well. Cover, and let stand 15 minutes. Slowly add the remaining whole wheat flour and gluten, and mix until a dough forms. Knead the dough in the mixer with the dough hook, on medium to high speed, adding flour as necessary, until the dough pulls away from the sides of the bowl and is smooth and springy but still soft to the touch. Remove the dough hook, cover the bowl, and let the dough rise until doubled, about 1 hour.

TO MIX THE DOUGH IN THE FOOD PROCESSOR Place the plastic dough blade into the work bowl. Heat the water until very warm, between 105° and 115°F; set aside. Place the remaining ingredients into the work bowl. Turn the processor on, and slowly pour the water through the feed tube, processing until the dough is smooth and pulls away from the sides of the bowl. If the dough is wet and sticky, add more flour, 1 tablespoon at a time, until the dough is smooth yet soft to the touch. If the dough is not soft to the touch but is very firm, add 1 tablespoon of water at a time, and process until the dough is smooth yet soft to the touch. Cover the work bowl, and let the dough rise until doubled, about 1 hour. Or remove the dough to a lightly greased bowl, cover, and let rise until doubled, about 1 hour.

TO MIX THE DOUGH IN THE BREAD MACHINE Pour the water (at room temperature) into the pan, and add the remaining ingredients, except the yeast. Make a small indentation in the dry ingredients, and add the yeast. Select *Dough,* and press *Start.* If the dough is wet and sticky, add more flour, 1 tablespoon at a time, until the dough is smooth yet soft to the touch. If the dough is not soft to the touch but is very firm, add 1 teaspoon of water at a time, until the dough is smooth yet soft to the touch. The machine will stop when the dough is ready to shape and bake.

TO MIX AND BAKE THE BREAD IN THE BREAD MACHINE Pour the water (at room temperature) into the pan, and add the remaining ingredients, except the yeast. Make a small indentation in the dry ingredients, and add the yeast. Select the *Basic* or *Whole Wheat* cycle, set the crust on *Medium,* and press *Start.* During the mixing cycle, if the dough is wet and sticky, add more flour, 1 tablespoon at a time, until the dough is smooth yet soft to the touch. If the dough is not soft to the touch but is very firm, add 1 teaspoon of water at a time, until the dough is smooth yet soft to the touch.

TO SHAPE AND BAKE IN THE OVEN Lightly grease a 9 × 5-inch loaf pan or an 8- or 9-inch round cake pan. Turn the dough out onto a lightly floured board or lightly oiled surface. Punch the dough down, and shape it into an oblong or round loaf. Place the loaf, with the smooth side up, into the pan. Cover and let rise in a warm place until almost doubled, 45 to 60 minutes. Preheat the oven to 375°F. Bake 25 to 30 minutes, until the loaf is golden and a wooden skewer inserted into the loaf comes out clean and dry. Brush the top of the loaf while it's still hot with melted butter, if desired. Remove from the pan and cool on a wire rack.

BEAUTIFUL LIGHT WHEAT BREAD

This is a perfect everyday bread, the kind you'll want to set on *Delay-Start* for breakfast the next morning. If you do, be sure to add the dry milk on top of the flour as indicated in the recipe so that it will stay dry until the machine begins to mix in the morning.

Sampler Loaf

$^2/_3$ cup water

1 tablespoon packed brown sugar

1 tablespoon butter, soft

1 teaspoon salt

$^1/_3$ cup whole wheat flour

$1^2/_3$ cups bread flour

$^1/_4$ cup nonfat dry milk

1 teaspoon rapid-rising or active dry yeast

Regular Loaf

1 cup water

2 tablespoons packed brown sugar

$1^1/_2$ tablespoons butter, soft

$1^1/_2$ teaspoons salt

$^2/_3$ cup whole wheat flour

$2^1/_2$ cups bread flour

$^1/_2$ cup nonfat dry milk

$1^1/_2$ teaspoons rapid-rising or active dry yeast

Large Loaf

$1^1/_3$ cups water

3 tablespoons packed brown sugar

2 tablespoons butter, soft

2 teaspoons salt

$^3/_4$ cup whole wheat flour

$3^1/_4$ cups bread flour

$^3/_4$ cup nonfat dry milk

2 teaspoons rapid-rising or active dry yeast

TO MIX THE DOUGH BY HAND Heat the water until warm, between 105° and 115°F; pour it into a large, warmed bowl, and add the yeast and brown sugar. Let stand 5 minutes, until the yeast begins to bubble. Stir in the butter, salt, whole wheat flour, half of the bread flour, and the dry milk. Beat well. Cover, and let stand 15 minutes. Slowly add the remaining bread flour, and beat until a smooth dough forms. Turn the dough out onto a very lightly floured board, and knead, adding flour if necessary, until smooth and springy, about 5 minutes. Wash the bowl and grease it; place the dough back in the bowl, and turn it over to grease the top. Cover, and let rise until doubled, about 1 hour.

TO MIX THE DOUGH WITH A HEAVY-DUTY MIXER Heat the water until warm, between 105° and 115°F; pour it into the warmed mixing bowl, and add the yeast and brown sugar. Let stand 5 minutes, until the yeast begins to bubble. Add the butter, salt, whole wheat flour, half of the bread flour, and the dry milk. Beat well. Cover, and let stand 15 minutes. Slowly add the remaining bread flour, and beat until a smooth dough forms. Knead the dough in the mixer with the dough hook, on medium to high speed, adding flour as necessary, until the dough pulls away from the sides of the bowl and is smooth and springy but still soft to the touch. Remove the dough hook, cover the bowl, and let the dough rise until doubled, about 1 hour.

TO MIX THE DOUGH IN THE FOOD PROCESSOR Place the plastic dough blade into the work bowl. Heat the water until very warm, between 120° and 130°F; set aside. Place the remaining ingredients into the work bowl. With the processor running, slowly pour the water through the feed tube, processing until the dough is smooth and pulls away from the sides of the bowl. If the dough is wet and sticky, add more flour, 1 tablespoon at a time, until the dough is smooth yet soft to the touch. If the dough is not soft to the touch but is very firm, add 1 tablespoon of water at a time, and process until the dough is smooth yet soft to the touch. Cover the work bowl, and let the dough rise until doubled, about 1 hour. Or remove the dough to a lightly greased bowl, cover, and let rise until doubled, about 1 hour.

TO MIX THE DOUGH IN THE BREAD MACHINE Pour the water (at room temperature) into the pan, and add the remaining ingredients, except the yeast. Make a small indentation in the dry ingredients, and add the yeast. Select *Dough,* and press *Start.* If the dough is wet and sticky, add more flour, 1 tablespoon at a time, until the dough is smooth yet soft to the touch. If the dough is not soft to the touch but is very firm, add 1 teaspoon of water at a time, until the dough is smooth yet soft to the touch. The machine will stop when the dough is ready to shape and bake.

TO MIX AND BAKE THE BREAD IN THE BREAD MACHINE Pour the water (at room temperature) into the pan, and add the remaining ingredients, except the yeast. Make a small indentation in the dry ingredients, and add the yeast. Select the *Basic* cycle, set the crust on *Medium,* and press *Start.* During the mixing cycle, if the dough is wet and sticky, add more flour, 1 tablespoon at a time, until the dough is smooth yet soft to the touch. If the dough is not soft to the touch but is very firm, add 1 teaspoon of water at a time, until the dough is smooth yet soft to the touch.

TO SHAPE AND BAKE IN THE OVEN Lightly grease a 8 × 4-inch or 9 × 5-inch loaf pan. Turn the dough out onto a lightly floured board or lightly oiled surface. Punch the dough down, and shape it into an oblong loaf. Place the loaf, with the smooth side up, into the pan. Cover and let rise in a warm place until almost doubled, 45 to 60 minutes. Preheat the oven to 375°F. Bake 25 to 30 minutes, until the loaf is golden and a wooden skewer inserted into the loaf comes out clean and dry. Brush the top of the loaf while it's still hot with melted butter, if desired. Remove from the pan and cool on a wire rack.

Apple Brown Bread Betty

To use a few slices of yesterday's bread, make Apple Brown Bread Betty, which is an old-fashioned dessert layered with bread and topped with a crumb mixture before baking.

6 SERVINGS

2 cups ($^1/_2$-inch) bread cubes made from Beautiful
    Light Wheat Bread
$^1/_4$ cup chopped walnuts
$^1/_4$ cup all-purpose flour
$^3/_4$ teaspoon cinnamon
$^1/_8$ teaspoon salt
1/4 cup ($^1/_2$ stick) cold butter

$^1/_3$ cup melted butter
1 cup golden raisins soaked in 2 tablespoons rum,
    port, or cognac
4 Granny Smith or Golden Delicious apples, peeled,
    cored, quartered, and sliced
Vanilla ice cream for serving

Preheat the oven to 375°F. Lightly butter a 1-quart shallow casserole or 9-inch cake pan. Spread the bread cubes on a cookie sheet and toast for 10 minutes. Remove from the oven, and cool.

Combine the walnuts, flour, cinnamon, and salt. Cut in the cold butter until the mixture resembles coarse crumbs; set aside.

Toss the bread cubes with the melted butter, then toss with the raisins and apples. Turn the bread and fruit mixture into the baking dish. Top with the walnut and flour mixture. Bake 45 minutes, until crisp. Serve warm with soft ice cream.

Green Salad with Spicy Wheat Croutons

My favorite salad consists of mixed baby greens, simply tossed with spicy oil and vinegar and then topped with chili-spiced toasted wheat bread croutons.

4 TO 6 SERVINGS

1 cup bread cubes, cut $1/2$ inch, made from day-old Cracked Wheat Bread or other whole wheat bread

2 teaspoons chili oil

$1/2$ teaspoon chili powder

$1/2$ teaspoon coarse (kosher) salt

1 large garlic clove, finely chopped

1 tablespoon Dijon-style mustard

2 teaspoons red wine or balsamic vinegar

$1/4$ teaspoon salt

$1/4$ teaspoon freshly ground black pepper

3 tablespoons extra-virgin olive oil

1 quart loosely packed mixed salad greens, torn into 2-inch pieces

Preheat the oven to 400°F. In a medium bowl, toss the bread cubes with the chili oil, chili spices, and salt. Spread on a baking sheet, and bake 10 minutes, until the cubes are lightly browned. In a salad bowl, mix the garlic, mustard, vinegar, salt, and pepper. Whisk in the olive oil. Just before serving, add the mixed greens to the bowl and toss with the dressing. Sprinkle with the croutons.

CRACKED WHEAT BREAD

Add the cracked wheat to the water when beginning to mix the dough, so the wheat has a bit of extra time to absorb enough water to be tenderized but not enough to lose its crunch.

Sampler Loaf

2/3 cup water

1/4 cup cracked wheat

1 tablespoon packed brown sugar

3/4 teaspoon salt

1/3 cup 8-grain* or whole wheat flour

1 1/3 cups bread flour

1 teaspoon gluten

1 teaspoon rapid-rising or active dry yeast

Regular Loaf

1 cup water

1/3 cup cracked wheat

2 tablespoons packed brown sugar

1 teaspoon salt

3/3 cup 8-grain* or whole wheat flour

1 2/3 cups bread flour

2 teaspoons gluten

1 1/2 teaspoons rapid-rising or active dry yeast

Large Loaf

1 1/3 cups water

1/2 cup cracked wheat

3 tablespoons packed brown sugar

1 1/2 teaspoons salt

1 cup 8-grain* or whole wheat flour

2 cups bread flour

1 tablespoon gluten

2 teaspoons rapid-rising or active dry yeast

TO MIX THE DOUGH BY HAND Heat the water until warm, between 105° and 115°F; pour it into a large bowl, and add the yeast and cracked wheat. Let stand 5 minutes, until the yeast begins to bubble. Stir in the brown sugar, salt, 8-grain flour, half of the bread flour, and the gluten. Beat well, until a smooth dough forms. Cover, and let stand 15 minutes. Stir in the remaining bread flour to make a stiff dough. Turn the dough out onto a very lightly floured board, and knead, adding flour if necessary, until smooth and springy, about 5 minutes. Wash the bowl and grease it; place the dough back in the bowl, and turn it over to grease the top. Cover, and let rise until doubled, about 1 hour.

TO MIX THE DOUGH WITH A HEAVY-DUTY MIXER Heat the water until warm, between 105° and 115°F; pour it into the mixing bowl, and add the yeast and cracked wheat. Let stand 5 minutes, until the yeast begins to bubble. Add the brown sugar, salt, 8-grain flour, half of the bread flour, and the gluten. Beat until a smooth dough forms. Cover, and let stand 15 minutes. Stir in the remaining bread flour to make a stiff dough. Knead the dough in the mixer with the

__Note__ *8-grain flour includes wheat, triticale, rye, millet, oat, buckwheat, barley, and soy flours and can be found in most health food stores or sections of supermarkets devoted to organic health foods.*

dough hook, on medium to high speed, adding flour as necessary, until the dough pulls away from the sides of the bowl and is smooth and springy but still soft to the touch. Remove the dough hook, cover the bowl, and let the dough rise until doubled, about 1 hour.

TO MIX THE DOUGH IN THE FOOD PROCESSOR
Place the plastic dough blade into the work bowl. Heat the water until very warm, between 120° and 130°F; pour half of the water into the work bowl, and add the cracked wheat. Let sit 5 minutes. Place the remaining ingredients into the work bowl, except the reserved water. Turn the processor on, and slowly pour the remaining water through the feed tube, processing until the dough is smooth and pulls away from the sides of the bowl. If the dough is wet and sticky, add more flour, 1 tablespoon at a time, until the dough is smooth yet soft to the touch. If the dough is not soft to the touch but is very firm, add 1 tablespoon of water at a time, and process until the dough is smooth yet soft to the touch. Cover the work bowl, and let the dough rise until doubled, about 1 hour. Or remove the dough to a lightly greased bowl, cover, and let rise until doubled, about 1 hour.

TO MIX THE DOUGH IN THE BREAD MACHINE Pour the water (at room temperature) into the pan; add the cracked wheat and stir. Add the remaining ingredients. Make a small indentation in the dry ingredients and add the yeast. Select *Dough,* and press *Start.* If the dough is wet and sticky, add more flour, 1 tablespoon at a time, until the dough is smooth yet soft to the touch. If the dough is not soft to the touch but is very firm, add 1 teaspoon of water at a time, until the dough is smooth yet soft to the touch. The machine will stop when the dough is ready to shape and bake.

TO MIX AND BAKE THE BREAD IN THE BREAD MACHINE Pour the water (at room temperature) into the pan; add the cracked wheat and stir. Add the remaining ingredients. Make a small indentation in the dry ingredients and add the yeast. Select the *Basic* or *Whole Wheat* cycle, set the crust on *Medium,* and press *Start.* During the mixing cycle, if the dough is wet and sticky, add more flour, 1 tablespoon at a time, until the dough is smooth yet soft to the touch. If the dough is not soft to the touch but is very firm, add 1 teaspoon of water at a time, until the dough is smooth yet soft to the touch.

TO SHAPE AND BAKE IN THE OVEN Lightly grease an 8 × 4-inch or 9 × 5-inch loaf pan or baking sheet. Turn the dough out onto a lightly floured board or lightly oiled surface. Punch the dough down, and shape it into an oblong or round loaf. Place the loaf, with the smooth side up, into the pan. Cover and let rise in a warm place until almost doubled, about 1 hour. Preheat the oven to 375°F. Bake 35 to 45 minutes, until the loaf is golden and a wooden skewer inserted into the loaf comes out clean and dry. Remove from the pan and cool on a wire rack.

ENGLISH GRANARY BREAD

This bread is 50% whole wheat, giving it a close texture and a nutty flavor. English Golden Syrup brings out the flavor of wheat in this bread. I find it in specialty food stores. I first learned to know this thick syrup when we lived in England many years ago. If you can't find English Golden Syrup a mild-flavored honey is a delicious substitute.

Sampler Loaf

²/₃ cup water

1 tablespoon English Golden Syrup or honey

¹/₂ tablespoon butter

1 teaspoon salt

1 cup whole wheat flour

1 cup bread flour

1 teaspoon rapid-rising or active dry yeast

Regular Loaf

1 cup water

2 tablespoons English Golden Syrup or honey

1 tablespoon butter

1¹/₂ teaspoons salt

1¹/₂ cups whole wheat flour

1¹/₂ cups bread flour

1¹/₂ teaspoons rapid-rising or active dry yeast

Large Loaf

1¹/₃ cups water

3 tablespoons English Golden Syrup or honey

2 tablespoons butter

2 teaspoons salt

2 cups whole wheat flour

2 cups bread flour

2 teaspoons rapid-rising or active dry yeast

GLAZE FOR BREAD BAKED CONVENTIONALLY

1 egg white, beaten

Wheat germ

Sesame seeds

TO MIX THE DOUGH BY HAND Heat the water until warm, between 105° and 115°F; pour it into a large, warmed bowl, and add the yeast and syrup. Let stand 5 minutes, until the yeast begins to bubble. Stir in the butter, salt, whole wheat flour, and half of the bread flour. Beat well. Cover, and let stand 15 minutes. Slowly add the remaining bread flour, and beat until a soft dough forms. Turn the dough out onto a very lightly floured board, and knead, adding flour if necessary, until smooth and springy, about 5 minutes. Wash the bowl and grease it; place the dough back in the bowl, and turn it over to grease the top. Cover, and let rise until doubled, about 1 hour.

TO MIX THE DOUGH WITH A HEAVY-DUTY MIXER Heat the water until warm, between 105° and 115°F; pour it into the warmed mixing bowl, and add the yeast and syrup. Let stand 5 minutes, until the yeast begins to bubble. Add the butter, salt, whole wheat flour, and half of the bread flour. Beat well. Cover, and let stand 15 minutes. Slowly add the remaining bread flour, and beat until a soft dough forms. Knead the dough in the mixer with the dough hook, on medium to high speed, adding flour as necessary, until the dough pulls away from the sides of the bowl and is smooth and springy but still soft to the touch. Remove the dough hook, cover the bowl, and let the dough rise until doubled, about 1 hour.

TO MIX THE DOUGH IN THE FOOD PROCESSOR   Place the plastic dough blade into the work bowl. Heat the water until very warm, between 120° and 130°F; set aside. Place the dry ingredients into the work bowl. Process until blended. Combine the water and syrup in a large measuring cup. Turn the processor on, and slowly pour the liquid through the feed tube, processing until the dough is smooth and pulls away from the sides of the bowl. If the dough is wet and sticky, add more flour, 1 tablespoon at a time, until the dough is smooth yet soft to the touch. If the dough is not soft to the touch but is very firm, add 1 tablespoon of water at a time, and process until the dough is smooth yet soft to the touch. Cover the work bowl, and let the dough rise until doubled, about 1 hour. Or remove the dough to a lightly greased bowl, cover, and let rise until doubled, about 1 hour.

TO MIX THE DOUGH IN THE BREAD MACHINE   Pour the water (at room temperature) into the pan, and add the remaining ingredients, except the yeast. Make a small indentation in the dry ingredients, and add the yeast. Select *Dough,* and press *Start.* If the dough is wet and sticky, add more flour, 1 tablespoon at a time, until the dough is smooth yet soft to the touch. If the dough is not soft to the touch but is very firm, add 1 teaspoon of water at a time, until the dough is smooth yet soft to the touch. The machine will stop when the dough is ready to shape and bake.

TO MIX AND BAKE THE BREAD IN THE BREAD MACHINE   Pour the water (at room temperature) into the pan, and add the remaining ingredients, except the yeast. Make a small indentation in the dry ingredients, and add the yeast. Select the *Basic* or *Whole Wheat* cycle, set the crust on *Medium,* and press *Start.* During the mixing cycle, if the dough is wet and sticky, add more flour, 1 tablespoon at a time, until the dough is smooth yet soft to the touch. If the dough is not soft to the touch but is very firm, add 1 teaspoon of water at a time, until the dough is smooth yet soft to the touch.

TO SHAPE AND BAKE IN THE OVEN   Lightly grease a baking sheet or cover it with parchment paper. Turn the dough out onto a lightly floured board or lightly oiled surface. Punch the dough down, and shape it into a round loaf. Place the loaf, with the smooth side up, onto the pan. Cover and let rise in a warm place until almost doubled, 45 to 60 minutes. Preheat the oven to 375°F. To glaze, brush the top of the loaf with beaten egg white and sprinkle on the wheat germ and sesame seeds. Using a serrated knife or a razor blade, slash the loaf four or five times. (The cuts open up during baking to make a pretty design on top of the loaf.) Bake 35 to 40 minutes, until the loaf is golden and a wooden skewer inserted into the loaf comes out clean and dry. Remove from the pan and cool on a wire rack.

LIGHT WHEAT BRIOCHE

Brioche is a delicious bread to have on hand. The classic shape is the top hat with a fluted base; it's a showy bread to include with a selection of other breads. The butter is added after the flour in the classic method, which produces a bread with small pores and a delicate texture. I like it the best when baked in the conventional oven, but you can use the convenience of the bread machine, especially if you plan to use the loaf for appetizers, or for Summer Pudding with Raspberry Sauce (page 24).

Sampler Loaf	Regular Loaf	Large Loaf
1 large egg plus 1 egg yolk plus water to equal 2/3 cup	3 large eggs plus water to equal 1 cup	4 large eggs plus water to equal 1 1/3 cups
1 teaspoon salt	1 1/2 teaspoons salt	2 teaspoons salt
2 teaspoons sugar	4 teaspoons sugar	2 tablespoons sugar
1/2 cup whole wheat flour	3/4 cup whole wheat flour	1 cup whole wheat flour
1 1/2 cups bread flour	2 1/2 cups bread flour	3 cups bread flour
4 tablespoons butter, softened	1/2 cup butter, softened	3/4 cup butter, softened
3/4 teaspoon rapid-rising or active dry yeast	1 teaspoon rapid-rising or active dry yeast	1 1/2 teaspoons rapid-rising or active dry yeast

TO MIX THE DOUGH BY HAND Warm the eggs under hot tap water, and crack into a measuring cup. Heat the water until warm, between 105° and 115°F, and add it to the eggs. Pour the mixture into a large, warmed bowl, and add the yeast. Let stand 5 minutes, until the yeast begins to bubble. Stir in the salt, sugar, whole wheat flour, and half of the bread flour. Beat well. Cover, and let stand 15 minutes. Slowly add the remaining bread flour, and beat until a dough forms. Cut the butter into pieces, and add to the dough. Turn the dough out onto a very lightly floured board, and knead, adding flour if necessary, until smooth and springy, about 5 minutes. Wash the bowl and grease it; place the dough back in the bowl, and turn it over to grease the top. Cover, and let rise until doubled, about 1 hour.

TO MIX THE DOUGH WITH A HEAVY-DUTY MIXER Warm the eggs under hot tap water, and crack into a measuring cup. Heat the water until warm, between 105° and 115°F, and add it to the eggs. Pour the mixture into the warmed mixing bowl, and add the yeast. Let stand 5 minutes, until the yeast begins to bubble. Add the salt, sugar, whole wheat flour, and half of the bread flour. Beat well. Cover, and let stand 15 minutes. Slowly add the remaining bread flour, and beat until a dough forms. Cut the butter into pieces, and add it to the dough. Knead the dough in the mixer with the dough hook, on medium to high speed, adding flour as necessary, until the dough pulls away from the sides of the bowl and is smooth and springy but still soft to the touch. Remove the dough hook, cover the bowl, and let the dough rise until doubled, about 1 hour.

TO MIX THE DOUGH IN THE FOOD PROCESSOR Place the plastic dough blade into the work bowl. Warm the eggs under hot tap water, and crack into a measuring cup. Heat the water until very warm, between 120° and 130°F, and add it to the eggs. Place the remaining ingredients, except the butter, into the work bowl. Turn the processor on, and slowly pour the water mixture through the feed tube, processing until the dough is smooth and pulls away from the sides of the bowl. If the dough is wet and sticky, add more flour, 1 tablespoon at a time, until the dough is smooth yet soft to the touch. If the dough is not soft to the touch but is very firm, add 1 tablespoon of water at a time, and process until the dough is smooth yet soft to the touch. Cut up the butter, and add it to the dough; process until blended. Cover the work bowl, and let the dough rise until doubled, about 1 hour. Or remove the dough to a lightly greased bowl, cover, and let rise until doubled, about 1 hour.

TO MIX THE DOUGH IN THE BREAD MACHINE Warm the eggs under hot tap water and crack into a measuring cup. Add the water (at room temperature) to the eggs; pour the mixture into the pan. Add the salt, sugar, whole wheat flour, and bread flour. Make a small indentation in the dry ingredients, and add the yeast. Select *Dough,* and press *Start.* Add the butter about 20 minutes into the cycle. If the dough is wet and sticky, add more flour, 1 tablespoon at a time,

until the dough is smooth yet soft to the touch. If the dough is not soft to the touch but is very firm, add 1 teaspoon of water at a time, until the dough is smooth yet soft to the touch. The machine will stop when the dough is ready to shape and bake.

TO MIX AND BAKE THE DOUGH IN THE BREAD MACHINE Place the eggs in a measuring cup, and add the water (at room temperature); pour the mixture into the pan. Add the salt, sugar, whole wheat flour, and bread flour. Make a small indentation in the dry ingredients, and add the yeast. Select *Basic* cycle, and press *Start.* Add the butter about 20 minutes into the cycle. If the dough is wet and sticky, add more flour, 1 tablespoon at a time, until the dough is smooth yet soft to the touch. If the dough is not soft to the touch but is very firm, add 1 teaspoon of water at a time, until the dough is smooth yet soft to the touch.

TO SHAPE AND BAKE IN THE OVEN Lightly grease a fluted brioche pan, a 9-inch round cake pan, or a 9 × 5-inch loaf pan. Turn the dough out onto a lightly floured board or lightly oiled surface. For the traditional brioche shape, punch the dough down and pinch off one-quarter of the dough. Shape the remaining dough into a round loaf. Place the loaf, smooth side up, in the brioche or cake pan. Make an indentation in the center of the loaf. Form the pinched-off portion into a teardrop shape, and place, pointed side down, into the hole in the loaf. Or press the dough into the loaf pan. Cover and let rise in a warm place until doubled, 1 to 1 1/2 hours. Preheat the oven to 350°F. Brush or spray the loaf with water. Bake 45 to 50 minutes, until a wooden skewer inserted through the loaf comes out clean. Remove from the pan and cool on a wire rack.

Summer Pudding with Raspberry Sauce

This classic English dessert is refreshing in the summertime, and is usually made by lining a pudding mold or bowl with thin slices of white bread. My version uses the rich Light Wheat Brioche (page 22). Making it in individual servings makes a pretty presentation, and is easy to serve.

8 SERVINGS

1 pint fresh strawberries, hulled and quartered

1 pint fresh blackberries

1 pint fresh raspberries

$1/2$ cup sugar

1 teaspoon freshly squeezed lemon juice

4 slices Light Wheat Brioche, $1/4$ inch thick

Raspberry Sauce (recipe follows)

Lightly whipped cream

Combine the berries and sugar in a nonaluminum saucepan. Heat to simmering over medium heat and cook gently stirring occasionally, for 10 minutes, until the berries just begin to break apart. Add the lemon juice and cool.

Cut 4 small circles of bread from each slice of brioche (2 to $2^1/2$ inches in diameter), without getting any of the crust. Spoon about 1 tablespoon of the berry mixture into the bottom of each of 4 custard cups. Dip 4 circles of brioche into the berry mixture, and place 1 into each of the custard cups. Top each with 1 tablespoon of the berry mixture. Dip 4 more circles of brioche, and place 1 into each custard cup, and top with 1 tablespoon of the berry mixture. Repeat the process until you have layered 4 pieces of brioche with berry sauce in each custard cup. The cups should be filled to the very top, to almost overflowing. Place the cups onto a baking sheet and cover them with plastic wrap. Place another baking sheet over the plastic wrap and set a weight on top to compress the puddings. Refrigerate overnight.

To serve, unmold the puddings by running a thin spatula or a butter knife around the inside edge of each pudding. Invert them onto a serving plate. Cut each pudding in half, and serve with the Raspberry Sauce and lightly whipped cream.

Raspberry Sauce

1 pint raspberries

1/2 cup sugar
1 teaspoon freshly squeezed lemon juice
1 tablespoon framboise

Puree the raspberries in the food processor or blender and strain into a bowl. Add the sugar and stir until dissolved. Add the lemon juice and framboise.

MILK AND HONEY WHEAT BREAD

Here's a good, basic bread that's good with any meal, for sandwiches, or for toasting. If you want to bake this in the bread machine using the *Delay-Start* option, use water instead of the liquid milk and add the equivalent of nonfat dry milk to the top of the dry ingredients. This is to prevent any possibility of spoiling.

Sampler Loaf	Regular Loaf	Large Loaf
2/3 cup milk	1 cup milk	1 1/3 cups milk
1 tablespoon honey	2 tablespoons honey	3 tablespoons honey
1 tablespoon canola oil	2 tablespoons canola oil	3 tablespoons canola oil
1 teaspoon salt	1 1/2 teaspoons salt	2 teaspoons salt
2/3 cup whole wheat flour	1 cup whole wheat flour	1 1/4 cups whole wheat flour
1/4 cup toasted wheat germ	1/3 cup toasted wheat germ	1/2 cup toasted wheat germ
3/4 cup bread flour	1 3/4 cups bread flour	2 1/2 cups bread flour
1 teaspoon rapid-rising or active dry yeast	1 1/2 teaspoons rapid-rising or active dry yeast	2 teaspoons rapid-rising or active dry yeast

TO MIX THE DOUGH BY HAND Scald the milk; cool it until warm, between 105° and 115°F; and pour it into a large, warmed bowl. Add the yeast and honey. Let stand 5 minutes, until the yeast begins to bubble. Stir in the oil, salt, whole wheat flour, and wheat germ. Beat until smooth. Cover, and let stand 15 minutes. Stir in the bread flour to make a soft, rough dough. Turn the dough out onto a very lightly floured board, and knead, adding flour if necessary, until smooth and springy, about 5 minutes. Wash the bowl and grease it; place the dough back in the bowl, and turn it over to grease the top. Cover, and let rise until doubled, about 1 hour.

TO MIX THE DOUGH WITH A HEAVY-DUTY MIXER Scald the milk; cool until warm, between 105° and 115°F; and pour it into the warmed mixing bowl. Add the yeast and honey. Let stand 5 minutes, until the yeast begins to bubble. Add the oil, salt, whole wheat flour, and wheat germ. Beat until smooth. Cover, and let stand 15 minutes. Stir in the bread flour to make a soft, rough dough. Knead the dough in the mixer with the dough hook, on medium to high speed, adding flour as necessary, until the dough pulls away from the sides of the bowl and is smooth and springy but still soft to the touch. Remove the dough hook, cover the bowl, and let the dough rise until doubled, about 1 hour.

TO MIX THE DOUGH IN THE FOOD PROCESSOR   Place the plastic dough blade into the work bowl. Scald the milk; cool until very warm, between 120° and 130°F; add the honey and oil, and set aside. Place the remaining ingredients into the work bowl. Turn the processor on, and slowly pour the liquids through the feed tube, processing until the dough is smooth and pulls away from the sides of the bowl. If the dough is wet and sticky, add more flour, 1 tablespoon at a time, until the dough is smooth yet soft to the touch. If the dough is not soft to the touch but is very firm, add 1 tablespoon of water at a time, and process until the dough is smooth yet soft to the touch. Cover the work bowl, and let the dough rise until doubled, about 1 hour. Or remove the dough to a lightly greased bowl, cover, and let rise until doubled, about 1 hour.

TO MIX THE DOUGH IN THE BREAD MACHINE   Scald the milk; cool to room temperature, and pour into the pan. Add the remaining ingredients in the order listed. Make an indentation in the dry ingredients and add the yeast. Select *Dough,* and press *Start.* If the dough is wet and sticky, add more flour, 1 tablespoon at a time, until the dough is smooth yet soft to the touch. If the dough is not soft to the touch but is very firm, add 1 teaspoon of water at a time, until the dough is smooth yet soft to the touch. The machine will stop when the dough is ready to shape and bake.

TO MIX AND BAKE THE BREAD IN THE BREAD MACHINE   Scald the milk; cool to room temperature, and pour into the pan. Add the remaining ingredients in the order listed. Make an indentation in the dry ingredients and add the yeast. Select the *Basic* or *Whole Wheat* cycle, set the crust on *Light,* and press *Start.* During the mixing cycle, if the dough is wet and sticky, add more flour, 1 tablespoon at a time, until the dough is smooth yet soft to the touch. If the dough is not soft to the touch but is very firm, add 1 teaspoon of water at a time, until the dough is smooth yet soft to the touch.

TO SHAPE AND BAKE IN THE OVEN   Lightly grease an 8 × 4-inch or 9 × 5-inch loaf pan or 9-inch round cake pan. Turn the dough out onto a lightly floured board or lightly oiled surface. Punch the dough down, and shape it into an oblong or round loaf. Place the loaf, with the smooth side up, into the pan. Cover and let rise in a warm place until almost doubled, 45 to 60 minutes. Preheat the oven to 350°F. Bake 30 to 35 minutes, until the loaf is golden. Remove from the pan and cool on a wire rack.

Herbed Wild Mushroom Pâté

A slice of whole wheat bread thickens this delicious mushroom pâté which is perfect as a starter for a casual meal or as a satisfying snack.

2 CUPS

1 slice, about 3/4-inch thick, English Granary Bread (page 20), whole wheat, or multigrain bread

1/2 cup heavy cream

2 tablespoons butter

1/2 pound fresh chantrelle, morel, button, or portabello mushrooms, chopped

1/4 cup minced onion

1 tablespoon minced fresh parsley

1/8 teaspoon dried oregano

1/8 teaspoon dried basil

2 ounces cream cheese, softened

1 tablespoon dry sherry

Salt and freshly ground pepper to taste

Plain crouton slices, for serving (page 304)

Crumble the bread into a small bowl, and add the cream. Melt the butter in a large skillet, and add the mushrooms and onion. Cook over medium-high heat, stirring occasionally, for 3 to 4 minutes, until the liquid is evaporated and the vegetables are softened. Transfer the mixture to a bowl; add the parsley, and let the mixture cool, stirring occasionally. Blend in the bread mixture, dried herbs, cream cheese, sherry, and salt and pepper. Turn into a serving bowl, and chill for 20 minutes to let the flavors blend. Serve with croutons or slices of lightly toasted bread.

Honey Orange Bread Pudding

Whole wheat breads are so good in bread puddings, I wonder why I hadn't thought of it before! Serve this warm with some cream to pour over.

8 SERVINGS

1/2 cup (1 stick) unsalted butter

8 slices (1/2-inch thick) Milk and Honey Wheat Bread (page 26), halved

2 cups milk

1 cup heavy cream or half-and-half

2/3 cup honey

1 large seedless navel orange

5 eggs

Preheat the oven to 325°F. Melt the butter, and dip one side of each bread slice into the butter; arrange the bread, butter-side up, overlapping slightly in a shallow 1 1/2-quart casserole.

In a medium saucepan, combine the milk, cream, and honey. Cut the zest from the orange with a potato peeler and add to the pan. Bring to a boil over moderate heat; remove from the heat, and let stand for 5 minutes.

In a large mixing bowl, whisk the eggs until just blended, then whisk in the hot milk mixture. Strain the custard over the bread in the casserole; the bread will rise to the top. Place the casserole into a larger pan, and pour warm water into the pan to reach halfway up the side of the casserole. Bake 45 minutes, until set.

NORWEGIAN WHEAT BREAD

This loaf has a creamy colored crumb, with a slightly sweet-and-sour flavor.

Sampler Loaf

1/3 cup water

1 large egg

1 tablespoon packed brown sugar

1 tablespoon soft butter

1 teaspoon salt

2 tablespoons buttermilk powder

1/2 cup whole wheat flour

1 1/2 cups bread flour

1 teaspoon rapid-rising or active
   dry yeast

Regular Loaf

3/4 cup water

1 large egg

1 1/2 tablespoons packed
   brown sugar

1 1/2 tablespoons soft butter

1 1/2 teaspoons salt

1/4 cup buttermilk powder

1 cup whole wheat flour

2 cups bread flour

1 1/2 teaspoons rapid-rising or
   active dry yeast

Large Loaf

1 cup water

1 large egg

2 tablespoons packed
   brown sugar

2 tablespoons soft butter

2 teaspoons salt

1/3 cup buttermilk powder

1 1/2 cups whole wheat flour

2 1/2 cups bread flour

2 teaspoons rapid-rising or active
   dry yeast

TO MIX THE DOUGH BY HAND Warm the egg in hot tap water. Heat the water until warm, between 105° and 115°F. Combine the egg, water, and brown sugar in a large, warmed bowl; add the yeast. Let stand 5 minutes, until the yeast begins to bubble. Stir in the salt, buttermilk powder, and whole wheat flour. Cover, and let stand 15 minutes. Slowly add the bread flour, and beat until a smooth dough forms. Turn the dough out onto a very lightly floured board, and knead, adding flour if necessary, until smooth and springy, about 5 minutes. Wash the bowl and grease it; place the dough back in the bowl, and turn it over to grease the top. Cover, and let rise until doubled, about 1 hour.

TO MIX THE DOUGH WITH A HEAVY-DUTY MIXER Warm the egg in hot tap water. Heat the water until warm, between 105° and 115°F. Combine the egg, water, and brown sugar in the warmed mixing bowl; add the yeast. Let stand 5 minutes, until the yeast begins to bubble. Add the salt, buttermilk powder, and the whole wheat flour. Cover, and let stand 15 minutes. Slowly add the bread flour, and beat until a smooth dough forms. Knead the dough in the mixer with the dough hook, on medium to high speed, adding flour as necessary, until the dough pulls away from the sides of the bowl and is smooth and springy but still soft to the touch. Remove the dough hook, cover the bowl, and let the dough rise until doubled, about 1 hour.

TO MIX THE DOUGH IN THE FOOD PROCESSOR   Place the plastic dough blade into the work bowl. Warm the egg in hot tap water. Heat the water until very warm, between 120° and 130°F; mix with the egg, and set aside. Place the remaining ingredients into the work bowl. Turn the processor on, and slowly pour the egg mixture through the feed tube, processing until the dough comes together in a ball and spins around the work bowl 25 times. If the dough is wet and sticky, add more flour, 1 tablespoon at a time, until the dough is smooth yet soft to the touch. If the dough is not soft to the touch but is very firm, add 1 tablespoon of water at a time, and process until the dough is smooth yet soft to the touch. Cover the work bowl, and let the dough rise until doubled, about 1 hour. Or remove the dough to a lightly greased bowl, cover, and let rise until doubled, about 1 hour.

TO MIX THE DOUGH IN THE BREAD MACHINE   Warm the egg in hot tap water. Pour the water (at room temperature) into the pan; add the egg. Add the remaining ingredients in the order listed. Make an indentation in the dry ingredients and add the yeast. Select *Dough,* and press *Start.* If the dough is wet and sticky, add

more flour, 1 tablespoon at a time, until the dough is smooth yet soft to the touch. If the dough is not soft to the touch but is very firm, add 1 teaspoon of water at a time, until the dough is smooth yet soft to the touch. The machine will stop when the dough is ready to shape and bake.

TO MIX AND BAKE THE BREAD IN THE BREAD MACHINE   Warm the egg in hot tap water. Pour the water (at room temperature) into the pan; add the egg. Add the remaining ingredients in the order listed. Make an indentation in the dry ingredients and add the yeast. Select the *Basic* or *Whole Wheat* cycle, set the crust on *Medium,* and press *Start.* During the mixing cycle, if the dough is wet and sticky, add more flour, 1 tablespoon at a time, until the dough is smooth yet soft to the touch. If the dough is not soft to the touch but is very firm, add 1 teaspoon of water at a time, until the dough is smooth yet soft to the touch.

TO SHAPE AND BAKE IN THE OVEN   Lightly grease a 9 × 5-inch loaf pan or an 8- or 9-inch round cake pan. Turn the dough out onto a lightly floured board or lightly oiled surface. Punch the dough down, and shape it into an oblong or round loaf. Place the loaf, with the smooth side up, into the pan. Cover and let rise in a warm place until almost doubled, about 45 minutes. Preheat the oven to 375°F. Bake 25 to 40 minutes, until the loaf is golden. Remove from the pan and cool on a wire rack.

TUSCAN BREAD

This is a very simple bread that traditionally does not have any salt added, which results in a texture that is open and porous. Salt controls the action of the yeast; so in this bread, I needed to reduce the amount of yeast considerably so that the dough wouldn't rise uncontrollably in the machine. I like to bake this loaf in the oven on preheated tiles with steam (see below). This produces a crunchy crust and a light, airy texture.

Sampler Loaf	Regular Loaf	Large Loaf
2/3 cup water	1 cup water	1 1/3 cups water
1/4 cup whole wheat flour	1/2 cup whole wheat flour	1 cup whole wheat flour
1 3/4 cups bread flour	2 1/2 cups bread flour	3 cups bread flour
1/4 teaspoon rapid-rising or active dry yeast	1/2 teaspoon rapid-rising or active dry yeast	3/4 teaspoon rapid-rising or active dry yeast

TO MIX THE DOUGH BY HAND Heat the water until warm, between 105° and 115°F; pour it into a large, warmed bowl, and add the yeast. Let stand 5 minutes, until the yeast begins to bubble. Slowly add the whole wheat flour and half of the bread flour. Beat until a smooth dough forms. Cover, and let stand 15 minutes. Turn the dough out onto a very lightly floured board, and knead, adding the remaining flour as necessary, until smooth and springy, about 5 minutes. Wash the bowl and grease it; place the dough back in the bowl, and turn it over to grease the top. Cover, and let rise until doubled, about 1 hour.

TO MIX THE DOUGH WITH A HEAVY-DUTY MIXER Heat the water until warm, between 105° and 115°F; pour it into the warmed mixing bowl, and add the yeast. Let stand 5 minutes, until the yeast begins to bubble. Slowly add the whole wheat flour and half of the bread flour. Beat until a smooth dough forms. Cover, and let stand 15 minutes. Knead the dough in the mixer with the dough hook, on medium to high speed, adding the remaining flour as necessary, until the dough pulls away from the sides of the bowl and is smooth and springy but still soft to the touch. Remove the dough hook, cover the bowl, and let the dough rise until doubled, about 1 hour.

TO MIX THE DOUGH IN THE FOOD PROCESSOR Place the plastic dough blade into the work bowl. Heat the water until very warm, between 120° and 130°F; set aside. Place the remaining ingredients into the work bowl, increasing the yeast to 1 to 2 teaspoons. Turn the processor on, and slowly pour the water through the feed tube, processing until the dough is smooth and pulls away from the sides of the bowl. If the dough is wet and sticky, add more flour, 1 tablespoon at a time, until the dough is smooth yet soft to the touch. If the dough is not soft to the touch but is very firm, add 1 tablespoon of water at a time, and process until the dough is smooth yet soft to the touch. Cover the work bowl, and let the dough rise until doubled, about 1 hour. Or remove the dough to a lightly greased bowl, cover, and let rise until doubled, about 1 hour.

TO MIX THE DOUGH IN THE BREAD MACHINE Pour the water (at room temperature) into the pan, and add the remaining ingredients in the order listed. Make an indentation in the dry ingredients and add yeast. Select *Dough,* and press *Start.* If the dough is wet and sticky, add more flour, 1 tablespoon at a time, until the dough is smooth yet soft to the touch. If the dough is not soft to the touch but is very firm, add 1 teaspoon of water at a time, until the dough is smooth yet soft to the touch. The machine will stop when the dough is ready to shape and bake.

TO MIX AND BAKE THE BREAD IN THE BREAD MACHINE Pour the water (at room temperature) into the pan, and add the remaining ingredients in the order listed. Make an indentation in the dry ingredients and add yeast. Select the *Basic* cycle, set the crust on *Medium,* and press *Start.* During the mixing cycle, if the dough is wet and sticky, add more flour, 1 tablespoon at a time, until the dough is smooth yet soft to the touch. If the dough is not soft to the touch but is very firm, add 1 teaspoon of water at a time, until the dough is smooth yet soft to the touch.

TO SHAPE AND BAKE IN THE OVEN Turn the dough out onto a lightly floured board or lightly oiled surface. Punch the dough down, and shape it into an oblong loaf.

To bake on baking tiles Place the loaf, with the smooth side up, on a bread board, or rimless cookie sheet, sprinkled with flour or cornmeal and let rise in a warm place until doubled, 45 to 60 minutes. Place baking tiles or a pizza stone on a rack in the center of the oven. Fill a rimmed, shallow baking pan with stones or river rock no larger than $1^1/2$ inches in diameter and place it on the bottom rack of the oven. Preheat the oven to 450°F for at least 30 minutes. (Rocks should be hot enough to sizzle when water is dropped on them.) Using a sharp knife or a razor, slash the risen loaf lengthwise to a depth of about $1/4$ inch. Transfer the loaf onto the preheated baking tiles or pizza stone in the oven. (This is best done by gently easing the loaf onto the baking tile with the assistance of a straight-edged tool such as a bench scraper.) Immediately pour 1 cup water into the pan of rocks on the bottom rack of the oven. (This is most easily done by squirting water from a sport bottle onto the rocks.) Bake for 15 to 20 minutes, until loaf is golden brown. Remove from the oven and cool on a wire rack. Brush the top of the loaf while it's still hot with soft butter, if desired.

To bake in a pan Lightly grease a baking sheet. Place the loaf, with the smooth side up, onto the sheet. Let rise in a warm place until almost doubled, 45 to 60 minutes. Preheat the oven to 400°F. Using a sharp knife or a razor, slash the top of the loaf lengthwise to a depth of about $1/4$ inch, and spritz or brush it with water. Bake 15 to 20 minutes, or until the loaf is golden. Remove from the oven and cool on a wire rack. Brush the top of the loaf while it's still hot with soft butter, if desired.

Tuscan Bruschetta

This is wonderful in the summertime when tomatoes are fresh off the vine!

8 SERVINGS

8 slices Tuscan Bread (page 32), cut into 1/2-inch-
    thick slices
2 garlic cloves, cut in half
1/4 cup extra-virgin olive oil

2 medium ripe tomatoes, thinly sliced
1/2 teaspoon freshly ground pepper
Fresh basil leaves

Toast the bread on both sides under the broiler or in a dry skillet. Rub one side of each slice with the garlic. Place the bread in a broiling pan. Sprinkle the oil over the bread, and top with the tomato slices and pepper.

Broil close to the flame for 1 minute, until the oil starts to sizzle. Garnish with fresh basil. Serve immediately.

Navy Bean Salad

Crisp Tuscan Bread croutons, bacon, and beans make this hearty salad a main dish for any time of year.

4 SERVINGS

1 cup dried navy beans, rinsed and soaked overnight in cold water

1 bay leaf

2 garlic cloves, lightly crushed

4 cups water

1 teaspoon salt

2 cups bread cubes, cut 3/4 inch, from Tuscan Bread (page 32)

1 tablespoon extra virgin olive oil

1/4 pound thick-sliced bacon, cut into 3/4-inch strips crosswise

3 large shallots, thinly sliced

3 tablespoons white wine vinegar

Freshly ground pepper to taste

1/2 pound frisée or mixed baby greens

1/2 cup halved red or yellow cherry tomatoes or seeded, diced fresh tomatoes

1/4 pound feta cheese, crumbled

Drain and rinse the beans. In a medium saucepan, combine the beans with the bay leaf, garlic, and water; bring to a boil over high heat. Reduce to low, cover, and simmer until the beans are tender but not mushy, about 1 hour. Add 1/2 teaspoon of the salt 10 minutes before the beans are done. Drain; let the beans cool to room temperature. Discard the bay leaf and garlic.

Preheat oven to 350°F. Toss the bread cubes with 2 teaspoons of the oil, and arrange them in a single layer in a baking dish. Bake about 8 minutes, until golden but not dry.

Fry the bacon until crisp. Drain on paper towels. Add the remaining 1 teaspoon of oil to fat in the skillet. Add the shallots, and cook over moderate heat, stirring, about 7 minutes, until they are just beginning to brown. Add the vinegar, and season with the remaining salt and the pepper; keep warm.

In large bowl, toss the frisée with the beans, bacon, croutons, and tomatoes. Add the dressing, and toss. Sprinkle with the feta cheese, and toss gently but thoroughly.

Panzanella (Italian Bread Salad)

I have a theory that the reasons Italians love their bread fresh is to inspire them to use any bread left from the day before in some creative way. I love fresh bread myself, so I'm always trying to find clever ways to use the bread I baked yesterday. I made this salad with a number of different nonsweet breads, while I was testing the recipes in this book; and all of them were delicious! This is a third idea for using day-old Tuscan Bread (page 32)!

6 TO 8 SERVINGS

4 cups bread cubes, cut 2 inches, preferably from
    Tuscan or French bread
1 shallot or small onion, finely chopped
1 garlic clove, pressed or chopped into a paste
1/4 cup balsamic vinegar
Salt and freshly ground pepper, to taste
1/2 cup extra-virgin olive oil

5 ripe plum tomatoes, seeded and chopped
1 red or yellow bell pepper, seeded and chopped
1 cucumber, peeled, seeded, and chopped
1/2 cup Niçoise or Greek olives, pitted and halved
1 quart mixed baby greens

Spread the bread cubes on a baking sheet and leave out, uncovered, to dry for 24 hours. Or bake in a 300°F oven 10 to 20 minutes, until dried but not toasted.

In a large bowl, whisk the shallot, garlic, and balsamic vinegar. Season with salt and pepper. Whisk in the oil until well combined. Add the tomatoes, bell peppers, cucumbers, and olives, tossing to combine. Adjust the season with salt and pepper.

Before serving, put the bread cubes into a bowl and cover with cold water. Let stand 5 minutes; then drain, and squeeze out the excess water. Toss the bread cubes with the olive oil mixture, and pour over greens. Serve immediately.

Honey Raspberry Toasts

This is one of the simplest, most delicious combinations I know. Fresh raspberries on top of cream, on top of toast, drizzled with honey makes a kind of "dessert bruschetta."

4 SERVINGS

4 slices Tuscan Bread (page 32)

2 teaspoons unsalted butter

1 cup mascarpone or 1/4 cup heavy cream mixed
   and whipped with 1/2 cup sour cream

1 cup fresh raspberries

2 tablespoons honey

Toast the bread until golden on both sides and spread with butter. Top each slice generously with mascarpone or the heavy cram and sour cream mixture. Top the cream with the raspberries and drizzle with honey. Serve immediately.

Barley Wheat Bread

Savory Apple Cranberry Stuffing

Beer and Mustard Rye Bread

Bohemian Rye Bread

Buckwheat and Cracked Wheat Bread

Buttermilk Oatmeal Bread

Baked Mushrooms with Cheese on Rye

Cheese Croutons

Cornmeal Molasses Bread

Cornmeal, Rye, and Whole Wheat Bread

Country White Bread

Black Bean and Sweet Corn Spread

Grilled Vegetable Salad with Grilled Bread

Eleven-Grain Buckwheat Bread

Steak in a Bag

Finnish Rye Bread

Gravlax on Rye with Caper and Dill

Finnish Sandwich Cake

Maple Oatmeal Bread

Old-Fashioned Oat and Rye Bread

Wild Mushroom and Nut Stuffing

Easy Chili Bean Spread

Yellow Cornmeal Yeast Bread (Pioneer Bread)

Rye Wheat and Millet Bread

Seven-Grain Bread

Ten-Grain Cereal Bread

Three-Grain Bread

Zuni Cornmeal Bread

Chili Cheese Strata

two

MULTIGRAIN BREADS

Many a novice bread baker gets tempted by the thought of combining grains to produce the best-tasting and most nutritious loaf of all time. But it is easy to go too far and end up with bread that is not rich and nutty flavored but is dry, firm, and tough to cut with a lackluster flavor. There is an art to mixing grains!

The baker needs to consider the flavors of different whole grain flours as well as their baking qualities. Because most whole grains other than wheat have little or no gluten, the best texture and dough development comes when at least 50 percent of the flour is high-gluten wheat-based bread flour. Wheat gluten, sometimes called vital gluten (available in the baking sections of many supermarkets), is a great way to boost the rising power of breads.

Not only is the art of mixing grains important for dough development, but different blends of grains produce different textures and flavors. Wheat, rye, and oats are the most commonly blended grains in yeast breads and can be used in amounts up to 50 percent of the flour in a recipe. Millet, cornmeal, and buckwheat have such pronounced flavors that a smaller percentage of these flours in a bread is more pleasing.

Multigrain cereals in selections from three to ten grains are wonderful in multigrain breads. They look granular, like cracked wheat, and require just a few minutes of soaking right in the bowl or bread machine container to soften. They contribute an interesting texture and whole grain flavor.

BARLEY WHEAT BREAD

Glazed and topped with seeds, this makes a pretty loaf. The texture is smooth and moist, with a mild whole grain flavor

Sampler Loaf

²/₃ cup water

1 tablespoon honey

³/₄ teaspoon salt

¹/₄ cup barley flour

¹/₄ cup whole wheat flour

1¹/₂ cups bread flour

1 teaspoon gluten

1 teaspoon rapid-rising or active
   dry yeast

Regular Loaf

1 cup water

1¹/₂ tablespoons honey

1 teaspoon salt

¹/₂ cup barley flour

¹/₂ cup whole wheat flour

2 cups bread flour

1 ¹/₂ teaspoons gluten

1¹/₂ teaspoons rapid-rising or
   active dry yeast

Large Loaf

1¹/₃ cups water

2 tablespoons honey

1¹/₂ teaspoons salt

³/₄ cup barley flour

³/₄ cup whole wheat flour

2¹/₂ cups bread flour

2 teaspoons gluten

2 teaspoons rapid-rising or active
   dry yeast

GLAZE FOR BREAD BAKED CONVENTIONALLY

1 egg, beaten

Sunflower seeds, sesame seeds, or poppy seeds (optional)

TO MIX THE DOUGH BY HAND Heat the water until warm, between 105° and 115°F; pour into a large, warmed bowl, and add the yeast. Let stand 5 minutes, until the yeast begins to bubble. Stir in the honey, salt, barley flour, whole wheat flour, half of the bread flour, and the gluten. Beat until smooth. Cover, and let stand 15 minutes. Slowly add the remaining bread flour, and beat until a soft dough forms. Turn the dough out onto a very lightly floured board, and knead, adding flour if necessary, until smooth and springy, about 5 minutes. Wash the bowl and grease it; place the dough back in the bowl, and turn it over to grease the top. Cover, and let rise until doubled, about 1 hour.

TO MIX THE DOUGH WITH A HEAVY-DUTY MIXER Heat the water until warm, between 105° and 115°F; pour it into the warmed mixing bowl, and add the yeast. Let stand 5 minutes, until the yeast begins to bubble. Add the honey, salt, barley flour, whole wheat flour, half of the bread flour, and the gluten. Beat until smooth. Cover, and let stand 15 minutes. Slowly add the remaining bread flour, and beat until a soft, rough dough forms. Knead the dough in the mixer with the dough hook, on medium to high speed, adding flour as necessary, until the dough pulls away from the sides of the bowl and is smooth and springy but still soft to the touch. Remove the dough hook, cover the bowl, and let the dough rise until doubled, about 1 hour.

TO MIX THE DOUGH IN THE FOOD PROCESSOR
Place the plastic dough blade into the work bowl. Heat the water until very warm, between 120° and 130°F; set aside. Place the remaining ingredients into the work bowl. Turn the processor on, and slowly pour the water through the feed tube, processing until the dough is smooth and pulls away from the sides of the bowl. If the dough is wet and sticky, add more flour, 1 tablespoon at a time, until the dough is smooth yet soft to the touch. If the dough is not soft to the touch but is very firm, add 1 tablespoon of water at a time, and process until the dough is smooth yet soft to the touch. Cover the work bowl, and let the dough rise until doubled, about 1 hour. Or remove the dough to a lightly greased bowl, cover, and let rise until doubled, about 1 hour.

TO MIX THE DOUGH IN THE BREAD MACHINE Pour the water (at room temperature) into the pan. Add the remaining ingredients, in the order listed. Make an indentation in the dry ingredients and add the yeast. Select *Dough,* and press *Start.* If the dough is wet and sticky, add more flour, 1 tablespoon at a time, until the dough is smooth yet soft to the touch. If the dough is not soft to the touch but is very firm, add 1 teaspoon of water at a time, until the dough is smooth yet soft to the touch. The machine will stop when the dough is ready to shape and bake.

TO MIX AND BAKE THE BREAD IN THE BREAD MACHINE Pour the water (at room temperature) into the pan. Add the remaining ingredients, in the order listed. Make an indentation in the dry ingredients and add the yeast. Select the *Basic* cycle, set the crust on *Medium,* and press *Start.* During the mixing cycle, if the dough is wet and sticky, add more flour, 1 tablespoon at a time, until the dough is smooth yet soft to the touch. If the dough is not soft to the touch but is very firm, add 1 teaspoon of water at a time, until the dough is smooth yet soft to the touch.

TO SHAPE AND BAKE IN THE OVEN Lightly grease a baking sheet. Turn the dough out onto a lightly floured board or lightly oiled surface. Punch the dough down, and shape it into a round loaf. Place the loaf, with the smooth side up, onto the baking sheet. Cover and let rise in a warm place until almost doubled, 45 minutes. Brush with the beaten egg, and sprinkle with sunflower seeds. Preheat the oven to 375°F. Bake 30 to 35 minutes, until the loaf is golden and a wooden skewer inserted into the loaf comes out clean and dry. Remove from the pan and cool on a wire rack.

Savory Apple Cranberry Stuffing

I hardly ever stuff a whole turkey anymore, although this stuffing would be just perfect for that. Turkey breasts in slices are lean and cook quickly. I flatten the slices out, put a spoonful of this stuffing onto the center of each, roll them up, and tie them into a neat little bundle—one per serving. It's perfect for a buffet menu.

12 SERVINGS

6 cups bread cubes, cut 1/2 inch, made from Barley Wheat Bread

6 tablespoons butter

4 large garlic cloves, minced or pressed

1 medium onion, finely chopped

1 1/2 cups finely chopped celery

2 cups chopped tart apple (2 apples)

1/2 cup dried cranberries

1 tablespoon minced fresh thyme

4 cups chicken stock, or canned low-sodium chicken broth

2 tablespoons freshly squeezed lemon juice

1 cup heavy cream

1 cup finely chopped flat-leaf parsley

3 large eggs, beaten

Preheat the oven to 350°F. Spread the bread cubes on a cookie sheet and toast for about 15 minutes, until dry.

In a large skillet, melt 5 tablespoons of the butter, and add the garlic, onion, celery, apple, and cranberries. Sauté for 3 to 5 minutes, until celery is tender. Add the thyme, 2 cups of the chicken broth, and the lemon juice; cook over medium to low heat, stirring occasionally, until most of the liquid has cooked away, about 10 minutes. Add the toasted bread cubes and mix until blended.

In a small bowl, mix the cream, parsley, and eggs. Combine the cream mixture with the bread mixture. Mix in the remaining 2 cups broth. Turn the mixture into a lightly greased, 2-quart shallow baking dish. Dot with the remaining tablespoon of butter. Place into the preheated oven, and bake about 45 minutes, until the top is golden and crisp and the stuffing is firm. Let rest 15 minutes before serving.

BEER AND MUSTARD RYE BREAD

The mustard, dark beer, and thyme in this bread make it perfect for corned beef sandwiches.

Sampler Loaf

2/3 cup flat, dark beer

1 tablespoon vegetable oil

1 tablespoon Dijon-style mustard

1 tablespoon sugar

3/4 teaspoon salt

3/4 teaspoon thyme leaves

1/3 cup rye flour

1 2/3 cups bread flour

1 teaspoon rapid-rising or active
   dry yeast

Regular Loaf

1 cup flat, dark beer

1 1/2 tablespoons vegetable oil

2 tablespoons
   Dijon-style mustard

2 tablespoons sugar

1 teaspoon salt

1 teaspoon thyme leaves

1/2 cup rye flour

2 1/2 cups bread flour

1 1/2 teaspoons rapid-rising or
   active dry yeast

Large Loaf

1 1/3 cups flat, dark beer

2 tablespoons vegetable oil

3 tablespoons
   Dijon-style mustard

3 tablespoons sugar

1 1/2 teaspoons salt

1 1/2 teaspoons thyme leaves

3/4 cup rye flour

3 1/4 cups bread flour

2 teaspoons rapid-rising or active
   dry yeast

GLAZE FOR BREAD BAKED CONVENTIONALLY

1 egg white, slightly beaten

Coarse (kosher) salt

TO MIX THE DOUGH BY HAND Heat the beer until warm, between 105° and 115°F; pour it into a large, warmed bowl, and add the yeast. Let stand 5 minutes, until the yeast begins to bubble. Stir in the oil, mustard, sugar, salt, thyme, and rye flour; beat until smooth. Beat in half of the bread flour. Cover, and let stand 15 minutes. Stir in the remaining bread flour to make a stiff dough. Turn the dough out onto a very lightly floured board, and knead, adding flour if necessary, until smooth and springy, about 5 minutes.

Wash the bowl and grease it; place the dough back in the bowl, and turn it over to grease the top. Cover, and let rise until doubled, about 1 hour.

TO MIX THE DOUGH WITH A HEAVY-DUTY MIXER Heat the beer until warm, between 105° and 115°F; pour it into the warmed mixing bowl, and add the yeast. Let stand 5 minutes, until the yeast begins to bubble. Add the oil, mustard, sugar, salt, thyme, and rye flour; beat until smooth. Beat in half of the bread flour. Cover, and let stand 15 minutes. Stir in the remaining bread flour to make a stiff dough. Knead the dough in the mixer with the dough hook, on medium to high speed, adding flour as necessary, until the dough pulls away from the sides of the bowl and is smooth and springy but still soft to the touch. Remove the dough hook, cover the bowl, and let the dough rise until doubled, about 1 hour.

TO MIX THE DOUGH IN THE FOOD PROCESSOR Place the plastic dough blade into the work bowl. Heat the beer until very warm, between 120° and 130°F; set aside. Place the dry ingredients into the work bowl; process just until blended. Add the oil and mustard. Turn the processor on, and slowly pour the beer through the feed tube, processing until the dough is smooth and pulls away from the sides of the bowl. If the dough is wet and sticky, add more flour, 1 tablespoon at a time, until the dough is smooth yet soft to the touch. If the dough is not soft to the touch but is very firm, add 1 tablespoon of water at a time, and process until the dough is smooth yet soft to the touch. Cover the work bowl, and let the dough rise until doubled, about 1 hour. Or remove the dough to a lightly greased bowl, cover, and let rise until doubled, about 1 hour.

TO MIX THE DOUGH IN THE BREAD MACHINE Pour the beer (at room temperature) into the pan. Add the remaining ingredients, in the order listed. Make an indentation in the dry ingredients and add the yeast. Select *Dough,* and press *Start.* If the dough is wet and sticky, add more flour, 1 tablespoon at a time, until the dough is smooth yet soft to the touch. If the dough is not soft to the touch but is very firm, add 1 teaspoon of water at a time, until the dough is smooth yet soft to the touch. The machine will stop when the dough is ready to shape and bake.

TO MIX AND BAKE THE BREAD IN THE BREAD MACHINE Pour the beer (at room temperature) into the pan. Add the remaining ingredients, in the order listed. Make an indentation in the dry ingredients and add the yeast. Select the *Basic* cycle, set the crust on *Medium,* and press *Start.* During the mixing cycle, if the dough is wet and sticky, add more flour, 1 tablespoon at a time, until the dough is smooth yet soft to the touch. If the dough is not soft to the touch but is very firm, add 1 teaspoon of water at a time, until the dough is smooth yet soft to the touch.

TO SHAPE AND BAKE IN THE OVEN Lightly grease an 8- or 9-inch round cake pan. Turn the dough out onto a lightly floured board or lightly oiled surface. Punch the dough down, and shape it into a round loaf. Place the loaf, with the smooth side up, into the pan. Cover and let rise in a warm place until almost doubled, 60 minutes. For a nice finish to the loaf, brush with the eggs white, and sprinkle with the coarse salt. Preheat the oven to 375°F. Bake 35 to 45 minutes, until a wooden skewer inserted into the loaf comes out clean and dry. Remove from the pan and cool on a wire rack.

BOHEMIAN RYE BREAD

Traditionally, the dough for this bread is placed into a coarsely woven basket for the final rising. Just before baking, the dough is inverted onto a baking sheet. The imprint of the basket remains on the loaf. Another option is to let the dough rise in a round bowl that is lined with a flour-dusted tea towel.

Sampler Loaf	Regular Loaf	Large Loaf
$^2/_3$ cup water	1 cup water	$1^1/_3$ cup water
$^1/_2$ teaspoon caraway seeds	$^3/_4$ teaspoon caraway seeds	1 teaspoon caraway seeds
1 tablespoon sugar	2 tablespoons sugar	3 tablespoons sugar
$^3/_4$ teaspoon salt	$1^1/_2$ teaspoons salt	2 teaspoons salt
$^1/_2$ tablespoon butter	1 tablespoon butter	$1^1/_2$ tablespoons butter
$^3/_4$ cup light rye flour	1 cup light rye flour	$1^1/_2$ cups light rye flour
$1^1/_4$ cups bread flour	2 cups bread flour	$2^1/_2$ cups bread flour
1 teaspoon rapid-rising or active dry yeast	$1^1/_2$ teaspoons rapid-rising or active dry yeast	2 teaspoons rapid-rising or active dry yeast

TO MIX THE DOUGH BY HAND Heat the water until warm, between 105° and 115°F; pour it into a large, warmed bowl, and add the yeast, caraway seeds, and sugar. Let stand 5 minutes, until the yeast begins to bubble. Stir in the salt, butter, and rye flour. Slowly add half the bread flour, and beat until a smooth batter forms. Cover, and let stand 15 minutes. Mix in the remaining flour to make dough. Turn the dough out onto a very lightly floured board, and knead, adding flour if necessary, until smooth and springy, about 5 minutes. Wash the bowl and grease it; place the dough back in the bowl, and turn it over to grease the top. Cover, and let rise until doubled, about 1 hour.

TO MIX THE DOUGH WITH A HEAVY-DUTY MIXER Heat the water until warm, between 105° and 115°F; pour it into the warmed mixing bowl, and add the yeast, caraway seeds, and sugar. Let stand 5 minutes, until the yeast begins to bubble. Add the salt, salt, butter, rye wheat flour, and half of the bread flour. Beat until a smooth batter forms. Cover, and let stand 15 minutes. Slowly add the remaining bread flour, and beat until a smooth dough forms. Knead the dough in the mixer with the dough hook, on medium to high speed, adding flour as necessary, until the dough pulls away from the sides of the bowl and is smooth and springy but still soft to the touch. Remove the dough hook, cover the bowl, and let the dough rise until doubled, about 1 hour.

TO MIX THE DOUGH IN THE FOOD PROCESSOR

Place the plastic dough blade into the work bowl. Heat the water until very warm, between 120° and 130°F; set aside. Place the remaining ingredients into the work bowl. Turn the processor on, and slowly pour the water through the feed tube, processing until the dough is smooth and pulls away from the sides of the bowl. If the dough is wet and sticky, add more flour, 1 tablespoon at a time, until the dough is smooth yet soft to the touch. If the dough is not soft to the touch but is very firm, add 1 tablespoon of water at a time, and process until the dough is smooth yet soft to the touch. Cover the work bowl, and let the dough rise until doubled, about 1 hour. Or remove the dough to a lightly greased bowl, cover, and let rise until doubled, about 1 hour.

TO MIX THE DOUGH IN THE BREAD MACHINE

Pour the water (at room temperature) into the pan. Add the remaining ingredients, in the order listed. Make an indentation in the dry ingredients and add the yeast. Select *Dough,* and press *Start.* If the dough is wet and sticky, add more flour, 1 tablespoon at a time, until the dough is smooth yet soft to the touch. If the dough is not soft to the touch but is very firm, add 1 teaspoon of water at a time, until the dough is smooth yet soft to the touch. The machine will stop when the dough is ready to shape and bake.

TO MIX AND BAKE THE BREAD IN THE BREAD MACHINE

Pour the water (at room temperature) into the pan. Add the remaining ingredients, in the order listed. Make an indentation in the dry ingredients and add the yeast. Select the *Basic* or *Whole Wheat* cycle, set the crust on *Medium,* and press *Start.* During the mixing cycle, if the dough is wet and sticky, add more flour, 1 tablespoon at a time, until the dough is smooth yet soft to the touch. If the dough is not soft to the touch but is very firm, add 1 teaspoon of water at a time, until the dough is smooth yet soft to the touch.

TO SHAPE AND BAKE IN THE OVEN

Coat a 10 × 3-inch round closely woven basket, or a smooth round bowl, with nonstick spray. Coat heavily with rye flour. Turn the dough out onto a lightly floured board or lightly oiled surface. Punch the dough down, and shape it into a ball. Place the loaf, with the smooth side down, into the basket or cloth-lined bowl. Cover, and let rise in a warm place until almost puffy, 45 minutes. Preheat the oven to 450°F. Coat a baking sheet with nonstick spray. Invert the risen dough onto the baking sheet, and remove the basket or towel. Bake 10 minutes, and then reduce the oven temperature to 350°F. Bake 45 minutes longer, until the loaf has browned and a wooden skewer inserted into the loaf comes out clean and dry. Remove from the pan and cool on a wire rack.

BUCKWHEAT AND
CRACKED WHEAT BREAD

Buckwheat adds an assertive flavor to this bread. It's no wonder; buckwheat is actually an herb, although it's thought of as a cereal. The flavor of this bread reminds me of the buckwheat blini that my husband and I enjoyed in eastern Finland and in Russia.

Sampler Loaf

2/3 cup water

1 tablespoon canola or corn oil

1 tablespoon honey

1 teaspoon salt

1 tablespoon cracked wheat

1/4 cup buckwheat flour

13/4 cups bread flour

1 teaspoon rapid-rising or active
   dry yeast

Regular Loaf

1 cup water

2 tablespoons canola or corn oil

2 tablespoons honey

1 1/2 teaspoons salt

2 tablespoons cracked wheat

1/3 cup buckwheat flour

2 2/3 cups bread flour

1 1/2 teaspoons rapid-rising or
   active dry yeast

Large Loaf

1 1/3 cups water

3 tablespoons canola or corn oil

3 tablespoons honey

2 teaspoons salt

3 tablespoons cracked wheat

1/2 cup buckwheat flour

3 1/2 cups bread flour

2 teaspoons rapid-rising or active
   dry yeast

TO MIX THE DOUGH BY HAND Heat the water until warm, between 105° and 115°F; pour it into a large, warmed bowl, and add the yeast. Let stand 5 minutes, until the yeast begins to bubble. Stir in the oil, honey, salt, cracked wheat, buckwheat flour, and half of the bread flour. Beat until a smooth dough forms. Cover, and let stand 15 minutes. Turn the dough out onto a very lightly floured board, and knead, adding the remaining flour as necessary, until smooth and springy, about 5 minutes. Wash the bowl and grease it; place the dough back in the bowl, and turn it over to grease the top. Cover, and let rise until doubled, about 1 hour.

TO MIX THE DOUGH WITH A HEAVY-DUTY MIXER Heat the water until warm, between 105° and 115°F; pour it into the warmed mixing bowl, and add the yeast. Let stand 5 minutes, until the yeast begins to bubble. Add the oil, honey, salt, cracked wheat, buckwheat flour, and half of the bread flour. Beat until a smooth dough forms. Cover, and let stand 15 minutes. Knead the dough in the mixer with the dough hook, on medium to high speed, adding the remaining flour as necessary, until the dough pulls away from the sides of the bowl and is smooth and springy but still soft to the touch. Remove the dough hook, cover the bowl, and let the dough rise until doubled, about 1 hour.

TO MIX THE DOUGH IN THE FOOD PROCESSOR Place the plastic dough blade into the work bowl. Heat the water until very warm, between 120° and 130°F; stir in the oil and honey, and set aside. Place the remaining ingredients into the work bowl. Turn the processor on, and slowly pour the water mixture through the feed tube, processing until the dough is smooth and pulls away from the sides of the bowl. If the dough is wet and sticky, add more flour, 1 tablespoon at a time, until the dough is smooth yet soft to the touch. If the dough is not soft to the touch but is very firm, add 1 tablespoon of water at a time, and process until the dough is smooth yet soft to the touch. Cover the work bowl, and let the dough rise until doubled, about 1 hour. Or remove the dough to a lightly greased bowl, cover, and let rise until doubled, about 1 hour.

TO MIX THE DOUGH IN THE BREAD MACHINE Pour the water (at room temperature) into the pan. Add the remaining ingredients, in the order listed. Make an indentation in the dry ingredients and add the yeast. Select *Dough,* and press *Start.* If the dough is wet and sticky, add more flour, 1 tablespoon at a time, until the dough is smooth yet soft to the touch. If the dough is not soft to the touch but is very firm, add 1 teaspoon of water at a time, until the dough is smooth yet soft to the touch. The machine will stop when the dough is ready to shape and bake.

TO MIX AND BAKE THE BREAD IN THE BREAD MACHINE Pour the water (at room temperature) into the pan. Add the remaining ingredients, in the order listed. Make an indentation in the dry ingredients and add the yeast. Select the *Basic* or *Whole Wheat* cycle, set the crust on *Medium,* and press *Start.* During the mixing cycle, if the dough is wet and sticky, add more flour, 1 tablespoon at a time, until the dough is smooth yet soft to the touch. If the dough is not soft to the touch but is very firm, add 1 teaspoon of water at a time, until the dough is smooth yet soft to the touch.

TO SHAPE AND BAKE IN THE OVEN Lightly grease a 4 × 8-inch or 5 × 9-inch loaf pan. Turn the dough out onto a lightly floured board or lightly oiled surface. Punch the dough down, and shape it into an oblong loaf. Place the loaf, with the smooth side up, into the pan. Cover, and let rise in a warm place until almost doubled, 45 minutes. Preheat the oven to 375°F. Bake 25 to 30 minutes, until the loaf is golden. Remove from the pan and cool on a wire rack.

BUTTERMILK OATMEAL BREAD

This homey, simple bread is a favorite of mine. It's absolutely delicious when it's warm, cut into thick slabs, buttered, and slathered with raspberry jam.

Sampler Loaf

2/3 cup boiling water

1/4 cup old-fashioned rolled oats

1 tablespoon butter or shortening

1 tablespoon sugar

3/4 teaspoon salt

1 1/2 tablespoons buttermilk powder

1/4 cup whole wheat flour

1 1/2 cups bread flour

1 teaspoon rapid-rising or active dry yeast

Regular Loaf

1 cup boiling water

1/3 cup old-fashioned rolled oats

2 tablespoons butter or shortening

2 tablespoons sugar

1 teaspoon salt

2 tablespoons buttermilk powder

1/3 cup whole wheat flour

2 1/3 cups bread flour

1 1/2 teaspoons rapid-rising or active dry yeast

Large Loaf

1 1/3 cups boiling water

1/2 cup old-fashioned rolled oats

3 tablespoons butter or shortening

3 tablespoons sugar

1 1/2 teaspoons salt

3 tablespoons buttermilk powder

1/2 cup whole wheat flour

3 cups bread flour

2 teaspoons rapid-rising or active dry yeast

GLAZE FOR BREAD BAKED CONVENTIONALLY

1 egg white, slightly beaten

Old-fashioned rolled oats

TO MIX THE DOUGH BY HAND Pour the water into a large bowl, and add the rolled oats. Let stand 15 minutes, until the mixture has cooled to warm, between 105° and 115°F. Add the yeast; let stand 5 minutes, until the yeast begins to bubble. Stir in the butter, sugar, salt, buttermilk powder, and whole wheat flour. Beat until a smooth dough forms. Cover, and let stand 15 minutes. Slowly add the bread flour, and beat until a stiff dough forms. Turn the dough out onto a very lightly floured board, and knead, adding flour if necessary, until smooth and springy, about 5 minutes. Wash the bowl and grease it; place the dough back in the bowl, and turn it over to grease the top. Cover, and let rise until doubled, about 1 hour.

TO MIX THE DOUGH WITH A HEAVY-DUTY MIXER Pour the water into the mixing bowl, and add the rolled oats. Let stand 15 minutes, until the mixture has cooled to warm, between 105° and 115°F. Add the yeast; let stand

5 minutes, until the yeast begins to bubble. Add the butter, sugar, salt, buttermilk powder, and the whole wheat flour. Beat until a smooth dough forms. Cover, and let stand 15 minutes. Slowly add the bread flour, and beat until a stiff dough forms. Knead the dough in the mixer with the dough hook, on medium to high speed, adding flour as necessary, until the dough pulls away from the sides of the bowl and is smooth and springy but still soft to the touch. Remove the dough hook, cover the bowl, and let the dough rise until doubled, about 1 hour.

TO MIX THE DOUGH IN THE FOOD PROCESSOR

Place the plastic dough blade into the work bowl. Pour half of the water into the work bowl, and add the rolled oats. Let stand 10 minutes, until the mixture has cooled to very warm, between 120° and 130°F. Add the remaining ingredients into the work bowl; processes until just blended. Slowly pour the remaining water (cooled to 120° to 130°F) through the feed tube, processing until the dough is smooth and pulls away from the sides of the bowl. If the dough is wet and sticky, add more flour, 1 tablespoon at a time, until the dough is smooth yet soft to the touch. If the dough is not soft to the touch but is very firm, add 1 tablespoon of water at a time, and process until the dough is smooth yet soft to the touch. Cover the work bowl, and let the dough rise until doubled, about 1 hour. Or remove the dough to a lightly greased bowl, cover, and let rise until doubled, about 1 hour.

TO MIX THE DOUGH IN THE BREAD MACHINE

Pour the water into the pan, and add the rolled oats. Let stand about 15 minutes, until the mixture has cooled to room temperature. Add the remaining ingredients, in the order listed. Make an indentation in the dry ingredients and add the yeast. Select *Dough,* and press *Start.* If the dough is wet and sticky, add more flour, 1 tablespoon at a time, until the dough is smooth yet soft to the touch. If the dough is not soft to the touch but is very firm, add 1 teaspoon of water at a time, until the dough is smooth yet soft to the touch. The machine will stop when the dough is ready to shape and bake.

TO MIX AND BAKE THE BREAD IN THE BREAD MACHINE

Pour the water into the pan, and add the rolled oats. Let stand about 15 minutes, until the mixture has cooled room temperature. Add the remaining ingredients, in the order listed. Make an indentation in the dry ingredients and add the yeast. Select the *Basic* cycle, set the crust on *Medium,* and press *Start.* During the mixing cycle, if the dough is wet and sticky, add more flour, 1 tablespoon at a time, until the dough is smooth yet soft to the touch. If the dough is not soft to the touch but is very firm, add 1 teaspoon of water at a time, until the dough is smooth yet soft to the touch.

TO SHAPE AND BAKE IN THE OVEN

Lightly grease a baking sheet, or cover it with parchment paper. Turn the dough out onto a lightly floured board or lightly oiled surface. Punch the dough down, and shape it into a round loaf. Place the loaf, with the smooth side up, onto the baking sheet. Cover and let rise in a warm place until almost doubled, 1 hour. Preheat the oven to 375°F. To glaze, brush the loaf with the egg white, and sprinkle on the rolled oats. Bake 35 to 45 minutes, until a wooden skewer inserted into the loaf comes out clean and dry. Remove from the pan and cool on a wire rack.

Baked Mushrooms with Cheese on Rye

These make very nice appetizers; to serve with a soup or salad, cover whole slices of bread with this mixture.

10 TO 12 SERVINGS

1 tablespoon butter

1 pound mushrooms, sliced

1/4 teaspoon freshly ground nutmeg

Salt and pepper to taste

1/4 cup heavy cream or sour cream

8 slices stale Bohemian Rye Bread (page 46), cut into 2 1/2-inch squares

1/2 cup shredded Gruyère or Swiss cheese

Chopped fresh parsley, for garnish

Preheat the oven to 400°F. In a large skillet, melt the butter. Add the mushrooms and sauté over medium heat for 10 minutes, until the liquid has evaporated. Reduce the heat to medium low; stir in the nutmeg, salt, pepper, and cream. Cook until thickened, about 3 to 4 minutes. Arrange the bread slices on a 9 × 12-inch baking pan. Spoon the mushroom mixture over the slices and sprinkle with cheese. Bake, uncovered, for 10 minutes, until the cheese is melted. Garnish with parsley.

Cheese Croutons

4 slices of Buttermilk Oatmeal Bread (page 50) or
any savory whole grain bread, 1/2 inch thick

1/4 cup olive or canola oil
Freshly grated Parmesan cheese

Preheat the oven to 375°F. Cut the bread into 1/2-inch cubes; toss in a large bowl with oil. Spread in a single layer on a cookie sheet, and bake for 25 to 35 minutes until golden and crisp. Sprinkle with the cheese while still warm.

CORNMEAL MOLASSES BREAD

The classic name for this bread is *anadama bread*. According to legend, a nineteenth-century fisherman was enraged that his wife, Anna, would always served him cornmeal mush for dinner and refused to change the menu. One evening when he felt he had had enough, the fisherman took the mush, threw in flour and yeast, and baked the mush into bread. Then he sat down to eat mumbling, "Anna, damn her!" Whether or not this is a true story will never be known, but this makes a wonderful bread.

Sampler Loaf	Regular Loaf	Large Loaf
2/3 cup boiling water	1 cup boiling water	11/3 cups boiling water
1/4 cup yellow cornmeal	1/3 cup yellow cornmeal	1/2 cup yellow cornmeal
2 tablespoons dark molasses	3 tablespoons dark molasses	1/4 cup dark molasses
1 tablespoon soft butter	2 tablespoons soft butter	3 tablespoons soft butter
1 teaspoon salt	11/2 teaspoons salt	2 teaspoons salt
13/4 cups bread flour	22/3 cups bread flour	31/2 cups bread flour
1 teaspoon rapid-rising or active dry yeast	11/2 teaspoons rapid-rising or active dry yeast	2 teaspoons rapid-rising or active dry yeast

TO MIX THE DOUGH BY HAND Pour the boiling water into a large bowl, add the cornmeal, and stir. Let stand until the mixture has cooled to warm, between 105° and 115°F. Add the molasses and yeast. Let stand 5 minutes, until the yeast begins to bubble. Stir in the butter, salt, and half of the bread flour. Beat until smooth. Cover, and let stand 15 minutes. Slowly add the remaining bread flour, and beat until a soft dough forms. Turn the dough out onto a very lightly floured board, and knead, adding flour if necessary, until smooth and springy, about 5 minutes. Wash the bowl and grease it; place the dough back in the bowl, and turn it over to grease the top. Cover, and let rise until doubled, about 1 hour.

TO MIX THE DOUGH WITH A HEAVY-DUTY MIXER Pour the boiling water in the mixing bowl, add the cornmeal, and stir. Let stand until the mixture has cooled to warm, between 105° and 115°F. Add the molasses and yeast. Let stand 5 minutes, until the yeast begins to bubble. Add the butter, salt, and half of the bread flour. Beat until smooth. Cover, and let stand 15 minutes. Slowly add the remaining bread flour, and beat until a soft dough forms. Knead the dough in the mixer with the dough hook, on medium to high speed, adding flour as necessary, until the dough pulls away from the sides of the bowl and is smooth and springy but still soft to the touch. Remove the dough hook, cover the bowl, and let the dough rise until doubled, about 1 hour.

TO MIX THE DOUGH IN THE FOOD PROCESSOR Place the plastic dough blade into the work bowl. Pour the water into the work bowl, add the cornmeal, and stir. Let stand until the mixture cools to very warm, between 120° and 130°F. Place the remaining ingredients into the work bowl; process until the dough is smooth and pulls away from the sides of the bowl. If the dough is wet and sticky, add more flour, 1 tablespoon at a time, until the dough is smooth yet soft to the touch. If the dough is not soft to the touch but is very firm, add 1 tablespoon of water at a time, and process until the dough is smooth yet soft to the touch. Cover the work bowl, and let the dough rise until doubled, about 1 hour. Or remove the dough to a lightly greased bowl, cover, and let rise until doubled, about 1 hour.

TO MIX THE DOUGH IN THE BREAD MACHINE Pour the boiling water into the pan, add the cornmeal, and stir. Let cool until the mixture is at room temperature. Add the remaining ingredients, in the order listed. Make an indentation in the dry ingredients and add the yeast. Select *Dough,* and press *Start.* If the dough is wet and sticky, add more flour, 1 tablespoon at a time, until the dough is smooth yet soft to the touch. If the dough is not soft to the touch but is very firm, add 1 teaspoon of water at a time, until the dough is smooth yet soft to the touch. The machine will stop when the dough is ready to shape and bake.

TO MIX AND BAKE THE BREAD IN THE BREAD MACHINE Pour the boiling water into the pan, add the cornmeal, and stir. Let cool until the mixture is at room temperature. Add the remaining ingredients, in the order listed. Make an indentation in the dry ingredients and add the yeast. Select the *Basic* cycle, set the crust on *Medium,* and press *Start.* During the mixing cycle, if the dough is wet and sticky, add more flour, 1 tablespoon at a time, until the dough is smooth yet soft to the touch. If the dough is not soft to the touch but is very firm, add 1 teaspoon of water at a time, until the dough is smooth yet soft to the touch.

TO SHAPE AND BAKE IN THE OVEN Lightly grease an 8- or 9-inch round cake pan. Turn the dough out onto a lightly floured board or lightly oiled surface. Punch the dough down, and shape it into a round loaf. Place the loaf, with the smooth side up, into the pan. Cover and let rise in a warm place until almost doubled, 45 minutes. Preheat the oven to 375°F. Bake 30 to 35 minutes, until the loaf is golden and a wooden skewer inserted into the loaf comes out clean and dry. Remove from the pan and cool on a wire rack.

CORNMEAL, RYE, AND WHOLE WHEAT BREAD

This is a perfect bread for everyday use. Dark rye flour is unsifted; therefore, it has the bran kernel in it. Although any whole wheat flour works well in this bread, I prefer graham whole wheat flour, because it contains the bran of the wheat, which gives a wonderful grainy texture to the bread.

Sampler Loaf	Regular Loaf	Large Loaf
3/4 cup water	1 cup water	1 1/2 cups water
2 tablespoons cornmeal	1/4 cup cornmeal	1/3 cup cornmeal
1 teaspoon salt	1 1/2 teaspoons salt	2 teaspoons salt
1 tablespoon packed brown sugar	2 tablespoons packed brown sugar	3 tablespoons packed brown sugar
2 teaspoons vegetable oil	1 tablespoon vegetable oil	2 tablespoons vegetable oil
1/4 cup dark rye flour	1/2 cup dark rye flour	3/4 cup dark rye flour
1/4 cup whole wheat flour	1/2 cup whole wheat flour	3/4 cup whole wheat flour
1 1/2 cups bread flour	1 1/2 cups bread flour	2 1/2 cups bread flour
1 teaspoon rapid-rising or active dry yeast	1 1/2 teaspoons rapid-rising or active dry yeast	2 teaspoons rapid-rising or active dry yeast

TO MIX THE DOUGH BY HAND Heat the water until warm, between 105° and 115°F; pour it along into a large, warmed bowl, and add the cornmeal and yeast. Let stand 5 minutes, until the yeast begins to bubble. Stir in the salt, brown sugar, oil, rye flour, whole wheat flour, and bread flour. Beat to make a stiff dough. Cover, and let stand 15 minutes. Turn the dough out onto a very lightly floured board, and knead, adding flour if necessary, until smooth and springy, about 5 minutes. Wash the bowl and grease it;

place the dough back in the bowl, and turn it over to grease the top. Cover, and let rise until doubled, about 1 hour.

TO MIX THE DOUGH WITH A HEAVY-DUTY MIXER Heat the water until warm, between 105° and 115°F; pour into the warmed mixing bowl, and add the cornmeal and yeast. Let stand 5 minutes, until the yeast begins to bubble. Add the salt, brown sugar, oil, rye flour, whole wheat flour, and bread flour. Beat to make a stiff dough.

Cover, and let stand 15 minutes. Knead the dough in the mixer with the dough hook, on medium to high speed, adding flour as necessary, until the dough pulls away from the sides of the bowl and is smooth and springy but still soft to the touch. Remove the dough hook, cover the bowl, and let the dough rise until doubled, about 1 hour.

TO MIX THE DOUGH IN THE FOOD PROCESSOR

Place the plastic dough blade into the work bowl. Heat the water until very warm, between 120° and 130°F; set aside. Place the remaining ingredients into the work bowl; process until well mixed. Turn the processor on, and slowly pour the water through the feed tube, processing until the dough is smooth and pulls away from the sides of the bowl. If the dough is wet and sticky, add more flour, 1 tablespoon at a time, until the dough is smooth yet soft to the touch. If the dough is not soft to the touch but is very firm, add 1 tablespoon of water at a time, and process until the dough is smooth yet soft to the touch. Cover the work bowl, and let the dough rise until doubled, about 1 hour. Or remove the dough to a lightly greased bowl, cover, and let rise until doubled, about 1 hour.

TO MIX THE DOUGH IN THE BREAD MACHINE

Pour the water (at room temperature) into the pan. Add the remaining ingredients, in the order listed. Make an indentation in the dry ingredients and add the yeast. Select *Dough,* and press *Start.* If the dough is wet and sticky, add more flour, 1 tablespoon at a time, until the dough is smooth yet soft to the touch. If the dough is not soft to the touch but is very firm, add 1 teaspoon of water at a time, until the dough is smooth yet soft to the touch. The machine will stop when the dough is ready to shape and bake.

TO MIX AND BAKE THE BREAD IN THE BREAD MACHINE

Pour the water (at room temperature) into the pan. Add the remaining ingredients, in the order listed. Make an indentation in the dry ingredients and add the yeast. Select the *Basic* or *Whole Wheat* cycle, set the crust on *Medium,* and press *Start.* During the mixing cycle, if the dough is wet and sticky, add more flour, 1 tablespoon at a time, until the dough is smooth yet soft to the touch. If the dough is not soft to the touch but is very firm, add 1 teaspoon of water at a time, until the dough is smooth yet soft to the touch.

TO SHAPE AND BAKE IN THE OVEN

Lightly grease rimless baking sheet. Turn the dough out onto a lightly floured board or lightly oiled surface. Punch the dough down, and shape it into a round loaf. Place the loaf, with the smooth side up, onto the baking sheet. Cover, and let rise in a warm place until almost doubled, 45 minutes. Preheat the oven to 375°F. Brush the loaf with water, and slash the top with a sharp knife to make a crisscross pattern. Bake 40 to 45 minutes, until the loaf is golden. Remove from the pan and cool on a wire rack.

COUNTRY WHITE BREAD

This old-fashioned loaf has just a bit of either barley or oat flour, which gives it a rich, nutty flavor and a creamy colored crumb.

Sampler Loaf	Regular Loaf	Large Loaf
2/3 cup water	1 cup water	1 1/3 cups water
3/4 teaspoon salt	1 teaspoon salt	1 1/2 teaspoons salt
2 teaspoons sugar	1 tablespoon sugar	1 1/2 tablespoons sugar
1/4 cup barley or oat flour	1/3 cup barley or oat flour	1/2 cup barley or oat flour
1 3/4 cups bread flour	2 2/3 cup bread flour	3 1/2 cups bread flour
1 teaspoon rapid-rising or active dry yeast	1 1/2 teaspoons rapid-rising or active dry yeast	2 teaspoons rapid-rising or active dry yeast

TO MIX THE DOUGH BY HAND Heat the water until warm, between 105° and 115°F; pour it into a large, warmed bowl, and add the yeast. Let stand 5 minutes, until the yeast begins to bubble. Stir in the salt, sugar, barley flour, and half of the bread flour. Beat until smooth. Cover, and let stand 15 minutes. Slowly add the remaining bread flour, and beat until a soft dough forms. Turn the dough out onto a very lightly floured board, and knead, adding flour if necessary, until smooth and springy, about 5 minutes. Wash the bowl and grease it; place the dough back in the bowl, and turn it over to grease the top. Cover, and let rise until doubled, about 1 hour.

TO MIX THE DOUGH WITH A HEAVY-DUTY MIXER Heat the water until warm, between 105° and 115°F; pour it into the warmed mixing bowl, and add the yeast. Let stand 5 minutes, until the yeast begins to bubble. Add the salt, sugar, barley flour, and half of the bread flour. Beat until smooth. Cover, and let stand 15 minutes. Slowly add the remaining bread flour, and beat until a soft dough forms. Knead the dough in the mixer with the dough hook, on medium to high speed, adding flour as necessary, until the dough pulls away from the sides of the bowl and is smooth and springy but still soft to the touch. Remove the dough hook, cover the bowl, and let the dough rise until doubled, about 1 hour.

TO MIX THE DOUGH IN THE FOOD PROCESSOR
Place the plastic dough blade into the work bowl. Heat the water until very warm, between 120° and 130°F; set aside. Place the remaining ingredients into the work bowl. Turn the processor on, and slowly pour the water through the feed tube, processing until the dough is smooth and pulls away from the sides of the bowl. If the dough is wet and sticky, add more flour, 1 tablespoon at a time, until the dough is smooth yet soft to the touch. If the dough is not soft to the touch but is very firm, add 1 tablespoon of water at a time, and process until the dough is smooth yet soft to the touch. Cover the work bowl, and let the dough rise until doubled, about 1 hour. Or remove the dough to a lightly greased bowl, cover, and let rise until doubled, about 1 hour.

TO MIX THE DOUGH IN THE BREAD MACHINE Pour the water (at room temperature) into the pan. Add the remaining ingredients, in the order listed. Make an indentation in the dry ingredients and add the yeast. Select *Dough,* and press *Start.* If the dough is wet and sticky, add more flour, 1 tablespoon at a time, until the dough is smooth yet soft to the touch. If the dough is not soft to the touch but is very firm, add 1 teaspoon of water at a time, until the dough is smooth yet soft to the touch. The machine will stop when the dough is ready to shape and bake.

TO MIX AND BAKE THE BREAD IN THE BREAD MACHINE Pour the water (at room temperature) into the pan. Add the remaining ingredients, in the order listed. Make an indentation in the dry ingredients and add the yeast. Select the *Basic* cycle, set the crust on *Medium,* and press *Start.* During the mixing cycle, if the dough is wet and sticky, add more flour, 1 tablespoon at a time, until the dough is smooth yet soft to the touch. If the dough is not soft to the touch but is very firm, add 1 teaspoon of water at a time, until the dough is smooth yet soft to the touch.

TO SHAPE AND BAKE IN THE OVEN Lightly grease a baking sheet, or cover it with parchment paper. Turn the dough out onto a lightly floured board or lightly oiled surface. Punch the dough down, and shape it into a round loaf, dusting it on all sides with flour. Place the loaf, with the smooth side up, onto the baking sheet. Cover and let rise in a warm place until almost doubled, 45 minutes. Preheat the oven to 375°F. Using a sharp knife or razor, slash a 3-inch circle on the very top of the loaf. Bake 30 to 35 minutes, until the loaf is golden and a wooden skewer inserted into the loaf comes out clean and dry. Remove from the pan and cool on a wire rack.

Black Bean and Sweet Corn Spread

This spread turns slices of almost any bread that contains cornmeal into a meal. Even though there are several steps involved in making this dish, it is worth the effort. It's the best served warm; so if you make it ahead, reheat it in the microwave oven before serving. When handling hot peppers, use gloves and be careful not to touch your eyes.

3 CUPS

1 cup dried black beans
1 small onion, finely diced
1 jalapeño pepper, seeded and minced
2 garlic cloves, minced
1 teaspoon salt
1 cup sweet corn kernels, or frozen
    whole-kernel corn
1 tablespoon extra-virgin olive oil

1 meaty large tomato
1 large poblano chili
1 cup shredded Monterey Jack cheese
1/2 cup shredded sharp Cheddar cheese
2 green onions, thinly sliced, including the
    green part
Cornmeal, Rye, and Whole Wheat Bread (page 56),
    fresh, or made into croutons

Wash and pick over the beans. Place in a large saucepan, and add cold water to cover. Bring to a boil, turn the heat off, and let stand 1 hour. Drain, rinse beans, and add fresh water to cover. Add the onion, jalapeño pepper, and garlic. Bring to a boil, reduce the heat, and simmer for 2 hours, until the beans are tender. Add more water if the beans become dry. Add the salt.

Meanwhile, preheat the oven to 450°F. Toss the corn with 2 teaspoons of the oil. Rub the tomato and the poblano chili with the remaining 1 teaspoon of oil. Place all in a roasting pan together, and roast 15 to 20 minutes, until the tomato and chili are charred. Remove from the oven, and place the tomato and chili into a paper bag. Place the corn into a small bowl.

Slip the skins off the tomato and chili. Deseed the chili. Chop the tomato and chili and add, along with the corn, to the beans. Simmer 15 minutes, stirring and mashing the beans until thick and creamy. Reduce the heat to low, and add the cheeses; taste, and add additional salt, if necessary. Mix and transfer to a serving dish and garnish with the green onions.

Grilled Vegetable Salad with Grilled Bread

This is absolutely perfect for a summer menu for entertaining! But I love this salad so much, that I'll serve it for lunch through the autumn, as long as we have the vegetables on hand. Sometimes I substitute other vegetables for those in the list. Most of the year though, where we live, outdoor grilling is impossible; so I roast the vegetables in a 500°F oven. Lately, I've been able to find sweet onions almost all year round—in the summer it's Vidalia; for the rest of the year there are other sweet onions, from Texas to Maui Sweet.

6 TO 8 SERVING

3/4 cup extra-virgin olive oil

1/4 cup balsamic vinegar

1 large sweet onion, cut into 3/4-inch-thick rounds

12 small red-skinned potatoes, unpeeled, halved

3 small zucchini, cut lengthwise into 4 slices

3 Japanese or Thai eggplants, cut lengthwise into quarters

1 large red bell pepper, stemmed, seeded, and cut into 1-inch-wide strips

1 large yellow bell pepper, stemmed, seeded, and cut into 1-inch-wide strips

1 teaspoon coarse (kosher) salt

1/2 teaspoon freshly ground coarse black pepper

6 thick slices (1/2 to 3/4 inches) Country White Bread (page 58)

Additional extra-virgin olive oil

FOR SERVING

10 cups mixed baby greens

4 large tomatoes, sliced

3 tablespoons chopped fresh basil

2 tablespoons chopped fresh chives or green onions

4 ounces crumbled feta cheese

1/2 cup freshly grated Parmigiano-Reggiano cheese

3/4 cup kalamata olives

Prepare the grill or preheat the oven to 500°F. Mix the 3/4 cup olive oil and vinegar. Brush the mixture onto the onion slices. Toss the mixture with the potatoes, zucchini, eggplants, and bell peppers. Sprinkle the vegetables with salt and black pepper. Grill the vegetables until just cooked through, about 10 minutes per side for the potatoes, 6 minutes per side for the onion, and 4 minutes per side for the zucchini, eggplants, and peppers. Or spread all of the vegetables in a single layer on a foil-covered baking sheet and roast the lot for 15 to 20 minutes.

Brush the bread with the additional olive oil and sprinkle with black pepper. Grill or roast the bread until it is just beginning to brown, about 2 minutes per side on the grill or 4 minutes in the oven.

To serve, arrange the greens on a large platter. Overlap the tomatoes on top of the greens in the center. Sprinkle with salt and pepper. Arrange the grilled vegetables around the edges. Sprinkle with the chopped basil, chives, cheeses, and olives. Surround with the bread, and serve immediately.

ELEVEN-GRAIN BUCKWHEAT BREAD

Ten-grain breakfast cereal looks like cracked wheat and usually comes in small 1-pound bags at the super-market. If you cannot find 10-grain cereal, you can use cracked wheat or any other multigrain cereal. Buckwheat flour adds its aromatic, bitter flavor to this bread. Buckwheat flour also comes in 1-pound bags; if you cannot find it, substitute light rye flour.

Sampler Loaf

$2/3$ cup boiling water

$1/4$ cup 10-grain breakfast cereal

1 tablespoon light molasses

1 teaspoon salt

$1/2$ tablespoon canola oil

$1/4$ cup buckwheat flour

$1^1/2$ cups bread flour

1 teaspoon rapid-rising or active
   dry yeast

$1/4$ cup raisins

Regular Loaf

1 cup boiling water

$1/2$ cup 10-grain breakfast cereal

2 tablespoons light molasses

$1^1/2$ teaspoons salt

1 tablespoon canola oil

$1/2$ cup buckwheat flour

2 cups bread flour

$1^1/2$ teaspoons rapid-rising or
   active dry yeast

$1/3$ cup raisins

Large Loaf

$1^1/3$ cups boiling water

$3/4$ cup 10-grain breakfast cereal

3 tablespoons light molasses

2 teaspoons salt

2 tablespoons canola oil

$3/4$ cup buckwheat flour

3 cups bread flour

2 teaspoons rapid-rising or active
   dry yeast

$1/2$ cup raisins

GLAZE FOR BREAD BAKED CONVENTIONALLY

1 tablespoon dark or light molasses

1 tablespoon water

TO MIX THE DOUGH BY HAND   Pour the boiling water in a large bowl, add the cereal, and stir. Let stand 25 minutes, until the mixture cools to warm, between 105° and 115°F. Add the yeast and molasses. Let stand 5 minutes, until the yeast begins to bubble. Stir in the salt, oil, buckwheat flour, and half of the bread flour. Beat until a smooth dough forms. Cover, and let stand 15 minutes. Stir in most of the remaining bread flour. Turn the dough out onto a very lightly floured board, and knead, adding flour if necessary, until smooth and springy, about 5 minutes. Knead in the raisins. Wash the bowl and grease it; place the dough back in the bowl, and turn it over to grease the top. Cover, and let rise until doubled, about 1 hour.

TO MIX THE DOUGH WITH A HEAVY-DUTY MIXER Pour the boiling water in the mixing bowl, add the cereal, and stir. Let stand 25 minutes, until the mixture cools to warm, between 105° and 115°F. add the yeast and molasses. Let stand 5 minutes, until the yeast begins to bubble. Add the salt, oil, buckwheat flour, and half of the bread flour. Beat until a smooth dough forms. Cover, and let stand 15 minutes. Beat in most of the remaining bread flour. Knead the dough in the mixer with the dough hook, on medium to high speed, adding flour as necessary, until the dough pulls away from the sides of the bowl and is smooth and springy but still soft to the touch. Knead in the raisins. Remove the dough hook, cover the bowl, and let the dough rise until doubled, about 1 hour.

TO MIX THE DOUGH IN THE FOOD PROCESSOR Place the plastic dough blade into the work bowl. Pour the boiling water into the work bowl, add the cereal, and stir. Let stand 25 minutes, until the mixture cools to very warm, between 120° and 130°F. Place the remaining ingredients, except the raisins, into the work bowl. Process until the dough is smooth and pulls away from the sides of the bowl. If the dough is wet and sticky, add more flour, 1 tablespoon at a time, until the dough is smooth yet soft to the touch. If the dough is not soft to the touch but is very firm, add 1 tablespoon of water at a time, and process until the dough is smooth yet soft to the touch. Mix in the raisins. Cover the work bowl, and let the dough rise until doubled, about 1 hour. Or remove the dough to a lightly greased bowl, cover, and let rise until doubled, about 1 hour.

TO MIX THE DOUGH IN THE BREAD MACHINE Pour the boiling water into the pan, add the cereal, and stir. Let stand 25 to 30 minutes, until the mixture cools to room temperature. Add the remaining ingredients, except the raisins, in the order listed. Make an indentation in the dry ingredients and add the yeast. If desired, the raisins can be added 20 to 25 minutes after the mixing begins. Select *Dough*, and press *Start*. If the dough is wet and sticky, add more flour, 1 tablespoon at a time, until the dough is smooth yet soft to the touch. If the dough is not soft to the touch but is very firm, add 1 teaspoon of water at a time, until the dough is smooth yet soft to the touch. Add the raisins when the machine signals it's time to add ingredients or when the cycle ends. The machine will stop when the dough is ready to shape and bake.

TO MIX AND BAKE THE BREAD IN THE BREAD MACHINE Pour the boiling water into the pan, add the cereal, and stir. Let stand 25 to 30 minutes, until the mixture cools to room temperature. Add the remaining ingredients, except the raisins, in the order listed. Make an indentation in the dry ingredients and add the yeast. If desired, the raisins can be added 20 to 25 minutes after the mixing begins. Select the *Fruit and Nut, Basic,* or *Whole Wheat* cycle; set the crust on *Medium;* and press *Start*. During the mixing cycle, if the dough is wet and sticky, add more flour, 1 tablespoon at a time, until the dough is smooth yet soft to the touch. If the dough is not soft to the touch but is very firm, add 1 teaspoon of water at a time, until the dough is smooth yet soft to the touch. Add the raisins when the machine signals it's time to add ingredients.

TO SHAPE AND BAKE IN THE OVEN Lightly grease an 8- or 9-inch round cake pan. Turn the dough out onto a lightly floured board or lightly oiled surface. Punch the dough down, and shape it into a round loaf. Place the loaf, with the smooth side up, into the pan. Cover and let rise in a warm place until almost doubled, 45 minutes. Preheat the oven to 375°F. To glaze, mix the molasses and water, and brush on the loaf. Bake 35 to 40 minutes, until a wooden skewer inserted into the loaf comes out clean and dry. Remove from the pan and cool on a wire rack.

Steak in a Bag

The spicy crumbs stay crispy and the steak is cooked to perfection—all in a brown paper bag.

6 SERVINGS

1 boneless sirloin steak (3-pound), 2 inches thick

4 tablespoons extra-virgin olive oil

2 large garlic cloves, minced or pressed

1 teaspoon slightly crushed fresh rosemary

1 teaspoon coarse (kosher) salt

1/2 teaspoon freshly ground coarse pepper

1 cup coarse bread crumbs made from Eleven-Grain Buckwheat Bread (page 62) or other wheat bread

Preheat the oven to 375°F. Pat the steak dry with paper towels. Blend the remaining ingredients together, until the crumbs are all coated with the oil. Place the crumbs on a piece of waxed paper, and press the steak into the crumbs to coat on all sides. Place the steak into a brown paper bag, close with paper clips, and place the bag on a cookie sheet. Bake 1 hour 15 minutes for rare. For more well-done meat, bake 30 to 45 minutes longer. Open the bag, and check for doneness by inserting a thermometer from the side of the steak into the center. Allow to stand 20 minutes before carving. Cut into slices on the diagonal.

FINNISH RYE BREAD

This is the simple rye flour bread I grew up with on a farm in northern Minnesota. My mother baked more than twenty loaves of it twice a week!

Sampler Loaf

²/₃ cup water

1 teaspoon packed brown sugar

2 teaspoons butter or oil

1 teaspoon salt

¹/₂ cup dark rye flour

1¹/₂ cups bread flour

1 teaspoon rapid-rising or active
  dry yeast

Regular Loaf

1 cup water

2 teaspoons packed brown sugar

1 tablespoons butter or oil

1¹/₂ teaspoons salt

³/₄ cup dark rye flour

2¹/₄ cups bread flour

1¹/₂ teaspoons rapid-rising or
  active dry yeast

Large Loaf

1¹/₃ cups water

1 tablespoon packed brown sugar

1¹/₂ tablespoons butter or oil

2 teaspoons salt

1 cup dark rye flour

3 cups bread flour

2 teaspoons rapid-rising or active
  dry yeast

TO MIX THE DOUGH BY HAND Heat the water until warm, between 105° and 115°F; pour it into a large, warmed bowl, and add the yeast. Let stand 5 minutes, until the yeast begins to bubble. Stir in the brown sugar, butter, salt, and rye flour. Beat well. Slowly add half of the bread flour, and beat until a smooth dough forms. Cover, and let stand 15 minutes. Turn the dough out onto a very lightly floured board, and knead, adding the remaining flour as necessary, until smooth and springy, about 5 minutes. Wash the bowl and grease it; place the dough back in the bowl, and turn it over to grease the top. Cover, and let rise until doubled, about 1 hour.

TO MIX THE DOUGH WITH A HEAVY-DUTY MIXER Heat the water until warm, between 105° and 115°F; pour it into the warmed mixing bowl, and add the yeast. Let stand 5 minutes, until the yeast begins to bubble. Add the brown sugar, butter, salt, and rye flour. Beat well. Slowly add half of the bread flour, and beat until a soft dough forms. Cover, and let stand 15 minutes. Knead the dough in the mixer with the dough hook, on medium to high speed, adding the remaining flour as necessary, until the dough pulls away from the sides of the bowl and is smooth and springy but still soft to the touch. Remove the dough hook, cover the bowl, and let the dough rise until doubled, about 1 hour.

TO MIX THE DOUGH IN THE FOOD PROCESSOR Place the plastic dough blade into the work bowl. Heat the water until very warm, between 120° and 130°F; set aside. Place the remaining ingredients into the work bowl. Turn the processor on, and slowly pour the water through the feed tube, processing until the dough is smooth and pulls away from the sides of the bowl. If the dough is wet and sticky, add more flour, 1 tablespoon at a time, until the dough is smooth yet soft to the touch. If the dough is not soft to the touch but is very firm, add 1 tablespoon of water at a time, and process until the dough is smooth yet soft to the touch. Cover the work bowl, and let the dough rise until doubled, about 1 hour. Or remove the dough to a lightly greased bowl, cover, and let rise until doubled, about 1 hour.

TO MIX THE DOUGH IN THE BREAD MACHINE Pour the water (at room temperature) into the pan. Add the remaining ingredients, in the order listed. Make an indentation in the dry ingredients and add the yeast. Select *Dough,* and press *Start.* If the dough is wet and sticky, add more flour, 1 tablespoon at a time, until the dough is smooth yet soft to the touch. If the dough is not soft to the touch but is very firm, add 1 teaspoon of water at a time, until the dough is smooth yet soft to the touch. The machine will stop when the dough is ready to shape and bake.

TO MIX AND BAKE THE BREAD IN THE BREAD MACHINE Pour the water (at room temperature) into the pan. Add the remaining ingredients, in the order listed. Make an indentation in the dry ingredients and add the yeast. Select the *Basic* or *Whole Wheat* cycle, set the crust on *Medium,* and press *Start.* During the mixing cycle, if the dough is wet and sticky, add more flour, 1 tablespoon at a time, until the dough is smooth yet soft to the touch. If the dough is not soft to the touch but is very firm, add 1 teaspoon

of water at a time, until the dough is smooth yet soft to the touch.

TO SHAPE AND BAKE IN THE OVEN Lightly grease an 8- or 9-inch round cake pan or a rimless baking sheet. Turn the dough out onto a lightly floured board or lightly oiled surface. Punch the dough down, and shape it into a round loaf. Place the loaf, with the smooth side up, into the pan. Cover and let rise in a warm place until almost doubled, 45 to 60 minutes. Preheat the oven to 375°F. Bake 35 to 40 minutes, until the loaf is golden and a wooden skewer inserted into the loaf comes out clean and dry. Brush the top of the loaf while it's still hot with melted butter, if desired. Remove from the pan and cool on a wire rack.

Gravlax on Rye with Caper and Dill

This elegant starter is a fabulous combination of flavors and is perfect for a special occasion. It is really a quick-and-easy, last-minute put-together, once you have the bread and the gravlax made. Gravlax is easy to make yourself, but you do need to start 24 hours before you want to serve it.

4 SERVINGS

8 thin slices Finnish Rye Bread or sourdough rye bread baked in baguettes

8 teaspoons unsalted butter

4 ounces gravlax, purchased or freshly made (recipe follows)

1/4 cup sour cream

2 tablespoons capers, drained

2 tablespoons finely chopped sweet onion

8 fresh dill sprigs or 2 teaspoons dried dillweed

Toast the bread until lightly browned. Spread each slice with 1 tablespoon unsalted butter. With a sharp knife, cut the gravlax into thin slices on the diagonal, and crumple them equally onto the toasted bread. Top each with 1/2 tablespoon sour cream. Sprinkle each with the capers and onion, and top each with a dill sprig.

Gravlax

It's simple to make your own gravlax, and you do not need to make a huge amount. If you can get fresh

salmon, you can do it in 24 hours.

1/2 POUND

1/2 pound salmon fillet
1 tablespoon coarse (kosher) salt
1 tablespoon packed brown sugar
1/8 teaspoon white pepper

Place the salmon into a glass or nonreactive pan. (An 8- or 9-inch glass cake pan is perfect.)

Mix the salt, sugar, and pepper. Rub the mixture onto the salmon on all sides, and place the fish back into the pan with the skin side down. Cover lightly with plastic wrap and place a weight on top. (I use a foil-covered brick.) Refrigerate 24 hours.

Remove the weight and plastic wrap; drain the pan of any juices that might have accumulated. With a paper towel, brush off the excess salt-sugar mixture.

With a sharp knife, cut the gravlax into very thin slices on the diagonal. Store, wrapped in plastic, in the refrigerator for 2 to 3 days, or freeze to keep for a longer time.

Finnish Sandwich Cake

I was talking with a Finnish friend one day, and she commented that the only time she uses her bread machine is when she wants to make a *voileipäkakku* (sandwich cake). Of course, I explained to her that she can mix almost any bread dough in the bread machine; then shape and bake it conventionally. She expressed surprise and thought that would be a real convenience. But I got an idea from her too: that bread baked in the machine makes the perfect shape for a sandwich loaf such as this. You can substitute all kinds of fillings. Although this recipe looks long and involved, it's really not difficult to make.

8 SERVINGS

1 large loaf of Finnish Rye Bread baked in
   the machine (page 66)
1/4 cup cold chicken or vegetable broth

EGG SALAD FILLING

4 hard-cooked eggs, shelled and chopped
1/4 cup mayonnaise
2 tablespoons chopped fresh dill
Salt and freshly ground black, to taste

MEAT FILLING

1 cup ground cooked chicken, turkey, or
   smoked ham
1/4 cup mayonnaise
2 teaspoon Dijon-style mustard
1 teaspoon prepared horseradish

CUCUMBER FILLING

1 cup shredded, deseeded cucumber (peeled, if it
   has been waxed)
1 tablespoon dillweed
1 tablespoon finely chopped parsley
1 tablespoon chopped fresh chives or grated onion
2 tablespoons sour cream or mayonnaise
2 teaspoon white vinegar
1 teaspoon sugar
Salt and freshly ground black, to taste

CREAM CHEESE FROSTING

1 package (8 ounces) regular or light cream cheese
1/4 cup sour cream

GARNISHES

1/2 chopped fresh herbs such as dill, parsley, chives,
   and savory
Thinly sliced ham
Thinly sliced cucumber
Cherry tomatoes

The day before serving, bake the large-sized loaf of bread in the bread machine, or make two regular-sized loaves. Loaf should be thoroughly cooled for easiest slicing. Trim the crusts.* Cut the loaf from top to bottom, assuming your machine has a square bread pan, into 4 slices.

Make the fillings. In separate bowls, mix all the ingredients for each of the fillings.

Place one slice of bread on a plate or board and sprinkle with 1 tablespoon of the broth. Spread the Egg Salad Filling evenly over the bread. Top a slice of bread, and sprinkle with 1 tablespoon of the broth. Spread the Meat Filling evenly over the bread. Top with a slice of bread, and sprinkle with 1 tablespoon of the broth. Spread the Cucumber Filling evenly over the bread. Top with the remaining slice of bread, and sprinkle with the remaining 1 tablespoon of broth. Wrap the loaf tightly with plastic wrap, and place onto a pan or board. Top with another board and a weight. Refrigerate overnight.

The next day, soften the cream cheese and mix with the sour cream using a hand mixer until well blended. Frost the sandwich loaf with this mixture, and garnish with the chopped herbs, ham, cucumber, and cherry tomatoes. Cut crosswise into slices to serve.

*Note   The crusts make great crumbs for all kinds of uses; bag and freeze them.

MAPLE OATMEAL BREAD

My husband and I really enjoy fresh bread in the morning. To wake up to the aroma of freshly baked bread was something you once could do only if you lived next to a bakery or traveled in Europe! This is a perfect bread for breakfast, if you set your machine to the *Delay-Start* cycle.

Sampler Loaf

2/3 cup water

1/4 cup old-fashioned rolled oats

1/2 tablespoon butter

1 tablespoon 100% pure maple syrup

3/4 teaspoon salt

1/4 cup whole wheat flour

1 1/2 cups bread flour

1 teaspoon rapid-rising or active dry yeast

Regular Loaf

1 cup water

1/2 cup old-fashioned rolled oats

1 tablespoon butter

2 tablespoons 100% pure maple syrup

1 teaspoon salt

1/2 cup whole wheat flour

2 cups bread flour

1 1/2 teaspoons rapid-rising or active dry yeast

Large Loaf

1 1/3 cups water

3/4 cup old-fashioned rolled oats

2 tablespoons butter

3 tablespoons 100% pure maple syrup

1 1/2 teaspoons salt

1 cup whole wheat flour

2 1/4 cups bread flour

2 teaspoons rapid-rising or active dry yeast

TO MIX THE DOUGH BY HAND Heat the water until warm, between 105° and 115°F; pour it into a large, warmed bowl, and add the yeast and rolled oats. Let stand 5 minutes, until the yeast begins to bubble. Stir in the butter, syrup, salt, and whole wheat flour. Beat until a smooth batter forms. Cover, and let stand 15 minutes. Slowly add the bread flour, and beat until a stiff dough forms. Turn the dough out onto a very lightly floured board, and knead, adding flour if necessary, until smooth and springy, about 5 minutes. Wash the bowl and grease it; place the dough back in the bowl, and turn it over to grease the top. Cover, and let rise until doubled, about 1 hour.

TO MIX THE DOUGH WITH A HEAVY-DUTY MIXER Heat the water until warm, between 105° and 115°F; pour it into the warmed mixing bowl, and add the yeast and rolled oats. Let stand 5 minutes, until the yeast begins to bubble. Add the butter, syrup, salt, and the whole wheat flour. Beat until a smooth batter forms. Cover, and let stand 15 minutes. Slowly add the bread flour, and beat until a stiff dough forms. Knead the dough in the mixer with the dough hook, on medium to high speed, adding flour as necessary, until the dough pulls away from the sides of the bowl and is smooth and springy but still soft to the touch. Remove the dough hook, cover the bowl, and let the dough rise until doubled, about 1 hour.

TO MIX THE DOUGH IN THE FOOD PROCESSOR
Place the plastic dough blade into the work bowl.
Heat the water until very warm, between 120°
and 130°F; set aside. Place the remaining ingredients into the work bowl. Turn the processor on,
and slowly pour the water through the feed tube,
processing until the dough is smooth and pulls
away from the sides of the bowl. If the dough is
wet and sticky, add more flour, 1 tablespoon at a
time, until the dough is smooth yet soft to the
touch. If the dough is not soft to the touch but is
very firm, add 1 tablespoon of water at a time,
and process until the dough is smooth yet soft to
the touch. Cover the work bowl, and let the
dough rise until doubled, about 1 hour. Or
remove the dough to a lightly greased bowl, cover,
and let rise until doubled, about 1 hour.

**TO MIX THE DOUGH IN THE BREAD
MACHINE** Pour the water (at room temperature) into the pan. Add the remaining ingredients, in the order listed. Make an indentation in
the dry ingredients and add the yeast. Select
Dough, and press *Start.* If the dough is wet and
sticky, add more flour, 1 tablespoon at a time,
until the dough is smooth yet soft to the touch. If
the dough is not soft to the touch but is very
firm, add 1 teaspoon of water at a time, until the
dough is smooth yet soft to the touch. The
machine will stop when the dough is ready to
shape and bake.

**TO MIX AND BAKE THE BREAD IN THE
BREAD MACHINE** Pour the water (at room
temperature) into the pan. Add the remaining
ingredients, in the order listed. Make an indentation in the dry ingredients and add the yeast.
Select the *Basic* cycle, set the crust on *Medium,*

and press *Start.* During the mixing cycle, if the
dough is wet and sticky, add more flour, 1 tablespoon at a time, until the dough is smooth yet
soft to the touch. If the dough is not soft to the
touch but is very firm, add 1 teaspoon of water at
a time, until the dough is smooth yet soft to the
touch.

TO SHAPE AND BAKE IN THE OVEN Lightly
grease an 8- or 9-inch round cake pan. Turn the
dough out onto a lightly floured board or lightly
oiled surface. Punch the dough down, and shape
it into a round loaf. Place the loaf, with the
smooth side up, into the pan. Cover and let rise in
a warm place until almost doubled, 1 hour.
Preheat the oven to 375°F. Bake 35 to 40 minutes, until a wooden skewer inserted into the loaf
comes out clean. Remove from the pan and cool
on a wire rack.

OLD-FASHIONED OAT
AND RYE BREAD

This is a great bread for breakfast, whether it's baked on the *Delay-Start* cycle or baked conventionally in advance. If you do decide to bake this loaf on the *Delay-Start* cycle, be sure to place the dry milk on top of the flour so that it will not get wet until the mixing begins.

Sampler Loaf	Regular Loaf	Large Loaf
3/4 cup boiling water	1 cup boiling water	1 1/2 cups boiling water
1/4 cup old-fashioned rolled oats	1/2 cup old-fashioned rolled oats	3/4 cup old-fashioned rolled oats
1 tablespoon butter or oil	2 tablespoons butter or oil	1/4 cup butter or oil
2 tablespoons packed brown sugar	1/4 cup packed brown sugar	6 tablespoons packed brown sugar
3/4 teaspoon salt	1 teaspoon salt	1 1/2 teaspoons salt
1/2 cup stone-ground rye flour	3/4 cup stone-ground rye flour	1 cup stone-ground rye flour
1 1/4 cups bread flour	1 3/4 cups bread flour	2 1/4 cups bread flour
2 tablespoons nonfat dry milk	1/4 cup nonfat dry milk	1/2 cup nonfat dry milk
1 teaspoon rapid-rising or active dry yeast	1 1/2 teaspoons rapid-rising or active dry yeast	2 teaspoons rapid-rising or active dry yeast

TO MIX THE DOUGH BY HAND   Pour the boiling water into a large bowl, and add the rolled oats. Let stand 25 to 35 minutes, until the mixture has cooled to warm, between 105° and 115°F. Add the yeast; let stand 5 minutes, until the yeast begins to bubble. Stir in the butter, sugar, salt, and rye flour. Beat until a smooth dough forms. Cover, and let stand 15 minutes. Slowly add the bread flour and dry milk, and beat until a stiff dough forms. Turn the dough out onto a very lightly floured board, and knead, adding flour if necessary, until smooth and springy, about 5 minutes. Wash the bowl and grease it; place the dough back in the bowl, and turn it over to grease the top. Cover, and let rise until doubled, about 1 hour.

TO MIX THE DOUGH WITH A HEAVY-DUTY MIXER   Pour the boiling water into the mixing bowl, and add the rolled oats. Let stand 25 to 35 minutes until the mixture cools to warm, between 105° and 115°F. Add the yeast; let stand 5 minutes, until the yeast begins to bubble. Add the butter, sugar, salt, and rye flour. Beat until a smooth dough forms. Cover, and let stand 15 minutes. Slowly add the bread flour and dry milk, and beat until a stiff dough forms. Knead the dough in the mixer with the dough hook, on medium to high speed, adding flour as necessary, until the dough pulls away from the sides of the bowl and is smooth and springy but still soft to the touch. Remove the dough hook, cover the bowl, and let the dough rise until doubled, about 1 hour.

TO MIX THE DOUGH IN THE FOOD PROCESSOR Place the plastic dough blade into the work bowl. Pour the boiling water into the work bowl, and add the rolled oats. Let stand 25 to 35 minutes until the mixture cools to very warm, between 120° and 130°F. Place the remaining ingredients into the work bowl. Process until the dough is smooth and pulls away from the sides of the bowl. If the dough is wet and sticky, add more flour, 1 tablespoon at a time, until the dough is smooth yet soft to the touch. If the dough is not soft to the touch but is very firm, add 1 tablespoon of water at a time, and process until the dough is smooth yet soft to the touch. Cover the work bowl, and let the dough rise until doubled, about 1 hour. Or remove the dough to a lightly greased bowl, cover, and let rise until doubled, about 1 hour.

TO MIX THE DOUGH IN THE BREAD MACHINE Pour the boiling water into the pan, and add the rolled oats. Let stand 35 to 45 minutes until the mixture cools to room temperature. Add the remaining ingredients, in the order

listed. Make an indentation in the dry ingredients and add the yeast. Select *Dough,* and press *Start.* If the dough is wet and sticky, add more flour, 1 tablespoon at a time, until the dough is smooth yet soft to the touch. If the dough is not soft to the touch but is very firm, add 1 teaspoon of water at a time, until the dough is smooth yet soft to the touch. The machine will stop when the dough is ready to shape and bake.

TO MIX AND BAKE THE BREAD IN THE BREAD MACHINE Pour the boiling water into the pan, and add the rolled oats. Let stand 35 to 45 minutes until the mixture cools to room temperature. Add the remaining ingredients, in the order listed. Make an indentation in the dry ingredients and add the yeast. Select the *Basic* cycle, set the crust on *Medium,* and press *Start.* During the mixing cycle, if the dough is wet and sticky, add more flour, 1 tablespoon at a time, until the dough is smooth yet soft to the touch. If the dough is not soft to the touch but is very firm, add 1 teaspoon of water at a time, until the dough is smooth yet soft to the touch.

TO SHAPE AND BAKE IN THE OVEN Lightly grease an 8- or 9-inch round cake pan. Turn the dough out onto a lightly floured board or lightly oiled surface. Punch the dough down, and shape it into a round loaf. Place the loaf, with the smooth side up, into the pan. Cover and let rise in a warm place until almost doubled, 1 hour. Preheat the oven to 375°F. Bake 35 to 45 minutes, until a wooden skewer inserted into the loaf comes out clean and dry. Remove from the pan and cool on a wire rack.

Wild Mushroom and Nut Stuffing

Wild mushrooms have such a rich, meaty flavor that they are satisfying enough to be the main course for a meatless meal. Use this stuffing for your Thanksgiving bird or Christmas goose. You can use most any day-old bread you have on hand, but Old-Fashioned Oat and Rye Bread (page 74) is especially good.

6 SERVINGS

1/3 cup finely chopped onion

1 rib celery, finely chopped

1 pound mixed fresh mushrooms, tough stems removed, coarsely chopped

3 tablespoons butter

6 cups 1/2-inch bread cubes made from whole grain bread, toasted until dry

1/2 cup chopped walnuts or pecans

1 tablespoon fresh sage leaves, chopped, or 1 teaspoon dried

1/2 teaspoon salt

1/4 teaspoon freshly ground pepper

1 cup low-sodium chicken broth

Preheat the oven to 350°F. In a large skillet over medium heat, cook the onion, celery, and mushrooms in the butter, about 5 minutes, stirring occasionally until the onion is soft. In a large bowl, combine the bread cubes, walnuts, sage, salt, and pepper. Add the mushroom mixture and broth to the bread cube mixture, and toss gently but thoroughly. Use to stuff a large bird or turn the mixture into a lightly greased 2-quart shallow baking dish. Bake 30 to 35 minutes, until top is lightly browned.

Easy Chili Bean Spread

This is a quick-fix spread, which when offered with sliced vine-ripened tomatoes, sharp Cheddar cheese, and leaves of garden lettuce can turn a slice of fresh bread into a mini-meal!

ABOUT 2 CUPS

1 can (15 or 16 ounces) chili beans, well drained
1 to 2 teaspoons chopped jalapeño peppers
1/2 cup sweet onion, coarsely chopped
1/2 to 1 teaspoon salt

Chopped cilantro, for garnish
Slices of Yellow Cornmeal Yeast Bread (page 78) or other whole grain bread

Place the chili beans, jalapeño peppers, and onions into the food processor fitted with the steel blade. Process in on/off pulses just until the entire mixture is coarsely chopped. Add salt. Turn into a serving bowl, and garnish with the cilantro. Serve with the bread.

YELLOW CORNMEAL YEAST BREAD
(PIONEER BREAD)

Cornmeal was a staple ingredient of the pioneers who settled the American frontier. Pioneer women used cornmeal to make both yeast-raised and quick breads. I love to serve this bread with a bowl of vegetable chowder. Do not use the delay-start option here because of the eggs.

Sampler Loaf

1 large egg plus water to equal
    2/3 cup

1 tablespoon corn oil

1/4 cup yellow cornmeal

2 tablespoons packed
    brown sugar

1 teaspoon salt

13/4 cups bread flour

1 teaspoon rapid-rising or active
    dry yeast

Regular Loaf

1 large egg plus water to equal
    1 cup

11/2 tablespoons corn oil

1/3 cup yellow cornmeal

1/4 cup packed brown sugar

11/2 teaspoons salt

22/3 cups bread flour

11/2 teaspoons rapid-rising or
    active dry yeast

Large Loaf

2 large eggs plus water to equal
    11/3 cups

2 tablespoons corn oil

1/2 cup yellow cornmeal

1/3 cup packed brown sugar

2 teaspoons salt

31/2 cups bread flour

2 teaspoons rapid-rising or active
    dry yeast

TO MIX THE DOUGH BY HAND Warm the eggs under hot tap water and crack into a measuring cup. Heat the water until warm, between 105° and 115°F, and add it to the eggs. Pour the mixture into a large, warmed bowl, and add the yeast. Place the water mixture into a large, warmed bowl, and add the yeast. Let stand 5 minutes, until the yeast begins to bubble. Stir in the oil, cornmeal, sugar, salt, and half of the bread flour. Beat until smooth. Cover, and let stand 15 minutes. Slowly add the remaining bread flour, and beat until a soft dough forms. Turn the dough out onto a very lightly floured board, and knead, adding flour if necessary, until smooth and springy, about 5 minutes. Wash the bowl and grease it; place the dough back in the bowl, and turn it over to grease the top. Cover, and let rise until doubled, about 1 hour.

TO MIX THE DOUGH WITH A HEAVY-DUTY MIXER Warm the eggs under hot tap water and crack into a measuring cup. Heat the water until warm, between 105° and 115°F, and add it to the eggs. Pour the mixture into the warmed mixing bowl; add the yeast. Let stand 5 minutes, until the yeast begins to bubble. Add the oil, cornmeal, sugar, salt, and half of the bread flour. Beat until smooth. Cover, and let stand 15 minutes.

Slowly add the remaining bread flour, and beat until a soft dough forms. Knead the dough in the mixer with the dough hook, on medium to high speed, adding flour as necessary, until the dough pulls away from the sides of the bowl and is smooth and springy but still soft to the touch. Remove the dough hook, cover the bowl, and let the dough rise until doubled, about 1 hour.

TO MIX THE DOUGH IN THE FOOD PROCESSOR
Place the plastic dough blade into the work bowl. Warm the eggs under hot tap water and crack into a measuring cup. Heat the water until very warm, between 120° and 130°F, and add it to the eggs; set aside. Place the remaining ingredients into the work bowl. Turn the processor on, and slowly pour the water mixture through the feed tube, processing until the dough is smooth and pulls away from the sides of the bowl. If the dough is wet and sticky, add more flour, 1 tablespoon at a time, until the dough is smooth yet soft to the touch. If the dough is not soft to the touch but is very firm, add 1 tablespoon of water at a time, and process until the dough is smooth yet soft to the touch. Cover the work bowl, and let the dough rise until doubled, about 1 hour. Or remove the dough to a lightly greased bowl, cover, and let rise until doubled, about 1 hour.

TO MIX THE DOUGH IN THE BREAD MACHINE Warm the eggs under hot tap water and crack into a measuring cup; add the water (at room temperature) to the eggs. Pour the mixture into the pan. Add the remaining ingredients, in the order listed. Make an indentation in the dry ingredients and add the yeast. Select *Dough,* and press *Start.* If the dough is wet and sticky, add more flour, 1 tablespoon at a time, until the dough is smooth yet soft to the touch. If the dough is not soft to the touch but is very firm, add 1 teaspoon of water at a time, until the dough is smooth yet soft to the touch. The machine will stop when the dough is ready to shape and bake.

TO MIX AND BAKE THE BREAD IN THE BREAD MACHINE Warm the eggs under hot tap water, and crack into a measuring cup; add the water (at room temperature) to the eggs. Pour the mixture into the pan. Add the remaining ingredients, in the order listed. Make an indentation in the dry ingredients and add the yeast. Select the *Basic* cycle, set the crust on *Medium,* and press *Start.* During the mixing cycle, if the dough is wet and sticky, add more flour, 1 tablespoon at a time, until the dough is smooth yet soft to the touch. If the dough is not soft to the touch but is very firm, add 1 teaspoon of water at a time, until the dough is smooth yet soft to the touch.

TO SHAPE AND BAKE IN THE OVEN Lightly grease an 8- or 9-inch round cake pan or a baking sheet. Turn the dough out onto a lightly floured board or lightly oiled surface. Punch the dough down, and shape it into a round loaf. Place the loaf, with the smooth side up, into the pan. Cover and let rise in a warm place until almost doubled, 45 minutes. Preheat the oven to 375°F. Bake 30 to 35 minutes, until the loaf is golden and a wooden skewer inserted into the loaf comes out clean and dry. Remove from the pan and cool on a wire rack.

RYE WHEAT AND MILLET BREAD

Millet seeds add crunch to this bread. You can buy them in health food stores, whole food markets, and by mail from baking catalogs.

Sampler Loaf

2/3 cup water

2 teaspoons packed brown sugar

3/4 teaspoon salt

1/4 cup lightly toasted
    millet seeds

1/4 cup stone-ground rye flour

1/2 cup whole wheat flour

1 1/4 cups bread flour

1 teaspoon rapid-rising or active
    dry yeast

Regular Loaf

1 cup water

1 tablespoon packed brown sugar

1 teaspoon salt

1/3 cup lightly toasted
    millet seeds

1/2 cup stone-ground rye flour

3/4 cup whole wheat flour

1 3/4 cups bread flour

1 1/2 teaspoons rapid-rising or
    active dry yeast

Large Loaf

1 1/3 cup water

1 1/2 tablespoons packed
    brown sugar

1 1/2 teaspoons salt

1/2 cup lightly toasted
    millet seeds

3/4 cup stone-ground rye flour

1 cup whole wheat flour

2 1/4 cups bread flour

2 teaspoons rapid-rising or active
    dry yeast

TO MIX THE DOUGH BY HAND Heat the water until warm, between 105° and 115°F; pour it into a large, warmed bowl, and add the yeast. Let stand 5 minutes, until the yeast begins to bubble. Stir in the sugar, salt, millet seeds, rye flour, and whole wheat flour. Beat until a smooth dough forms. Cover, and let stand 15 minutes. Slowly add the bread flour, and beat until a stiff dough forms. Turn the dough out onto a very lightly floured board, and knead, adding flour if necessary, until smooth and springy, about 5 minutes. Wash the bowl and grease it; place the dough back in the bowl, and turn it over to grease the top. Cover, and let rise until doubled, about 1 hour.

TO MIX THE DOUGH WITH A HEAVY-DUTY MIXER Heat the water until warm, between 105° and 115°F; pour it into the warmed mixing bowl, and add the yeast. Let stand 5 minutes, until the yeast begins to bubble. Add the sugar, salt, millet seeds, rye flour, and whole wheat flour. Beat until a smooth dough forms. Cover, and let stand 15 minutes. Slowly add the bread flour, and beat until a stiff dough forms. Knead the dough in the mixer with the dough hook, on medium to high speed, adding flour as necessary, until the dough pulls away from the sides of the bowl and is smooth and springy but still soft to the touch. Remove the dough hook, cover the bowl, and let the dough rise until doubled, about 1 hour.

TO MIX THE DOUGH IN THE FOOD PROCESSOR
Place the plastic dough blade into the work bowl. Heat the water until very warm, between 120° and 130°F; set aside. Place the remaining ingredients into the work bowl. Turn the processor on, and slowly pour the water through the feed tube, processing until the dough is smooth and pulls away from the sides of the bowl. If the dough is wet and sticky, add more flour, 1 tablespoon at a time, until the dough is smooth yet soft to the touch. If the dough is not soft to the touch but is very firm, add 1 tablespoon of water at a time, and process until the dough is smooth yet soft to the touch. Cover the work bowl, and let the dough rise until doubled, about 1 hour. Or remove the dough to a lightly greased bowl, cover, and let rise until doubled, about 1 hour.

TO MIX THE DOUGH IN THE BREAD MACHINE Pour the water (at room temperature) into the pan. Add the remaining ingredients, in the order listed. Make an indentation in the dry ingredients and add the yeast. Select *Dough,* and press *Start.* If the dough is wet and sticky, add more flour, 1 tablespoon at a time, until the dough is smooth yet soft to the touch. If the dough is not soft to the touch but is very firm, add 1 teaspoon of water at a time, until the dough is smooth yet soft to the touch. The machine will stop when the dough is ready to shape and bake.

TO MIX AND BAKE THE BREAD IN THE BREAD MACHINE Pour the water (at room temperature) into the pan. Add the remaining ingredients, in the order listed. Make an indentation in the dry ingredients and add the yeast. Select the *Basic* cycle, set the crust on *Medium,*

and press *Start.* During the mixing cycle, if the dough is wet and sticky, add more flour, 1 tablespoon at a time, until the dough is smooth yet soft to the touch. If the dough is not soft to the touch but is very firm, add 1 teaspoon of water at a time, until the dough is smooth yet soft to the touch.

TO SHAPE AND BAKE IN THE OVEN Lightly grease an 8- or 9-inch round cake pan. Turn the dough out onto a lightly floured board or lightly oiled surface. Punch the dough down, and shape it into a round loaf. Place the loaf, with the smooth side up, into the pan. Cover and let rise in a warm place until almost doubled, 1 hour. Preheat the oven to 375°F. Bake 35 to 45 minutes, until a wooden skewer inserted into the loaf comes out clean. Remove from the pan and cool on a wire rack.

SEVEN-GRAIN BREAD

I buy a granular 7-grain cereal either at a whole foods cooperative or in the health foods section of my supermarket. Such a mix includes stone-ground wheat, rye, triticale, oats, oat bran, barley, rice, and flax seeds. I buy oat flour from the same sources; although sometimes it is handier to put rolled oats into the blender or food processor, and process it until it is ground into a flour. The pumpkin seed oil I use is available in health food and nutrition stores and is processed in Austria. Normally, it's used for salads and as a nutritional additive to diets; but it gives this bread an additional nuttiness. If you cannot find pumpkin seed oil, you can substitute grapeseed or canola oil.

Sampler Loaf

2/3 cup water

3 tablespoons 7-grain cereal

2 tablespoons oat flour or quick-cooking rolled oats

3/4 teaspoon salt

1 tablespoon light molasses

2 teaspoons extra-virgin olive oil

1 teaspoon pumpkin seed oil

1 2/3 cups bread flour

1 teaspoon rapid-rising or active dry yeast

Regular Loaf

1 cup water

1/4 cup 7-grain cereal

1/4 cup oat flour or quick-cooking rolled oats

1 1/4 teaspoons salt

2 tablespoons light molasses

1 tablespoon extra-virgin olive oil

1 1/2 teaspoons pumpkin seed oil

2 1/2 cups bread flour

1 1/2 teaspoons rapid-rising or active dry yeast

Large Loaf

1 1/3 cups water

1/2 cup 7-grain cereal

1/2 cup oat flour or quick-cooking rolled oats

1 1/2 teaspoons salt

3 tablespoons light molasses

2 tablespoons extra-virgin olive oil

2 teaspoons pumpkin seed oil

3 1/2 cups bread flour

2 teaspoons rapid-rising or active dry yeast

TO MIX THE DOUGH BY HAND Heat the water to 130°F; pour it into a large bowl, and add the cereal. Let stand 10 minutes, until the mixture cools to 115°F. Add the yeast, oat flour, salt, molasses, and oils. Beat well. Cover, and let stand 15 minutes. Slowly add the bread flour, and beat until a smooth dough forms. Turn the dough out onto a very lightly floured board, and knead, adding flour if necessary, until smooth and springy, about 5 minutes. Wash the bowl and grease it; place the dough back in the bowl, and turn it over to grease the top. Cover, and let rise until doubled, about 1 hour.

TO MIX THE DOUGH WITH A HEAVY-DUTY MIXER Heat the water to 130°F; pour it into the mixing bowl, and add the cereal. Let stand 10 minutes, until the mixture cools to 115°F. Add the yeast, oat flour, salt, molasses, and oils. Beat well. Cover, and let stand 15 minutes. Slowly add the bread flour, and beat until a smooth dough forms. Knead the dough in the mixer with the dough hook, on medium to high speed, adding flour as necessary, until the dough pulls away from the sides of the bowl and is smooth and springy but still soft to the touch. Remove the dough hook, cover the bowl, and let the dough rise until doubled, about 1 hour.

TO MIX THE DOUGH IN THE FOOD PROCESSOR Place the plastic dough blade into the work bowl. Heat the water until very warm, between 120° and 130°F, and pour it into a large bowl; add the cereal, and set aside. Place the remaining ingredients into the work bowl. Turn the processor on, and slowly pour the water mixture through the feed tube, processing until the dough is smooth and pulls away from the sides of the bowl. If the dough is wet and sticky, add more flour, 1 tablespoon at a time, until the dough is smooth yet soft to the touch. If the dough is not soft to the touch but is very firm, add 1 tablespoon of water at a time, and process until the dough is smooth yet soft to the touch. Cover the work bowl, and let the dough rise until doubled, about 1 hour. Or remove the dough to a lightly greased bowl, cover, and let rise until doubled, about 1 hour.

TO MIX THE DOUGH IN THE BREAD MACHINE Pour the water (at room temperature) into the pan. Add the remaining ingredients, in the order listed. Make an indentation in the dry ingredients and add the yeast. Select *Dough,* and press *Start.* If the dough is wet and sticky, add more flour, 1 tablespoon at a time, until the dough is smooth yet soft to the touch. If the dough is not soft to the touch but is very firm, add 1 teaspoon of water at a time, until the

dough is smooth yet soft to the touch. The machine will stop when the dough is ready to shape and bake.

TO MIX AND BAKE THE BREAD IN THE BREAD MACHINE Pour the water (at room temperature) into the pan. Add the remaining ingredients, in the order listed. Make an indentation in the dry ingredients and add the yeast. Select the *Basic* or *Whole Wheat* cycle, set the crust on *Medium,* and press *Start.* During the mixing cycle, if the dough is wet and sticky, add more flour, 1 tablespoon at a time, until the dough is smooth yet soft to the touch. If the dough is not soft to the touch but is very firm, add 1 teaspoon of water at a time, until the dough is smooth yet soft to the touch.

TO SHAPE AND BAKE IN THE OVEN Lightly grease a 9 × 5-inch loaf pan or an 8- or 9-inch round cake pan. Turn the dough out onto a lightly floured board or lightly oiled surface. Punch the dough down, and shape it into an oblong or round loaf. Place the loaf, with the smooth side up, into the pan. Cover and let rise in a warm place until almost doubled, 45 minutes. Preheat the oven to 375°F. Bake 25 to 30 minutes, until the loaf is golden. Remove from the pan and cool on a wire rack.

TEN-GRAIN CEREAL BREAD

With the same texture as cracked wheat, 10-grain cereals are available not only in health food and whole foods markets but also in specialty departments of larger supermarkets. The combination of grains may vary from one brand to another, but the success in this bread is universal to all.

Sampler Loaf

2/3 cup boiling water

1/4 cup 10-grain cereal*

1/2 tablespoon butter or oil

1 tablespoon 100% pure maple syrup

3/4 teaspoon salt

1/4 cup whole wheat flour

1 1/2 cups bread flour

1 teaspoon rapid-rising or active dry yeast

Regular Loaf

1 cup boiling water

1/2 cup 10-grain cereal*

1 tablespoon butter or oil

2 tablespoons 100% pure maple syrup

1 teaspoon salt

1/2 cup whole wheat flour

2 cups bread flour

1 1/2 teaspoons rapid-rising or active dry yeast

Large Loaf

1 1/3 cups boiling water

3/4 cup 10-grain cereal*

2 tablespoons butter or oil

3 tablespoons 100% pure maple syrup

1 1/2 teaspoons salt

3/4 cup whole wheat flour

2 1/2 cups bread flour

2 teaspoons rapid-rising or active dry yeast

TO MIX THE DOUGH BY HAND   Pour the boiling water into a large bowl, add the cereal, and stir. Let stand 30 minutes, until the mixture cools to warm, between 105° and 115°F. Add the yeast; let stand 5 minutes, until the yeast begins to bubble. Stir in the butter, syrup, salt, and whole wheat flour. Beat well. Cover, and let stand 15 minutes. Slowly add the bread flour, and beat until a smooth dough forms. Turn the dough out onto a very lightly floured board, and knead, adding flour if necessary, until smooth and springy, about 5 minutes. Wash the bowl and grease it; place the dough back in the bowl, and turn it over to grease the top. Cover, and let rise until doubled, about 1 hour.

TO MIX THE DOUGH WITH A HEAVY-DUTY MIXER   Pour the boiling water into the mixing bowl, add the cereal, and stir. Let stand 30 minutes, until the mixture cools to warm, between 105° and 115°F. Add the yeast; let stand 5 minutes, until the yeast begins to bubble. Add the butter, syrup, salt, and whole wheat flour. Beat well. Cover, and let stand 15 minutes. Slowly add

Note   *The cereal I use is a mixture of wheat, rye, triticale, oats, corn, barley, soy, brown rice, millet, and flaxseed.*

the bread flour, and beat until a smooth dough forms. Knead the dough in the mixer with the dough hook, on medium to high speed, adding flour as necessary, until the dough pulls away from the sides of the bowl and is smooth and springy but still soft to the touch. Remove the dough hook, cover the bowl, and let the dough rise until doubled, about 1 hour.

TO MIX THE DOUGH IN THE FOOD PROCESSOR Place the plastic dough blade into the work bowl. Pour the boiling water into the work bowl, add the cereal, and stir. Let stand 30 minutes, until the mixture cools to very warm, between 120° and 130°F. Place the remaining ingredients into the work bowl. Process until the dough is smooth and pulls away from the sides of the bowl. If the dough is wet and sticky, add more flour, 1 tablespoon at a time, until the dough is smooth yet soft to the touch. If the dough is not soft to the touch but is very firm, add 1 tablespoon of water at a time, and process until the dough is smooth yet soft to the touch. Cover the work bowl, and let the dough rise until doubled, about 1 hour. Or remove the dough to a lightly greased bowl, cover, and let rise until doubled, about 1 hour.

TO MIX THE DOUGH IN THE BREAD MACHINE Pour the boiling water into the pan, add the cereal, and stir. Let stand 30 minutes, until the mixture cools to room temperature. Add the remaining ingredients, except the yeast. Make a small indentation in the dry ingredients, and add the yeast. Select *Dough,* and press *Start.* If the dough is wet and sticky, add more flour, 1 tablespoon at a time, until the dough is smooth yet soft to the touch. If the dough is not soft to the touch but is very firm, add 1 teaspoon of water at a time, until the dough is smooth yet soft to the touch. The machine will stop when the dough is ready to shape and bake.

TO MIX AND BAKE THE BREAD IN THE BREAD MACHINE Pour the boiling water into the pan, add the cereal, and stir. Let stand 30 minutes, until the mixture cools to room temperature. Add the remaining ingredients, except the yeast. Make a small indentation in the dry ingredients, and add the yeast. Select the *Basic* or *Whole Wheat* cycle, set the crust on *Medium,* and press *Start.* During the mixing cycle, if the dough is wet and sticky, add more flour, 1 tablespoon at a time, until the dough is smooth yet soft to the touch. If the dough is not soft to the touch but is very firm, add 1 teaspoon of water at a time, until the dough is smooth yet soft to the touch.

TO SHAPE AND BAKE IN THE OVEN Lightly grease an 8- or 9-inch round cake pan. Turn the dough out onto a lightly floured board or lightly oiled surface. Punch the dough down, and shape it into a round loaf. Place the loaf, with the smooth side up, into the pan. Cover and let rise in a warm place until almost doubled, 45 to 60 minutes. Preheat the oven to 375°F. Bake 25 to 30 minutes, until the loaf is golden and a wooden skewer inserted into the loaf comes out clean and dry. Brush the top of the loaf while it's still hot with melted butter, if desired. Remove from the pan and cool on a wire rack.

THREE-GRAIN BREAD

I use a 3-grain cereal that contains cracked wheat, cracked rye, and cracked flax and is sold under the brand name Red River. It makes a nutty, wonderful loaf with a crunchy crust and a great grainy flavor. If you cannot buy such a cereal, check out your local whole foods cooperative and use any cereal that looks like cracked wheat, whether 3-, 4- or 5-grain. The method requires that you soften the cereal in boiling water, and then let it stand until it cools down before proceeding. Bread machine bakers can do this right in the bread pan or in a mixing bowl.

Sampler Loaf	Regular Loaf	Large Loaf
3/4 cup boiling water	1 1/4 cups boiling water	1 1/2 cups boiling water
1/2 cup 3-grain cereal	3/4 cup 3-grain cereal	1 cup 3-grain cereal
1 teaspoon salt	1 1/2 teaspoons salt	2 teaspoons salt
1 1/2 tablespoons packed brown sugar	2 tablespoons packed brown sugar	3 tablespoons packed brown sugar
1 tablespoon unsalted butter, softened	2 tablespoons unsalted butter, softened	3 tablespoons unsalted butter, softened
2 cups bread flour	2 1/2 cups bread flour	3 cups bread flour
1 teaspoon rapid-rising or active dry yeast	1 1/2 teaspoons rapid-rising or active dry yeast	2 teaspoons rapid-rising or active dry yeast

TO MIX THE DOUGH BY HAND   Pour the boiling water into a large bowl, add the cereal, and stir. Let stand 30 minutes , until the mixture cools to warm, between 105° and 115°F. Add the yeast, salt, brown sugar, and butter. Beat well. Cover, and let stand 15 minutes. Slowly add the bread flour, and beat until a smooth dough forms. Turn the dough out onto a very lightly floured board, and knead, adding flour if necessary, until smooth and springy, about 5 minutes. Wash the bowl and grease it; place the dough back in the bowl, and turn it over to grease the top. Cover, and let rise until doubled, about 1 hour.

TO MIX THE DOUGH WITH A HEAVY-DUTY MIXER   Pour the boiling water into the mixing bowl, add the cereal, and stir. Let stand 30 minutes, until the mixture cools to warm, between 105° and 115°F. Add the yeast, salt, brown sugar, and butter. Beat well. Cover, and let stand 15 minutes. Slowly add the bread flour, and beat until a smooth dough forms. Knead the dough in the mixer with the dough hook, on medium to high speed, adding flour as necessary, until the dough pulls away from the sides of the bowl and is smooth and springy but still soft to the touch. Remove the dough hook, cover the bowl, and let the dough rise until doubled, about 1 hour.

TO MIX THE DOUGH IN THE FOOD PROCESSOR Place the plastic dough blade into the work bowl. Pour the boiling water into the work bowl, add the cereal, and stir. Let stand 30 minutes, until the mixture cools to very warm, between 120° and 130°F. Place the remaining ingredients into the work bowl. Process until the dough is smooth and pulls away from the sides of the bowl. If the dough is wet and sticky, add more flour, 1 table-spoon at a time, until the dough is smooth yet soft to the touch. If the dough is not soft to the touch but is very firm, add 1 tablespoon of water at a time, and process until the dough is smooth yet soft to the touch. Cover the work bowl, and let the dough rise until doubled, about 1 hour. Or remove the dough to a lightly greased bowl, cover, and let rise until doubled, about 1 hour.

TO MIX THE DOUGH IN THE BREAD MACHINE Pour the boiling water into the pan, add the cereal, and stir. Let stand 30 minutes, until the mixture cools to room temperature. Add the remaining ingredients, in the order list-ed. Make an indentation in the dry ingredients and add the yeast. Select *Dough,* and press *Start.* If the dough is wet and sticky, add more flour, 1 tablespoon at a time, until the dough is smooth yet soft to the touch. If the dough is not soft to the touch but is very firm, add 1 teaspoon of water at a time, until the dough is smooth yet soft

to the touch. The machine will stop when the dough is ready to shape and bake.

TO MIX AND BAKE THE BREAD IN THE BREAD MACHINE Pour the boiling water into the pan, add the cereal, and stir. Let stand 30 min-utes, until the mixture cools to room tempera-ture. Add the remaining ingredients, in the order listed. Make an indentation in the dry ingredients and add the yeast. Select the *Basic* or *Whole Wheat* cycle, set the crust on *Medium,* and press *Start.* During the mixing cycle, if the dough is wet and sticky, add more flour, 1 tablespoon at a time, until the dough is smooth yet soft to the touch. If the dough is not soft to the touch but is very firm, add 1 teaspoon of water at a time, until the dough is smooth yet soft to the touch.

TO SHAPE AND BAKE IN THE OVEN Lightly grease a 9 × 5-inch loaf pan or an 8- or 9-inch round cake pan. Turn the dough out onto a light-ly floured board or lightly oiled surface. Punch the dough down, and shape it into an oblong or round loaf. Place the loaf, with the smooth side up, into the pan. Cover and let rise in a warm place until almost doubled, 45 minutes. Preheat the oven to 375°F. Bake 25 to 30 minutes, until the loaf is golden. Remove from the pan and cool on a wire rack.

ZUNI CORNMEAL BREAD

The Pueblo people of the U.S. Southwest bake this bread in rustic outdoor earth ovens in burnished black pottery. This is a modernized version, made with incredible convenience in modern machines. Although there's no comparison to a loaf baked in a wood-fired oven, you'll still get a wonderfully tasty, crusty loaf in your conventional oven. Masa harina is a very finely ground cornmeal that is found either in the foreign foods section or in the baking section of most grocery stores. I've also found it in health food stores and whole food markets.

Sampler Loaf	Regular Loaf	Large Loaf
$2/3$ cup water	1 cup water	$1^{1}/3$ cups water
$1/4$ cup masa harina	$1/3$ cup masa harina	$1/2$ cup masa harina
$1/4$ cup yellow cornmeal	$1/3$ cup yellow cornmeal	$1/2$ cup yellow cornmeal
1 tablespoon extra-virgin olive oil	2 tablespoons extra-virgin olive oil	3 tablespoons extra-virgin olive oil
1 tablespoon dark molasses	2 tablespoons dark molasses	3 tablespoon dark molasses
1 teaspoon salt	$1^{1}/2$ teaspoons salt	2 teaspoons salt
$1^{1}/2$ cups bread flour	$2^{1}/3$ cups bread flour	3 cups bread flour
1 teaspoon rapid-rising or active dry yeast	$1^{1}/2$ teaspoons rapid-rising or active dry yeast	2 teaspoons rapid-rising or active dry yeast

TO MIX THE DOUGH BY HAND Heat the water until warm, between 105° and 115°F; pour it into a large, warmed bowl. Add the masa harina, cornmeal, and yeast. Let stand 5 minutes, until the yeast begins to bubble. Stir in the oil, salt, and half of the bread flour. Beat well. Cover, and let stand 15 minutes. Slowly add the remaining bread flour, and beat until a soft dough forms. Turn the dough out onto a very lightly floured board, and knead, adding flour if necessary, until smooth and springy, about 5 minutes.

Wash the bowl and grease it; place the dough back in the bowl, and turn it over to grease the top. Cover, and let rise until doubled, about 1 hour.

TO MIX THE DOUGH WITH A HEAVY-DUTY MIXER Heat the water until warm, between 105° and 115°F; pour it into the warmed mixing bowl. Add the masa harina, cornmeal, and yeast. Let stand 5 minutes, until the yeast begins to bubble. Add the oil, salt, and half of the bread flour. Beat well. Cover, and let stand 15 minutes. Slowly add the remaining bread flour, and beat until a soft dough forms. Knead the dough in the mixer with the dough hook, on medium to high speed, adding flour as necessary, until the dough pulls away from the sides of the bowl and is smooth and springy but still soft to the touch. Remove the dough hook, cover the bowl, and let the dough rise until doubled, about 1 hour.

TO MIX THE DOUGH IN THE FOOD PROCESSOR
Place the plastic dough blade into the work bowl. Heat the water until very warm, between 120° and 130°F; set aside. Place the remaining ingredients into the work bowl. Turn the processor on, and slowly pour the water through the feed tube, processing until the dough is smooth and pulls away from the sides of the bowl. If the dough is wet and sticky, add more flour, 1 tablespoon at a time, until the dough is smooth yet soft to the touch. If the dough is not soft to the touch but is very firm, add 1 tablespoon of water at a time, and process until the dough is smooth yet soft to the touch. Cover the work bowl, and let the dough rise until doubled, about 1 hour. Or remove the dough to a lightly greased bowl, cover, and let rise until doubled, about 1 hour.

TO MIX THE DOUGH IN THE BREAD MACHINE Pour the water (at room temperature) into the pan. Add the remaining ingredients, in the order listed. Make an indentation in the dry ingredients and add the yeast. Select *Dough,* and press *Start.* If the dough is wet and sticky, add more flour, 1 tablespoon at a time, until the dough is smooth yet soft to the touch. If the dough is not soft to the touch but is very firm, add 1 teaspoon of water at a time, until the dough is smooth yet soft to the touch. The machine will stop when the dough is ready to shape and bake.

TO MIX AND BAKE THE BREAD IN THE BREAD MACHINE Pour the water (at room temperature) into the pan. Add the remaining ingredients, in the order listed. Make an indentation in the dry ingredients and add the yeast. Select the *Basic* cycle, medium crust, and press *Start.* During the mixing cycle, if the dough is wet and sticky, add more flour, 1 tablespoon at a time, until the dough is smooth yet soft to the touch. If the dough is not soft to the touch but is very firm, add 1 teaspoon of water at a time, until the dough is smooth yet soft to the touch.

TO SHAPE AND BAKE IN THE OVEN Lightly grease a baking sheet or cover it with parchment paper. Turn the dough out onto a lightly floured board or lightly oiled surface. Punch the dough down, and shape it into a round loaf. Place the loaf, with the smooth side up, onto the baking sheet. Cover and let rise in a warm place until almost doubled, 45 minutes. Preheat the oven to 375°F. Bake 30 to 35 minutes, until the loaf is golden and a wooden skewer inserted into the loaf comes out clean and dry. Remove from the pan and cool on a wire rack.

Chili Cheese Strata

Although this is just fine assembled and baked immediately, for convenience, you can make it a day ahead.

Cover it with plastic wrap, and refrigerate; then bake it the next morning for a late and leisurely breakfast.

When I serve it with my favorite mango salsa, it's a real hit!

8 SERVINGS

1 cup milk

2 large eggs

1/2 teaspoon salt

1/2 teaspoon freshly ground black pepper

1 cup shredded Monterey Jack cheese

3 tablespoons sliced green onions

2 teaspoons minced jalapeño pepper

2 cups cubed day-old Zuni Cornmeal Bread
  (page 88)

FOR SERVING

Mango Salsa (recipe follows)

Chopped cilantro

Preheat the oven to 400°F. Lightly grease a 9-inch pie pan or 1-quart shallow casserole. In a small bowl or 2-cup measure, mix the milk, eggs, salt, and black pepper. In a large bowl, toss the cheese, onions, jalapeño pepper, and bread together. Turn the bread mixture into the prepared pan. Pour the milk mixture over. Bake 25 minutes, until set. To serve, top with the salsa and cilantro, and cut into wedges.

Mango Salsa

Mango salsa, served like a relish, goes well with any breakfast strata, as well as smoked or poached fresh salmon and grilled halibut or tuna steaks. Mangoes are readily available for most of the year.

ABOUT 4 CUPS

3 mangoes, seeded, peeled and cut into cubes
1/4 cup freshly squeezed lime juice
1 cup fresh or canned, drained pineapple chunks
1 large sweet (Vidalia) onion, finely diced
2 teaspoons finely diced jalapeño pepper
1/4 cup chopped cilantro

Combine all of the ingredients in a serving bowl, folding them together gently. Cover and let stand at room temperature for about 30 minutes, so the flavors can blend.

Eight-Grain Honey Sunflower Seed Bread

Goat Cheese, Walnut, and Fresh Herb Spread

Apple Cinnamon Bread

Cheddar Cheese Nut Bread

Chocolate, Walnut, and Wheat Bread

Chocolate Bread Pudding

Cinnamon-Pecan Wheat and Rye Bread

Fresh Pear Slices and Blue Castello on Toast

Cinnamon Crouton Cubes

Country Currant Rye Bread

Cranberry Graham Bread

Cranberry Oatmeal Nut Loaf

Date and Nut Buttermilk Wheat Bread

Dried Fig and Walnut Bread

French Walnut and Wheat Bread

Breakfast Bread with Dried Fruit, Almonds,
and Oatmeal

Golden Raisin and Oatmeal Pecan Bread

Honey Walnut Egg Bread

Baked Cheese Fondue

Oatmeal Maple Nut Bread

Orange Cranberry Cornmeal Bread

Raisin Pumpernickel

Raisin Rye Bread

Raisin, Cinnamon, and Nut Wheat Bread

Peach and Whole Wheat Bread Pudding

Rustic Grains and Honey Pecan Bread

Sesame, Oat, and Cinnamon Swirl Loaf

Toasted Sesame Graham Wheat Bread

Toasted Grains and Honey Pecan Bread

Tropical Fruits Wheat Bread

Walnut Wheat Bread

Wheat and Sunflower Bread

Wheat Berry and Raisin Bread

Cranberry Semolina Bread

Whole Wheat Raisin-Nut Bread

Wild Rice and Three-Grain Bread

Hummus

three

WHOLE GRAIN BREADS
WITH FRUITS AND NUTS

I suppose this has to be my favorite chapter of all! I love breads with moisture, texture, and chewiness. These whole grain breads coupled with the sweet and chewiness of fruits and the crunch of nuts make them perfect for round-the-clock eating, for snacks or with a meal. Their flavors go together with all kinds of spreads and sandwich makings.

Here is a selection of breads that can be a springboard to your own creativity. Try Apple Cinnamon Bread; Cheddar Cheese Nut Bread; Chocolate, Walnut, and Wheat Bread; or Cinnamon-Pecan Wheat and Rye Bread, for example. Use these recipes as models for your own creative combinations. As long as the ingredients you select do not change the liquid-to-flour balance of the recipe, they should work out perfectly.

One warning: If you mix the bread in the bread machine and add the dried fruit with the flour before pressing *Start*, they will be mashed right into the dough. If the bread will be baked in the machine, choose the *Fruit and Nut* cycle, and wait until you hear the signal before adding the fruit to the pan. If your machine does not have this cycle, just wait until the end of the first kneading cycle; and without stopping the machine or pulling out the bread pan, lift the dough out, and knead the added ingredients in by hand. Then simply place the dough back into the pan, close the lid, and let the machine do the rest. Especially for whole grain breads with fruits and nuts, I prefer to have the machine make the dough, and then to bake the breads in the oven, because I like the traditional loaf shape the best. If the bread will be shaped and baked conventionally, select *Dough* and program your machine to tell you when to add the fruit. If your machine can't do this, simply add the fruit when the machine signals that the *Dough* cycle is over; then push *Dough* and *Start* again. Stop the machine when the fruit has been mixed in. Or you can knead the fruit in by hand just before you shape the loaf.

EIGHT-GRAIN HONEY
SUNFLOWER SEED BREAD

The eight grains in King Arthur Flour's 8-Grain Flour are wheat, triticale, rye, millet, oat, buckwheat, barley, and soy. Other 8-grain flours are sold in health food and whole foods markets; and though they might have a slightly different mixture of grains, they also work well in this recipe. Honey brings out the nutty flavor of all the grains. Hulled and toasted sunflower seeds add a nice crunch and flavor.

Sampler Loaf	Regular Loaf	Large Loaf
$2/3$ cup water	1 cup water	$1^1/3$ cups water
$3/4$ teaspoon salt	1 teaspoon salt	$1^1/2$ teaspoons salt
1 tablespoon canola oil	2 tablespoons canola oil	3 tablespoons canola oil
2 tablespoons honey	$1/4$ cup honey	$1/3$ cup honey
$1/4$ cup sunflower seeds	$1/3$ cup sunflower seeds	$1/2$ cup sunflower seeds
$1/2$ cup 8-grain or other multigrain flour	1 cup 8-grain or other multigrain flour	$1^1/4$ cup 8-grain or other multigrain flour
$1^1/2$ cups bread flour	2 cups bread flour	3 cups bread flour
1 teaspoon rapid-rising or active dry yeast	$1^1/2$ teaspoons rapid-rising or active dry yeast	2 teaspoons rapid-rising or active dry yeast

GLAZE FOR BREAD BAKED CONVENTIONALLY*
1 egg
1 tablespoon water or milk
Sunflower seeds

TO MIX THE DOUGH BY HAND Heat the water until warm, between 105° and 115°F; pour it into a large, warmed bowl. Add the yeast, salt, oil, honey, sunflower seeds, 8-grain flour and half of the bread flour. Let stand 5 minutes until the yeast begins to bubble. Beat until a smooth dough forms. Cover, and let stand 15 minutes. Add the sunflower seeds. Slowly add the remaining bread flour, and beat until a soft dough forms. Turn the dough out onto a very lightly floured board, and knead, adding flour if necessary, until smooth and springy, about 5 minutes.

*Note   *The egg glaze, which is optional for most recipes, is simply a whole egg beaten with a little water or milk. It "glues" toppings, such as seeds, rolled grains, and nuts, onto the top of the loaf as it bakes. Keep leftover glaze in a covered jar in the refrigerator for up to three days.*

Wash the bowl and grease it; place the dough back in the bowl, and turn it over to grease the top. Cover, and let rise until doubled, about 1 hour.

TO MIX THE DOUGH WITH A HEAVY-DUTY MIXER Heat the water until warm, between 105° and 115°F; pour it into the warmed mixing bowl. Add the yeast. Let stand 5 minutes until the yeast begins to bubble. Add salt, oil, honey, sunflower seeds, 8-grain flour, and half of the bread flour. Beat until a smooth dough forms. Cover, and let stand 15 minutes. Add the sunflower seeds. Slowly add the remaining bread flour, and beat until a soft dough forms. Knead the dough in the mixer with the dough hook, on medium to high speed, adding flour as necessary, until the dough pulls away from the sides of the bowl and is smooth and springy but still soft to the touch. Remove the dough hook, cover the bowl, and let the dough rise until doubled, about 1 hour.

TO MIX THE DOUGH IN THE FOOD PROCESSOR Place the plastic dough blade into the work bowl. Heat the water until very warm, between 120° and 130°F; set aside. Place the remaining ingredients into the work bowl. Turn the processor on, and slowly pour the water through the feed tube, processing until the dough is smooth and pulls away from the sides of the bowl. If the dough is wet and sticky, add more flour, 1 tablespoon at a time, until the dough is smooth yet soft to the touch. If the dough is not soft to the touch but is very firm, add 1 tablespoon of water at a time, and process until the dough is smooth yet soft to the touch. Cover the work bowl, and let the dough rise until doubled, about 1 hour. Or remove the dough to a lightly greased bowl, cover, and let rise until doubled, about 1 hour.

TO MIX THE DOUGH IN THE BREAD MACHINE Pour the water (at room temperature) into the pan. Add the remaining ingredients, in the order listed. Make an indentation in the dry ingredients and add the yeast. Select *Dough,* and press *Start.* If the dough is wet and sticky, add more flour, 1 tablespoon at a time, until the dough is smooth yet soft to the touch. If the dough is not soft to the touch but is very firm, add 1 teaspoon of water at a time, until the dough is smooth yet soft to the touch. The machine will stop when the dough is ready to shape and bake.

TO MIX AND BAKE THE BREAD IN THE BREAD MACHINE Pour the water (at room temperature) into the pan. Add the remaining ingredients, in the order listed. Make an indentation in the dry ingredients and add the yeast. Select the *Basic* or *Whole Wheat* cycle, set the crust on *Medium,* and press *Start.* During the mixing cycle, if the dough is wet and sticky, add more flour, 1 tablespoon at a time, until the dough is smooth yet soft to the touch. If the dough is not soft to the touch but is very firm, add 1 teaspoon of water at a time, until the dough is smooth yet soft to the touch.

TO SHAPE AND BAKE IN THE OVEN Lightly grease a 9 × 5-inch loaf pan or an 8- or 9-inch round cake pan. Turn the dough out onto a lightly floured board or lightly oiled surface. Punch the dough down, and shape it into an oblong or round loaf. Place the loaf, with the smooth side up, into the pan. Cover and let rise in a warm place until almost doubled, 45 minutes. To glaze, beat the egg with the water, brush the mixture on the loaf, and sprinkle on the sunflower seeds. Preheat the oven to 375°F. Bake 25 to 35 minutes, until the loaf is golden. Remove from the pan and cool on a wire rack.

Goat Cheese, Walnut, and Fresh Herb Spread

Here's a quick and savory spread that you can put on almost any thinly sliced, plain or toasted whole grain bread.

ABOUT 1 1/2 CUPS

1 package (6 ounces) domestic or imported chèvre* cheese, softened

1/2 cup finely minced walnuts

3 tablespoons heavy cream

1 tablespoon extra-virgin olive oil

2 teaspoons chopped fresh savory

2 teaspoons chopped fresh Italian parsley

1 teaspoon chopped fresh thyme

Salt and freshly ground pepper, to taste

Measure all of the ingredients into a small bowl. Using a hand-held electric mixer, blend until smooth. Adjust the seasonings. Pack into a serving crock, and refrigerate until ready to serve.

*Note   *You can substitute cream cheese for the chèvre.*

APPLE CINNAMON BREAD

Barley flour adds a nutty flavor and smooth texture to this bread. It is usually available in the whole foods section of a supermarket or at a whole foods coop. You can, however, substitute an equal amount of rye, whole wheat, or all-purpose flour. Dried apples add flavor as well as moistness and texture to this bread.

Sampler Loaf	Regular Loaf	Large Loaf
2/3 cup water	1 cup water	1 1/3 cups water
3/4 teaspoon salt	1 teaspoon salt	1 1/2 teaspoon salt
1/2 teaspoon cinnamon	3/4 teaspoon cinnamon	1 teaspoon cinnamon
1 tablespoon sugar	2 tablespoons sugar	3 tablespoons sugar
1/3 cup barley flour	1/2 cup barley flour	3/4 cup barley flour
1/3 cup whole wheat flour	1/2 cup whole wheat flour	3/4 cup whole wheat flour
1 1/3 cups bread flour	2 cups bread flour	2 1/2 cups bread flour
1/4 cup chopped dried apple	1/3 cup chopped dried apple	1/2 cup chopped dried apple
1 teaspoon rapid-rising or active dry yeast	1 1/2 teaspoons rapid-rising or active dry yeast	2 teaspoons rapid-rising or active dry yeast

TO MIX THE DOUGH BY HAND Heat the water until warm, between 105° and 115°F; pour it into a large, warmed bowl, and add the yeast. Let stand 5 minutes, until the yeast begins to bubble. Stir in the salt, cinnamon, sugar, barley flour, whole wheat flour, and half of the bread flour. Beat until smooth. Cover, and let stand 15 minutes. Slowly add the remaining bread flour, and beat until a soft dough forms. Turn the dough out onto a very lightly floured board, and knead, adding flour if necessary, until smooth and springy, about 5 minutes. Knead in the apple. Wash the bowl and grease it; place the dough back in the bowl, and turn it over to grease the top. Cover, and let rise until doubled, about 1 hour.

TO MIX THE DOUGH WITH A HEAVY-DUTY MIXER Heat the water until warm, between 105° and 115°F; pour it into the warmed mixing bowl, and add the yeast. Let stand 5 minutes, until the yeast begins to bubble. Add the salt, cinnamon, sugar, barley flour, whole wheat flour, and half of the bread flour. Beat until smooth. Cover, and let stand 15 minutes. Slowly add the remaining bread flour, and beat until a soft dough forms.

Knead the dough in the mixer with the dough hook, on medium to high speed, adding flour as necessary, until the dough pulls away from the sides of the bowl and is smooth and springy but still soft to the touch. Knead in the apple. Remove the dough hook, cover the bowl, and let the dough rise until doubled, about 1 hour.

TO MIX THE DOUGH IN THE FOOD PROCESSOR

Place the plastic dough blade into the work bowl. Heat the water until very warm, between 120° and 130°F; set aside. Place the remaining ingredients, except the apple, into the work bowl. Turn the processor on, and slowly pour the water through the feed tube, processing until the dough is smooth and pulls away from the sides of the bowl. If the dough is wet and sticky, add more flour, 1 tablespoon at a time, until the dough is smooth yet soft to the touch. If the dough is not soft to the touch but is very firm, add 1 tablespoon of water at a time, and process until the dough is smooth yet soft to the touch. Mix in the apples. Cover the work bowl, and let the dough rise until doubled, about 1 hour. Or remove the dough to a lightly greased bowl, cover, and let rise until doubled, about 1 hour.

TO MIX THE DOUGH IN THE BREAD MACHINE

Pour the water (at room temperature) into the pan. Add the remaining ingredients, except the apples. Make an indentation in the dry ingredients and add the yeast. Select *Dough,* and press *Start.* If the dough is wet and sticky, add more flour, 1 tablespoon at a time, until the dough is smooth yet soft to the touch. If the dough is not soft to the touch but is very firm, add 1 teaspoon of water at a time, until the dough is smooth yet soft to the touch. Add the apples when the machine signals it's time to add ingredients or when the cycle ends. The machine will stop when the dough is ready to shape and bake.

TO MIX AND BAKE THE BREAD IN THE BREAD MACHINE

Pour the water (at room temperature) into the pan. Add the remaining ingredients, except the apples. Make an indentation in the dry ingredients and add the yeast. Select the *Fruit and Nut, Basic,* or *Whole Wheat* cycle; set the crust on *Medium;* and press *Start.* During the mixing cycle, if the dough is wet and sticky, add more flour, 1 tablespoon at a time, until the dough is smooth yet soft to the touch. If the dough is not soft to the touch but is very firm, add 1 teaspoon of water at a time, until the dough is smooth yet soft to the touch. Add the apples when the machine signals it's time to add ingredients.

TO SHAPE AND BAKE IN THE OVEN

Lightly grease an 8- or 9-inch round cake pan. Turn the dough out onto a lightly floured board or lightly oiled surface. Punch the dough down, and shape it into a round loaf. Place the loaf, with the smooth side up, into the pan. Cover and let rise in a warm place until almost doubled, 45 minutes. Preheat the oven to 375°F. Bake 30 to 35 minutes, until the loaf is golden and a wooden skewer inserted into the loaf comes out clean and dry. Remove from the pan and cool on a wire rack.

CHEDDAR CHEESE NUT BREAD

This is adapted from my recipe for Chunk-o-Cheese Bread, which I entered in the ninth Pillsbury Bake-Off and which won second grand prize! I sometimes make this bread without the nuts, which is the way my original recipe went. I like to use a robust sharp Cheddar cheese; but any firm, mild to sharp, yellow or white cheese will be great. Good-sized chunks make a loaf with open, large, cheese-lined pockets through-out the bread, reminding me of the openings in Swiss cheese. You will not get the pockets of cheese when you bake it in the machine, because the machine mixes and mashes the cheese right into the dough—which makes a great tasting, but different kind of loaf. For that reason I like this bread the best when it is shaped by hand and baked in the conventional oven.

Sampler Loaf	Regular Loaf	Large Loaf
2/3 cup boiling water	1 cup boiling water	1 1/3 cups boiling water
1/4 cup yellow cornmeal	1/3 cup yellow cornmeal	1/2 cup yellow cornmeal
2 tablespoons dark molasses	3 tablespoons dark molasses	1/4 cup dark molasses
1 tablespoon soft butter	2 tablespoons soft butter	3 tablespoons soft butter
1 teaspoon salt	1 1/2 teaspoons salt	2 teaspoons salt
1 3/4 cups bread flour	2 2/3 cups bread flour	3 1/2 cups bread flour
1 teaspoon rapid-rising or active dry yeast	1 1/2 teaspoons rapid-rising or active dry yeast	2 teaspoons rapid-rising or active dry yeast
1 cup sharp Cheddar cheese cubes (1-inch cubes)	1 1/2 cups sharp Cheddar cheese cubes (1-inch cubes)	2 cups sharp Cheddar cheese cubes (1-inch cubes)
1/4 cup chopped toasted walnuts	1/2 cup chopped toasted walnuts	2/3 cup chopped toasted walnuts

TO MIX THE DOUGH BY HAND Pour the boiling water into a large bowl, add the cornmeal, and stir. Let stand 25 to 35 minutes, until the mixture cools to warm, between 105° and 115°F. Add the molasses and yeast; let stand 5 minutes, until the yeast begins to bubble. Stir in the butter, salt, and half of the bread flour. Beat until smooth. Cover, and let stand 15 minutes. Slowly add the remaining bread flour, and beat until a soft dough forms. Turn the dough out onto a very lightly floured board, and knead, adding flour if necessary, until smooth and springy, about 5 minutes. Knead in the cheese and walnuts. Wash the bowl and grease it; place the dough back in the bowl, and turn it over to grease the top. Cover, and let rise until doubled, about 1 hour.

TO MIX THE DOUGH WITH A HEAVY-DUTY MIXER Pour the boiling water into the mixing bowl, add the cornmeal, stir. Let stand 25 to 35 minutes, until the mixture cools to warm, between 105° and 115°F. Add the molasses and yeast; let stand 5 minutes, until the yeast begins to bubble. Add the butter, salt, and half of the bread flour. Beat until smooth. Cover, and let stand 15 minutes. Slowly add the remaining bread flour, and beat until a soft dough forms. Knead the dough in the mixer with the dough hook, on medium to high speed, adding flour as necessary, until the dough pulls away from the sides of the bowl and is smooth and springy but still soft to the touch. Knead in the cheese and walnuts. Remove the dough hook, cover the bowl, and let the dough rise until doubled, about 1 hour.

TO MIX THE DOUGH IN THE FOOD PROCESSOR Place the plastic dough blade into the work bowl. Pour the boiling water into the work bowl, add the cornmeal, and stir. Let stand about 25 minutes, until the mixture cools to very warm, between 120° and 130°F. Place the remaining ingredients, except the cheese and walnuts, into the work bowl. Turn the processor on, and slowly pour the water through the feed tube, processing

until the dough is smooth and pulls away from the sides of the bowl. If the dough is wet and sticky, add more flour, 1 tablespoon at a time, until the dough is smooth yet soft to the touch. If the dough is not soft to the touch but is very firm, add 1 tablespoon of water at a time, and process until the dough is smooth yet soft to the touch. Mix in the cheese and walnuts. Cover the work bowl, and let the dough rise until doubled, about 1 hour. Or remove the dough to a lightly greased bowl, cover, and let rise until doubled, about 1 hour.

TO MIX THE DOUGH IN THE BREAD MACHINE Pour the boiling water into the pan, add the cornmeal, and stir. Let stand until the mixture cools to room temperature. Add the remaining ingredients, except the cheese and nuts. Make an indentation in the dry ingredients and add the yeast. Select *Dough,* and press *Start.* If the dough is wet and sticky, add more flour, 1 tablespoon at a time, until the dough is smooth yet soft to the touch. If the dough is not soft to the touch but is very firm, add 1 teaspoon of water at a time, until the dough is smooth yet soft to the touch. Add the cheese and walnuts when the machine signals it's time to add ingredients or when the cycle ends. The machine will stop when the dough is ready to shape and bake.

TO MIX AND BAKE THE BREAD IN THE BREAD MACHINE Pour the boiling water into the pan, add the cornmeal, and stir. Let stand 35 to 45 minutes, until the mixture cools to room temperature. Add the remaining ingredients, except the cheese and nuts. Make an indentation in the dry ingredients and add the yeast. Select the *Fruit and Nut, Basic,* or *Whole Wheat* cycle; set the crust on *Medium;* and press *Start.* During the mixing cycle, if the dough is wet and sticky, add more flour, 1 tablespoon at a time, until the dough is smooth yet soft to the touch. If the dough is not soft to the touch but is very firm, add 1 teaspoon of water at a time, until the dough is smooth yet soft to the touch. Add the cheese and walnuts when the machine signals it's time to add ingredients.

TO SHAPE AND BAKE IN THE OVEN Lightly grease an 8- or 9-inch round cake pan. Turn the dough out onto a lightly floured board or lightly oiled surface. Punch the dough down, and shape it into a round loaf. Place the loaf, with the smooth side up, into the pan. Cover and let rise in a warm place until almost doubled, 45 minutes. Preheat the oven to 375°F. Bake 30 to 35 minutes, until the loaf is golden and a wooden skewer inserted into the loaf comes out clean and dry. Remove from the pan and cool on a wire rack.

TOASTING NUTS

To toast nuts, preheat the oven to 350°F. Spread the nuts on a baking sheet, and toast in the oven 10 to 12 minutes.

CHOCOLATE, WALNUT, AND WHEAT BREAD

This seemed like a totally crazy idea until I tried it. The whole wheat, chocolate, and nuts make a delicious combination: a bread that, when sliced still warm, reveals little pockets of melted chocolate. It isn't sweet. When baked in the bread machine, it has a reddish crumb, because the chocolate gets mixed into the dough.

Sampler Loaf

2/3 cup water

3/4 teaspoon salt

1 cup whole wheat flour

1 cup bread flour

2 teaspoons gluten

1 1/2 teaspoons rapid-rising or active dry yeast

1/2 cup chopped toasted walnuts

1/2 cup semisweet chocolate chips

Regular Loaf

1 cup water

1 teaspoon salt

1 1/2 cups whole wheat flour

1 1/2 cups bread flour

1 tablespoon gluten

2 teaspoons rapid-rising or active dry yeast

1 cup chopped toasted walnuts

1 cup semisweet chocolate chips

Large Loaf

1 1/3 cups water

1 1/2 teaspoons salt

2 cups whole wheat flour

2 cups bread flour

4 teaspoons gluten

2 1/4 teaspoons rapid-rising or active dry yeast

1 1/2 cups chopped toasted walnuts

1 1/2 cups semisweet chocolate chips

TO MIX THE DOUGH BY HAND Heat the water until warm, between 105° and 115°F; pour it into a large, warmed bowl, and add the yeast. Let stand 5 minutes, until the yeast begins to bubble. Stir in the salt, whole wheat flour, half of the bread flour, and the gluten. Beat well. Cover, and let stand 15 minutes. Slowly add the remaining bread flour, and beat until a dough forms. Turn the dough out onto a very lightly floured board, and knead, adding flour if necessary, until smooth and springy, about 5 minutes. Knead in the walnuts and chocolate. Wash the bowl and grease it; place the dough back in the bowl, and turn it over to grease the top. Cover, and let rise until doubled, about 1 hour.

TO MIX THE DOUGH WITH A HEAVY-DUTY MIXER Heat the water until warm, between 105° and 115°F; pour it into the warmed mixing bowl, and add the yeast. Let stand 5 minutes, until the yeast begins to bubble. Add the salt, whole wheat flour, half of the bread flour, the gluten. butter, salt, dry milk, and the whole wheat flour. Beat until a smooth dough forms.

Cover, and let stand 15 minutes. Slowly add the remaining bread flour, and beat until a smooth dough forms. Knead the dough in the mixer with the dough hook, on medium to high speed, adding flour as necessary, until the dough pulls away from the sides of the bowl and is smooth and springy but still soft to the touch. Knead in the walnuts and chocolate. Remove the dough hook, cover the bowl, and let the dough rise until doubled, about 1 hour.

TO MIX THE DOUGH IN THE FOOD PROCESSOR
Place the plastic dough blade into the work bowl. Heat the water until very warm, between 120° and 130°F; set aside. Place the remaining ingredients, except the chocolate and walnuts, into the work bowl. Turn the processor on, and slowly pour the water through the feed tube, processing until the dough is smooth and pulls away from the sides of the bowl. If the dough is wet and sticky, add more flour, 1 tablespoon at a time, until the dough is smooth yet soft to the touch. If the dough is not soft to the touch but is very firm, add 1 tablespoon of water at a time, and process until the dough is smooth yet soft to the touch. Mix in the walnuts and chocolate. Cover the work bowl, and let the dough rise until doubled, about 1 hour. Or remove the dough to a lightly greased bowl, cover, and let rise until doubled, about 1 hour.

TO MIX THE DOUGH IN THE BREAD MACHINE Pour the water (at room temperature) into the pan. Add the salt, whole wheat flour, bread flour, and gluten. Make a small indentation in the dry ingredients and add the yeast. Select *Dough,* and press *Start.* If the dough is wet and sticky, add more flour, 1 tablespoon at a time, until the dough is smooth yet soft to the touch. If the dough is not soft to the touch but is very firm, add 1 teaspoon of water at a time, until the dough is smooth yet soft to the touch. Add the walnuts and chocolate when the machine signals it's time to add ingredients or when the cycle ends. The machine will stop when the dough is ready to shape and bake.

TO MIX AND BAKE THE BREAD IN THE BREAD MACHINE Pour the water (at room temperature) into the pan. Add the salt, whole wheat flour, bread flour, and gluten. Make a small indentation in the dry ingredients and add the yeast. Select the *Fruit and Nut, Basic,* or *Whole Wheat* cycle; set the crust on *Medium;* and press *Start.* During the mixing cycle, if the dough is wet and sticky, add more flour, 1 tablespoon at a time, until the dough is smooth yet soft to the touch. If the dough is not soft to the touch but is very firm, add 1 teaspoon of water at a time, until the dough is smooth yet soft to the touch. Add the walnuts and chocolate when the machine signals it's time to add ingredients or when the cycle ends.

TO SHAPE AND BAKE IN THE OVEN Lightly grease a baking sheet or cover it with parchment paper. Turn the dough out onto a lightly floured board or lightly oiled surface. Punch the dough down, and shape it into a round loaf. Place the loaf, with the smooth side up, onto the baking sheet. Cover and let rise in warm place until puffy, 45 to 60 minutes. Preheat the oven to 350°F. Brush or spray the loaf with water; Using a serrated knife or razor, make three shallow cuts (about $1/8$ inch deep) across the top of the loaf. Bake 35 to 40 minutes, until a wooden skewer inserted into the loaf comes out clean and dry. Remove from the pan and cool on a wire rack.

Chocolate Bread Pudding

This is really delicious made with crumbs from either Chocolate, Walnut, and Wheat Bread (page 103) or Light Wheat Brioche (page 22). It's quick, easy, and foolproof. Make it in individual ramekins or in one large pan. Warm, it is custard-like, but chilled it resembles a chocolate mousse cake. Because it is rich, you need only small servings. I served it as dessert for a luncheon wedding shower for my niece, topped with lightly whipped cream and sliced fresh peaches.

12 SERVINGS

3/4 cup sugar

1 cup milk

8 ounces (1 1/2 cups) semisweet chocolate bits

5 eggs, separated

1/2 cup (1 stick) unsalted butter, cut up

1 tablespoon vanilla

2 cups Chocolate, Walnut, and
  Wheat Bread crumbs

Lightly sweetened whipped cream

Sliced fresh peaches or strawberries

Preheat the oven to 350°F. Butter an 8-inch soufflé dish and dust with 1 1/2 tablespoons of the sugar.

In a heavy saucepan, heat the milk to simmering. Put the chocolate bits into the work bowl of a food processor fitted with the steel blade. Process until the chocolate is chopped fine. With the processor on, pour in the hot milk, and process until smooth. Add half of the remaining sugar along with the egg yolks. Add the butter and vanilla. Process just until smooth.

In a large bowl, mix the bread crumbs with the chocolate mixture.

Beat the egg whites until soft peaks form, and gradually beat in the remaining sugar, beating until the whites are glossy and stand in stiff peaks. Stir one-third of the egg whites into the chocolate mixture to lighten it. Fold in the remaining whites until no white streaks remain.

Turn the mixture into the soufflé dish. Place the dish into a larger pan, and add warm water to reach halfway up the side of the dish. Bake in the center of the oven for 45 to 50 minutes, until the pudding is set and a knife inserted into the center comes out clean. Remove from the oven, and let cool 10 minutes. Serve warm with lightly whipped cream and sliced fresh peaches spooned over. Or refrigerate until ready to serve, invert the pudding onto a serving plate, and cut into wedges. Top with the whipped cream and peaches.

CINNAMON-PECAN WHEAT AND RYE BREAD

This is a terrific combination of flavors! The toasted pecans add a nice crunch to the bread, and the cinnamon brings out the whole grain flavors.

Small Loaf	Regular Loaf	Large Loaf
$2/3$ cup water	1 cup water	$1^1/3$ cups water
$1^1/2$ tablespoons packed brown sugar	2 tablespoons packed brown sugar	3 tablespoons packed brown sugar
$3/4$ teaspoon salt	1 teaspoon salt	$1^1/2$ teaspoons salt
1 teaspoon cinnamon	2 teaspoons cinnamon	1 tablespoon cinnamon
1 tablespoon butter, softened	2 tablespoons butter, softened	3 tablespoons butter, softened
1 tablespoon nonfat dry milk	2 tablespoons nonfat dry milk	3 tablespoons nonfat dry milk
$1/3$ cup whole wheat flour	$1/2$ cup whole wheat flour	$3/4$ cup whole wheat flour
$1/3$ cup light rye flour	$1/2$ cup light rye flour	$3/4$ cup light rye flour
$1^1/3$ cups bread flour	2 cups bread flour	$2^1/2$ cups bread flour
1 teaspoon rapid-rising or active dry yeast	$1^1/2$ teaspoons rapid-rising or active dry yeast	2 teaspoons rapid-rising or active dry yeast
$1/4$ cup chopped toasted pecans	$1/2$ cup chopped toasted pecans	$3/4$ cup chopped toasted pecans

TO MIX THE DOUGH BY HAND Heat the water until warm, between 105° and 115°F; pour it into a large, warmed bowl, and add the yeast, brown sugar, salt, and cinammon. Let stand 5 minutes, until the yeast begins to bubble. Stir in the butter, dry milk, and whole wheat flour, and rye flour. Beat until smooth. Cover, and let stand 15 minutes. Slowly add the bread flour, and beat until a smooth dough forms. Turn the dough out onto a very lightly floured board, and knead, adding flour if necessary, until smooth and springy, about 5 minutes. Knead in the pecans. Wash the bowl and grease it; place the dough back in the bowl, and turn it over to grease the top. Cover, and let rise until doubled, about 1 hour.

TO MIX THE DOUGH WITH A HEAVY-DUTY MIXER Heat the water until warm, between 105° and 115°F; pour it into the warmed mixing bowl, and add the yeast, brown sugar, salt, and cinammon. Let stand 5 minutes, until the yeast begins to bubble. Add the butter, dry milk, whole wheat flour, and rye flour. Beat until smooth. Cover, and let stand 15 minutes. Slowly add the bread flour, and beat until a smooth dough forms. Knead the dough in the mixer with the dough hook, on medium to high speed, adding flour as necessary, until the dough pulls away from the sides of the bowl and is smooth and springy but still soft to the touch. Knead in the pecans. Remove the dough hook, cover the bowl, and let the dough rise until doubled, about 1 hour.

TO MIX THE DOUGH IN THE FOOD PROCESSOR Place the plastic dough blade into the work bowl. Heat the water until very warm, between 120° and 130°F; set aside. Place the remaining ingredients, except the nuts, into the work bowl. Turn the processor on, and slowly pour the water through the feed tube, processing until the dough is smooth and pulls away from the sides of the bowl. If the dough is wet and sticky, add more flour, 1 tablespoon at a time, until the dough is smooth yet soft to the touch. If the dough is not soft to the touch but is very firm, add 1 tablespoon of water at a time, and process until the dough is smooth yet soft to the touch. Add nuts and process until blended into dough. Cover the work bowl, and let the dough rise until doubled, about 1 hour. Or remove the dough to a lightly greased bowl, cover, and let rise until doubled, about 1 hour.

TO MIX THE DOUGH IN THE BREAD MACHINE Pour the water (at room temperature) into the pan. Add the remaining ingredients, in the order listed. Make an indentation in the dry ingredients and add the yeast. Select *Dough,* and press *Start.* If the dough is wet and sticky, add more flour, 1 tablespoon at a time, until the dough is smooth yet soft to the touch. If the dough is not soft to the touch but is very firm, add 1 teaspoon of water at a time, until the dough is smooth yet soft to the touch. The machine will stop when the dough is ready to shape and bake.

TO MIX AND BAKE THE BREAD IN THE BREAD MACHINE Pour the water (at room temperature) into the pan. Add the remaining ingredients, in the order listed. Make an indentation in the dry ingredients and add the yeast. Select the *Basic* cycle, set the crust on *Medium,* and press *Start.* During the mixing cycle, if the dough is wet and sticky, add more flour, 1 tablespoon at a time, until the dough is smooth yet soft to the touch. If the dough is not soft to the touch but is very firm, add 1 teaspoon of water at a time, until the dough is smooth yet soft to the touch.

TO SHAPE AND BAKE IN THE OVEN Lightly grease a 9 × 5-inch loaf pan or an 8- or 9-inch round cake pan. Turn the dough out onto a lightly floured board or lightly oiled surface. Punch the dough down, and shape it into an oblong or round loaf. Place the loaf, with the smooth side up, into the pan. Cover and let rise in a warm place until almost doubled, 45 minutes. Preheat the oven to 375°F. Bake 25 to 30 minutes, until the loaf is golden. Remove from the pan and cool on a wire rack.

Fresh Pear Slices and Blue Castello on Toast

The Danish Blue Castello cheese is creamy and rich and perfect with fruit and a whole grain bread. Cinnamon-Pecan Wheat and Rye Bread (page 106) is my favorite with this combination. This dish is ideal as an appetizer or a small sandwich at tea time.

6 SERVINGS

6 slices Cinnamon-Pecan Wheat and Rye Bread,
   1/2 inch thick
1 package (8 ounces) Danish Blue Castello cheese or
   Gorgonzola

18 thin slices ripe Bosc or Red Bartlett
   pear, unpeeled
2 to 3 teaspoons walnut oil

Preheat the oven to 350°F. Cut each bread slice into a 2 × 3-inch square (save the edges for crumbs or another use).

Place on baking sheet and toast the bread for 10 minutes or until lightly browned, turning once. Top each square with some cheese, gently mashing it down to cover the bread. Top each with 3 slices of fresh pear. Return to the oven for 3 minutes or until the cheese melts.

Sprinkle with walnut oil and cut each square in half, diagonally. Serve warm with a rich red wine or with hot tea.

Cinnamon Crouton Cubes

I make flavored crouton cubes with almost any kind of bread, but this works especially well with whole wheat breads that have raisins, dried cranberries, or nuts added. Use them to garnish fruit plates, fruit salads, and fruit soups or just pour into a bowl and serve as a snack.

4 CUPS

1 quart bread cubes, cut 1/2 inch, made from stale
   sweet or spiced bread

3 tablespoons butter, melted

3 tablespoons sugar

2 teaspoons cinnamon

Preheat the oven to 350°F. Put the bread cubes into a large bowl and toss with the melted butter, sugar, and cinnamon until evenly coated. Spread the cubes out onto a cookie sheet in a single layer. Bake 10 to 15 minutes or until crispy. Cool and store in an airtight container.

COUNTRY CURRANT RYE BREAD

This bread is loaded with so many dried currants that they sweeten the loaf. It's a dense, dark loaf, because of the high percentage of rye flour; when thinly sliced this bread makes a wonderful addition to any cheese board, served with sweet butter, Brie, cream, or a pungent blue cheese. If the currants are very dry, cover them with warm water for 10 minutes; then drain thoroughly.

Sampler Loaf	Regular Loaf	Large Loaf
2/3 cup water	1 cup water	1 1/3 cups water
1 teaspoon salt	1 1/2 teaspoons salt	2 teaspoons salt
1 tablespoon butter	2 tablespoons butter	3 tablespoons butter
1 cup dark rye flour	1 1/2 cups dark rye flour	2 cups dark rye flour
1 cup bread flour	1 1/2 cups bread flour	2 cups bread flour
1 tablespoon gluten	1 1/2 tablespoons gluten	2 tablespoons gluten
1 1/4 teaspoons rapid-rising or active dry yeast	1 1/2 teaspoons rapid-rising or active dry yeast	2 teaspoons rapid-rising or active dry yeast
1/2 cup currants	1 cup currants	1 1/2 cups currants

TO MIX THE DOUGH BY HAND Heat the water until warm, between 105° and 115°F; pour it into a large, warmed bowl, and add the yeast. Let stand 5 minutes, until the yeast begins to bubble. Stir in the salt, butter, and rye flour. Beat until smooth. Cover, and let stand 15 minutes. Slowly add the bread flour and the gluten, and beat until a smooth dough forms. Turn the dough out onto a very lightly floured board, and knead, adding flour if necessary, until smooth and springy, about 5 minutes. Knead in the currants. Wash the bowl and grease it; place the dough back in the bowl, and turn it over to grease the top. Cover, and let rise until doubled, about 1 hour.

TO MIX THE DOUGH WITH A HEAVY-DUTY MIXER Heat the water until warm, between 105° and 115°F; pour it into the warmed mixing bowl, and add the yeast. Let stand 5 minutes, until the yeast begins to bubble. Add the salt, butter, and rye flour. Beat until smooth. Cover, and let stand 15 minutes. Slowly add the bread flour and gluten, and beat until a smooth dough forms. Knead the dough in the mixer with the dough hook, on medium to high speed, adding flour as necessary, until the dough pulls away from the sides of the bowl and is smooth and springy but still soft to the touch. Knead in the currants. Remove the dough hook, cover the bowl, and let the dough rise until doubled, about 1 hour.

TO MIX THE DOUGH IN THE FOOD PROCESSOR
Place the plastic dough blade into the work bowl. Heat the water until very warm, between 120° and 130°F; set aside. Place the remaining ingredients, except the currants, into the work bowl. Turn the processor on, and slowly pour the water through the feed tube, processing until the dough is smooth and pulls away from the sides of the bowl. If the dough is wet and sticky, add more flour, 1 tablespoon at a time, until the dough is smooth yet soft to the touch. If the dough is not soft to the touch but is very firm, add 1 tablespoon of water at a time, and process until the dough is smooth yet soft to the touch. Mix in the currants. Cover the work bowl, and let the dough rise until doubled, about 1 hour. Or remove the dough to a lightly greased bowl, cover, and let rise until doubled, about 1 hour.

TO MIX THE DOUGH IN THE BREAD MACHINE Pour the water (at room temperature) into the pan, and add the remaining ingredients, except the currants. Make an indentation in the dry ingredients and add the yeast. Select *Dough,* and press *Start.* If the dough is wet and sticky, add more flour, 1 tablespoon at a time, until the dough is smooth yet soft to the touch. If the dough is not soft to the touch but is very firm, add 1 teaspoon of water at a time, until the dough is smooth yet soft to the touch. Add the currants when the machine signals it's time to add ingredients or when the cycle ends. The machine will stop when the dough is ready to shape and bake.

TO MIX AND BAKE THE BREAD IN THE BREAD MACHINE Pour the water (at room temperature) into the pan, and add the remaining ingredients, except the currants. Make an indentation in the dry ingredients and add the yeast. Select the *Basic* cycle, set the crust on *Medium,* and press *Start.* During the mixing cycle, if the dough is wet and sticky, add more flour, 1 tablespoon at a time, until the dough is smooth yet soft to the touch. If the dough is not soft to the touch but is very firm, add 1 teaspoon of water at a time, until the dough is smooth yet soft to the touch. Add the currants when the machine signals it's time to add ingredients.

TO SHAPE AND BAKE IN THE OVEN Lightly grease a baking sheet or cover with parchment paper. Turn the dough out onto a lightly floured board or lightly oiled surface. Punch the dough down, and shape it into a round loaf. Place the loaf, with the smooth side up, onto the baking sheet. Cover and let rise in a warm place until almost doubled, 45 minutes. Preheat the oven to 350°F. Bake 30 to 35 minutes, until the loaf is golden and a wooden skewer inserted into the loaf comes out clean and dry. Remove from the pan and cool on a wire rack.

CRANBERRY GRAHAM BREAD

Graham flour, interchangeable with whole wheat flour, has the wheat bran in the flour. Side by side, graham flour usually looks coarser than whole wheat flour, although there is variation among brands. Either flour works fine in this recipe, which has a creamy colored crumb. Sunflower seeds add texture and dried cranberries add a tangy bite to this bread.

Sampler Loaf	Regular Loaf	Large Loaf
2/3 cup water	1 cup water	1 1/3 cups water
1/2 tablespoon sugar	1 tablespoon sugar	1 1/2 tablespoons sugar
2 tablespoons nonfat dry milk	3 tablespoons nonfat dry milk	1/4 cup nonfat dry milk
1 tablespoon butter, soft	1 1/2 tablespoons butter, soft	2 tablespoons butter, soft
1/2 teaspoon salt	1 teaspoon salt	1 1/2 teaspoons salt
1/2 cup graham flour or whole wheat flour	1 cup graham flour or whole wheat flour	1 1/2 cups graham flour or whole wheat flour
1 1/2 cups bread flour	2 cups bread flour	2 1/2 cups bread flour
3/4 teaspoon rapid-rising or active dry yeast	1 1/2 teaspoon rapid-rising or active dry yeast	2 teaspoons rapid-rising or active dry yeast
1/4 cup dried cranberries	1/3 cup dried cranberries	1/2 cup dried cranberries
2 tablespoons roasted sunflower seeds	3 tablespoons roasted sunflower seeds	1/4 cup roasted sunflower seeds

TO MIX THE DOUGH BY HAND Heat the water until warm, between 105° and 115°F; pour it into a large, warmed bowl, and add the yeast, sugar, and dry milk. Let stand 5 minutes, until the yeast begins to bubble. Stir in the butter, salt, and graham flour. Cover, and let stand 15 minutes. Slowly add the bread flour, and beat until a smooth dough forms. Turn the dough out onto a very lightly floured board, and knead, adding flour if necessary, until smooth and springy, about 5 minutes. Knead in the cranberries and sunflower seeds. Wash the bowl and grease it; place the dough back in the bowl, and turn it over to grease the top. Cover, and let rise until doubled, about 1 hour.

TO MIX THE DOUGH WITH A HEAVY-DUTY MIXER Heat the water until warm, between 105° and 115°F; pour it into the warmed mixing bowl, and add the yeast, sugar, and dry milk. Let stand 5 minutes, until the yeast begins to bubble. Add the butter, salt, and graham flour. Cover, and let stand 15 minutes. Slowly add the bread flour, and beat until a smooth dough forms. Knead the dough in the mixer with the dough hook, on medium to high speed, adding flour as necessary, until the dough pulls away from the sides of the bowl and is smooth and springy but still soft to the touch. Knead in the cranberries and sunflower seeds. Remove the dough hook, cover the bowl, and let the dough rise until doubled, about 1 hour.

TO MIX THE DOUGH IN THE FOOD PROCESSOR Place the plastic dough blade into the work bowl. Heat the water until very warm, between 120° and 130°F; set aside. Place the remaining ingredients, except the cranberries and sunflower seeds, into the work bowl. Turn the processor on, and slowly pour the water through the feed tube, processing until the dough is smooth and pulls away from the sides of the bowl. If the dough is wet and sticky, add more flour, 1 tablespoon at a time, until the dough is smooth yet soft to the touch. If the dough is not soft to the touch but is very firm, add 1 tablespoon of water at a time, and process until the dough is smooth yet soft to the touch. Mix in the cranberries and sunflower seeds. Cover the work bowl, and let the dough rise until doubled, about 1 hour. Or remove the dough to a lightly greased bowl, cover, and let rise until doubled, about 1 hour.

TO MIX THE DOUGH IN THE BREAD MACHINE Pour the water (at room temperature) into the pan. Add the remaining ingredients, except the cranberries and sunflower seeds, in the order listed. Make an indentation in the dry ingredients and add the yeast. Select *Dough*, and press *Start*. If the dough is wet and sticky, add more flour, 1 tablespoon at a time, until the

dough is smooth yet soft to the touch. If the dough is not soft to the touch but is very firm, add 1 teaspoon of water at a time, until the dough is smooth yet soft to the touch. Add the cranberries and sunflower seeds when the machine signals it's time to add ingredients or when the cycle ends. The machine will stop when the dough is ready to shape and bake.

TO MIX AND BAKE THE BREAD IN THE BREAD MACHINE Pour the water (at room temperature) into the pan. Add the remaining ingredients, except the cranberries and sunflower seeds, in the order listed. Make an indentation in the dry ingredients and add the yeast. Select the *Fruit and Nut, Basic,* or *Whole Wheat* cycle; set the crust on *Medium;* and press *Start*. During the mixing cycle, if the dough is wet and sticky, add more flour, 1 tablespoon at a time, until the dough is smooth yet soft to the touch. If the dough is not soft to the touch but is very firm, add 1 teaspoon of water at a time, until the dough is smooth yet soft to the touch. Add the cranberries and sunflower seeds when the machine signals it's time to add ingredients.

TO SHAPE AND BAKE IN THE OVEN Lightly grease a 9 × 5-inch loaf pan or an 8- or 9-inch round cake pan. Turn the dough out onto a lightly floured board or lightly oiled surface. Punch the dough down, and shape it into an oblong or round loaf. Place the loaf, with the smooth side up, into the pan. Cover and let rise in a warm place until almost doubled, 45 minutes. Preheat the oven to 350°F. Bake 30 to 35 minutes, until the loaf is golden and a wooden skewer inserted into the loaf comes out clean and dry. Remove from the pan and cool on a wire rack.

CRANBERRY OATMEAL NUT LOAF

Instead of raisins, the perky, tart taste of cranberries, along with orange and nuts, makes this an irresistibly delicious bread. A bit of lemon juice enhances the flavor.

Sampler Loaf

2/3 cup water

1 teaspoon freshly squeezed lemon juice

2 teaspoons butter or shortening

1 tablespoon sugar

3 tablespoons nonfat dry milk

3/4 teaspoon salt

2 teaspoons grated orange zest

1/4 cup quick-cooking rolled oats

1/4 cup whole wheat or rye flour

1 1/2 cups bread flour

1 teaspoon rapid-rising or active dry yeast

1/3 cup dried sweetened cranberries

1/3 cup chopped toasted walnuts

Regular Loaf

1 cup water

1 1/2 teaspoons freshly squeezed lemon juice

1 tablespoon butter or shortening

2 tablespoons sugar

1/3 cup nonfat dry milk

1 teaspoon salt

1 tablespoon grated orange zest

1/3 cup quick-cooking rolled oats

1/3 cup whole wheat or rye flour

2 1/3 cups bread flour

1 1/2 teaspoons rapid-rising or active dry yeast

1/2 cup dried sweetened cranberries

1/2 cup chopped toasted walnuts

Large Loaf

1 1/3 cups water

2 teaspoons freshly squeezed lemon juice

1 1/2 tablespoons butter or shortening

3 tablespoons sugar

1/2 cup nonfat dry milk

1 1/2 teaspoons salt

1 1/2 tablespoons grated orange zest

1/2 cup quick-cooking rolled oats

1/2 cup whole wheat or rye flour

3 cups bread flour

2 teaspoons rapid-rising or active dry yeast

2/3 cup dried sweetened cranberries

2/3 cup chopped toasted walnuts

TO MIX THE DOUGH BY HAND Heat the water until warm, between 105° and 115°F; pour it into a large, warmed bowl, and add the yeast. Let stand 5 minutes, until the yeast begins to bubble. Stir in the lemon juice, butter, sugar, dry milk, salt, orange zest, rolled oats, and whole wheat flour. Beat until a smooth dough forms. Cover, and let stand 15 minutes. Slowly add the bread flour, and beat until a stiff dough forms. Turn the dough out onto a very lightly floured board, and knead, adding flour if necessary, until smooth and springy, about 5 minutes. Knead in the cranberries and walnuts. Wash the bowl and grease it; place the dough back in the bowl, and turn it over to grease the top. Cover, and let rise until doubled, about 1 hour.

TO MIX THE DOUGH WITH A HEAVY-DUTY MIXER Heat the water until warm, between 105° and 115°F; pour it into the warmed mixing

bowl, and add the yeast. Let stand 5 minutes, until the yeast begins to bubble. Add the lemon juice, butter, sugar, dry milk, salt, orange zest, rolled oats, and whole wheat flour. Beat until a smooth dough forms. Cover, and let stand 15 minutes. Slowly add the bread flour, and beat until a stiff dough forms. Knead the dough in the mixer with the dough hook, on medium to high speed, adding flour as necessary, until the dough pulls away from the sides of the bowl and is smooth and springy but still soft to the touch. Knead in the cranberries and walnuts. Remove the dough hook, cover the bowl, and let the dough rise until doubled, about 1 hour.

TO MIX THE DOUGH IN THE FOOD PROCESSOR
Place the plastic dough blade into the work bowl. Heat the water until very warm, between 120° and 130°F; set aside. Place the remaining ingredients, except the cranberries and walnuts, into the work bowl. Turn the processor on, and slowly pour the water through the feed tube, processing until the dough is smooth and pulls away from the sides of the bowl. If the dough is wet and sticky, add more flour, 1 tablespoon at a time, until the dough is smooth yet soft to the touch. If the dough is not soft to the touch but is very firm, add 1 tablespoon of water at a time, and process until the dough is smooth yet soft to the touch. Mix in the cranberries and walnuts. Cover the work bowl, and let the dough rise until doubled, about 1 hour. Or remove the dough to a lightly greased bowl, cover, and let rise until doubled, about 1 hour.

TO MIX THE DOUGH IN THE BREAD MACHINE   Pour the water (at room temperature) into the pan, and add the remaining ingredients, except the cranberries and walnuts. Make an

indentation in the dry ingredients and add the yeast. Select *Dough,* and press *Start.* If the dough is wet and sticky, add more flour, 1 tablespoon at a time, until the dough is smooth yet soft to the touch. If the dough is not soft to the touch but is very firm, add 1 teaspoon of water at a time, until the dough is smooth yet soft to the touch. Add the cranberries and walnuts when the machine signals it's time to add ingredients or when the cycle ends. The machine will stop when the dough is ready to shape and bake.

TO MIX AND BAKE THE BREAD IN THE BREAD MACHINE   Pour the water (at room temperature) into the pan, and add the remaining ingredients, except the cranberries and walnuts. Make an indentation in the dry ingredients and add the yeast. Select the *Fruit and Nut, Basic* or *Whole Wheat* cycle; set the crust on *Medium;* and press *Start.* During the mixing cycle, if the dough is wet and sticky, add more flour, 1 tablespoon at a time, until the dough is smooth yet soft to the touch. If the dough is not soft to the touch but is very firm, add 1 teaspoon of water at a time, until the dough is smooth yet soft to the touch. Add the cranberries walnuts when the machine signals it's time to add ingredients.

TO SHAPE AND BAKE IN THE OVEN   Lightly grease a baking sheet or cover it with parchment paper. Turn the dough out onto a lightly floured board or lightly oiled surface. Punch the dough down, and shape it into a round loaf. Place the loaf, with the smooth side up, onto the baking sheet. Cover and let rise in a warm place until almost doubled, 1 hour. Preheat the oven to 375°F. Bake 35 to 45 minutes, until a wooden skewer inserted into the loaf comes out clean and dry. Remove from the pan and cool on a wire rack.

DATE AND NUT
BUTTERMILK WHEAT BREAD

Buttermilk adds a tangy flavor to this bread with a tender yet crisp crust. If I don't have fresh buttermilk on hand, I use water instead, and then add buttermilk powder, according to the package instructions.

Sampler Loaf

2/3 cup buttermilk

1/2 teaspoon freshly squeezed lemon juice

1 tablespoon soft butter or oil

1 teaspoon salt

1 tablespoon packed brown sugar

1/2 cup whole wheat flour

1 1/2 cups bread flour

1 teaspoon rapid-rising or active dry yeast

2 tablespoons chopped dates

2 tablespoons toasted chopped walnuts

Regular Loaf

1 cup buttermilk

1 teaspoon freshly squeezed lemon juice

2 tablespoons soft butter or oil

1 1/2 teaspoons salt

2 tablespoons packed brown sugar

1 cup whole wheat flour

2 cups bread flour

1 1/2 teaspoons rapid-rising or active dry yeast

1/4 cup chopped dates

1/4 cup toasted chopped walnuts

Large Loaf

1 1/3 cups buttermilk

1 1/2 teaspoons freshly squeezed lemon juice

3 tablespoons soft butter or oil

2 teaspoons salt

3 tablespoons packed brown sugar

1 1/4 cups whole wheat flour

2 3/4 cups bread flour

2 teaspoons rapid-rising or active dry yeast

1/2 cup chopped dates

1/2 cup toasted chopped walnuts

GLAZE FOR BREAD BAKED CONVENTIONALLY

1 egg beaten

1 tablespoon water or milk

TO MIX THE DOUGH BY HAND Heat the buttermilk until warm, between 105° and 115°F; pour it into a large, warmed bowl, and add the yeast. Let stand 5 minutes, until the yeast begins to bubble. Stir in the lemon juice, butter, salt, sugar, and whole wheat flour. Cover, and let stand 15 minutes. Slowly add the bread flour, and beat until a smooth dough forms. Turn the dough out onto a very lightly floured board, and knead, adding flour if necessary, until smooth and springy, about 5 minutes. Knead in the dates and walnuts. Wash the bowl and grease it; place the dough back in the bowl, and turn it over to grease the top. Cover, and let rise until doubled, about 1 hour.

TO MIX THE DOUGH WITH A HEAVY-DUTY MIXER Heat the buttermilk until warm, between 105° and 115°F; pour it into the warmed mixing bowl, and add the yeast. Let stand 5 minutes, until the yeast begins to bubble. Add the lemon juice, butter, salt, sugar, and whole wheat flour. Cover, and let stand 15 minutes. Slowly add the bread flour, and beat until a smooth dough forms. Knead the dough in the mixer with the dough hook, on medium to high speed, adding flour as necessary, until the dough pulls away from the sides of the bowl and is smooth and springy but still soft to the touch. Knead in the dates and walnuts. Remove the dough hook, cover the bowl, and let the dough rise until doubled, about 1 hour.

TO MIX THE DOUGH IN THE FOOD PROCESSOR Place the plastic dough blade into the work bowl. Heat the buttermilk until very warm, between 120° and 130°F; set aside. Place the remaining ingredients, except the dates and walnuts, into the work bowl. Turn the processor on, and slowly pour the water through the feed tube, processing until the dough is smooth and pulls away from the sides of the bowl. If the dough is wet and sticky, add more flour, 1 tablespoon at a time, until the dough is smooth yet soft to the touch. If the dough is not soft to the touch but is very firm, add 1 tablespoon of water at a time, and process until the dough is smooth yet soft to the touch. Mix in the dates and walnuts. Cover the work bowl, and let the dough rise until doubled, about 1 hour. Or remove the dough to a lightly greased bowl, cover, and let rise until doubled, about 1 hour.

TO MIX THE DOUGH IN THE BREAD MACHINE Pour the buttermilk (at room temperature) into the pan, and add the remaining ingredients, except the dates and walnuts. Make an indentation in the dry ingredients and add the yeast. Select *Dough,* and press *Start.* If the dough is wet and sticky, add more flour, 1 tablespoon at a

time, until the dough is smooth yet soft to the touch. If the dough is not soft to the touch but is very firm, add 1 teaspoon of water at a time, until the dough is smooth yet soft to the touch. Add the dates and walnuts when the machine signals it's time to add ingredients or when the cycle ends. The machine will stop when the dough is ready to shape and bake.

TO MIX AND BAKE THE BREAD IN THE BREAD MACHINE Pour the buttermilk (at room temperature) into the pan, and add the remaining ingredients, except the dates and walnuts. Make an indentation in the dry ingredients and add the yeast. Select the *Fruit and Nut, Basic,* or *Whole Wheat* cycle; set the crust on *Medium;* and press *Start.* During the mixing cycle, if the dough is wet and sticky, add more flour, 1 tablespoon at a time, until the dough is smooth yet soft to the touch. If the dough is not soft to the touch but is very firm, add 1 teaspoon of water at a time, until the dough is smooth yet soft to the touch. Add the dates and walnuts when the machine signals it's time to add ingredients.

TO SHAPE AND BAKE IN THE OVEN Lightly grease a baking sheet. Turn the dough out onto a lightly floured board or lightly oiled surface. Punch the dough down, and shape it into a round loaf. Place the loaf, with the smooth side up, onto the baking sheet. Cover and let rise in a warm place until almost doubled, 1 hour. Preheat the oven to 375°F. To glaze, beat the egg with the water, and brush the mixture on the loaf. Bake 25 to 45 minutes, until the loaf sounds hollow when tapped and a wooden skewer inserted into the loaf comes out clean and dry. Remove from the pan and cool on a wire rack.

DRIED FIG AND WALNUT BREAD

Freshly packaged dried figs are usually succulent, soft, and delicious. But if they are very dry, just soak them in warm juice, wine, or water for 10 to 15 minutes. Blot dry with paper towels, then chop them up before adding them to the bread.

Sampler Loaf	Regular Loaf	Large Loaf
$2/3$ cup water	1 cup water	$1^1/3$ cups water
2 teaspoons honey	1 tablespoon honey	$1^1/2$ tablespoons honey
2 teaspoons soft butter	1 tablespoon soft butter	$1^1/2$ tablespoons soft butter
$3/4$ teaspoon salt	1 teaspoon salt	$1^1/2$ teaspoons salt
1 cup whole wheat flour	$1^1/2$ cups whole wheat flour	2 cups whole wheat flour
1 cup bread flour	$1^1/2$ cups bread flour	2 cups bread flour
1 teaspoon rapid-rising or active dry yeast	$1^1/2$ teaspoons rapid-rising or active dry yeast	2 teaspoons rapid-rising or active dry yeast
2 tablespoons chopped dried black figs	$1/4$ cup chopped dried black figs	$1/3$ cup chopped dried black figs
3 tablespoons toasted chopped walnuts	$1/3$ cup toasted chopped walnuts	$1/2$ cup toasted chopped walnuts

TO MIX THE DOUGH BY HAND   Heat the water until warm, between 105° and 115°F; pour it into a large, warmed bowl, and add the yeast. Let stand 5 minutes, until the yeast begins to bubble. Stir in the honey, butter, salt, and whole wheat flour. Beat until smooth. Cover, and let stand 15 minutes. Slowly add the bread flour, and beat until a smooth dough forms. Turn the dough out onto a very lightly floured board, and knead, adding flour if necessary, until smooth and springy, about 5 minutes. Knead in the figs and walnuts. Wash the bowl and grease it; place the dough back in the bowl, and turn it over to grease the top. Cover, and let rise until doubled, about 1 hour.

TO MIX THE DOUGH WITH A HEAVY-DUTY MIXER   Heat the water until warm, between 105° and 115°F; pour it into the warmed mixing bowl, and add the yeast. Let stand 5 minutes, until the yeast begins to bubble. Add the honey, butter, salt, and whole wheat flour. Beat until smooth. Cover, and let stand 15 minutes. Slowly add the bread flour, and beat until a smooth dough forms. Knead the dough in the mixer with the dough hook, on medium to high speed, adding flour as necessary, until the dough pulls away from the sides of the bowl and is smooth and springy but still soft to the touch. Knead in the figs and walnuts. Remove the dough hook, cover the bowl, and let the dough rise until doubled, about 1 hour.

TO MIX THE DOUGH IN THE FOOD PROCESSOR Place the plastic dough blade into the work bowl. Heat the water until very warm, between 120° and 130°F; set aside. Place the remaining ingredients, except the figs and walnuts, into the work bowl. Turn the processor on, and slowly pour the water through the feed tube, processing until the dough is smooth and pulls away from the sides of the bowl. If the dough is wet and sticky, add more flour, 1 tablespoon at a time, until the dough is smooth yet soft to the touch. If the dough is not soft to the touch but is very firm, add 1 tablespoon of water at a time, and process until the dough is smooth yet soft to the touch. Mix in the figs and walnuts. Cover the work bowl, and let the dough rise until doubled, about 1 hour. Or remove the dough to a lightly greased bowl, cover, and let rise until doubled, about 1 hour.

TO MIX THE DOUGH IN THE BREAD MACHINE Pour the water (at room temperature) into the pan, and add the remaining ingredients, except the figs and walnuts. Make an indentation in the dry ingredients and add the yeast. Select *Dough,* and press *Start.* If the dough is wet and sticky, add more flour, 1 tablespoon at a time, until the dough is smooth yet soft to the touch. If the dough is not soft to the touch but is

very firm, add 1 teaspoon of water at a time, until the dough is smooth yet soft to the touch. Add the figs and walnuts when the machine signals it's time to add ingredients or when the cycle ends. The machine will stop when the dough is ready to shape and bake.

TO MIX AND BAKE THE BREAD IN THE BREAD MACHINE Pour the water (at room temperature) into the pan, and add the remaining ingredients, except figs and walnuts. Make an indentation in the dry ingredients and add the yeast. Select the *Fruit and Nut* or *Basic* cycle, set the crust on *Medium,* and press *Start.* During the mixing cycle, if the dough is wet and sticky, add more flour, 1 tablespoon at a time, until the dough is smooth yet soft to the touch. If the dough is not soft to the touch but is very firm, add 1 teaspoon of water at a time, until the dough is smooth yet soft to the touch. Add the figs and walnuts when the machine signals it's time to add ingredients.

TO SHAPE AND BAKE IN THE OVEN Lightly grease baking sheet or cover it in parchment paper. Turn the dough out onto a lightly floured board or lightly oiled surface. Punch the dough down, and shape it into an oblong or round loaf. Place the loaf, with the smooth side up, onto the baking sheet. Cover and let rise in a warm place until almost doubled, 45 minutes. Preheat the oven to 375°F. Bake 35 to 45 minutes, until the loaf is nicely browned. Remove from the pan and cool on a wire rack.

FRENCH WALNUT
AND WHEAT BREAD

Pain aux noix originates in the Alsace region of France, where walnuts are abundant. The combination of walnuts and whole wheat flour gives the loaf a rich, reddish brown–colored crumb. No sugar and shortening are used in this classic recipe. It is wonderful sliced thin and spread with sweet butter and topped with domestic blue cheese. The loaf, hand shaped and conventionally baked is not only delicious but beautiful to look at.

Sampler Loaf	Regular Loaf	Large Loaf
2/3 cup water	1 cup water	1 1/3 cups water
1 teaspoon salt	1 1/2 teaspoons salt	2 teaspoons salt
3/4 cup whole wheat flour	1 cup whole wheat flour	1 1/2 cups whole wheat flour
1 1/4 cups bread flour	2 cups bread flour	2 1/2 cups bread flour
1/2 tablespoon gluten	1 tablespoon gluten	1 1/2 tablespoons gluten
1/2 cup finely ground walnuts	1 cup finely ground walnuts	1 1/2 cups finely ground walnuts
1 1/2 teaspoons rapid-rising or active dry yeast	2 teaspoons rapid-rising or active dry yeast	2 1/4 teaspoons rapid-rising or active dry yeast
1/4 cup coarsely chopped walnuts	1/3 cup coarsely chopped walnuts	1/2 cup coarsely chopped walnuts

TO MIX THE DOUGH BY HAND Heat the water until warm, between 105° and 115°F; pour it into a large, warmed bowl, and add the yeast. Let stand 5 minutes, until the yeast begins to bubble. Stir in the salt and whole wheat flour. Beat until smooth. Cover, and let stand 15 minutes. Slowly add the bread flour, gluten, and ground walnuts; beat well. Turn the dough out onto a very lightly floured board, and knead, adding flour if necessary, until smooth and springy, about 5 minutes. Knead in the chopped walnuts. Wash the bowl and grease it; place the dough back in the bowl, and turn it over to grease the top. Cover, and let rise until doubled, about 1 hour.

TO MIX THE DOUGH WITH A HEAVY-DUTY MIXER Heat the water until warm, between 105° and 115°F; pour it into the warmed mixing bowl, and add the yeast. Let stand 5 minutes, until the yeast begins to bubble. Add the salt and whole wheat flour. Beat until smooth. Cover, and let stand 15 minutes. Slowly add the bread flour, gluten, and ground walnuts; beat well. Knead the dough in the mixer with the dough hook, on medium to high speed, adding flour as necessary, until the dough pulls away from the sides of the bowl and is smooth and springy but still soft to the touch. Knead in the chopped walnuts. Remove the dough hook, cover the bowl, and let the dough rise until doubled, about 1 hour.

TO MIX THE DOUGH IN THE FOOD PROCESSOR
Place the plastic dough blade into the work bowl. Heat the water until very warm, between 120° and 130°F; set aside. Place the remaining ingredients, except the chopped walnuts, into the work bowl. Turn the processor on, and slowly pour the water through the feed tube, processing until the dough is smooth and pulls away from the sides of the bowl. If the dough is wet and sticky, add more flour, 1 tablespoon at a time, until the dough is smooth yet soft to the touch. If the dough is not soft to the touch but is very firm, add 1 tablespoon of water at a time, and process until the dough is smooth yet soft to the touch. Mix in the chopped walnuts. Cover the work bowl, and let the dough rise until doubled, about 1 hour. Or remove the dough to a lightly greased bowl, cover, and let rise until doubled, about 1 hour.

TO MIX THE DOUGH IN THE BREAD MACHINE Pour the water (at room temperature) into the pan. Add the remaining ingredients, except the chopped walnuts, in the order listed. Make an indentation in the dry ingredients and add the yeast. Select *Dough,* and press *Start.* If the dough is wet and sticky, add more flour, 1 tablespoon at a time, until the dough is smooth yet soft to the touch. If the dough is not soft to

the touch but is very firm, add 1 teaspoon of water at a time, until the dough is smooth yet soft to the touch. Add the walnuts when the machine signals it's time to add ingredients or when the cycle ends. The machine will stop when the dough is ready to shape and bake.

TO MIX AND BAKE THE BREAD IN THE BREAD MACHINE Pour the water (at room temperature) into the pan. Add the remaining ingredients, except the chopped walnuts, in the order listed. Make an indentation in the dry ingredients and add the yeast. Select the *Basic* cycle, set the crust on *Medium,* and press *Start.* During the mixing cycle, if the dough is wet and sticky, add more flour, 1 tablespoon at a time, until the dough is smooth yet soft to the touch. If the dough is not soft to the touch but is very firm, add 1 teaspoon of water at a time, until the dough is smooth yet soft to the touch. Add the walnuts when the machine signals it's time to add ingredients.

TO SHAPE AND BAKE IN THE OVEN Lightly grease a 9 × 5-inch loaf pan, an 8- or 9-inch round cake pan, or a baking sheet. Turn the dough out onto a lightly floured board or lightly oiled surface. Punch the dough down, and shape it into an oblong or round loaf. Place the loaf, with the smooth side up, into the pan. Cover and let rise in a warm place until almost doubled, 45 minutes. Preheat the oven to 375°F. Bake 35 to 45 minutes, until the loaf is nicely browned. Remove from the pan and cool on a wire rack.

BREAKFAST BREAD WITH DRIED FRUIT, ALMONDS, AND OATMEAL

I had a bag of mixed dried fruit bits, which included dried apples, apricots, raisins and other fruits, leftover from snacks I bought for the grandkids. The fruit added flavor and chewiness to this oatmeal bread. The fruit bits do not need to be reconstituted or soaked before adding them to bread, because they're so moist already. I added almonds for crunch and flavor. I suppose any other kind of nut would be good, too.

Sampler Loaf	Regular Loaf	Large Loaf
2/3 cup water	1 cup water	1 1/3 cups water
1/3 cup old-fashioned rolled oats	1/2 cup old-fashioned rolled oats	3/4 cup old-fashioned rolled oats
1 tablespoon butter	2 tablespoons butter	3 tablespoons butter
1 tablespoon sugar	2 tablespoons sugar	3 tablespoons sugar
1 teaspoon salt	1 1/2 teaspoons salt	2 teaspoons salt
1 2/3 cups bread flour	2 1/2 cups bread flour	3 1/4 cups bread flour
1 teaspoon rapid-rising or active dry yeast	1 1/2 teaspoons rapid-rising or active dry yeast	2 teaspoons rapid-rising or active dry yeast
1/4 cup dried fruit bits	1/3 cup dried fruit bits	1/2 cup dried fruit bits
2 tablespoons slivered almonds	1/4 cup slivered almonds	1/3 cup slivered almonds

GLAZE FOR BREAD BAKED CONVENTIONALLY

1 egg

1 tablespoon water or milk

Cinnamon sugar

TO MIX THE DOUGH BY HAND Heat the water until warm, between 105° and 115°F; pour it into a large, warmed bowl, and add the yeast and rolled oats. Let stand 5 minutes, until the yeast begins to bubble. Stir in the butter, sugar, salt, and half of the bread flour. Beat until a smooth dough forms. Cover, and let stand 15 minutes. Slowly add the remaining bread flour, and beat until a stiff dough forms. Turn the dough out onto a very lightly floured board, and knead, adding flour if necessary, until smooth and springy, about 5 minutes. Knead in the fruit and almonds. Wash the bowl and grease it; place the dough back in the bowl, and turn it over to grease the top. Cover, and let rise until doubled, about 1 hour.

TO MIX THE DOUGH WITH A HEAVY-DUTY MIXER Heat the water until warm, between 105° and 115°F; pour it into the warmed mixing bowl, and add the yeast and rolled oats. Let stand 5 minutes, until the yeast begins to bubble. Add the butter, sugar, salt, and half of the bread flour. Beat until a smooth dough forms. Cover, and let stand 15 minutes. Slowly add the remaining bread flour, and beat until a stiff dough forms. Knead the dough in the mixer with the dough hook, on medium to high speed, adding flour as necessary, until the dough pulls away from the sides of the bowl and is smooth and springy but still soft to the touch. Knead in the fruit and almonds. Remove the dough hook, cover the bowl, and let the dough rise until doubled, about 1 hour.

TO MIX THE DOUGH IN THE FOOD PROCESSOR Place the plastic dough blade into the work bowl. Heat the water until very warm, between 120° and 130°F; set aside. Place the remaining ingredients, except the fruit and almonds, into the work bowl. Turn the processor on, and slowly pour the water through the feed tube, processing until the dough is smooth and pulls away from the sides of the bowl. If the dough is wet and sticky, add more flour, 1 tablespoon at a time, until the dough is smooth yet soft to the touch. If the dough is not soft to the touch but is very firm, add 1 tablespoon of water at a time, and process until the

dough is smooth yet soft to the touch. Mix in the fruit and almonds. Cover the work bowl, and let the dough rise until doubled, about 1 hour. Or remove the dough to a lightly greased bowl, cover, and let rise until doubled, about 1 hour.

TO MIX THE DOUGH IN THE BREAD MACHINE Pour the water (at room temperature) into the pan. Add the remaining ingredients, except the fruit and almonds, in the order listed. Make an indentation in the dry ingredients and add the yeast. Select *Dough,* and press *Start.* If the dough is wet and sticky, add more flour, 1 tablespoon at a time, until the dough is smooth yet soft to the touch. If the dough is not soft to the touch but is very firm, add 1 teaspoon of water at a time, until the dough is smooth yet soft to the touch. Add the fruit and almonds when the machine signals it's time to add ingredients or when the cycle ends. The machine will stop when the dough is ready to shape and bake.

TO MIX AND BAKE THE BREAD IN THE BREAD MACHINE Pour the water (at room temperature) into the pan. Add the remaining ingredients, except the fruit and almonds, in the order listed. Make an indentation in the dry ingredients and add the yeast. Select the *Basic* cycle, set the crust on *Medium,* and press *Start.* During the mixing cycle, if the dough is wet and sticky, add more flour, 1 tablespoon at a time, until the dough is smooth yet soft to the touch. If the dough is not soft to the touch but is very firm, add 1 teaspoon of water at a time, until the dough is smooth yet soft to the touch. If desired, sprinkle the loaf with cinnamon sugar after the final rise, just before the bread begins to bake.

Add the fruit and almonds when the machine signals it's time to add ingredients.

TO SHAPE AND BAKE IN THE OVEN Lightly grease an 8- or 9-inch round cake pan. Turn the dough out onto a lightly floured board or lightly oiled surface. Punch the dough down, and shape it into a round loaf. Place the loaf, with the smooth side up, into the pan. Cover and let rise in a warm place until almost doubled, 45 to 60 minutes. Preheat the oven to 375°F. To glaze, beat the egg with the water, brush the mixture on the loaf, and sprinkle on the cinnamon sugar. Bake 35 to 45 minutes, until a wooden skewer inserted into the loaf comes out clean and dry. Remove from the pan and cool on a wire rack.

GOLDEN RAISIN AND OATMEAL PECAN BREAD

This is a wonderful bread for any time of day. I love to spread it with honey butter for breakfast and with a vegetable cream cheese spread to accompany soup for lunch. For a snack, I enjoy it drizzled with a bit of lemon oil or a thick smear of butter.

Sampler Loaf	Regular Loaf	Large Loaf
2/3 cup boiling water	1 cup boiling water	1 1/3 cups boiling water
1/3 cup old-fashioned rolled oats	1/2 cup old-fashioned rolled oats	2/3 cup old-fashioned rolled oats
1 1/2 tablespoons molasses	2 tablespoons molasses	3 tablespoons molasses
1 1/2 tablespoons canola oil	2 tablespoons canola oil	3 tablespoons canola oil
3/4 teaspoon salt	1 teaspoon salt	1 1/2 teaspoons salt
1 2/3 cups bread flour	2 1/2 cups bread flour	3 1/3 cups bread flour
1 teaspoon yeast	1 1/2 teaspoons yeast	2 teaspoons yeast
1/2 cup raisins (optional)	3/4 cup raisins (optional)	1 cup raisins (optional)
1/2 cup coarsely chopped pecans	3/4 cup coarsely chopped pecans	1 cup coarsely chopped pecans

GLAZE FOR BREAD BAKED CONVENTIONALLY
1 egg
1 tablespoon water or milk

TO MIX THE DOUGH BY HAND   Pour the boiling water into a large bowl, add the rolled oats, and stir. Let stand until the mixture cools to warm, between 105° and 115°F. Add the molasses and yeast; let stand 5 minutes, until the yeast begins to bubble. Stir in the oil, salt, and half of the bread flour. Beat until a smooth dough forms. Cover, and let stand 15 minutes. Slowly add the remaining bread flour, and beat until a stiff dough forms. Turn the dough out onto a very lightly floured board, and knead, adding flour if necessary, until smooth and springy, about 5 minutes. Knead in the raisins and pecans. Wash the bowl and grease it; place the dough back in the bowl, and turn it over to grease the top. Cover, and let rise until doubled, about 1 hour.

TO MIX THE DOUGH WITH A HEAVY-DUTY MIXER Pour the boiling water in the mixing bowl, add the rolled oats, and stir. Let stand until the mixture cools to warm, between 105° and 115°F. Add the molasses and yeast; let stand 5 minutes, until the yeast begins to bubble. Add the oil, salt, and half of the bread flour. Beat until a smooth dough forms. Cover, and let stand 15 minutes. Slowly add the remaining bread flour, and beat until a stiff dough forms. Knead the dough in the mixer with the dough hook, on medium to high speed, adding flour as necessary, until the dough pulls away from the sides of the bowl and is smooth and springy but still soft to the touch. Knead in the raisins and pecans. Remove the dough hook, cover the bowl, and let the dough rise until doubled, about 1 hour.

TO MIX THE DOUGH IN THE FOOD PROCESSOR Place the plastic dough blade into the work bowl. Pour the boiling water into the work bowl, add the rolled oats, and stir. Let stand until the mixture cools to very warm, between 120° and 130°F. Place the remaining ingredients, except the raisins and pecans, into the work bowl. Process until the dough is smooth and pulls away from the sides of the bowl. If the dough is wet and sticky, add more flour, 1 tablespoon at a time, until the dough is smooth yet soft to the touch. If the dough is not soft to the touch but is very firm, add 1 tablespoon of water at a time, and process until the dough is smooth yet soft to the touch. Mix in the raisins and pecans. Cover the work bowl, and let the dough rise until doubled,

about 1 hour. Or remove the dough to a lightly greased bowl, cover, and let rise until doubled, about 1 hour.

TO MIX THE DOUGH IN THE BREAD MACHINE Pour the boiling water into the pan, add the rolled oats, and stir. Let stand until the mixture has cooled to room temperature. Add the remaining ingredients, except the raisins and pecans. Make an indentation in the dry ingredients and add the yeast. Select *Dough,* and press *Start.* If the dough is wet and sticky, add more flour, 1 tablespoon at a time, until the dough is smooth yet soft to the touch. If the dough is not soft to the touch but is very firm, add 1 teaspoon of water at a time, until the dough is smooth yet soft to the touch. Add the raisins and pecans when the machine signals it's time to add ingredients or when the cycle ends. The machine will stop when the dough is ready to shape and bake.

TO MIX AND BAKE THE BREAD IN THE BREAD MACHINE Pour the boiling water into the pan, add the rolled oats, and stir. Let stand until the mixture has cooled to room temperature. Add the remaining ingredients, except the raisins and pecans. Make an indentation in the dry ingredients and add the yeast. Select the *Fruit and Nut, Basic,* or *Whole Wheat* cycle; set the crust on *Medium;* and press *Start.* During the mixing cycle, if the dough is wet and sticky, add more flour, 1 tablespoon at a time, until the dough is smooth yet soft to the touch. If the dough is not soft to the touch but is very firm, add 1 teaspoon of water at a time, until the dough is smooth yet soft to the touch. Add the raisins and pecans when the machine signals it's time to add ingredients.

TO SHAPE AND BAKE IN THE OVEN Lightly grease a baking sheet or cover it with parchment paper. Turn the dough out onto a lightly floured board or lightly oiled surface. Punch the dough down, and shape it into a round loaf. Place the loaf, with the smooth side up, onto the baking sheet. Cover and let rise in a warm place until almost doubled, 45 to 60 minutes. Preheat the oven to 375°F. To glaze, beat the egg with the water, and brush the mixture on the loaf. Bake 35 to 45 minutes, until a wooden skewer inserted into the loaf comes out clean and dry. Remove from the pan and cool on a wire rack.

HONEY WALNUT EGG BREAD

This modernized version of a classic bread is so easy and convenient to make using the bread machine. Add walnut pieces directly to the mixture; they get chopped in the process of mixing in the bread machine. You'll have to chop them before adding them to dough mixed by hand, heavy-duty mixer, or food processor.

Sampler Loaf	Regular Loaf	Large Loaf
1 large egg plus water to equal 2/3 cup	1 large egg plus water to equal 1 cup	2 large eggs plus water to equal 1 1/3 cups
1 tablespoon honey	1 1/2 tablespoons honey	2 tablespoons honey
1/4 cup toasted walnut halves	1/3 cup toasted walnut halves	1/2 cup toasted walnut halves
3/4 teaspoon salt	1 teaspoon salt	1 1/2 teaspoons salt
1 tablespoon softened butter	1 1/2 tablespoons softened butter	2 tablespoons softened butter
1/4 cup nonfat dry milk	1/3 cup nonfat dry milk	1/2 cup nonfat dry milk
1/2 cup whole wheat bread	3/4 cup whole wheat bread	1 cup whole wheat bread
1 1/2 cups bread flour	2 1/4 cups bread flour	3 cups bread flour
1 teaspoon rapid-rising or active dry yeast	1 1/2 teaspoons rapid-rising or active dry yeast	2 teaspoons rapid-rising or active dry yeast

GLAZE FOR BREAD BAKED CONVENTIONALLY

1 egg

1 tablespoon water or milk

TO MIX THE DOUGH BY HAND Warm the eggs under hot tap water, and crack into a measuring cup. Heat the water until warm, between 105° and 115°F, and add it to the eggs. Pour the mixture into a large, warmed bowl, and add the yeast. Let stand 5 minutes, until the yeast begins to bubble. Meanwhile, chop the walnuts, and set aside. Stir in the honey, salt, butter, dry milk, whole wheat flour, and half of the bread flour. Beat until smooth. Cover, and let stand 15 minutes. Slowly add the remaining bread flour, and beat until a soft dough forms. Turn the dough out onto a very lightly floured board, and knead, adding flour if necessary, until smooth and springy, about 5 minutes. Knead in the walnuts. Wash the bowl and grease it; place the dough back in the bowl, and turn it over to grease the top. Cover, and let rise until doubled, about 1 hour.

TO MIX THE DOUGH WITH A HEAVY-DUTY MIXER Warm the eggs under hot tap water, and crack into a measuring cup. Heat the water until warm, between 105° and 115°F, and add it to the eggs. Pour the mixture into the warmed mixing bowl, and add the yeast. Let stand 5 minutes, until the yeast begins to bubble. Meanwhile, chop the walnuts, and set aside. Add the honey, salt, butter, dry milk, whole wheat flour, and half of the bread flour. Beat until smooth. Cover, and let stand 15 minutes. Slowly add the remaining bread flour, and beat until a soft dough forms. Knead the dough in the mixer with the dough hook, on medium to high speed, adding flour as necessary, until the dough pulls away from the sides of the bowl and is smooth and springy but still soft to the touch. Knead in the walnuts. Remove the dough hook, cover the bowl, and let the dough rise until doubled, about 1 hour.

TO MIX THE DOUGH IN THE FOOD PROCESSOR Place the plastic dough blade into the work bowl. Warm the eggs under hot tap water, and crack into a measuring cup. Heat the water until very warm, between 120° and 130°F, and add it to the eggs; set aside. Place the remaining ingredients, except the walnuts into the work bowl. Chop the walnuts, and set aside. Turn the processor on, and slowly pour the water mixture through the feed tube, processing until the dough is smooth and

pulls away from the sides of the bowl. If the dough is wet and sticky, add more flour, 1 tablespoon at a time, until the dough is smooth yet soft to the touch. If the dough is not soft to the touch but is very firm, add 1 tablespoon of water at a time, and process until the dough is smooth yet soft to the touch. Mix in the walnuts. Cover the work bowl, and let the dough rise until doubled, about 1 hour. Or remove the dough to a lightly greased bowl, cover, and let rise until doubled, about 1 hour.

TO MIX THE DOUGH IN THE BREAD MACHINE Warm the eggs under hot tap water, and crack into a measuring cup. Add the water (at room temperature) to the eggs, and pour the mixture into the pan. Add the remaining ingredients, in the order listed. Make an indentation in the dry ingredients and add the yeast. Select *Dough,* and press *Start.* If the dough is wet and sticky, add more flour, 1 tablespoon at a time, until the dough is smooth yet soft to the touch. If the dough is not soft to the touch but is very firm, add 1 teaspoon of water at a time, until the dough is smooth yet soft to the touch. The machine will stop when the dough is ready to shape and bake.

TO MIX AND BAKE THE BREAD IN THE BREAD MACHINE Warm the eggs under hot tap water, and crack into a measuring cup. Add the water (at room temperature) to the eggs, and pour the mixture into the pan. Add the remaining ingredients, in the order listed. Make an indentation in the dry ingredients and add the yeast. Select the *Basic* cycle, set the crust on

Medium, and press *Start.* During the mixing cycle, if the dough is wet and sticky, add more flour, 1 tablespoon at a time, until the dough is smooth yet soft to the touch. If the dough is not soft to the touch but is very firm, add 1 teaspoon of water at a time, until the dough is smooth yet soft to the touch.

TO SHAPE AND BAKE IN THE OVEN Lightly grease a baking sheet or cover it in parchment paper. Turn the dough out onto a lightly floured board or lightly oiled surface. Punch the dough down, and shape it into a round loaf. Place the loaf, with the smooth side up, onto the baking sheet. Cover and let rise in a warm place until almost doubled, 45 to 60 minutes. Preheat the oven to 375°F. To glaze, beat the egg with the water, and brush the mixture on the loaf. Bake 35 to 45 minutes, until a wooden skewer inserted into the loaf comes out clean and dry. Remove from the pan and cool on a wire rack.

Baked Cheese Fondue

There are all kinds of variations to this classic dish. You can add cooked seafood, ham, chicken, herbs, spices, and bits and ends of odd cheeses to create a new taste every time. You can even use all different kinds of breads or a mixture of breads, depending on what you have on hand. My favorite thing to do is to dice up ends of bread into 1-inch cubes, bag, and freeze them. Then, the night before I'm going to serve it, I put this simple fondue together for an effortless brunch dish.

8 SERVINGS

6 cups ¹/₂-inch bread cubes made from Honey
   Walnut Egg Bread (page 128) or other whole
   grain bread

2 tablespoons butter, melted

1 medium onion, very finely minced

1 large carrot, finely shredded

¹/₄ cup minced parsley

2 tablespoons minced chives

1 teaspoon chopped fresh thyme

1 teaspoon chopped fresh basil

2 cups shredded sharp Cheddar cheese

4 large eggs, lightly beaten

2¹/₂ cups milk

2 tablespoons Dijon-style mustard

¹/₈ teaspoon paprika (sweet or hot)

Mushroom Dill Sauce (recipe follows)

In a large bowl, toss the bread with the melted butter. Place half of the bread cubes into a 2-quart soufflé dish or casserole and sprinkle with half of the onion, carrot, herbs, and cheese. Repeat.

Beat the eggs with the milk, mustard, and paprika. Pour over the bread and cheese mixture. Cover and refrigerate overnight.

Remove from the refrigerator and allow to stand at room temperature for 45 minutes to warm up a little. Preheat the oven to 350°F. Bake 1 hour, until puffed and golden brown. Serve with the Mushroom Dill Sauce, if desired.

Mushroom Dill Sauce

1 pound fresh mushrooms, sliced
2 tablespoons butter
3 tablespoons all-purpose flour
2 cups half-and-half
1 teaspoon dillweed
Salt and freshly ground black, to taste

In a large skillet, sauté the mushrooms in the butter on medium heat about 10 minutes, until tender. Sprinkle with the flour and mix well. Stir in the half-and-half. Bring to a boil; cook, stirring 3-4 minutes, until thickened. Add the dillweed, salt, and pepper. Serve hot over squares of the Baked Cheese Fondue.

OATMEAL MAPLE NUT BREAD

When you use 100% pure maple syrup in this bread you get the best maple flavor. Toasting the nuts and the rolled oats brings out their nutty flavor.

Sampler Loaf

2/3 cup water

2 tablespoons 100% pure
    maple syrup

1 teaspoon salt

1/4 cup chopped toasted walnuts

1/4 cup old-fashioned rolled
    oats, toasted

1/4 cup whole wheat flour

1 1/2 cups bread flour

1 teaspoon rapid-rising or active
    dry yeast

Regular Loaf

1 cup water

1/4 cup 100% pure maple syrup

1 1/2 teaspoons salt

1/3 cup chopped toasted walnuts

1/3 cup old-fashioned rolled
    oats, toasted

1/3 cup whole wheat flour

2 1/3 cups bread flour

1 1/2 teaspoons rapid-rising or
    active dry yeast

Large Loaf

1 1/3 cups water

6 tablespoons 100% pure
    maple syrup

2 teaspoons salt

1/2 cup chopped toasted walnuts

1/2 cup old-fashioned rolled
    oats, toasted

1/2 cup whole wheat flour

3 cups bread flour

2 teaspoons rapid-rising or active
    dry yeast

GLAZE FOR BREAD BAKED CONVENTIONALLY

1 egg

1 tablespoon water or milk

Rolled oats

TO MIX THE DOUGH BY HAND Heat the water until warm, between 105° and 115°F; pour it into a large, warmed bowl, and add the yeast and maple syrup. Let stand 5 minutes, until the yeast begins to bubble. Stir in the salt, rolled oats, whole wheat flour, and half of the bread flour. Beat well. Cover, and let stand 15 minutes. Slowly add the remaining bread flour, and beat until a dough forms. Turn the dough out onto a very lightly floured board, and knead, adding flour if necessary, until smooth and springy, about 5 minutes. Knead in the walnuts. Wash the bowl and grease it; place the dough back in the bowl, and turn it over to grease the top. Cover, and let rise until doubled, about 1 hour.

TO MIX THE DOUGH WITH A HEAVY-DUTY MIXER
Heat the water until warm, between 105° and 115°F; pour it along with the into the warmed mixing bowl, and add the yeast and maple syrup. Let stand 5 minutes, until the yeast begins to bubble. Add the salt, rolled oats, whole wheat flour, and half of the bread flour. Beat well. Cover, and let stand 15 minutes. Slowly add the remaining bread flour, and beat until a dough forms. Knead the dough in the mixer with the dough hook, on medium to high speed, adding flour as necessary, until the dough pulls away from the sides of the bowl and is smooth and springy but still soft to the touch. Knead in the walnuts. Remove the dough hook, cover the bowl, and let the dough rise until doubled, about 1 hour.

TO MIX THE DOUGH IN THE FOOD PROCESSOR
Place the plastic dough blade into the work bowl. Heat the water until very warm, between 120° and 130°F; set aside. Place the remaining ingredients, except the walnuts, into the work bowl. Turn the processor on, and slowly pour the water through the feed tube, processing until the dough is smooth and pulls away from the sides of the bowl. If the dough is wet and sticky, add more flour, 1 tablespoon at a time, until the dough is smooth yet soft to the touch. If the dough is not soft to the touch but is very firm,

add 1 tablespoon of water at a time, and process until the dough is smooth yet soft to the touch. Mix in the walnuts. Cover the work bowl, and let the dough rise until doubled, about 1 hour. Or remove the dough to a lightly greased bowl, cover, and let rise until doubled, about 1 hour.

TO MIX THE DOUGH IN THE BREAD MACHINE Pour the water (at room temperature) into the pan, and add the remaining ingredients, except the yeast, in the order listed. Make a small indentation in the dry ingredients, and add the yeast. Select *Dough,* and press *Start.* If the dough is wet and sticky, add more flour, 1 tablespoon at a time, until the dough is smooth yet soft to the touch. If the dough is not soft to the touch but is very firm, add 1 teaspoon of water at a time, until the dough is smooth yet soft to the touch. The machine will stop when the dough is ready to shape and bake.

TO MIX AND BAKE THE BREAD IN THE BREAD MACHINE Pour the water (at room temperature) into the pan, and add the remaining ingredients, except the yeast, in the order listed. Make a small indentation in the dry ingredients, and add the yeast. Select the *Basic* cycle, set the crust on *Medium,* and press *Start.* During the mixing cycle, if the dough is wet and sticky, add more flour, 1 tablespoon at a time, until the dough is smooth yet soft to the touch. If the dough is not soft to the touch but is very firm, add 1 teaspoon of water at a time, until the dough is smooth yet soft to the touch.

TO SHAPE AND BAKE IN THE OVEN Lightly grease a baking sheet or cover it with parchment paper. Turn the dough out onto a lightly floured board or lightly oiled surface. Punch the dough down, and shape it into a round loaf. Place the loaf, with the smooth side up, onto the baking sheet. Cover and let rise in a warm place until almost doubled, 45 to 60 minutes. Preheat the oven to 375°F. To glaze, beat the egg with the water, brush the mixture on the loaf, and sprinkle on the rolled oats. Using a serrated knife or razor, make three shallow cuts (about $1/8$ inch deep) across the loaf. Bake 35 to 40 minutes, until a wooden skewer inserted into the loaf comes out clean and dry. Remove from the pan and cool on a wire rack.

TOASTING ROLLED OATS

To toast rolled oats, preheat the oven to 350°F. Spread the oats on a baking sheet, and toast in the oven 10 minutes, stirring once, until aromatic.

ORANGE CRANBERRY
CORNMEAL BREAD

This is so good for breakfast!

Sampler Loaf

2/3 cup water

1 tablespoon sugar

2 tablespoons yellow cornmeal

1 tablespoon soft shortening

1 teaspoon grated orange zest

3/4 teaspoon salt

1/2 cup whole wheat flour

1 1/2 cups bread flour

1 teaspoon rapid-rising or active
    dry yeast

1/2 cup dried cranberries*

Regular Loaf

1 cup water

2 tablespoons sugar

1/4 cup yellow cornmeal

2 tablespoons soft shortening

2 teaspoons grated orange zest

1 teaspoon salt

3/4 cup whole wheat flour

2 1/4 cups bread flour

1 1/2 teaspoons rapid-rising or
    active dry yeast

3/4 cup dried cranberries*

Large Loaf

1 1/3 cups water

3 tablespoons sugar

1/2 cup yellow cornmeal

3 tablespoons soft shortening

1 tablespoon grated orange zest

1 1/2 teaspoons salt

1 cup whole wheat flour

3 cups bread flour

2 teaspoons rapid-rising or active
    dry yeast

1 cup dried cranberries*

GLAZE FOR BREAD BAKED CONVENTIONALLY

1 egg

1 tablespoon water or milk

TO MIX THE DOUGH BY HAND Heat the water until warm, between 105° and 115°F; pour it into a large, warmed bowl, and add the sugar and yeast. Let stand 5 minutes, until the yeast begins to bubble. Stir in the cornmeal, shortening, orange zest, salt, whole wheat flour, and half of the bread flour. Beat until smooth. Cover, and let stand 15 minutes. Slowly add the remaining bread flour, and beat until a stiff dough forms. Turn the dough out onto a very lightly floured board, and knead, adding flour if necessary, until smooth and springy, about 5 minutes. Knead in the cranberries. Wash the bowl and grease it; place the dough back in the bowl, and turn it over to grease the top. Cover, and let rise until doubled, about 1 hour.

*Note *If the cranberries are very dry, cover them with hot water, and let soak for 10 minutes. Drain thoroughly before using.*

TO MIX THE DOUGH WITH A HEAVY-DUTY MIXER Heat the water until warm, between 105° and 115°F; pour it into the warmed mixing bowl, and add the sugar and yeast. Let stand 5 minutes, until the yeast begins to bubble. Add the cornmeal, shortening, orange zest, salt, whole wheat flour, and half of the bread flour. Beat until smooth. Cover, and let stand 15 minutes. Slowly add the remaining bread flour, and beat until a soft dough forms. Knead the dough in the mixer with the dough hook, on medium to high speed, adding flour as necessary, until the dough pulls away from the sides of the bowl and is smooth and springy but still soft to the touch. Knead in the cranberries. Remove the dough hook, cover the bowl, and let the dough rise until doubled, about 1 hour.

TO MIX THE DOUGH IN THE FOOD PROCESSOR Place the plastic dough blade into the work bowl. Heat the water until very warm, between 120° and 130°F; set aside. Place the remaining ingredients, except the cranberries, into the work bowl. Turn the processor on, and slowly pour the water through the feed tube, processing until the dough is smooth and pulls away from the sides of the bowl. If the dough is wet and sticky, add more flour, 1 tablespoon at a time, until the dough is smooth yet soft to the touch. If the dough is not soft to the touch but is very firm, add 1 tablespoon of water at a time, and process until the dough is smooth yet soft to the touch. Mix in the cranberries. Cover the work bowl, and let the dough rise until doubled, about 1 hour. Or remove the dough to a lightly greased bowl, cover, and let rise until doubled, about 1 hour.

TO MIX THE DOUGH IN THE BREAD MACHINE Pour the water (at room temperature) into the pan, and add the remaining ingredients, except the cranberries. Make indentation in the dry ingredients and add yeast. Select *Dough,* and press *Start.* If the dough is wet and sticky, add more flour, 1 tablespoon at a time, until the dough is smooth yet soft to the touch. If the dough is not soft to the touch but is very firm, add 1 teaspoon of water at a time, until the dough is smooth yet soft to the touch. Add the cranberries when the machine signals it's time to add ingredients or when the cycle ends. The machine will stop when the dough is ready to shape and bake.

TO MIX AND BAKE THE BREAD IN THE BREAD MACHINE Pour the water (at room temperature) into the pan, and add the remaining ingredients, except the cranberries. Make indentation in the dry ingredients and add yeast. Select the *Fruit and Nut, Basic,* or *Whole Wheat* cycle; set the crust on *Medium;* and press *Start.* During the mixing cycle, if the dough is wet and sticky, add more flour, 1 tablespoon at a time, until the dough is smooth yet soft to the touch. If the dough is not soft to the touch but is very firm, add 1 teaspoon of water at a time, until the dough is smooth yet soft to the touch. Add the cranberries when the machine signals it's time to add ingredients.

TO SHAPE AND BAKE IN THE OVEN Lightly grease a 9 × 5-inch loaf pan or an 8- or 9-inch round cake pan. Turn the dough out onto a lightly floured board or lightly oiled surface. Punch the dough down, and shape it into an oblong or round loaf. Place the loaf, with the smooth side up, into the pan. Cover and let rise in a warm place until almost doubled, 45 minutes. Preheat the oven to 375°F. If desired, beat the egg with the water, and brush the mixture on the loaf. Bake 30 to 40 minutes, until the loaf is golden and a wooden skewer inserted into the loaf comes out clean and dry. Remove from the pan and cool on a wire rack.

RAISIN PUMPERNICKEL

This rye and wheat bread is studded with raisins and makes a great base for open-faced sandwiches.

Sampler Loaf	Regular Loaf	Large Loaf
2/3 cup water	1 cup water	1 1/3 cups water
1 tablespoon light molasses	1 1/2 tablespoons light molasses	2 tablespoons light molasses
1 tablespoon butter, melted	1 1/2 tablespoons butter, melted	2 tablespoons butter, melted
1 teaspoon salt	1 1/2 teaspoons salt	2 teaspoons salt
1 1/2 teaspoons caraway seeds	2 teaspoons caraway seeds	1 tablespoon caraway seeds
1/4 cup light or medium rye flour	1/2 cup light or medium rye flour	3/4 cup light or medium rye flour
1/4 cup whole wheat flour	1/2 cup whole wheat flour	3/4 cup whole wheat flour
1 1/2 cups bread flour	2 cups bread flour	2 1/2 cups bread flour
1 1/2 tablespoons gluten	2 tablespoons gluten	3 tablespoons gluten
1 teaspoon rapid-rising or active dry yeast	1 1/2 teaspoons rapid-rising or active dry yeast	2 teaspoons rapid-rising or active dry yeast
1 cup dark raisins	1 1/2 cups dark raisins	2 cups dark raisins

TO MIX THE DOUGH BY HAND Heat the water until warm, between 105° and 115°F; pour it into a large, warmed bowl, and add the yeast, molasses, and butter. Let stand 5 minutes, until the yeast begins to bubble. Stir in the salt, caraway seeds, rye flour, and wheat flour. Cover, and let stand 15 minutes. Slowly add the bread flour and gluten, and beat until a smooth dough forms. Turn the dough out onto a very lightly floured board, and knead, adding flour if necessary, until smooth and springy, about 5 minutes. Knead in the raisins. Wash the bowl and grease it; place the dough back in the bowl, and turn it over to grease the top. Cover, and let rise until doubled, about 1 hour.

TO MIX THE DOUGH WITH A HEAVY-DUTY MIXER Heat the water until warm, between 105° and 115°F; pour it the warmed mixing bowl, and add the yeast, molasses, and butter. Let stand 5 minutes, until the yeast begins to bubble. Stir in the salt, caraway seeds, rye flour, and wheat flour. Cover, and let stand 15 minutes. Slowly add the bread flour and gluten, and beat until a smooth dough forms. Knead the dough in the mixer with the dough hook, on medium to high speed, adding flour as necessary, until the dough pulls away from the sides of the bowl and is smooth and springy but still soft to the touch. Knead in the raisins. Remove the dough hook, cover the bowl, and let the dough rise until doubled, about 1 hour.

TO MIX THE DOUGH IN THE FOOD PROCESSOR
Place the plastic dough blade into the work bowl. Heat the water until very warm, between 120° and 130°F; set aside. Place the remaining ingredients, except the raisins, into the work bowl. Turn the processor on, and slowly pour the water through the feed tube, processing until the dough is smooth and pulls away from the sides of the bowl. If the dough is wet and sticky, add more flour, 1 tablespoon at a time, until the dough is smooth yet soft to the touch. If the dough is not soft to the touch but is very firm, add 1 tablespoon of water at a time, and process until the dough is smooth yet soft to the touch. Mix in the raisins. Cover the work bowl, and let the dough rise until doubled, about 1 hour. Or remove the dough to a lightly greased bowl, cover, and let rise until doubled, about 1 hour.

TO MIX THE DOUGH IN THE BREAD MACHINE Pour the water (at room temperature) into the pan, and add the remaining ingredients, except the raisins. Make indentation in the dry ingredients and add yeast. Select *Dough,* and press *Start.* If the dough is wet and sticky, add more flour, 1 tablespoon at a time, until the dough is smooth yet soft to the touch. If the dough is not soft to the touch but is very firm,

add 1 teaspoon of water at a time, until the dough is smooth yet soft to the touch. Add the raisins when the machine signals it's time to add ingredients or when the cycle ends. The machine will stop when the dough is ready to shape and bake.

TO MIX AND BAKE THE BREAD IN THE BREAD MACHINE Pour the water (at room temperature) into the pan, and add the remaining ingredients, except the raisins. Make indentation in the dry ingredients and add yeast. Select the *Basic,* or *Whole Wheat* cycle; set the crust on *Medium;* and press *Start.* During the mixing cycle, if the dough is wet and sticky, add more flour, 1 tablespoon at a time, until the dough is smooth yet soft to the touch. If the dough is not soft to the touch but is very firm, add 1 teaspoon of water at a time, until the dough is smooth yet soft to the touch. Add the raisins when the machine signals it's time to add ingredients.

TO SHAPE AND BAKE IN THE OVEN Lightly grease a baking sheet or cover it with parchment paper. Turn the dough out onto a lightly floured board or lightly oiled surface. Punch the dough down, and shape it into an oblong or round loaf. Place the loaf, with the smooth side up, onto the baking sheet. Cover it with a towel, and let rise in warm place until almost doubled, 1 hour. Preheat the oven to 350°F. Bake 35 to 45 minutes, until a wooden skewer inserted into the loaf comes out clean and dry. Remove from the pan and cool on a wire rack.

RAISIN RYE BREAD

Loaded with raisins, this bread is great as a base for smorrebrod—traditional Danish sandwiches. The raisins make the bread a little bit sweet.

Sampler Loaf

²/₃ cup water

³/₄ cup raisins

³/₄ teaspoon salt

1 tablespoon shortening or
    canola, corn, or olive oil

¹/₂ cup dark rye flour

1¹/₂ cups bread flour

1¹/₄ teaspoons rapid-rising or
    active dry yeast

Regular Loaf

1 cup water

1 cup raisins

1 teaspoon salt

2 tablespoons shortening or
    canola, corn, or olive oil

1 cup dark rye flour

2 cups bread flour

1¹/₂ teaspoons rapid-rising or
    active dry yeast

Large Loaf

1¹/₃ cup water

1¹/₂ cups dried raisins

1¹/₂ teaspoons salt

3 tablespoons shortening or
    canola, corn, or olive oil

1¹/₂ cups dark rye flour

2¹/₂ cups bread flour

2 teaspoons rapid-rising or active
    dry yeast

TO MIX THE DOUGH BY HAND Heat the water until warm, between 105° and 115°F; pour it into a large, warmed bowl, and add the yeast. Let stand 5 minutes, until the yeast begins to bubble. Stir in the raisins, salt, shortening, rye flour, and half of the bread flour. Beat until a smooth dough forms. Cover, and let stand 15 minutes. Turn the dough out onto a very lightly floured board, and knead, adding the remaining flour as necessary, until smooth and springy, about 5 minutes. Wash the bowl and grease it; place the dough back in the bowl, and turn it over to grease the top. Cover, and let rise until doubled, about 1 hour.

TO MIX THE DOUGH WITH A HEAVY-DUTY MIXER Heat the water until warm, between 105° and 115°F; pour it into a large, warmed bowl, and add the yeast. Let stand 5 minutes, until the yeast begins to bubble. Stir in the raisins, salt, shortening, rye flour, and half of the bread flour. Beat until a smooth dough forms. Cover, and let stand 15 minutes. Knead the dough in the mixer with the dough hook, on medium to high speed, adding the remaining flour as necessary, until the dough pulls away from the sides of the bowl and is smooth and springy but still soft to the touch. Remove the dough hook, cover the bowl, and let the dough rise until doubled, about 1 hour.

TO MIX THE DOUGH IN THE FOOD PROCESSOR Place the plastic dough blade into the work bowl. Heat the water until very warm, between 120° and 130°F; set aside. Place the remaining ingredients into the work bowl. Turn the processor on, and slowly pour the water through the feed tube, processing until the dough is smooth and pulls away from the sides of the bowl. If the dough is wet and sticky, add more flour, 1 tablespoon at a time, until the dough is smooth yet soft to the touch. If the dough is not soft to the touch but is very firm, add 1 tablespoon of water at a time, and process until the dough is smooth yet soft to the touch. Cover the work bowl, and let the dough rise until doubled, about 1 hour. Or remove the dough to a lightly greased bowl, cover, and let rise until doubled, about 1 hour.

TO MIX THE DOUGH IN THE BREAD MACHINE Pour the water (at room temperature) into the pan, and add the remaining ingredients. Make indentation in the dry ingredients and add yeast. Select *Dough,* and press *Start.* If the dough is wet and sticky, add more flour, 1 tablespoon at a time, until the dough is smooth yet soft to the touch. If the dough is not soft to the touch but is very firm, add 1 teaspoon of water at

a time, until the dough is smooth yet soft to the touch. The machine will stop when the dough is ready to shape and bake.

TO MIX AND BAKE THE BREAD IN THE BREAD MACHINE Pour the water (at room temperature) into the pan, and add the remaining ingredients. Make indentation in the dry ingredients and add yeast. Select the *Basic* or *Whole Wheat* cycle, set the crust on *Medium,* and press *Start.* During the mixing cycle, if the dough is wet and sticky, add more flour, 1 tablespoon at a time, until the dough is smooth yet soft to the touch. If the dough is not soft to the touch but is very firm, add 1 teaspoon of water at a time, until the dough is smooth yet soft to the touch.

TO SHAPE AND BAKE IN THE OVEN Lightly grease a baking sheet or cover it with parchment paper. Turn the dough out onto a lightly floured board or lightly oiled surface. Punch the dough down, and shape it into an oblong or round loaf. Place the loaf, with the smooth side up, onto the baking sheet. Cover and let rise in a warm place until almost doubled, 1 hour. Preheat the oven to 350°F. Bake 25 to 40 minutes, until the loaf sound hollow when tapped and a wooden skewer inserted into the loaf comes out clean and dry. Remove from the pan and cool on a wire rack.

RAISIN, CINNAMON, AND NUT WHEAT BREAD

Cinnamon and walnuts together bring out the nutty whole wheat flavor, and raisins add a sweet bite.

Sampler Loaf

2/3 cup water

3/4 teaspoon salt

3/4 teaspoon cinnamon

2 teaspoons packed brown sugar

1/4 cup nonfat dry milk

1 tablespoon butter

1 cup whole wheat flour

1 cup bread flour

1 1/4 teaspoons rapid-rising or active dry yeast

1/4 cup raisins

1/4 cup chopped walnuts

Regular Loaf

1 cup water

1 teaspoon salt

1 teaspoon cinnamon

1 tablespoon packed brown sugar

1/3 cup nonfat dry milk

1 1/2 tablespoons butter

1 1/2 cups whole wheat flour

1 1/2 cups bread flour

1 1/2 teaspoons rapid-rising or active dry yeast

1/2 cup raisins

1/2 cup chopped walnuts

Large Loaf

1 1/3 cups water

1 1/2 teaspoons salt

1 1/2 teaspoons cinnamon

1 1/2 tablespoons packed brown sugar

1/2 cup nonfat dry milk

2 tablespoons butter

2 cups whole wheat flour

2 cups bread flour

2 teaspoons rapid-rising or active dry yeast

3/4 cup raisins

3/4 cup chopped walnuts

TO MIX THE DOUGH BY HAND Heat the water until warm, between 105° and 115°F; pour it into a large, warmed bowl, and add the yeast, salt, cinnamon, sugar, and dry milk. Let stand 5 minutes, until the yeast begins to bubble. Stir in the butter and whole wheat flour. Beat until smooth. Cover, and let stand 15 minutes. Slowly add the bread flour, and beat until a soft dough forms. Turn the dough out onto a very lightly floured board, and knead, adding flour if necessary, until smooth and springy, about 5 minutes. Knead in the raisins and walnuts. Wash the bowl and grease it; place the dough back in the bowl, and turn it over to grease the top. Cover, and let rise until doubled, about 1 hour.

TO MIX THE DOUGH WITH A HEAVY-DUTY MIXER Heat the water until warm, between 105° and 115°F; pour it into a large, warmed bowl, and add the yeast, salt, cinnamon, sugar, and dry milk. Let stand 5 minutes, until the yeast begins to bubble. Stir in the butter and whole wheat flour. Beat until smooth. Cover, and let stand 15 minutes. Slowly add the bread flour, and beat until a soft dough forms. Knead the dough in the mixer with the dough hook, on medium to high speed, adding flour as necessary, until the dough pulls away from the sides of the bowl and is smooth and springy but still soft to the touch. Knead in the raisins and walnuts. Remove the dough hook, cover the bowl, and let the dough rise until doubled, about 1 hour.

TO MIX THE DOUGH IN THE FOOD PROCESSOR Place the plastic dough blade into the work bowl. Heat the water until very warm, between 120° and 130°F; set aside. Place the remaining ingredients, except the raisins and walnuts, into the work bowl. Turn the processor on, and slowly pour the water through the feed tube, processing until the dough is smooth and pulls away from the sides of the bowl. If the dough is wet and sticky, add more flour, 1 tablespoon at a time, until the dough is smooth yet soft to the touch. If the dough is not soft to the touch but is very firm, add 1 tablespoon of water at a time, and process until the dough is smooth yet soft to the touch. Mix in the raisins and walnuts. Cover the work bowl, and let the dough rise until doubled, about 1 hour. Or remove the dough to a lightly greased bowl, cover, and let rise until doubled, about 1 hour.

TO MIX THE DOUGH IN THE BREAD MACHINE Pour the water (at room temperature) into the pan, and add the remaining ingredients, except the raisins and walnuts. Make indentation in the dry ingredients and add yeast. Select *Dough,* and press *Start.* If the dough is wet and sticky, add more flour, 1 tablespoon at a time, until the dough is smooth yet soft to the touch. If

the dough is not soft to the touch but is very firm, add 1 teaspoon of water at a time, until the dough is smooth yet soft to the touch. Add the raisins and walnuts when the machine signals it's time to add ingredients or when the cycle ends. The machine will stop when the dough is ready to shape and bake.

TO MIX AND BAKE THE BREAD IN THE BREAD MACHINE Pour the water (at room temperature) into the pan, and add the remaining ingredients, except the raisins and walnuts. Make indentation in the dry ingredients and add yeast. Select the *Fruit and Nut, Basic,* or *Whole Wheat* cycle; set the crust on *Medium;* and press *Start.* During the mixing cycle, if the dough is wet and sticky, add more flour, 1 tablespoon at a time, until the dough is smooth yet soft to the touch. If the dough is not soft to the touch but is very firm, add 1 teaspoon of water at a time, until the dough is smooth yet soft to the touch. Add the raisins and walnuts when the machine signals it's time to add ingredients.

TO SHAPE AND BAKE IN THE OVEN Lightly grease an 8 × 4-inch or 9 × 5-inch loaf pan, an 8- or 9-inch round cake pan, or a baking sheet. Turn the dough out onto a lightly floured board or lightly oiled surface. Punch the dough down, and shape it into an oblong or round loaf. Place the loaf, with the smooth side up, into the pan. Cover and let rise in a warm place until almost doubled, 45 to 60 minutes. Preheat the oven to 375°F. Bake 30 to 35 minutes, until the loaf is golden. Remove from the pan and cool on a wire rack.

Peach and Whole Wheat Bread Pudding

This is a rich custard that includes both puréed and diced peaches, which are baked with bread cubes.

8 SERVINGS

4 cups bread cubes, cut 1/2 inch, made from any whole wheat bread that has raisins and/or nuts added

6 tablespoons butter, melted and cooled

6 eggs

3 cups milk

1 cup sugar

2 teaspoons vanilla

3 large fresh peaches, blanched and peeled, diced into 1/2-inch cubes

1/4 teaspoon cinnamon

1 1/2 cups whipping cream or half-and-half

1 tablespoon powdered sugar

1 teaspoon rum

Preheat oven to 350°F. Toss the bread cubes in the butter and divide them between two baking sheets. Bake 10 minutes or until lightly toasted. Let the bread cubes cool.

In a large bowl, whisk the eggs, milk and 3/4 cup of the sugar and the vanilla together until well blended. In a food processor or blender, purée one of the peaches. Stir the purée into the custard mixture with the remaining diced peaches.

Butter eight 1-cup individual baking dishes. In a small bowl, stir the cinnamon and the remaining 1/4 cup of sugar together. Add the bread cubes to the peach mixture. Divide the mixture among the baking dishes. Sprinkle with the cinnamon sugar. Bake 30 to 40 minutes, until just set. Allow to cool for 10 minutes.

In a bowl, beat the cream with the powdered sugar until it holds soft peaks. Add the rum. Run a knife around the edge of each pudding and invert each onto a heated plate. Spoon some of the cream onto each plate and dust with powdered sugar.

RUSTIC GRAINS AND HONEY PECAN BREAD

This appealing bread has a pale crumb flecked with rolled and whole grains and seeds. The mixture contains wheat; rye; millet; and sunflower, sesame, poppy, and flax seeds.

Sampler Loaf

$2/3$ cup water

1 tablespoon honey

1 tablespoon butter or shortening

$3/4$ teaspoon salt

$1/4$ cup toasted Rustic Grains Mixture (recipe follows)

2 cups bread flour

1 teaspoon rapid-rising or active dry yeast

$1/2$ cup raisins

$1/2$ cup chopped toasted pecans

Regular Loaf

1 cup water

$1^1/2$ tablespoons honey

$1^1/2$ tablespoons butter or shortening

$1^1/2$ teaspoons salt

$1/3$ cup toasted Rustic Grains Mixture (recipe follows)

3 cups bread flour

$1^1/2$ teaspoons rapid-rising or active dry yeast

1 cup raisins

1 cup chopped toasted pecans

Regular Loaf

$1^1/3$ cups water

2 tablespoons honey

2 tablespoons butter or shortening

2 teaspoons salt

$1/2$ cup toasted Rustic Grains Mixture (recipe follows)

4 cups bread flour

2 teaspoons rapid-rising or active dry yeast

$1^1/2$ cups raisins

$1^1/2$ cups chopped toasted pecans

GLAZE FOR BREAD BAKED CONVENTIONALLY

1 egg

1 tablespoon water or milk

TO MIX THE DOUGH BY HAND Heat the water until warm, between 105° and 115°F; pour it into a large, warmed bowl, and add the yeast. Let stand 5 minutes, until the yeast begins to bubble. Stir in the honey, butter, salt, toasted grains, and $1/2$ cup of the bread flour. Beat well. Cover, and let stand 15 minutes. Slowly add the remaining bread flour, and beat until a smooth dough forms. Turn the dough out onto a very lightly floured board, and knead, adding flour if necessary, until smooth and springy, about 5 minutes. Knead in the raisins and pecans. Wash the bowl and grease it; place the dough back in the bowl, and turn it over to grease the top. Cover, and let rise until doubled, about 1 hour.

TO MIX THE DOUGH WITH A HEAVY-DUTY MIXER Heat the water until warm, between

105° and 115°F; pour it into the warmed mixing bowl, and add the yeast. Let stand 5 minutes, until the yeast begins to bubble. Add the honey, butter, salt, toasted grains, and $1/2$ cup of the bread flour. Beat well. Slowly add the bread flour, and beat until a smooth dough forms. Cover, and let stand 15 minutes. Knead the dough in the mixer with the dough hook, on medium to high speed, adding flour as necessary, until the dough pulls away from the sides of the bowl and is smooth and springy but still soft to the touch. Knead in the raisins and pecans. Remove the dough hook, cover the bowl, and let the dough rise until doubled, about 1 hour.

TO MIX THE DOUGH IN THE FOOD PROCESSOR
Place the plastic dough blade into the work bowl. Heat the water until very warm, between 120° and 130°F; set aside. Place the remaining ingredients, except the raisins and pecans, into the work bowl. Turn the processor on, and slowly pour the water through the feed tube, processing until the dough is smooth and pulls away from the sides of the bowl. If the dough is wet and sticky, add more flour, 1 tablespoon at a time, until the dough is smooth yet soft to the touch. If the dough is not soft to the touch but is very firm, add 1 tablespoon of water at a time, and process until the dough is smooth yet soft to the touch. Mix in the raisins and pecans. Cover the work bowl, and let the dough rise until doubled, about 1 hour. Or remove the dough to a lightly greased bowl, cover, and let rise until doubled, about 1 hour.

TO MIX THE DOUGH IN THE BREAD MACHINE Pour the water (at room temperature) into the pan. Add the remaining ingredients, except the raisins and pecans, in the order listed. Make an indentation in the dry ingredients and add the yeast. Select *Dough,* and press *Start.* If the dough is wet and sticky, add more flour, 1 tablespoon at a time, until the dough is smooth yet soft to the touch. If the dough is not soft to the touch but is very firm, add 1 teaspoon of water at a time, until the dough is smooth yet soft to the touch. Add the raisins and pecans when the machine signals it's time to add ingredients or when the cycle ends. The machine will stop when the dough is ready to shape and bake.

TO MIX AND BAKE THE BREAD IN THE BREAD MACHINE Pour the water (at room temperature) into the pan. Add the remaining ingredients, except the raisins and pecans, in the order listed. Make an indentation in the dry ingredients and add the yeast. Select the *Fruit and Nut, Basic,* or *Whole Wheat* cycle; set the crust on *Medium;* and press *Start.* During the mixing cycle, if the dough is wet and sticky, add more flour, 1 tablespoon at a time, until the dough is smooth yet soft to the touch. If the dough is not soft to the touch but is very firm, add 1 teaspoon of water at a time, until the dough is smooth yet soft to the touch. Add the raisins and pecans when the machine signals it's time to add ingredients.

TO SHAPE AND BAKE IN THE OVEN Lightly grease a 9 × 5-inch loaf pan, an 8- or 9-inch round cake pan, or a baking sheet. Turn the dough out onto a lightly floured board or lightly oiled surface. Punch the dough down, and shape it into an oblong or round loaf. Place the loaf, with the smooth side up, into the pan. Cover and let rise in a warm place until almost doubled, 45 to 60 minutes. Preheat the oven to 375°F. To glaze, beat the egg with the water, and brush the mixture on the loaf. Bake 35 to 40 minutes, until the loaf is golden and a wooden skewer inserted into the loaf comes out clean and dry. Remove from the pan and cool on a wire rack.

Rustic Grains Mixture

This approximates a commercial mixture that is available by mail order from King Arthur Flour. The ingredients are available in most health food and whole foods markets.

3 CUPS

1 cup rolled wheat flakes
1 cup rolled rye flakes
3/4 cup unroasted sunflower seeds
1/4 cup sesame seeds
3 tablespoons whole millet
2 tablespoons poppy seeds
1 tablespoon whole flax seeds

Combine all of the ingredients, and store in an airtight container. To toast, preheat the oven to 350°F. Spread the mix in an ungreased, shallow baking pan and bake 10 minutes until toasted, stirring once.

SESAME, OAT, AND CINNAMON SWIRL LOAF

This is a great loaf for Sunday brunch or an afternoon tea. Spread the slices with cream cheese and top with a thin slice of fresh apple or pear. In this recipe, the rolled oats are added to the liquid ingredients at the beginning, so they partially cook as the water cools. If you want to bake this loaf in the machine, just add the cinnamon along with the rest of the ingredients. You won't get a swirl loaf, but you'll still have the delicious flavor of cinnamon.

Sampler Loaf

2/3 cup boiling water

1/4 cup quick-cooking rolled oats

1 tablespoon butter

1 teaspoon salt

1 tablespoon toasted
  sesame seeds

1 tablespoon packed brown sugar

3/4 cup whole wheat flour

1 cup bread flour

1 teaspoon rapid-rising or active
  dry yeast

1 teaspoon cinnamon

Regular Loaf

1 cup boiling water

1/3 cup quick-cooking rolled oats

1 1/2 tablespoons butter

1 1/2 teaspoons salt

1 1/2 tablespoons toasted
  sesame seeds

1 1/2 tablespoons packed
  brown sugar

1 cup whole wheat flour

1 2/3 cups bread flour

1 1/2 teaspoons rapid-rising or
  active dry yeast

1 1/2 teaspoon cinnamon

Large Loaf

1 1/3 cups boiling water

1/2 cup quick-cooking rolled oats

2 tablespoons butter

2 teaspoons salt

2 tablespoons toasted
  sesame seeds

2 tablespoons packed
  brown sugar

1 1/2 cups whole wheat flour

2 cups bread flour

2 teaspoons rapid-rising or active
  dry yeast

2 teaspoons cinnamon

TO MIX THE DOUGH BY HAND Pour the boiling water into a large bowl, add the rolled oats, and stir. Let stand until the mixture cools to warm, between 105° and 115°F. Add the yeast; let stand 5 minutes, until the yeast begins to bubble. Stir in the butter, salt, sesame seeds, sugar, and whole wheat flour. Beat well. Cover, and let stand 15 minutes. Slowly add the bread flour, and beat until a stiff dough forms. Turn the dough out onto a very lightly floured board, and knead, adding flour if necessary, until smooth and springy, about 5 minutes. Wash the bowl and grease it; place the dough back in the bowl, and turn it over to grease the top. Cover, and let rise until doubled, about 1 hour.

TO MIX THE DOUGH WITH A HEAVY-DUTY MIXER   Pour the boiling water into the mixing bowl, add the rolled oats, and stir. Let stand until the mixture cools to warm, between 105° and 115°F. Add the yeast; let stand 5 minutes, until the yeast begins to bubble. Add the butter, salt, sesame seeds, sugar, and whole wheat flour. Beat well. Cover, and let stand 15 minutes. Slowly add the bread flour, and beat until a stiff dough forms. Knead the dough in the mixer with the dough hook, on medium to high speed, adding flour as necessary, until the dough pulls away from the sides of the bowl and is smooth and springy but still soft to the touch. Remove the dough hook, cover the bowl, and let the dough rise until doubled, about 1 hour.

TO MIX THE DOUGH IN THE FOOD PROCESSOR Place the plastic dough blade into the work bowl. Place the boiling water into a medium bowl, add the rolled oats, and stir. Let stand until the mixture cools to very warm, between 120° and 130°F. Place the remaining ingredients, except the cinnamon, into the work bowl. Add the water mixture. Process until the dough is smooth and pulls away from the sides of the bowl. If the dough is wet and sticky, add more flour, 1 tablespoon at a time, until the dough is smooth yet soft to the touch. If the dough is not soft to the touch but is very firm, add 1 tablespoon of water at a time, and process until the dough is smooth yet soft to the touch. Cover the work bowl, and

let the dough rise until doubled, about 1 hour. Or remove the dough to a lightly greased bowl, cover, and let rise until doubled, about 1 hour.

TO MIX THE DOUGH IN THE BREAD MACHINE   Pour the boiling water into the pan, add the rolled oats, and stir. Let stand until the mixture cools to room temperature. Add the remaining ingredients, except the cinnamon. Make an indentation in the dry ingredients and add yeast. Select *Dough,* and press *Start.* If the dough is wet and sticky, add more flour, 1 tablespoon at a time, until the dough is smooth yet soft to the touch. If the dough is not soft to the touch but is very firm, add 1 teaspoon of water at a time, until the dough is smooth yet soft to the touch. The machine will stop when the dough is ready to shape and bake.

TO MIX AND BAKE THE BREAD IN THE BREAD MACHINE   Pour the boiling water into the pan, add the rolled oats, and stir. Let stand until the mixture cools to room temperature. Add the remaining ingredients, including the cinnamon. Make an indentation in the dry ingredients and add yeast. Select the *Basic* or *Whole Wheat* cycle, set the crust on *Medium,* and press *Start.* During the mixing cycle, if the dough is wet and sticky, add more flour, 1 tablespoon at a time, until the dough is smooth yet soft to the touch. If the dough is not soft to the touch but is very firm, add 1 teaspoon of water at a time, until the dough is smooth yet soft to the touch.

TO SHAPE AND BAKE IN THE OVEN   Lightly grease a $8^{1}/_{2} \times 4^{1}/_{2}$-inch loaf pan. Turn the dough out onto a lightly floured board or lightly oiled surface. Punch the dough down, and roll it out into a 8 × 12-inch rectangle. Sprinkle evenly with the cinnamon, and roll up tightly, sealing the seam and ends. Place the loaf, with the smooth side up, into the pan. Cover, and let rise in a warm place until almost doubled, 45 to 60 minutes. Preheat the oven to 375°F. Bake 30 to 35 minutes, until the loaf is golden and a wooden skewer inserted into the loaf comes out clean and dry. Remove from the pan and cool on a wire rack.

TOASTING SESAME SEEDS

To toast sesame seeds, spread them in a dry skillet and place over medium heat. Cover loosely (they pop as they heat). Cook, shaking the pan occasionally, about 10 minutes, until the seeds are golden.

TOASTED SESAME GRAHAM WHEAT BREAD

Toasted sesame oil adds a delightful flavor to this whole wheat bread, which is an adaptation of a Greek classic. If you do not have sesame oil, you can substitute another oil, but the sesame flavor will not be as intense. Although you can bake this bread in the bread machine, I prefer to make the dough and shape it into the traditional, beautiful braid.

Sampler Loaf

2/3 cup water

1 1/2 teaspoons honey

1 tablespoon sesame oil

1 teaspoon salt

1 cup graham wheat flour

1 cup bread flour

2 tablespoons toasted
   sesame seeds

1 teaspoon rapid-rising or active
   dry yeast

Regular Loaf

1 cup water

2 teaspoons honey

1 1/2 tablespoons sesame oil

1 1/2 teaspoons salt

1 1/2 cups graham flour

1 1/2 cups bread flour

3 tablespoons toasted
   sesame seeds

1 1/2 teaspoons rapid-rising or
   active dry yeast

Large Loaf

1 1/3 cups water

1 tablespoon honey

2 tablespoons sesame oil

2 teaspoons salt

2 cups graham wheat flour

2 cups bread flour

1/4 cup toasted sesame seeds

2 teaspoons rapid-rising or active
   dry yeast

TOPPING FOR BREAD BAKED CONVENTIONALLY
Toasted sesame seeds

TO MIX THE DOUGH BY HAND Heat the water until warm, between 105° and 115°F; pour it into a large, warmed bowl, and add the yeast. Let stand 5 minutes, until the yeast begins to bubble. Stir in the honey, oil, salt, and graham flour. Beat well. Cover, and let stand 15 minutes. Slowly add the bread flour and sesame seeds, and beat until a stiff dough forms. Turn the dough out onto a very lightly floured board, and knead,

adding flour if necessary, until smooth and springy, about 5 minutes. Wash the bowl and grease it; place the dough back in the bowl, and turn it over to grease the top. Cover, and let rise until doubled, about 1 hour.

TO MIX THE DOUGH WITH A HEAVY-DUTY MIXER Heat the water until warm, between 105° and 115°F; pour it into the warmed mixing

bowl, and add the yeast. Let stand 5 minutes, until the yeast begins to bubble. Add the honey, oil, salt, and graham flour. Beat well. Cover, and let stand 15 minutes. Slowly add the bread flour and sesame seeds, and beat until a stiff dough forms. Knead the dough in the mixer with the dough hook, on medium to high speed, adding flour as necessary, until the dough pulls away from the sides of the bowl and is smooth and springy but still soft to the touch. Remove the dough hook, cover the bowl, and let the dough rise until doubled, about 1 hour.

TO MIX THE DOUGH IN THE FOOD PROCESSOR
Place the plastic dough blade into the work bowl. Heat the water until very warm, between 120° and 130°F; set aside. Place the remaining ingredients into the work bowl. Turn the processor on, and slowly pour the water through the feed tube, processing until the dough is smooth and pulls away from the sides of the bowl. If the dough is wet and sticky, add more flour, 1 tablespoon at a time, until the dough is smooth yet soft to the touch. If the dough is not soft to the touch but is very firm, add 1 tablespoon of water at a time, and process until the dough is smooth yet soft to the touch. Cover the work bowl, and let the dough rise until doubled, about 1 hour. Or remove the dough to a lightly greased bowl, cover, and let rise until doubled, about 1 hour.

TO MIX THE DOUGH IN THE BREAD MACHINE Pour the water (at room temperature) into the pan, and add the remaining ingredients, except the yeast. Make a small indentation in the dry ingredients and add the yeast. Select *Dough,* and press *Start.* If the dough is wet and

sticky, add more flour, 1 tablespoon at a time, until the dough is smooth yet soft to the touch. If the dough is not soft to the touch but is very firm, add 1 teaspoon of water at a time, until the dough is smooth yet soft to the touch. The machine will stop when the dough is ready to shape and bake.

TO MIX AND BAKE THE BREAD IN THE BREAD MACHINE Pour the water (at room temperature) into the pan, and add the remaining ingredients, except the yeast. Make a small indentation in the dry ingredients and add the yeast. Select the *Basic* or *Whole Wheat* cycle, set the crust on *Medium,* and press *Start.* During the mixing cycle, if the dough is wet and sticky, add more flour, 1 tablespoon at a time, until the dough is smooth yet soft to the touch. If the dough is not soft to the touch but is very firm, add 1 teaspoon of water at a time, until the dough is smooth yet soft to the touch.

TO SHAPE AND BAKE IN THE OVEN Lightly grease a baking sheet. Turn the dough out onto a lightly floured board or lightly oiled surface. Punch the dough down, and divide into three parts. Shape each part into a strand, about 12 inches long. Braid the three strands together, pinching the ends to seal. Place the loaf, with the smooth side up, onto the baking sheet. Cover and let rise in a warm place until almost doubled, 45 to 60 minutes. Preheat the oven to 375°F. To top, brush the loaf with water, and sprinkle on the sesame seeds. Bake 25 to 35 minutes, until the loaf is golden and a wooden skewer inserted into the loaf comes out clean and dry. Remove from the pan and cool on a wire rack.

TOASTED GRAINS AND HONEY PECAN BREAD

This appealing bread has a pale crumb flecked with rolled whole grains and seeds. The mixture contains rolled wheat, rye, sunflower seeds, sesame seeds, whole millet, poppy seeds, and flax seeds. The flavors are nuttier when the mixture is toasted before using.

Sampler Loaf	Regular Loaf	Large Loaf
2/3 cup water	1 cup water	1 1/3 cups water
1 tablespoon honey	1 1/2 tablespoons honey	2 tablespoons honey
1 tablespoon butter or shortening	1 1/2 tablespoons butter or shortening	2 tablespoons butter or shortening
3/4 teaspoon salt	1 1/2 teaspoons salt	2 teaspoons salt
1/4 cup toasted rustic grains mixture (page 147)	1/3 cup toasted rustic grains mixture (page 147)	1/2 cup toasted rustic grains mixture (page 147)
2 cups bread flour	3 cups bread flour	4 cups bread flour
1 teaspoon rapid-rising or active dry yeast	1 1/2 teaspoons rapid-rising or active dry yeast	2 teaspoons rapid-rising or active dry yeast
1/2 cup chopped toasted pecans	1 cup chopped toasted pecans	1 1/2 cups chopped toasted pecans

GLAZE FOR BREAD BAKED CONVENTIONALLY
1 egg
1 tablespoon water or milk

TO MIX THE DOUGH BY HAND Heat the water until warm, between 105° and 115°F; pour it into a large, warmed bowl, and add the yeast. Let stand 5 minutes, until the yeast begins to bubble. Stir in the honey, butter, salt, rustic grains, and 1/2 cup of the bread flour. Beat well. Cover, and let stand 15 minutes. Slowly add the remaining bread flour, and beat until a smooth dough forms. Turn the dough out onto a very lightly floured board, and knead, adding flour if necessary, until smooth and springy, about 5 minutes. Knead in the pecans. Wash the bowl and grease it; place the dough back in the bowl, and turn it over to grease the top. Cover, and let rise until doubled, about 1 hour.

TO MIX THE DOUGH WITH A HEAVY-DUTY MIXER

Heat the water until warm, between 105° and 115°F; pour it into the warmed mixing bowl, and add the yeast. Let stand 5 minutes, until the yeast begins to bubble. Add the honey, butter, salt, rustic grains, and $1/2$ cup of the bread flour. Beat well. Cover, and let stand 15 minutes. Slowly add the bread flour, and beat until a smooth dough forms. Knead the dough in the mixer with the dough hook, on medium to high speed, adding flour as necessary, until the dough pulls away from the sides of the bowl and is smooth and springy but still soft to the touch. Knead in the pecans. Remove the dough hook, cover the bowl, and let the dough rise until doubled, about 1 hour.

TO MIX THE DOUGH IN THE FOOD PROCESSOR

Place the plastic dough blade into the work bowl. Heat the water until very warm, between 120° and 130°F; set aside. Place the remaining ingredients into the work bowl. Turn the processor on, and slowly pour the water through the feed tube, processing until the dough is smooth and pulls away from the sides of the bowl. If the dough is wet and sticky, add more flour, 1 tablespoon at a time, until the dough is smooth yet soft to the touch. If the dough is not soft to the touch but is very firm, add 1 tablespoon of water at a time, and process until the dough is smooth yet soft to the touch. Cover the work bowl, and let the dough rise until doubled, about 1 hour. Or remove the dough to a lightly greased bowl, cover, and let rise until doubled, about 1 hour.

TO MIX THE DOUGH IN THE BREAD MACHINE

Pour the water (at room temperature) into the pan. Add the remaining ingredients, except the pecans, in the order listed. Make indentation in the dry ingredients and add yeast. Select *Dough,* and press *Start.* If the dough is wet and sticky, add more flour, 1 tablespoon at a time, until the dough is smooth yet soft to the touch. If the dough is not soft to the touch but is very firm, add 1 teaspoon of water at a time, until the dough is smooth yet soft to the touch. Add the pecans when the machine signals it's time to add ingredients or when the cycle ends. The machine will stop when the dough is ready to shape and bake.

TO MIX AND BAKE THE BREAD IN THE BREAD MACHINE

Pour the water (at room temperature) into the pan. Add the remaining ingredients, except the pecans, in the order listed. Make indentation in the dry ingredients and add yeast. Select the *Fruit and Nut, Basic,* or *Whole Wheat* cycle; set the crust on *Medium;* and press *Start.* During the mixing cycle, if the dough is wet and sticky, add more flour, 1 tablespoon at a time, until the dough is smooth yet soft to the touch. If the dough is not soft to the touch but is very firm, add 1 teaspoon of water at a time, until the dough is smooth yet soft to the touch. Add the pecans when the machine signals it's time to add ingredients.

TO SHAPE AND BAKE IN THE OVEN

Lightly grease a 9 × 5-inch loaf pan, an 8- or 9-inch round cake pan, or a baking sheet. Turn the dough out onto a lightly floured board or lightly oiled surface. Punch the dough down, and shape it into an oblong or round loaf. Place the loaf, with the smooth side up, into the pan. Cover and let rise in a warm place until almost doubled, 45 to 60 minutes. Preheat the oven to 375°F. To glaze, beat the egg with the water, and brush the mixture on the loaf. Bake 35 to 40 minutes, until the loaf is golden and a wooden skewer inserted into the loaf comes out clean and dry. Remove from the pan and cool on a wire rack.

TROPICAL FRUITS WHEAT BREAD

Dried papaya, mango, and pineapple slices, are found in the bulk foods department of a supermarket. These fruits may seem like an unlikely pairing with the decidedly untropical whole wheat, but the combination is irresistible.

Sampler Loaf	Regular Loaf	Large Loaf
2/3 cup water	1 cup water	1 1/3 cups water
1 tablespoon soft butter	1 1/2 tablespoons soft butter	2 tablespoons soft butter
3/4 teaspoon salt	1 teaspoon salt	1 1/2 teaspoons salt
1 tablespoon sugar	1 1/2 tablespoons sugar	2 tablespoons sugar
3/4 teaspoon cinnamon	1 teaspoon cinnamon	1 1/2 teaspoons cinnamon
1/4 teaspoon freshly grated nutmeg	1/2 teaspoon freshly grated nutmeg	3/4 teaspoon freshly grated nutmeg
1/4 cup nonfat dry milk	1/3 cup nonfat dry milk	1/2 cup nonfat dry milk
2/3 cup whole wheat flour	1 cup whole wheat flour	1 1/3 cups whole wheat flour
1 1/3 cups bread flour	2 cups bread flour	2 2/3 cups bread flour
1 teaspoon rapid-rising or active dry yeast	1 1/2 teaspoons rapid-rising or active dry yeast	2 teaspoons rapid-rising or active dry yeast
1/4 cup chopped dried papaya, mango, and/or pineapple	1/2 cup chopped dried papaya, mango, and/or pineapple	3/4 cup chopped dried papaya, mango, and/or pineapple
1/4 slivered or sliced almonds	1/2 slivered or sliced almonds	3/4 slivered or sliced almonds

TO MIX THE DOUGH BY HAND Heat the water until warm, between 105° and 115°F; pour it into a large, warmed bowl, and add the yeast. Let stand 5 minutes, until the yeast begins to bubble. Stir in the butter, salt, sugar, cinnamon, nutmeg, dry milk, whole wheat flour, and half of the bread flour. Beat well. Cover, and let stand 15 minutes. Slowly add the remaining bread flour, and beat until a smooth dough forms. Turn the dough out onto a very lightly floured board, and knead, adding flour if necessary, until smooth and springy, about 5 minutes. Knead in the fruit and almonds. Wash the bowl and grease it; place the dough back in the bowl, and turn it over to grease the top. Cover, and let rise until doubled, about 1 hour.

TO MIX THE DOUGH WITH A HEAVY-DUTY MIXER Heat the water until warm, between 105° and 115°F; pour it into the warmed mixing bowl, and add the yeast. Let stand 5 minutes, until the yeast begins to bubble. Add the butter, salt, sugar, cinnamon, nutmeg, dry milk, whole wheat flour, and half of the bread flour. Beat well. Cover, and let stand 15 minutes. Slowly add the remaining bread flour, and beat until a smooth dough forms. Knead the dough in the mixer with the dough hook, on medium to high speed, adding flour as necessary, until the dough pulls away from the sides of the bowl and is smooth and springy but still soft to the touch. Knead in the fruit and almonds. Remove the dough hook, cover the bowl, and let the dough rise until doubled, about 1 hour.

TO MIX THE DOUGH IN THE FOOD PROCESSOR Place the plastic dough blade into the work bowl. Heat the water until very warm, between 120° and 130°F; set aside. Place the remaining ingredients, except the fruit and almonds, into the work bowl. Turn the processor on, and slowly pour the water through the feed tube, processing until the dough is smooth and pulls away from the sides of the bowl. If the dough is wet and sticky, add more flour, 1 tablespoon at a time, until the dough is smooth yet soft to the touch. If the dough is not soft to the touch but is very firm, add 1 tablespoon of water at a time, and process until the dough is smooth yet soft to the touch. Mix in the fruit and almonds. Cover the work bowl, and let the dough rise until doubled, about 1 hour. Or remove the dough to a lightly greased bowl, cover, and let rise until doubled, about 1 hour.

TO MIX THE DOUGH IN THE BREAD MACHINE Pour the water (at room temperature) into the pan, and add the salt, sugar, cinnamon, nutmeg, dry milk, whole wheat flour, and bread flour. Make a small indentation in the dry ingredients, and add the yeast. Select *Dough,* and press *Start.* If the dough is wet and sticky, add

more flour, 1 tablespoon at a time, until the dough is smooth yet soft to the touch. If the dough is not soft to the touch but is very firm, add 1 teaspoon of water at a time, until the dough is smooth yet soft to the touch. Add the fruit and almonds when the machine signals it's time to add ingredients or when the cycle ends. The machine will stop when the dough is ready to shape and bake.

TO MIX AND BAKE THE BREAD IN THE BREAD MACHINE Pour the water (at room temperature) into the pan, add the salt, sugar, cinnamon, nutmeg, dry milk, whole wheat flour, and bread flour. Make a small indentation in the dry ingredients, and add the yeast. Select the *Fruit and Nut, Basic,* or *Whole Wheat* cycle; set the crust on *Medium;* and press *Start.* During the mixing cycle, if the dough is wet and sticky, add more flour, 1 tablespoon at a time, until the dough is smooth yet soft to the touch. If the dough is not soft to the touch but is very firm, add 1 teaspoon of water at a time, until the dough is smooth yet soft to the touch. Add the fruit and almonds when the machine signals it's time to add ingredients.

TO SHAPE AND BAKE IN THE OVEN Lightly grease a 9 × 5-inch loaf pan, an 8- or 9-inch round cake pan, or a baking sheet. Turn the dough out onto a lightly floured board or lightly oiled surface. Punch the dough down, and shape it into an oblong or round loaf. Place the loaf, with the smooth side up, into the pan. Cover and let rise in a warm place until almost doubled, 45 minutes. Preheat the oven to 375°F. Bake 35 to 45 minutes, until the loaf is nicely browned. Remove from the pan and cool on a wire rack.

WALNUT WHEAT BREAD

This is a rich wheat bread, but not as rich as classic brioche. Eggs add a tenderness to the crumb and a wonderful flavor.

Sampler Loaf

1 large egg plus water to equal
   2/3 cup

3 tablespoons butter, softened

1 teaspoon salt

2 teaspoons sugar

2 tablespoons nonfat dry milk

3/4 cup whole wheat flour

1 1/4 cups bread flour

1/4 cup coarsely chopped walnuts

1 teaspoon rapid-rising or active
   dry yeast

Regular Loaf

2 large eggs plus water to equal
   1 cup

1/3 cup butter, softened

1 1/2 teaspoons salt

4 teaspoons sugar

1/4 cup nonfat dry milk

1 cup whole wheat flour

2 cups bread flour

1/3 cup coarsely chopped walnuts

1 1/2 teaspoons rapid-rising or
   active dry yeast

Large Loaf

3 large eggs plus water to equal
   1 1/3 cups

1/2 cup (1 stick) butter, softened

2 teaspoons salt

2 tablespoons sugar

1/3 cup nonfat dry milk

1 1/2 cups whole wheat flour

2 1/2 cups bread flour

1/2 cup coarsely chopped walnuts

2 teaspoons rapid-rising or active
   dry yeast

TO MIX THE DOUGH BY HAND Warm the eggs under hot tap water, and crack into a measuring cup. Heat the water until warm, between 105° and 115°F, and add it to the eggs. Pour the mixture into a large, warmed bowl, and add the yeast. Let stand 5 minutes, until the yeast begins to bubble. Stir in the butter, salt, sugar, dry milk, whole wheat flour, and half of the bread flour. Beat well. Cover, and let stand 15 minutes. Slowly add the remaining bread flour, and beat until a dough forms. Turn the dough out onto a very lightly floured board, and knead, adding flour if necessary, until smooth and springy, about 5 minutes. Knead in the walnuts. Wash the bowl and grease it; place the dough back in the bowl, and turn it over to grease the top. Cover, and let rise until doubled, about 1 hour.

TO MIX THE DOUGH WITH A HEAVY-DUTY MIXER Warm the eggs under hot tap water, and crack into a measuring cup. Heat the water until warm, between 105° and 115°F, and add it to the eggs. Pour the mixture into the warmed mixing bowl, and add the yeast. Let stand 5 minutes, until the yeast begins to bubble. Add the butter, salt, sugar, dry milk, whole wheat flour, and half of the bread flour. Beat well. Cover, and let stand 15 minutes. Slowly add the remaining bread flour, and beat until a dough forms. Knead the dough in the mixer with the dough hook, on medium to high speed, adding flour as necessary, until the dough pulls away from the sides of the bowl and is smooth and springy but still soft to the touch. Knead in the walnuts. Remove the dough hook, cover the bowl, and let the dough rise until doubled, about 1 hour.

TO MIX THE DOUGH IN THE FOOD PROCESSOR Warm the eggs under hot tap water, and crack into a measuring cup. Heat the water until very warm, between 120° and 130°F, and add it to the eggs; set aside. Place the remaining ingredients, except the walnuts, into the work bowl. Turn the processor on, and slowly pour the water mixture through the feed tube, processing until the dough is smooth and pulls away from the sides of the bowl. If the dough is wet and sticky, add more flour, 1 tablespoon at a time, until the dough is smooth yet soft to the touch. If the dough is not soft to the touch but is very firm, add 1 tablespoon of water at a time, and process until the dough is smooth yet soft to the touch. Mix in the walnuts. Cover the work bowl, and let the dough rise until doubled, about 1 hour. Or remove the dough to a lightly greased bowl, cover, and let rise until doubled, about 1 hour.

TO MIX THE DOUGH IN THE BREAD MACHINE Warm the eggs under hot tap water, and crack into a measuring cup. Add the water (at room temperature) to the eggs, and pour into the pan. Add the remaining ingredients, except the yeast. Make a small indentation in the dry ingredients, and add the yeast. Select *Dough,* and press

Start. If the dough is wet and sticky, add more flour, 1 tablespoon at a time, until the dough is smooth yet soft to the touch. If the dough is not soft to the touch but is very firm, add 1 teaspoon of water at a time, until the dough is smooth yet soft to the touch. The machine will stop when the dough is ready to shape and bake.

TO MIX AND BAKE THE BREAD IN THE BREAD MACHINE Warm the eggs under hot tap water, and crack into a measuring cup. Add the water (at room temperature) to the eggs, and pour into the pan. Add the remaining ingredients, except the yeast. Make a small indentation in the dry ingredients, and add the yeast. Select the *Basic* cycle, set the crust on *Light,* and press *Start.* During the mixing cycle, if the dough is wet and sticky, add more flour, 1 tablespoon at a time, until the dough is smooth yet soft to the touch. If the dough is not soft to the touch but is very firm, add 1 teaspoon of water at a time, until the dough is smooth yet soft to the touch.

TO SHAPE AND BAKE IN THE OVEN Lightly grease a 9 × 5-inch loaf pan, an 8- or 9-inch round cake pan, or a baking sheet. Turn the dough out onto a lightly floured board or lightly oiled surface. Punch the dough down, and shape it into an oblong or round loaf. Place the loaf, with the smooth side up, into the pan. Cover and let rise in a warm place until almost doubled, 45 to 60 minutes. Preheat the oven to 350°F. Brush or spray the loaf with water. Bake 30 to 35 minutes, until a wooden skewer inserted into the loaf comes out clean and dry. Remove from the pan and cool on a wire rack.

WHEAT AND SUNFLOWER BREAD

Nutty tasting sunflower seeds inside and on the top of the loaf make this bread irresistible.

Sampler Loaf	Regular Loaf	Large Loaf
$2/3$ cup water	1 cup water	$1^1/3$ cups water
$1^1/2$ teaspoons freshly squeezed lemon juice	2 teaspoons freshly squeezed lemon juice	1 tablespoons freshly squeezed lemon juice
1 tablespoon canola oil	$1^1/2$ tablespoons canola oil	2 tablespoons canola oil
1 tablespoon molasses	$1^1/2$ tablespoons molasses	2 tablespoons molasses
$3/4$ teaspoon grated orange zest	1 teaspoon grated orange zest	$1^1/2$ teaspoons grated orange zest
1 teaspoon salt	$1^1/2$ teaspoons salt	2 teaspoons salt
$1/4$ cup nonfat dry milk	$1/3$ cup nonfat dry milk	$1/2$ cup nonfat dry milk
1 tablespoon toasted wheat germ	$1^1/2$ tablespoons toasted wheat germ	2 tablespoons toasted wheat germ
1 tablespoon cracked wheat	$1^1/2$ tablespoons cracked wheat	2 tablespoons cracked wheat
$1/4$ cup whole wheat flour	$1/3$ cup whole wheat flour	$1/2$ cup whole wheat flour
$1^2/3$ cups bread flour	$2^2/3$ cups bread flour	$3^1/2$ cups bread flour
3 tablespoons sunflower seeds	$1/4$ cup sunflower seeds	6 tablespoons sunflower seeds
1 teaspoon rapid-rising or active dry yeast	$1^1/2$ teaspoons rapid-rising or active dry yeast	2 teaspoons rapid-rising or active dry yeast

GLAZE FOR BREAD BAKED CONVENTIONALLY

1 egg

1 tablespoon water

Wheat germ and sesame seeds

TO MIX THE DOUGH BY HAND Heat the water until warm, between 105° and 115°F; pour it into a large, warmed bowl, and add the yeast. Let stand 5 minutes, until the yeast begins to bubble. Stir in the remaining ingredients, except the bread flour. Beat well. Cover, and let stand 15 minutes. Slowly add the bread flour, and beat until a smooth dough forms. Turn the dough out onto a very lightly floured board, and knead, adding flour if necessary, until smooth and springy, about 5 minutes. Wash the bowl and grease it; place the dough back in the bowl, and turn it over to grease the top. Cover, and let rise until doubled, about 1 hour.

TO MIX THE DOUGH WITH A HEAVY-DUTY MIXER Heat the water until warm, between 105° and 115°F; pour it into the warmed mixing bowl, and add the yeast. Let stand 5 minutes, until the yeast begins to bubble. Add the remaining ingredients, except the bread flour. Beat well. Cover, and let stand 15 minutes. Slowly add the bread flour, and beat until a smooth dough forms. Knead the dough in the mixer with the dough hook, on medium to high speed, adding flour as necessary, until the dough pulls away from the sides of the bowl and is smooth and springy but still soft to the touch. Remove the dough hook, cover the bowl, and let the dough rise until doubled, about 1 hour.

TO MIX THE DOUGH IN THE FOOD PROCESSOR Place the plastic dough blade into the work bowl. Heat the water until very warm, between 120° and 130°F; set aside. Place the remaining ingredients into the work bowl. Turn the processor on, and slowly pour the water through the feed tube, processing until the dough is smooth and pulls away from the sides of the bowl. If the dough is wet and sticky, add more flour, 1 tablespoon at a time, until the dough is smooth yet soft to the touch. If the dough is not soft to the touch but is very firm, add 1 tablespoon of water at a time, and process until the dough is smooth yet soft to the touch. Cover the work bowl, and let the dough rise until doubled, about 1 hour. Or remove the dough to a lightly greased bowl, cover, and let rise until doubled, about 1 hour.

TO MIX THE DOUGH IN THE BREAD MACHINE Pour the water (at room temperature) into the pan, and add the remaining ingredients, except the yeast. Make a small indentation in the dry ingredients, and add the yeast. Select *Dough,* and press *Start.* If the dough is wet and sticky, add more flour, 1 tablespoon at a time, until the dough is smooth yet soft to the touch. If the dough is not soft to the touch but is very firm, add 1 teaspoon of water at a time, until the dough is smooth yet soft to the touch. The machine will stop when the dough is ready to shape and bake.

TO MIX AND BAKE THE BREAD IN THE BREAD MACHINE Pour the water (at room temperature) into the pan, and add the remaining ingredients, except the yeast. Make a small indentation in the dry ingredients, and add the yeast. Select the *Basic* or *Whole Wheat* cycle, set the crust on *Medium,* and press *Start.* During the mixing cycle, if the dough is wet and sticky, add more flour, 1 tablespoon at a time, until the dough is smooth yet soft to the touch. If the dough is not soft to the touch but is very firm, add 1 teaspoon of water at a time, until the dough is smooth yet soft to the touch.

TO SHAPE AND BAKE IN THE OVEN Lightly grease a baking sheet or cover with parchment paper. Turn the dough out onto a lightly floured board or lightly oiled surface. Punch the dough down, and shape it into an oblong or round loaf. Place the loaf, with the smooth side up, onto the baking sheet. Cover and let rise until almost doubled, about 45 to 60 minutes. Preheat the oven to 375°F. To glaze, beat the egg with the water, brush the mixture on the loaf, and sprinkle on the wheat germ and sunflower seeds. Bake 35 to 45 minutes, until the loaf is nicely browned. Remove from the pan and cool on a wire rack.

WHEAT BERRY AND RAISIN BREAD

Wheat berries, or whole wheat kernels, cook to tender crunchiness in less than an hour and add a wonderful texture to this bread. Cook them according to the package instructions (or see below), and be sure to drain them well.

Sampler Loaf

2/3 cup water

3/4 teaspoon salt

1 tablespoon canola oil

1 tablespoon honey

1 tablespoon molasses

1 cup whole wheat flour

1 cup bread flour

1 teaspoon yeast

1/2 cup cooked wheat berries, well drained*

1/2 cup raisins

Regular Loaf

1 cup water

1 teaspoon salt

1 1/2 tablespoons canola oil

1 1/2 tablespoons honey

1 1/2 tablespoons molasses

1 1/2 cups whole wheat flour

1 1/2 cups bread flour

1 1/2 teaspoons yeast

3/4 cup cooked wheat berries, well drained*

3/4 cup raisins

Large Loaf

1 1/3 cups water

1 1/2 teaspoons salt

2 tablespoons canola oil

2 tablespoons honey

2 tablespoons molasses

2 cups whole wheat flour

2 cups bread flour

2 teaspoons yeast

1 cup cooked wheat berries, well drained*

1 cup raisins

GLAZE FOR BREAD BAKED CONVENTIONALLY

1 egg

1 tablespoon water or milk

1 to 2 tablespoons sesame seeds

Note   *If you are going to mix this dough in the bread machine, be extremely careful to drain the wheat berries very well. Furthermore, it's important to add the berries to the dough near the end of the kneading cycle. If the cooked wheat berries are added to the dough early in the kneading cycle, the grains will be totally mashed into the dough, adding lots of extra moisture. It will be difficult to add enough extra flour to the dough without affecting the flavor of the bread.*

TO MIX THE DOUGH BY HAND Heat the water until warm, between 105° and 115°F; pour it into a large, warmed bowl. Add the yeast, salt, oil, honey, and molasses. Let stand 5 minutes until yeast bubbles. Add the wheat berries, whole wheat flour, and half of the bread flour. Beat until a smooth dough forms. Cover, and let stand 15 minutes. Turn the dough out onto a very lightly floured board, and knead, adding the remaining flour as necessary, until smooth and springy, about 5 minutes. Knead in the raisins. Wash the bowl and grease it; place the dough back in the bowl, and turn it over to grease the top. Cover, and let rise until doubled, about 1 hour.

TO MIX THE DOUGH WITH A HEAVY-DUTY MIXER Heat the water until warm, between 105° and 115°F; pour it into the warmed mixing bowl. Add the yeast, salt, oil, honey, and molasses. Let stand 5 minutes until yeast bubbles. Add the wheat berries, whole wheat flour, and half of the bread flour. Beat until a smooth dough forms. Cover, and let stand 15 minutes. Knead the dough in the mixer with the dough hook, on medium to high speed, adding the remaining flour as necessary, until the dough pulls away from the sides of the bowl and is smooth and springy but still soft to the touch. Knead in the raisins. Remove the dough hook, cover the bowl, and let the dough rise until doubled, about 1 hour.

TO MIX THE DOUGH IN THE FOOD PROCESSOR Place the plastic dough blade into the work bowl. Heat the water until very warm, between 120° and 130°F; set aside. Place the remaining ingredients, except the raisins, into the work bowl. Turn the processor on, and slowly pour the water through the feed tube, processing until the dough is smooth and pulls away from the sides of the bowl. If the dough is wet and sticky, add more flour, 1 tablespoon at a time, until the dough is smooth yet soft to the touch. If the dough is not soft to the touch but is very firm, add 1 tablespoon of water at a time, and process until the dough is smooth yet soft to the touch. Mix in the raisins. Cover the work bowl, and let the dough rise until doubled, about 1 hour. Or remove the dough to a lightly greased bowl, cover, and let rise until doubled, about 1 hour.

TO MIX THE DOUGH IN THE BREAD MACHINE Pour the water (at room temperature) into the pan. Add the remaining ingredients, except the wheat berries and raisins, in the order listed. Make an indentation in the dry ingredients and add the yeast. Select *Dough,* and press *Start.* If the dough is wet and sticky, add more flour, 1 tablespoon at a time, until the dough is smooth yet soft to the touch. If the dough is not soft to the touch but is very firm, add 1 teaspoon of water at a time, until the dough is smooth yet soft to the touch. Add the wheat berries and raisins when the machine signals it's time to add ingredients or when the cycle ends. The machine will stop when the dough is ready to shape and bake.

TO MIX AND BAKE THE BREAD IN THE BREAD MACHINE Pour the water (at room temperature) into the pan. Add the remaining ingredients, except the raisins, in the order listed. Make an indentation in the dry ingredients and add the yeast. Select the *Fruit and Nut, Basic,* or *Whole Wheat* cycle; set the crust on *Medium;* and press *Start.* During the mixing cycle, if the dough is wet and sticky, add more flour, 1 tablespoon at a time, until the dough is smooth yet soft to the touch. If the dough is not soft to the touch but is very firm, add 1 teaspoon of water at a time, until the dough is smooth yet soft to the touch. Add the wheat berries and raisins when the machine signals it's time to add ingredients.

TO SHAPE AND BAKE IN THE OVEN Lightly grease a baking sheet or cover it in parchment paper. Turn the dough out onto a lightly floured board or lightly oiled surface. Punch the dough down, and shape it into a round loaf. Place the loaf, with the smooth side up, onto the baking sheet. Cover and let rise in a warm place until almost doubled, 45 minutes. Preheat the oven to 375°F. Bake 25 to 35 minutes, until the loaf is golden. Remove from the pan and cool on a wire rack.

COOKING WHEAT AND RYE BERRIES

To cook wheat and rye berries, place 1 cup grain and 3 cups water in a medium saucepan. Bring to a boil, lower the heat, cover, and simmer about 45 minutes, until the grain is tender. Cool; drain very well before adding the berries to the dough (I blot the grain with a paper towel). Store leftover cooked wheat and rye berries in a plastic bag in the refrigerator for up to 3 days, or freeze for longer storage.

CRANBERRY SEMOLINA BREAD

Semolina flour is more coarsely ground than normal white flour. It is made of hard Durum wheat and is usually used in making pasta. It is often used in making French bread, where it is mixed with white bread flour. In this recipe, semolina adds texture and flavor. Dried cranberries fleck the bread, adding tart bites.

Sampler Loaf	Regular Loaf	Large Loaf
1 large egg plus water to equal 2/3 cup	1 large egg plus water to equal 1 cup	2 large eggs plus water to equal 1 1/3 cups
1 tablespoon honey	2 tablespoons honey	3 tablespoons honey
1 teaspoon butter	2 teaspoons butter	1 tablespoon butter
1 teaspoon salt	1 1/2 teaspoons salt	2 teaspoons salt
2 tablespoons nonfat dry milk	3 tablespoons nonfat dry milk	1/4 cup nonfat dry milk
1/4 cup semolina flour	1/3 cup semolina flour	1/2 cup semolina flour
3/4 cup whole wheat flour	2/3 cup whole wheat flour	1 cup whole wheat flour
1 cup bread flour	1 1/2 cups bread flour	2 cups bread flour
1 teaspoon rapid-rising or active dry yeast	1 1/2 teaspoons rapid-rising or active dry yeast	2 teaspoons rapid-rising or active dry yeast
1/4 cup dried cranberries	1/3 cup dried cranberries	1/2 cup dried cranberries

TO MIX THE DOUGH BY HAND Warm the eggs under hot tap water, and crack into a measuring cup. Heat the water until warm, between 105° and 115°F, and add it to the eggs. Pour the mixture into a warmed large bowl, and add the yeast. Let stand 5 minutes, until the yeast begins to bubble. Stir in the honey, butter, salt, dry milk, semolina flour, whole wheat flour, and half of the bread flour. Beat until smooth. Cover, and let stand 15 minutes. Slowly add the remaining bread flour, and beat until a soft dough forms.

Turn the dough out onto a very lightly floured board, and knead, adding flour if necessary, until smooth and springy, about 5 minutes. Knead in the cranberries. Wash the bowl and grease it; place the dough back in the bowl, and turn it over to grease the top. Cover, and let rise until doubled, about 1 hour.

TO MIX THE DOUGH WITH A HEAVY-DUTY MIXER Warm the eggs under hot tap water, and crack into a measuring cup. Heat the water until warm, between 105° and 115°F, and add it to the eggs. Pour the mixture into the warmed mixing bowl, and add the yeast. Let stand 5 minutes, until the yeast begins to bubble. Add the honey, butter, salt, dry milk, semolina flour, whole wheat flour, and half of the bread flour. Beat until smooth. Cover, and let stand 15 minutes. Slowly add the remaining bread flour, and beat until a soft dough forms. Knead the dough in the mixer with the dough hook, on medium to high speed, adding flour as necessary, until the dough pulls away from the sides of the bowl and is smooth and springy but still soft to the touch. Knead in the cranberries. Remove the dough hook, cover the bowl, and let the dough rise until doubled, about 1 hour.

TO MIX THE DOUGH IN THE FOOD PROCESSOR Place the plastic dough blade into the work bowl. Warm the eggs under hot tap water, and crack into a measuring cup. Heat the water until very warm, between 120° and 130°, and add it to the eggs; set aside. Place the remaining ingredients, except the cranberries, into the work bowl. Turn the processor on, and slowly pour the water mixture through the feed tube, processing until the dough is smooth and pulls away from the sides of the bowl. If the dough is wet and sticky, add more flour, 1 tablespoon at a time, until the dough is smooth yet soft to the touch. If the dough is not soft to the touch but is very firm, add 1 tablespoon of water at a time, and process until the dough is smooth yet soft to the touch. Mix in the cranberries. Cover the work bowl, and let the dough rise until doubled, about 1 hour. Or remove the dough to a lightly greased bowl, cover, and let rise until doubled, about 1 hour.

TO MIX THE DOUGH IN THE BREAD MACHINE Warm the eggs under hot tap water, and crack into a measuring cup. Add the water (at room temperature) to the eggs. Pour the water mixture into the pan. Add the remaining ingredients, except the cranberries, in the order listed. Make an indentation in the dry ingredients and add the yeast. Select *Dough,* and press *Start.* If the dough is wet and sticky, add more flour, 1 tablespoon at a time, until the dough is smooth yet soft to the touch. If the dough is not soft to the touch but is very firm, add 1 teaspoon of water at a time, until the dough is smooth yet soft to the touch. Add the cranberries when the machine signals it's time to add ingredients or when the cycle ends. The machine will stop when the dough is ready to shape and bake.

TO MIX AND BAKE THE BREAD IN THE BREAD MACHINE Warm the eggs under hot tap water, and crack into a measuring cup. Add the water (at room temperature) to the eggs. Pour the water mixture into the pan. Add the remaining ingredients, except the cranberries, in the order listed. Make an indentation in the dry ingredients and add the yeast. Select the *Fruit and Nut, Basic,* or *Whole Wheat* cycle; set the crust on *Medium;* and press *Start.* During the mixing cycle, if the dough is wet and sticky, add more flour, 1 tablespoon at a time, until the dough is smooth yet soft to the touch. If the dough is not soft to the touch but is very firm, add 1 teaspoon of water at a time, until the dough is smooth yet soft to the touch. Add the cranberries when the machine signals it's time to add ingredients.

TO SHAPE AND BAKE IN THE OVEN Lightly grease an 8- or 9-inch round cake pan or baking sheet. Turn the dough out onto a lightly floured board or lightly oiled surface. Punch the dough down, and shape it into a round loaf. Place the loaf, with the smooth side up, into the pan. Cover and let rise in a warm place until almost doubled, 45 minutes. Preheat the oven to 375°F. Bake 30 to 35 minutes, until the loaf is golden and a wooden skewer inserted into the loaf comes out clean and dry. Remove from the pan and cool on a wire rack.

WHOLE WHEAT RAISIN-NUT BREAD

My favorite breads for snacking and sandwiches have fruit and nuts added. This bread is particularly good with thinly sliced sharp Cheddar cheese or Norwegian Gjetost.

Sampler Loaf

2/3 cup water

1 tablespoon butter

3/4 teaspoon salt

3/4 teaspoon cinnamon

1 1/2 teaspoons packed
    brown sugar

1 tablespoon nonfat dry milk

2 cups whole wheat flour

1 tablespoon gluten

1 1/4 teaspoons rapid-rising or
    active dry yeast

1/4 cup raisins

1/4 cup chopped walnuts

Regular Loaf

1 cup water

1 1/2 tablespoons butter

1 teaspoon salt

1 teaspoon cinnamon

1 tablespoon packed brown sugar

1 1/2 tablespoons nonfat dry milk

3 cups whole wheat flour

1 1/2 tablespoons gluten

1 1/2 teaspoons rapid-rising or
    active dry yeast

1/2 cup raisins

1/2 cup chopped walnuts

Large Loaf

1 1/3 cups water

2 tablespoons butter

1 1/2 teaspoons salt

1 1/2 teaspoons cinnamon

1 1/2 tablespoons packed
    brown sugar

2 tablespoons nonfat dry milk

4 cups whole wheat flour

2 tablespoons gluten

2 teaspoons rapid-rising or active
    dry yeast

3/4 cup raisins

3/4 cup chopped walnuts

TO MIX THE DOUGH BY HAND Heat the water until warm, between 105° and 115°F; pour it into a large, warmed bowl. Add the yeast, salt, cinnamon, sugar, and dry milk. Let stand 5 minutes, until the yeast begins to bubble. Stir in the butter and half of the whole wheat flour. Beat until smooth. Cover, and let stand 15 minutes. Slowly add the remaining whole wheat flour, and beat until a soft dough forms. Turn the dough out onto a very lightly floured board, and knead, adding flour if necessary, until smooth and springy, about 5 minutes. Knead in the raisins and the walnuts. Wash the bowl and grease it;

place the dough back in the bowl, and turn it over to grease the top. Cover, and let rise until doubled, about 1 hour.

TO MIX THE DOUGH WITH A HEAVY-DUTY MIXER Add the yeast, salt, cinnamon, sugar, and dry milk. Let stand 5 minutes, until the yeast begins to bubble. Stir in the butter and half of the whole wheat flour. Beat until smooth. Cover, and let stand 15 minutes. Slowly add the remaining whole wheat flour, and beat until a soft dough forms. Knead the dough in the mixer with the dough hook, on medium to high speed, adding flour as necessary, until the dough pulls away from the sides of the bowl and is smooth and springy but still soft to the touch. Knead in the raisins and nuts. Remove the dough hook, cover the bowl, and let the dough rise until doubled, about 1 hour.

TO MIX THE DOUGH IN THE FOOD PROCESSOR Place the plastic dough blade into the work bowl. Heat the water until very warm, between 120° and 130°F; set aside. Place the remaining ingredients, except the raisins and walnuts, into the work bowl. Turn the processor on, and slowly pour the water through the feed tube, processing until the dough is smooth and pulls away from the sides of the bowl. If the dough is wet and sticky, add more flour, 1 tablespoon at a time, until the dough is smooth yet soft to the touch. If the dough is not soft to the touch but is very firm, add 1 tablespoon of water at a time, and process until the dough is smooth yet soft to the touch. Mix in the raisins and walnuts. Cover the work bowl, and let the dough rise until doubled, about 1 hour. Or remove the dough to a lightly greased bowl, cover, and let rise until doubled, about 1 hour.

TO MIX THE DOUGH IN THE BREAD MACHINE Pour the water (at room temperature) into the pan. Add the remaining ingredients, except the raisins and walnuts, in the order listed. Make an indentation in the dry ingredients and add the yeast. Select *Dough,* and press *Start.* If the dough is wet and sticky, add more flour, 1 tablespoon at a time, until the dough is smooth yet soft to the touch. If the dough is not soft to the touch but is very firm, add 1 teaspoon of water at a time, until the dough is smooth yet soft

to the touch. Add the raisins and walnuts when the machine signals it's time to add ingredients or when the cycle ends. The machine will stop when the dough is ready to shape and bake.

TO MIX AND BAKE THE BREAD IN THE BREAD MACHINE Pour the water (at room temperature) into the pan. Add the remaining ingredients, except the raisins and walnuts, in the order listed. Make an indentation in the dry ingredients and add the yeast. Select the *Fruit and Nut, Basic,* or *Whole Wheat* cycle; set the crust on *Medium;* and press *Start.* During the mixing cycle, if the dough is wet and sticky, add more flour, 1 tablespoon at a time, until the dough is smooth yet soft to the touch. If the dough is not soft to the touch but is very firm, add 1 teaspoon of water at a time, until the dough is smooth yet soft to the touch. Add the raisins and walnuts when the machine signals it's time to add ingredients.

TO SHAPE AND BAKE IN THE OVEN Lightly grease an 8 × 4-inch or 9 × 5-inch loaf pan. Turn the dough out onto a lightly floured board or lightly oiled surface. Punch the dough down, and shape it into an oblong loaf. Place the loaf, with the smooth side up, into the pan. Cover and let rise in a warm place until almost doubled, 45 to 60 minutes. Preheat the oven to 375°F. Bake 30 to 35 minutes, until the loaf is golden. Remove from the pan and cool on a wire rack.

WILD RICE AND
THREE-GRAIN BREAD

After cooking, the wild rice needs to be very well drained before you add it to this bread. Sometimes I measure it onto a paper towel, so I can blot it before adding it to the dough. Cook the rice according to the package directions (or see below). For bread baked in the machine, the sunflower seeds will stay on the outside, encrusting the loaf.

Sampler Loaf	**Regular Loaf**	**Large Loaf**
2/3 cup water	1 cup water	1 1/3 cups water
1 tablespoon canola oil	2 tablespoons canola oil	3 tablespoons canola oil
1 teaspoon salt	1 1/2 teaspoons salt	2 teaspoons salt
1 tablespoon honey	2 tablespoons honey	3 tablespoons honey
2 tablespoons old-fashioned rolled oats	1/4 cup old-fashioned rolled oats	1/3 cup old-fashioned rolled oats
2 tablespoons rye flour	1/4 cup rye flour	1/3 cup rye flour
1/4 cup whole wheat flour	1/3 cup whole wheat flour	1/2 cup whole wheat flour
1 1/2 cups bread flour	2 1/3 cups bread flour	3 cups bread flour
1 teaspoon rapid-rising or active dry yeast	1 1/2 teaspoons rapid-rising or active dry yeast	2 teaspoons rapid-rising or active dry yeast
1/4 cup cooked wild rice*	1/3 cup cooked wild rice*	1/2 cup cooked wild rice*

TOPPING

2 to 3 tablespoons roasted and salted sunflower seeds

GLAZE FOR BREAD BAKED CONVENTIONALLY

1 egg

1 tablespoon water or milk

*Note   *Especially for bread mixed in the machine, the wild rice must be very well drained. If you are mixing the dough in the machine, you really need to watch the dough as it begins to be kneaded: Because of the added moisture in the cooked wild rice, the dough may need as much as 4 to 5 tablespoons of additional bread flour. Watch and feel the dough as it goes through its initial kneading. The extra trouble is worth the effort, since this is a very delicious, grainy bread. Even when the rice is added at the end of the cycle it may soften the dough, so it needs careful watching. It's very important that the rice be very well drained. The extra trouble is definitely worth it!*

TO MIX THE DOUGH BY HAND Heat the water until warm, between 105° and 115°F; pour it into a large, warmed bowl, and add the yeast. Let stand 5 minutes, until the yeast begins to bubble. Stir in the oil, salt, honey, rolled oats, rye flour, and whole wheat flour. Cover, and let stand 15 minutes. Slowly add the bread flour, and beat until a smooth dough forms. Cover, and let stand 15 minutes. Turn the dough out onto a very lightly floured board, and knead, adding flour if necessary, until smooth and springy, about 5 minutes. Knead in the wild rice. Wash the bowl and grease it; place the dough back in the bowl, and turn it over to grease the top. Cover, and let rise until doubled, about 1 hour.

TO MIX THE DOUGH WITH A HEAVY-DUTY MIXER Heat the water until warm, between 105° and 115°F; pour it into the warmed mixing bowl, and add the yeast. Let stand 5 minutes, until the yeast begins to bubble. Add the oil, salt, honey, rolled oats rye flour, and whole wheat flour. Cover, and let stand 15 minutes. Slowly add the bread flour, and beat until a smooth dough forms. Knead the dough in the mixer with the dough hook, on medium to high speed, adding flour as necessary, until the dough pulls away from the sides of the bowl and is smooth and springy but still soft to the touch. Knead in the wild rice. Remove the dough hook, cover the bowl, and let the dough rise until doubled, about 1 hour.

TO MIX THE DOUGH IN THE FOOD PROCESSOR Place the plastic dough blade into the work bowl. Heat the water until very warm, between 120° and 130°F; set aside. Place the remaining ingredients, except the wild rice, into the work bowl. Turn the processor on, and slowly pour the water through the feed tube, processing until the dough is smooth and pulls away from the sides of the bowl. If the dough is wet and sticky, add more flour, 1 tablespoon at a time, until the dough is smooth yet soft to the touch. If the dough is not soft to the touch but is very firm, add 1 tablespoon of water at a time, and process until the dough is smooth yet soft to the touch. Mix in the wild rice. Cover the work bowl, and let the dough rise until doubled, about 1 hour. Or remove the dough to a lightly greased bowl, cover, and let rise until doubled, about 1 hour.

TO MIX THE DOUGH IN THE BREAD MACHINE Pour the water (at room temperature) into the pan. Add the remaining ingredients, except the wild rice, in the order listed. Make an indentation in the dry ingredients and add the yeast. Select *Dough,* and press *Start.* If the dough is wet and sticky, add more flour, 1 tablespoon at a time, until the dough is smooth yet soft to the touch. If the dough is not soft to the touch but is very firm, add 1 teaspoon of water at a time, until the dough is smooth yet soft to the touch. Add the wild rice when the machine signals it's time to add ingredients or when the cycle ends. The machine will stop when the dough is ready to shape and bake.

TO MIX AND BAKE THE BREAD IN THE BREAD MACHINE Pour the water (at room temperature) into the pan. Add the remaining ingredients, except the wild rice, in the order listed. Make an indentation in the dry ingredients and add the yeast. Select the *Fruit and Nut, Basic,* or *Whole Wheat* cycle; set the crust on *Medium;* and press *Start.* During the mixing cycle, if the dough is wet and sticky, add more flour, 1 tablespoon at a time, until the dough is smooth yet soft to the touch. If the dough is not soft to the touch but is very firm, add 1 teaspoon of water at a time, until the dough is smooth yet soft to the touch. Add the wild rice when the machine signals it's time to add ingredients. When the second rising is done, just before the bread begins to bake, sprinkle on the sunflower seeds.

TO SHAPE AND BAKE IN THE OVEN Lightly grease a baking sheet or cover it with parchment paper. Turn the dough out onto a lightly floured board or lightly oiled surface. Punch the dough down, and shape it into a round loaf. Or divide the dough into three parts, roll each part into an 18-inch strand. Braid the strands, and form the loaf into a wreath shape; pinch and seal the seams and ends. Place the loaf, with the smooth side up, onto the baking sheet. Cover and let rise in a warm place until almost doubled, 45 minutes. Preheat the oven to 375°F. To glaze, beat the egg with the water, brush the mixture on the loaf, and sprinkle on the sunflower seeds. Bake 25 to 30 minutes, until the loaf is golden. Remove from the pan and cool on a wire rack.

COOKING WILD RICE

To cook wild rice, wash 1 cup rice in three changes of hot tap water to remove all dust and foreign particles. Place the rice into a medium saucepan and add 3 cups water. Bring to a boil, lower the heat, cover, and simmer for about 30 minutes, until the wild rice kernels are very well cooked. Let stand until cool, about 30 minutes. Pour into a sieve and drain very well.

Hummus

This popular Middle Eastern dip is basically a purée of chick-peas (garbanzo beans). I flavor it lots of different ways, depending on what I have on hand. Although it is traditionally served with pita bread, hummus makes a great spread for almost any whole grain bread. My personal favorite is to spread it on a multigrain bread and top it with a slice of fresh, juicy tomato! You can use canned chick-peas, but I think the flavor of the freshly cooked peas is always better. You do need to remember to soak them overnight; but they take only about 45 minutes to simmer to tenderness.

ABOUT 2 CUPS

1 cup dried chick-peas (garbanzo beans)
3 large garlic cloves
1/4 cup tahini*
2 tablespoons freshly squeezed lemon juice
1/4 cup minced green onion (optional)

1 tablespoon extra-virgin olive oil
1 to 2 teaspoons salt, or to taste
1/4 teaspoon freshly ground black pepper
Red pepper flakes, to taste

Rinse and pick over the chick-peas; drain. Place the peas in a large saucepan, cover with water, and let stand overnight until the peas have about doubled in size. Drain, return the peas to the saucepan, and cover with fresh water. Add the whole garlic cloves, and bring to a boil. Lower the heat, and simmer for about 45 minutes, until tender. Cool. Drain the chick-peas, saving the liquid.

Place the chick-peas in the work bowl of a food processor fitted with the steel blade. Process until smooth. Add the tahini, lemon juice, green onions, oil, salt, and black pepper. Process until smooth and creamy, adding some of the bean liquid as necessary to achieve the desired consistency. Transfer to a serving bowl. Sprinkle with red pepper flakes, if desired.

Curried Hummus: Add 1 to 2 teaspoons curry powder along with the salt and black pepper.

Hummus with Roasted Red Peppers: Add 1/2 cup well-drained, roasted, peeled, and seeded red bell peppers along with the green onions.

*Note   *Tahini is a thick paste made from ground sesame seeds. It resembles peanut butter in texture and is used in Middle Eastern cooking to flavor dishes such as hummus and baba ganoush.*

Caraway-Onion Rye Bread

Green Salad with Spicy Croutons

Carrot-Sunflower Wheat Bread

Carrot Wheat Bread with Walnuts and Raisins

Carrot Pudding with Buttery Sauce

Dill, Onion, Rye, and Wheat Bread

Crabmeat Crostini

Kalamata Olive and Herb Bread

Fresh Tomato and Corn Salad with Feta Cheese
and Garlic Croutons

Potato Rye Bread

Savory Rosemary and Cheese Bread Pudding

Potato Wheat Bread

Wild Mushroom Pudding

Rye and Sauerkraut Bread

Spinach-Feta Whole Wheat Bread

Sun-Dried Tomato and Pesto Bread

Sun-Dried Tomato and Parmesan Wheat Bread

Tomato-Basil Semolina Baguettes

Herbed Garlic Butter

Tomato Wheat Baguettes with Garlic and Rosemary

Tomato Basil Crostini

four

BREADS WITH WHOLE GRAINS AND VEGETABLES

Spinach, potatoes, tomatoes, sauerkraut, corn, onions, and carrots add color, flavor, and texture to whole grain yeast breads differently from the way they do for quick breads. Over the years, I've incorporated almost any vegetable you can think of into a bread.

As a penny-pinching student, I couldn't imagine throwing even a cup of soup away. Into the bread it would go! I would use whole grain rather than white flour for aesthetic reasons. Vegetable mixtures can turn a white dough into dirty gray, even though the flavor is wonderful; a whole grain bread, however, becomes enriched in color.

Leftover juices and soups and puréed cooked vegetables—added as part of the liquid component of a dough—combined with whole grain flour make delicious, hearty loaves. For example, try tomato juice or puréed tomatoes with garlic and rosemary in a wheat bread shaped into a baguette. Or put a purée of leftover cooked carrots in a whole wheat dough; add walnuts and raisins; and shape it into a fat, round loaf. Or bake mashed potatoes into a wheat bread and serve warm with Boursin.

The basic challenge of using puréed vegetables or leftover vegetables in a bread is maintaining the balance of liquid to flour. You need to be very watchful. Pay attention to the directions for adding extra flour or liquid to your dough (included with each recipe). When dehydrated vegetables are added to a bread dough (such as dried onions or potatoes), it is much easier to control the liquid to flour balance.

CARAWAY-ONION RYE BREAD

This bread is perfect for an Octoberfest menu, with sauerbraten or German sausages and garlic mashed potatoes. Sometimes I shape this dough into rolls to make chicken sandwiches for a picnic.

Sampler Loaf	Regular Loaf	Large Loaf
2/3 cup water	1 cup water	1 1/3 cups water
1 teaspoon freshly squeezed lemon juice	2 teaspoons freshly squeezed lemon juice	1 tablespoon freshly squeezed lemon juice
1 tablespoon sugar	2 tablespoons sugar	3 tablespoons sugar
1 teaspoon salt	1 1/2 teaspoons salt	2 teaspoons salt
1 teaspoon caraway seeds	1 1/2 teaspoons caraway seeds	2 teaspoons caraway seeds
2 tablespoons dried onion flakes	3 tablespoons dried onion flakes	1/4 cup dried onion flakes
2 teaspoons extra-virgin olive or canola oil	1 tablespoon extra-virgin olive or canola oil	1 1/2 tablespoons extra-virgin olive or canola oil
1/2 cup rye flour	3/4 cup rye flour	1 cup rye flour
1 1/2 cups bread flour	2 1/4 cups bread flour	3 cups bread flour
1 teaspoon gluten	1 tablespoon gluten	1 1/2 tablespoons gluten
1 teaspoon rapid-rising or active dry yeast	1 1/2 teaspoons rapid-rising or active dry yeast	2 teaspoons rapid-rising or active dry yeast

TO MIX THE DOUGH BY HAND Heat the water until warm, between 105° and 115°F; pour it into a large, warmed bowl, and add the yeast, caraway seeds, onion flakes, lemon juice, and sugar. Let stand 5 minutes, until the yeast begins to bubble. Stir in the salt, oil, and rye flour. Cover, and let stand 15 minutes. Slowly add the bread flour, and beat until a smooth dough forms. Turn the dough out onto a very lightly floured board, and knead, adding flour if necessary, until smooth and springy, about 5 minutes. Wash the bowl and grease it; place the dough back in the bowl, and turn it over to grease the top. Cover, and let rise until doubled, about 1 hour.

TO MIX THE DOUGH WITH A HEAVY-DUTY MIXER Heat the water until warm, between 105° and 115°F; pour it into the warmed mixing bowl, and add the yeast, lemon juice, and sugar. Let stand 5 minutes, until the yeast begins to bubble. Add the salt, caraway seeds, onion flakes, oil, and rye flour. Cover, and let stand 15 minutes.

Slowly add the bread flour, and beat until a smooth dough forms. Knead the dough in the mixer with the dough hook, on medium to high speed, adding flour as necessary, until the dough pulls away from the sides of the bowl and is smooth and springy but still soft to the touch. Remove the dough hook, cover the bowl, and let the dough rise until doubled, about 1 hour.

TO MIX THE DOUGH IN THE FOOD PROCESSOR Place the plastic dough blade into the work bowl. Heat the water until very warm, between 120° and 130°F; set aside. Place the remaining ingredients into the work bowl. Turn the processor on, and slowly pour the water through the feed tube, processing until the dough is smooth and pulls away from the sides of the bowl. If the dough is wet and sticky, add more flour, 1 tablespoon at a time, until the dough is smooth yet soft to the touch. If the dough is not soft to the touch but is very firm, add 1 tablespoon of water at a time, and process until the dough is smooth yet soft to the touch. Cover the work bowl, and let the dough rise until doubled, about 1 hour. Or remove the dough to a lightly greased bowl, cover, and let rise until doubled, about 1 hour.

TO MIX THE DOUGH IN THE BREAD MACHINE Pour the water (at room temperature) into the pan. Add the remaining ingredients, in the order listed. Make an indentation in the dry ingredients and add the yeast. Select *Dough,* and press *Start.* If the dough is wet and sticky, add more flour, 1 tablespoon at a time, until the dough is smooth yet soft to the touch. If the dough is not soft to the touch but is very firm, add 1 teaspoon of water at a time, until the dough is smooth yet soft to the touch. The machine will stop when the dough is ready to shape and bake.

TO MIX AND BAKE THE BREAD IN THE BREAD MACHINE Pour the water (at room temperature) into the pan. Add the remaining ingredients, in the order listed. Make an indentation in the dry ingredients and add the yeast. Select the *Basic* or *Whole Wheat* cycle, set the crust on *Medium,* and press *Start.* During the mixing cycle, if the dough is wet and sticky, add more flour, 1 tablespoon at a time, until the dough is smooth yet soft to the touch. If the dough is not soft to the touch but is very firm, add 1 teaspoon of water at a time, until the dough is smooth yet soft to the touch.

TO SHAPE AND BAKE IN THE OVEN Lightly grease a baking sheet or cover it with parchment paper. Turn the dough out on a lightly floured board or lightly oil surface. Punch the dough down, and shape it into an oblong loaf. Place the loaf, with the smooth side up, onto the baking sheet. Cover and let rise in a warm place until almost doubled, 1 hour. Preheat the oven to 350°F. Bake 35 to 45 minutes, until the loaf sounds hollow when tapped and a wooden skewer inserted into the loaf comes out clean and dry. Brush the top of the loaf while it's still hot with melted butter, if desired. Remove from the pan and cool on a wire rack.

FOR SANDWICH ROLLS Divide the dough into equal parts. You should get 6 parts from the sampler-size dough, 9 parts from the regular-size dough, and 12 parts from the large-size dough. Shape each part into a roll. Place the rolls in the prepared pan, with the smooth side up. Continue with the recipe, except bake 15 minutes, until lightly browned.

Green Salad with Spicy Croutons

My favorite salad is made up of mixed baby greens, tossed simply with spicy oil and vinegar and then topped with chili-spiced toasted wheat bread croutons.

4 TO 6 SERVINGS

1 cup bread cubes, cut $1/2$ inch, made from day-old wheat bread

2 teaspoons chili oil

$1/2$ teaspoon chili powder

$1/2$ teaspoon coarse (kosher) salt

1 large garlic clove, finely chopped

1 tablespoon Dijon-style mustard

2 teaspoons red wine or balsamic vinegar

$1/4$ teaspoon salt

$1/4$ teaspoon freshly ground pepper

3 tablespoons extra-virgin olive oil

1 quart loosely packed mixed salad greens, torn into 2-inch pieces

Preheat the oven to 400°F. In a medium bowl, toss the bread cubes with the chili oil, chili spices, and $1/2$ teaspoon coarse salt. Spread the cubes on a baking sheet, and bake 10 minutes, until the cubes are lightly browned, turning them once.

In a salad bowl, mix the garlic, mustard, vinegar, $1/4$ teaspoon salt, and pepper together. Whisk in the olive oil. Just before serving, add the mixed greens to the bowl and toss to coat with the dressing. Sprinkle with the croutons.

CARROT-SUNFLOWER WHEAT BREAD

Crunchy with sunflower seeds and flecked with carrot, this bread is wonderful spread with hummus (page 173) and topped with a slice of juicy garden-ripe tomato. Toasted pumpkin seeds from the health food store make a great substitute for the sunflower seeds.

Sampler Loaf

$2/3$ cup water

$3/4$ teaspoon salt

1 tablespoon extra-virgin olive oil

1 tablespoon honey

1 tablespoon nonfat dry milk

1 tablespoon wheat germ

$1/4$ cup bran flakes

$1/4$ cup shredded fresh carrot

$1/4$ cup sunflower seeds

$1/2$ cup whole wheat flour

$1^1/2$ cups bread flour

1 teaspoon rapid-rising or active dry yeast

Regular Loaf

1 cup water

1 teaspoon salt

$1^1/2$ tablespoons extra-virgin olive oil

$1^1/2$ tablespoons honey

$1^1/2$ tablespoons nonfat dry milk

$1^1/2$ tablespoons wheat germ

$1/3$ cup bran flakes

$1/3$ cup shredded fresh carrot

$1/4$ cup sunflower seeds

$3/4$ cup whole wheat flour

$2^1/4$ cups bread flour

$1^1/2$ teaspoons rapid-rising or active dry yeast

Large Loaf

$1^1/3$ cups water

$1^1/2$ teaspoons salt

2 tablespoons extra-virgin olive oil

2 tablespoons honey

2 tablespoons nonfat dry milk

2 tablespoons wheat germ

$1/2$ cup bran flakes

$1/2$ cup shredded fresh carrot

$1/2$ cup sunflower seeds

1 cup whole wheat flour

3 cups bread flour

2 teaspoons rapid-rising or active dry yeast

GLAZE FOR BREAD BAKED CONVENTIONALLY

1 egg, beaten

Roasted and salted
    sunflower seeds

TO MIX THE DOUGH BY HAND Heat the water until warm, between 105° and 115°F; pour it into a large, warmed bowl, and add the yeast. Let stand 5 minutes, until the yeast begins to bubble. Stir in the remaining ingredients, except the bread flour. Cover, and let stand 15 minutes. Slowly add the bread flour, and beat until a smooth dough forms. Turn the dough out onto a very lightly floured board, and knead, adding flour if necessary, until smooth and springy, about 5 minutes. Wash the bowl and grease it; place the dough back in the bowl, and turn it over to grease the top. Cover, and let rise until doubled, about 1 hour.

TO MIX THE DOUGH WITH A HEAVY-DUTY MIXER

Heat the water until warm, between 105° and 115°F; pour it into the warmed mixing bowl, and add the yeast. Let stand 5 minutes, until the yeast begins to bubble. Add the remaining ingredients, except the bread flour. Cover, and let stand 15 minutes. Slowly add the bread flour, and beat until a smooth dough forms. Knead the dough in the mixer with the dough hook, on medium to high speed, adding flour as necessary, until the dough pulls away from the sides of the bowl and is smooth and springy but still soft to the touch. Remove the dough hook, cover the bowl, and let the dough rise until doubled, about 1 hour.

TO MIX THE DOUGH IN THE FOOD PROCESSOR

Place the plastic dough blade into the work bowl. Heat the water until very warm, between 120° and 130°F; set aside. Place the remaining ingredients into the work bowl. Turn the processor on, and slowly pour the water through the feed tube, processing until the dough is smooth and pulls away from the sides of the bowl. If the dough is wet and sticky, add more flour, 1 tablespoon at a time, until the dough is smooth yet soft to the touch. If the dough is not soft to the touch but is very firm, add 1 tablespoon of water at a time, and process until the dough is smooth yet soft to the touch. Cover the work bowl, and let the dough rise until doubled, about 1 hour. Or remove the dough to a lightly greased bowl, cover, and let rise until doubled, about 1 hour.

TO MIX THE DOUGH IN THE BREAD MACHINE

Pour the water (at room temperature) into the pan. Add the remaining ingredients, in the order listed. Make an indentation in the dry ingredients and add the yeast. Select *Dough,* and press *Start.* If the dough is wet and sticky, add more flour, 1 tablespoon at a time, until the dough is smooth yet soft to the touch. If the dough is not soft to the touch but is very firm, add 1 teaspoon of water at a time, until the dough is smooth yet soft to the touch. The machine will stop when the dough is ready to shape and bake.

TO MIX AND BAKE THE BREAD IN THE BREAD MACHINE

Pour the water (at room temperature) into the pan. Add the remaining ingredients, in the order listed. Make an indentation in the dry ingredients and add the yeast. Select the *Basic* or *Whole Wheat* cycle, set the crust on *Medium,* and press *Start.* During the mixing cycle, if the dough is wet and sticky, add more flour, 1 tablespoon at a time, until the dough is smooth yet soft to the touch. If the dough is not soft to the touch but is very firm, add 1 teaspoon of water at a time, until the dough is smooth yet soft to the touch.

TO SHAPE AND BAKE IN THE OVEN

Lightly grease a baking sheet in a warm place. Punch the dough down, and shape it into a round loaf. Place the loaf, with the smooth side up, onto the baking sheet. Cover and let rise in a warm place until almost doubled, 60 minutes. Preheat the oven to 350°F. To glaze, brush the loaf with the egg, and sprinkle on the sunflower seeds. Bake 25 to 45 minutes, until the loaf is golden and a wooden skewer inserted into the loaf comes out clean and dry. Remove from the pan and cool on a wire rack.

CARROT WHEAT BREAD WITH WALNUTS AND RAISINS

Cook a few extra carrots when you're making dinner, just so you can make this bread. It's extra special thinly sliced and spread with cream cheese, served with a salad or at tea time.

Sampler Loaf

1/3 cup water

1/3 cup puréed cooked carrot

3/4 teaspoon salt

1 tablespoon vegetable oil

1 tablespoon honey

1/2 cup whole wheat flour

1 1/2 cups bread flour

1 teaspoon rapid-rising or active dry yeast

1/2 cup raisins

1/2 cup chopped walnuts

Regular Loaf

1/2 cup water

1/2 cup puréed cooked carrot

1 teaspoon salt

1 1/2 tablespoons vegetable oil

1 1/2 tablespoons honey

3/4 cup whole wheat flour

2 1/4 cups bread flour

1 1/2 teaspoons rapid-rising or active dry yeast

3/4 cup raisins

3/4 cup chopped walnuts

Large Loaf

2/3 cup water

2/3 cup puréed cooked carrot

1 1/2 teaspoons salt

2 tablespoons vegetable oil

2 tablespoons honey

1 cup whole wheat flour

3 cups bread flour

2 teaspoons rapid-rising or active dry yeast

1 cup raisins

1 cup chopped walnuts

TO MIX THE DOUGH BY HAND Mix the water and carrot purée, and heat until warm, between 105° and 115°F; pour the mixture into a large, warmed bowl, and add the yeast and honey. Let stand 5 minutes, until the yeast begins to bubble. Stir in the salt, oil, and whole wheat flour. Cover, and let stand 15 minutes. Slowly add the bread flour, and beat until a smooth dough forms. Turn the dough out onto a very lightly floured board, and knead, adding flour if necessary, until smooth and springy, about 5 minutes. Knead in the raisins and walnuts. Wash the bowl and grease it; place the dough back in the bowl, and turn it over to grease the top. Cover, and let rise until doubled, about 1 hour.

TO MIX THE DOUGH WITH A HEAVY-DUTY MIXER Mix the water and carrot purée, and heat until warm, between 105° and 115°F; pour the mixture into the warmed mixing bowl, and add the yeast. Let stand 5 minutes, until the yeast begins to bubble. Add the salt, oil, and whole wheat flour. Cover, and let stand 15 minutes. Slowly add the bread flour, and beat until a smooth dough forms. Knead the dough in the mixer with the dough hook, on medium to high speed, adding flour as necessary, until the dough pulls away from the sides of the bowl and is smooth and springy but still soft to the touch. Knead in the raisins and walnuts. Remove the dough hook, cover the bowl, and let the dough rise until doubled, about 1 hour.

TO MIX THE DOUGH IN THE FOOD PROCESSOR Place the plastic dough blade into the work bowl. Heat the water until very warm, between 120° and 130°F; set aside. Place the remaining ingredients, except the raisins and walnuts, into the work bowl. Turn the processor on, and slowly pour the water through the feed tube, processing until the dough is smooth and pulls away from the sides of the bowl. If the dough is wet and sticky, add more flour, 1 tablespoon at a time, until the dough is smooth yet soft to the touch. If the dough is not soft to the touch but is very firm, add 1 tablespoon of water at a time, and process until the dough is smooth yet soft to the touch. Mix in the raisins and walnuts. Cover the work bowl, and let the dough rise until doubled, about 1 hour. Or remove the dough to a lightly greased bowl, cover, and let rise until doubled, about 1 hour.

TO MIX THE DOUGH IN THE BREAD MACHINE Pour the water and carrot purée (both at room temperature) into the pan. Add the remaining ingredients, except the raisins and walnuts, in the order listed. Make an indentation in the dry ingredients and add the yeast. Select *Dough,* and press *Start.* If the dough is wet and sticky, add more flour, 1 tablespoon at a time, until the dough is smooth yet soft to the touch. If

the dough is not soft to the touch but is very firm, add 1 teaspoon of water at a time, until the dough is smooth yet soft to the touch. Add the raisins and walnuts when the machine signals it's time to add ingredients or when the cycle ends. The machine will stop when the dough is ready to shape and bake.

TO MIX AND BAKE THE BREAD IN THE BREAD MACHINE Pour the water and carrot purée (both at room temperature) into the pan. Add the remaining ingredients, except the raisins and walnuts, in the order listed. Make an indentation in the dry ingredients and add the yeast. Select the *Basic* or *Whole Wheat* cycle; set the crust on *Medium;* and press *Start.* During the mixing cycle, if the dough is wet and sticky, add more flour, 1 tablespoon at a time, until the dough is smooth yet soft to the touch. If the dough is not soft to the touch but is very firm, add 1 teaspoon of water at a time, until the dough is smooth yet soft to the touch. Add the raisins and walnuts when the machine signals it's time to add ingredients.

TO SHAPE AND BAKE IN THE OVEN Lightly grease a baking sheet. Turn the dough out onto a lightly floured board or lightly oiled surface. Punch the dough down, and shape it into a round loaf. Place the loaf, with the smooth side up, onto the baking sheet. Cover and let rise in a warm place until almost doubled, 1 hour. Preheat the oven to 350°F. Bake 25 to 45 minutes, until the loaf sounds hollow when tapped and a wooden skewer inserted into the loaf comes out clean and dry. Remove from the pan and cool on a wire rack.

Carrot Pudding with Buttery Sauce

Because of their sweetness and texture, carrots, though neither fruit nor berry, have been used since early colonial days as an ingredient in desserts. This pudding can be steamed or baked and is absolutely irresistible with the Buttery Sauce. I have to admit that it tastes the best to me in the autumn, when the leaves are turning and thoughts of the upcoming holidays are in my mind.

8 SERVINGS

1 cup all-purpose flour

1 teaspoon baking soda

1 teaspoon cinnamon

1 teaspoon freshly grated nutmeg

1 teaspoon allspice

1/2 teaspoon ground cloves

1/2 teaspoon salt

1 cup fine dry bread crumbs made from Carrot Wheat Bread with Walnuts and Raisins (page 182) or other whole wheat bread

1 cup packed brown sugar

1 cup finely shredded raw carrot

1 cup shredded raw potato

1 cup chopped raisins

1 cup chopped walnuts

1 cup chopped or ground suet

1 tablespoon dark molasses

2 eggs, lightly beaten

Butter Sauce (recipe follows)

If steaming the pudding, butter a 2-quart steaming or pudding mold, and boil a kettle of water. If baking the pudding, butter an 8-cup ring mold, and preheat the oven to 350°F.

In a large bowl, combine all of the ingredients, except the molasses and eggs, in the order given. Mix the molasses and eggs together, then stir into the vegetable mixture. Turn the mixture into the mold.

If steaming the pudding, cover the top of the mold with waxed paper and then with a square of folded muslin. Place the mold onto a rack in a deep steamer kettle or roaster. Add boiling water to the kettle, up to the level of the rack. Cover the kettle and maintain a simmer, adding water if necessary. Steam 3 hours, until a skewer inserted through the center comes out clean.

If baking the pudding, cover the mold tightly with foil. Place the mold into a larger pan and pour water in the pan to reach halfway up the side of the mold. Bake 1 hour, until a skewer inserted through the center comes out clean.

Remove the pudding from mold and serve warm. Or wrap and freeze; rewarm by steaming the pudding or heating in a microwave oven until it is warm. Be careful not to overheat the pudding. Serve with the Buttery Sauce.

Buttery Sauce

3 CUPS

1/2 cup (1 stick) butter
1 cup packed brown sugar
1 large egg
1 tablespoon white wine vinegar
Dash freshly grated nutmeg
1 teaspoon vanilla
1 cup heavy cream, whipped

Bring water in the bottom of a double boiler to boiling. In the top of the double boiler, off the heat, cream the butter and brown sugar. Add the egg and vinegar, and beat until light and fluffy. Add the nutmeg. Place over boiling water and cook, stirring constantly, 10 minutes, until thickened. Add the vanilla. Chill. Just before serving, fold in the whipped cream.

DILL, ONION, RYE, AND WHEAT BREAD

Delicious, tender, aromatic. I can't decide if I like it better for sandwiches or buttered and served with freshly made vegetable chowder.

Sampler Loaf	Regular Loaf	Large Loaf
1/3 cup water	1/2 cup water	2/3 cup water
1 1/2 teaspoons sugar	2 teaspoons sugar	1 tablespoon sugar
1 large egg	1 large egg	1 large egg
1/2 cup creamed cottage cheese	3/4 cup creamed cottage cheese	1 cup creamed cottage cheese
2 teaspoons butter	1 tablespoon butter	2 tablespoons butter
1 teaspoon salt	1 1/2 teaspoons salt	2 teaspoons salt
1 1/2 teaspoons dillweed	2 teaspoons dillweed	1 tablespoon dillweed
2 teaspoons dried onion flakes	1 tablespoon dried onion flakes	4 teaspoons dried onion flakes
1/4 cup dark rye flour	1/2 cup dark rye flour	3/4 cup dark rye flour
1/2 cup whole wheat flour	3/4 cup whole wheat flour	1 cup whole wheat flour
1 1/4 cups bread flour	2 cups bread flour	2 1/2 cups bread flour
1 teaspoon rapid-rising or active dry yeast	1 1/2 teaspoons rapid-rising or active dry yeast	2 teaspoons rapid-rising or active dry yeast

TO MIX THE DOUGH BY HAND Heat the water until warm, between 105° and 115°F; pour it into a large, warmed bowl, and add the yeast and sugar. Let stand 5 minutes, until the yeast begins to bubble. Stir in the remaining ingredients except the bread flour. Cover, and let stand 15 minutes. Slowly add the bread flour, and beat until a smooth dough forms. Turn the dough out onto a very lightly floured board, and knead, adding flour if necessary, until smooth and springy, about 5 minutes. Wash the bowl and grease it; place the dough back in the bowl, and turn it over to grease the top. Cover, and let rise until doubled, about 1 hour.

TO MIX THE DOUGH WITH A HEAVY-DUTY MIXER Heat the water until warm, between 105° and 115°F; pour it into the warmed mixing bowl, and add the yeast and sugar. Let stand 5 minutes, until the yeast begins to bubble. Add the remaining ingredients except the bread flour. Cover, and let stand 15 minutes. Slowly add the bread flour, and beat until a smooth dough forms. Knead the dough in the mixer with the dough hook, on medium to high speed, adding flour as necessary, until the dough pulls away from the sides of the bowl and is smooth and springy but still soft to the touch. Remove the dough hook, cover the bowl, and let the dough rise until doubled, about 1 hour.

TO MIX THE DOUGH IN THE FOOD PROCESSOR Place the plastic dough blade into the work bowl. Heat the water until very warm, between 120° and 130°F; set aside. Place the remaining ingredients into the work bowl. Turn the processor on, and slowly pour the water through the feed tube, processing until the dough is smooth and pulls away from the sides of the bowl. If the dough is wet and sticky, add more flour, 1 tablespoon at a time, until the dough is smooth yet soft to the touch. If the dough is not soft to the touch but is very firm, add 1 tablespoon of water at a time, and process until the dough is smooth yet soft to the touch. Cover the work bowl, and let the dough rise until doubled, about 1 hour. Or remove the dough to a lightly greased bowl, cover, and let rise until doubled, about 1 hour.

TO MIX THE DOUGH IN THE BREAD MACHINE Pour the water (at room temperature) into the pan. Add the remaining ingredients, in the order listed. Make an indentation in the dry ingredients and add the yeast. Select *Dough,* and press *Start.* If the dough is wet and sticky, add more flour, 1 tablespoon at a time, until the dough is smooth yet soft to the touch. If the dough is not soft to the touch but is very firm, add 1 teaspoon of water at a time, until the

dough is smooth yet soft to the touch. The machine will stop when the dough is ready to shape and bake.

TO MIX AND BAKE THE BREAD IN THE BREAD MACHINE Pour the water (at room temperature) into the pan. Add the remaining ingredients, in the order listed. Make an indentation in the dry ingredients and add the yeast. Select the *Basic* or *Whole Wheat* cycle, set the crust on *Medium,* and press *Start.* During the mixing cycle, if the dough is wet and sticky, add more flour, 1 tablespoon at a time, until the dough is smooth yet soft to the touch. If the dough is not soft to the touch but is very firm, add 1 teaspoon of water at a time, until the dough is smooth yet soft to the touch.

TO SHAPE AND BAKE IN THE OVEN Lightly grease a baking sheet. Turn the dough out onto a lightly floured board or lightly oiled surface. Punch the dough down, and shape it into an oblong loaf. Place the loaf, with the smooth side up, onto the baking sheet. Cover and let rise in a warm place until almost doubled, 1 hour. Preheat the oven to 350°F. Bake 35 to 45 minutes, until the loaf sounds hollow when tapped and a wooden skewer inserted into the loaf comes out clean and dry. Brush the top of the loaf while it's still hot with soft butter, if desired. Remove from the pan and cool on a wire rack.

Crabmeat Crostini

This is a quick and appealing appetizer that is not only good on toast made with Dill, Onion, Rye, and Wheat Bread (page 186) but also with Caraway, Onion, and Rye Bread (page 177). You can make the crostini ahead and pack them in a plastic bag or an airtight container; freeze until you are ready to use them.

24 APPETIZERS

6 slices (preferably day-old) Dill, Onion, Rye, and Wheat bread, crusts removed

Extra-virgin olive oil for brushing

2 green onions, chopped (including green parts)

$^1/_2$ cup shredded sharp Cheddar cheese

$^1/_8$ teaspoon cayenne

1 cup cooked crabmeat

$^1/_2$ cup chopped toasted almonds

Preheat the oven to 300°F. Cut each slice of bread into 4 squares; spread the squares in a single layer on a cookie sheet. Brush each slice with oil. Bake 30 to 45 minutes, until dry and crisp. Remove the baking sheet from the oven. Cool on the sheet and remove to a plate or container. Increase the oven to 400°F.

In a food processor fitted with the steel blade, combine the onions, cheese, cayenne, and crabmeat. Process until finely chopped, stopping before the mixture becomes a paste. Spread a spoonful of the crabmeat mixture onto each piece of toast, and top each with a few almonds. Place on cookie sheet. Bake 2 to 3 minutes, until hot. Remove when cool.

KALAMATA OLIVE AND HERB BREAD

Drizzle warm slices of this bread with a little olive oil! Or, for a delicious (and trendy) appetizer, top with roasted red bell pepper butter (page 311).

Sampler Loaf

2/3 cup water

1 teaspoon extra-virgin olive oil

1 teaspoon dried oregano

1 teaspoon minced garlic

1/2 teaspoon salt

1/4 cup whole wheat flour

1 3/4 cups bread flour

1 teaspoon rapid-rising or active dry yeast

1/4 cup coarsely chopped, well-drained, pitted Greek olives

Regular Loaf

1 cup water

1 1/2 teaspoons extra-virgin olive oil

1 1/2 teaspoons dried oregano

1 1/2 teaspoons minced garlic

3/4 teaspoon salt

1/2 cup whole wheat flour

2 1/2 cups bread flour

1 1/2 teaspoons rapid-rising or active dry yeast

1/3 cup coarsely chopped, well-drained pitted Greek olives

Large Loaf

1 1/3 cups water

1 tablespoon extra-virgin olive oil

1 tablespoon dried oregano

2 teaspoons minced garlic

1 teaspoon salt

3/4 cup whole wheat flour

3 1/4 cups bread flour

2 teaspoons rapid-rising or active dry yeast

1/2 cup coarsely chopped, well-drained pitted Greek olives

TO MIX THE DOUGH BY HAND Heat the water until warm, between 105° and 115°F; pour it into a large, warmed bowl, and add the yeast. Let stand 5 minutes, until the yeast begins to bubble. Stir in the oil, oregano, garlic, salt, whole wheat flour and half of the bread flour. Beat until smooth. Cover, and let stand 15 minutes. Slowly add the remaining bread flour, and beat until a soft dough forms. Turn the dough out onto a very lightly floured board, and knead, adding flour if necessary, until smooth and springy, about 5 minutes. Knead in the olives. Wash the bowl and grease it; place the dough back in the bowl, and turn it over to grease the top. Cover, and let rise until doubled, about 1 hour.

TO MIX THE DOUGH WITH A HEAVY-DUTY MIXER Heat the water until warm, between 105° and

115°F; pour it into the warmed mixing bowl, and add the yeast. Let stand 5 minutes, until the yeast begins to bubble. Add the oil, oregano, garlic, salt, whole wheat flour, and half of the bread flour. Beat until smooth. Cover, and let stand 15 minutes. Slowly add the remaining bread flour, and beat until a soft dough forms. Knead the dough in the mixer with the dough hook, on medium to high speed, adding flour as necessary, until the dough pulls away from the sides of the bowl and is smooth and springy but still soft to the touch. Knead in the olives. Remove the dough hook, cover the bowl, and let the dough rise until doubled, about 1 hour.

TO MIX THE DOUGH IN THE FOOD PROCESSOR Place the plastic dough blade into the work bowl. Heat the water until very warm, between 120° and

130°F; set aside. Place the remaining ingredients, except the olives, into the work bowl. Turn the processor on, and slowly pour the water through the feed tube, processing until the dough is smooth and pulls away from the sides of the bowl. If the dough is wet and sticky, add more flour, 1 tablespoon at a time, until the dough is smooth yet soft to the touch. If the dough is not soft to the touch but is very firm, add 1 tablespoon of water at a time, and process until the dough is smooth yet soft to the touch. Mix in the olives. Cover the work bowl, and let the dough rise until doubled, about 1 hour. Or remove the dough to a lightly greased bowl, cover, and let rise until doubled, about 1 hour.

TO MIX THE DOUGH IN THE BREAD MACHINE
Pour the water (at room temperature) into the pan. Add the remaining ingredients, except the olives, in the order listed. Make a well in the center of the dry ingredients and add the yeast. Select *Dough,* and press *Start.* If the dough is wet and sticky, add more flour, 1 tablespoon at a time, until the dough is smooth yet soft to the touch. If the dough is not soft to the touch but is very firm, add 1 teaspoon of water at a time, until the dough is smooth yet soft to the touch. Add the olives when the machine signals it's time to add ingredients or when the cycle ends. The machine will stop when the dough is ready to shape and bake.

TO MIX AND BAKE THE BREAD IN THE BREAD MACHINE
Pour the water (at room temperature) into the pan. Add the remaining ingredients, except the olives. Make a well in the center of the dry ingredients and add the yeast. Select the *Basic* cycle, set the crust on *Medium,* and press *Start.* During the mixing cycle, if the dough is wet and sticky, add more flour, 1 tablespoon at a time, until the dough is smooth yet soft to the touch. If the dough is not soft to the touch but is very firm, add 1 teaspoon of water at a time, until the dough is smooth yet soft to the touch. Add the olives when the machine signals it's time to add ingredients.

TO SHAPE AND BAKE IN THE OVEN
Turn the dough out onto a lightly floured board or lightly oiled surface. Punch the dough down, and shape it into a round loaf.

To bake on baking tiles Place the loaf, with the smooth side up, on a bread board, or rimless cookie sheet, sprinkled with flour or cornmeal and let rise in a warm place until doubled, 45 to 60 minutes. Place baking tiles or a pizza stone on a rack in the center of the oven. Fill a rimmed, shallow baking pan with stones or river rock no larger than $1^{1}/_{2}$ inches in diameter and place it on the bottom rack of the oven. Preheat the oven to 450°F for at least 30 minutes. (Rocks should be hot enough to sizzle when water is dropped on them.) Using a sharp knife or a razor, slash the risen loaf lengthwise to a depth of about $^{1}/_{4}$ inch. Transfer the loaf onto the preheated baking tiles or pizza stone in the oven. (This is best done by gently easing the loaf onto the baking tile with the assistance of a straight-edged tool such as a bench scraper.) Immediately pour 1 cup water into the pan of rocks on the bottom rack of the oven. (This is most easily done by squirting water from a sport bottle onto the rocks.) Bake for 15 to 20 minutes, until loaf is golden brown. Remove from the oven and cool on a wire rack.

To bake in a pan Lightly grease a baking pan. Place the loaf, with the smooth side up, into the pan. Cover and let rise in a warm place until almost doubled, 45 to 60 minutes. Preheat the oven to 375°F. Using a sharp knife or a razor, slash the top of the loaf, and brush it with water. Bake 30 to 35 minutes, until the loaf is golden. Remove from the oven and cool on a wire rack.

Fresh Tomato and Corn Salad with
Feta Cheese and Garlic Croutons

Freshly toasted garlic croutons are the best in this salad, but I usually make up a bunch ahead just to have them on hand.

6 SERVINGS

FOR THE CROUTONS

2 cups 1/2inch bread cubes made from day-old Kalamata Olive Herb Bread or other whole grain bread

2 tablespoons extra-virgin olive oil

1 garlic clove, minced or pressed

Kosher salt to taste

FOR THE SALAD

4 vine-ripened tomatoes

3/4 cup corn kernels, cut from 2 ears of cooked fresh corn

6 cups baby lettuce leaves

4 ounces crumbled feta cheese

FOR THE DRESSING

3/4 cup extra-virgin olive oil

1 tablespoon raspberry vinegar

1 tablespoon white rice vinegar

1/2 teaspoon salt

1/4 teaspoon freshly ground pepper

1 large garlic clove, minced or pressed

2 teaspoons minced fresh basil leaves

Make the croutons. Preheat the oven to 350°F. Toss the bread cubes with the oil, garlic and salt. Spread on a baking sheet in a single layer. Bake about 10 minutes, until crisp. Cool.

Make the salad. Remove the cores from the tomatoes, and cut them into 8 wedges each. Combine the tomatoes and corn in a mixing bowl. Arrange the lettuce on six salad plates or on a large salad platter.

Make the dressing. In a small bowl, whisk the oil, vinegars, salt, pepper, garlic and basil together.

To serve, toss the dressing with the tomatoes, feta, and corn. Arrange the mixture on top of the lettuce. Sprinkle on the croutons.

POTATO RYE BREAD

Although I often use mashed potatoes left over from Sunday dinner, I find that instant potato flakes produce much more consistent results for bread machine recipes. Potatoes add tenderness and moistness to rye bread and are often used in European country loaves.

Sampler Loaf

2/3 cup water

1/2 tablespoon molasses

1/2 tablespoon corn oil

1/2 teaspoon caraway seeds

1 teaspoon salt

2 tablespoons dried potato flakes or granules*

2 tablespoons nonfat dry milk powder

1/2 cup rye flour

1 1/2 cups bread flour

1 teaspoon rapid-rising or active dry yeast

Regular Loaf

1 cup water

1 tablespoon molasses

1 tablespoon corn oil

1 teaspoon caraway seeds

1 1/2 teaspoons salt

1/4 cup dried potato flakes or granules*

1/4 cup nonfat dry milk powder

3/4 cup rye flour

2 1/4 cups bread flour

1 1/2 teaspoons rapid-rising or active dry yeast

Large Loaf

1 1/3 cups water

2 tablespoons molasses

2 tablespoons corn oil

2 teaspoons caraway seeds

2 teaspoons salt

1/3 cup dried potato flakes or granules*

1/3 cup nonfat dry milk powder

1 cup rye flour

3 cups bread flour

2 teaspoons rapid-rising or active dry yeast

TO MIX THE DOUGH BY HAND Heat the water until warm, between 105° and 115°F; pour it into a large, warmed bowl, and add the yeast and molasses. Let stand 5 minutes, until the yeast begins to bubble. Stir in the oil, caraway seeds, salt, potato flakes, dry milk, and rye flour. Beat well. Slowly add half of the bread flour, and beat until a smooth dough forms.

Cover, and let stand 15 minutes. Turn the dough out onto a very lightly floured board, and knead, adding the remaining flour as necessary, until smooth and springy, about 5 minutes. Wash the bowl and grease it; place the dough back in the bowl, and turn it over to grease the top. Cover, and let rise until doubled, about 1 hour.

*Note   *Because the amount of liquid in mashed potatoes made from scratch varies so much, it is impossible to give an accurate substitution for use in this recipe.*

TO MIX THE DOUGH WITH A HEAVY-DUTY MIXER Heat the water until warm, between 105° and 115°F; pour it into the warmed mixing bowl, and add the yeast and molasses. Let stand 5 minutes, until the yeast begins to bubble. Add the oil, caraway seeds, salt, potato flakes, dry milk, and rye flour. Beat well. Slowly add half of the bread flour, and beat until a smooth dough forms. Cover, and let stand 15 minutes. Knead the dough in the mixer with the dough hook, on medium to high speed, adding the remaining flour as necessary, until the dough pulls away from the sides of the bowl and is smooth and springy but still soft to the touch. Remove the dough hook, cover the bowl, and let the dough rise until doubled, about 1 hour.

TO MIX THE DOUGH IN THE FOOD PROCESSOR Place the plastic dough blade into the work bowl. Heat the water until very warm, between 120° and 130°F; mix in the oil and set aside. Place the remaining ingredients into the work bowl. Turn the processor on, and slowly pour the water mixture through the feed tube, processing until the dough is smooth and pulls away from the sides of the bowl. If the dough is wet and sticky, add more flour, 1 tablespoon at a time, until the dough is smooth yet soft to the touch. If the dough is not soft to the touch but is very firm, add 1 tablespoon of water at a time, and process until the dough is smooth yet soft to the touch. Cover the work bowl, and let the dough rise until doubled, about 1 hour. Or remove the dough to a lightly greased bowl, cover, and let rise until doubled, about 1 hour.

TO MIX THE DOUGH IN THE BREAD MACHINE Pour the water (at room temperature) into the pan. Add the remaining ingredients, in the order listed. Make an indentation in the center of the dry ingredients and add the yeast. Select *Dough,* and press *Start.* If the dough is wet and sticky, add more flour, 1 tablespoon at a time, until the dough is smooth yet soft to the touch. If the dough is not soft to the touch but is very firm, add 1 teaspoon of water at a time, until the dough is smooth yet soft to the touch. The machine will stop when the dough is ready to shape and bake.

TO MIX AND BAKE THE BREAD IN THE BREAD MACHINE Pour the water (at room temperature) into the pan. Add the remaining ingredients, in the order listed. Make an indentation in the center of the dry ingredients and add the yeast. Select the *Basic* or *Whole Wheat* cycle, set the crust on *Medium,* and press *Start.* During the mixing cycle, if the dough is wet and sticky, add more flour, 1 tablespoon at a time, until the dough is smooth yet soft to the touch. If the dough is not soft to the touch but is very firm, add 1 teaspoon of water at a time, until the dough is smooth yet soft to the touch.

TO SHAPE AND BAKE IN THE OVEN Lightly grease a baking sheet. Turn the dough out onto a lightly floured board or lightly oiled surface.

Punch the dough down, and shape it into a round loaf. Place the loaf, with the smooth side up, onto the baking sheet. Cover and let rise in a warm place until almost doubled, 45 to 60 minutes. Preheat the oven to 375°F. Bake 35 to 40 minutes, until the loaf is golden and a wooden skewer inserted into the loaf comes out clean and dry. Brush the top of the loaf while it's still hot with melted butter, if desired. Remove from the pan and cool on a wire rack.

Savory Rosemary and Cheese Bread Pudding

You can use almost any flavor of bread in this easy, savory bread pudding, which is assembled the day before you plan to serve it. This is a great dish for a large party. To round out a brunch menu, offer a platter of melon spears, sautéed sausages, and freshly made coffee. You might even start out with an old-time favorite: mimosas (orange juice and champagne).

12 SERVINGS

1 large onion, chopped, about 1¹/₂ cups

2 tablespoons butter

6 slices of whole grain bread, crusts removed

3 cups light cream, half-and-half, or undiluted evaporated milk

10 large eggs

1 teaspoon salt

¹/₈ teaspoon cayenne (optional)

2 cups shredded Cheddar or Monterey Jack cheese

¹/₄ cup fresh rosemary leaves

Butter a shallow casserole, about 9 × 12-inches. In a medium skillet, cook the onion in the butter over medium heat, stirring occasionally, until golden. Toast the bread slices. In a bowl, whisk together the cream, eggs, salt, and cayenne.

Arrange 4 slices of the bread in the bottom of the casserole. Cut the remaining 2 slices of bread into ¹/₂-inch cubes. Sprinkle half of the bread cubes in the casserole; top with half of the cheese and the onion and rosemary. Top with the remaining bread cubes, and sprinkle with the remaining cheese. Pour the egg mixture evenly over all. Cover and chill at least 8 hours or overnight.

Preheat the oven to 375°F. Bake, uncovered, 40 minutes, until golden brown.

POTATO WHEAT BREAD

It's a little tricky to make a bread with fresh potatoes that you bake right in the bread machine, because potatoes vary in moistness. To make a perfect loaf, you must check the dough carefully during mixing. I prefer to make the dough for this bread in the bread machine but bake it in the oven. I use russet potatoes, since they cook up dry and mealy (for cooking instructions, see sidebar at the end of this recipe).

Sampler Loaf

$1/2$ cup potato water or plain
     water (see below)

1 tablespoon sugar

$1/2$ cup mashed potatoes (from
     1 medium potato—
     see below)

1 teaspoon freshly squeezed
     lemon juice

1 tablespoon corn oil

$1/2$ teaspoon salt

1 cup whole wheat flour

1 cup bread flour

2 tablespoons sunflower seeds

1 teaspoon rapid-rising or active
     dry yeast

Regular Loaf

$3/4$ cup potato water or plain
     water (see below)

2 tablespoons sugar

$3/4$ cup mashed potatoes (from
     1 large potato—see below)

$1^1/2$ teaspoons freshly squeezed
     lemon juice

2 tablespoons corn oil

1 teaspoon salt

$1^1/2$ cups whole wheat flour

$1^1/2$ cups bread flour

$1/4$ cup sunflower seeds

$1^1/2$ teaspoons rapid-rising or
     active dry yeast

Large Loaf

1 cup potato water or plain water
     (see below)

3 tablespoons sugar

1 cup mashed potatoes (from
     approximately 2 medium
     potatoes—see below)

2 teaspoons freshly squeezed
     lemon juice

3 tablespoons corn oil

$1^1/2$ teaspoons salt

2 cups whole wheat flour

2 cups bread flour

$1/2$ cup sunflower seeds

2 teaspoons rapid-rising or active
     dry yeast

TO MIX THE DOUGH BY HAND Heat the potato water until warm, between 105° and 115°F; pour it along with the sugar into a large, warmed bowl, and add the yeast. Let stand 5 minutes, until the yeast begins to bubble. Stir in the potatoes, lemon juice, oil, salt, and whole wheat flour. Slowly add half of the bread flour, and beat until a smooth dough forms. Cover, and let stand 15 minutes. Turn the dough out onto a very lightly floured board, and knead, adding the remaining flour as necessary, until smooth and springy, about 5 minutes. Knead in the sunflower seeds.

Wash the bowl and grease it; place the dough back in the bowl, and turn it over to grease the top. Cover, and let rise until doubled, about 1 hour.

TO MIX THE DOUGH WITH A HEAVY-DUTY MIXER Heat the potato water until warm, between 105° and 115°F; pour it along with the sugar into the warmed mixing bowl, and add the yeast. Let stand 5 minutes, until the yeast begins to bubble. Add the potatoes, lemon juice, oil, salt, and wheat flour. Slowly add half of the bread flour, and beat until a smooth dough forms. Cover, and let stand 15 minutes. Knead the dough in the mixer with the dough hook, on medium to high speed, adding the remaining flour as necessary, until the dough pulls away from the sides of the bowl and is smooth and springy but still soft to the touch. Knead in the sunflower seeds. Remove the dough hook, cover the bowl, and let the dough rise until doubled, about 1 hour.

TO MIX THE DOUGH IN THE FOOD PROCESSOR Place the plastic dough blade into the work bowl. Heat the potato water until very warm, between 120° and 130°F; mix in the oil, and set aside. Place the remaining ingredients into the work bowl. Turn the processor on, and slowly pour the water mixture through the feed tube, processing until the dough is smooth and pulls away from the sides of the bowl. If the dough is wet and sticky, add more flour, 1 tablespoon at a time, until the dough is smooth yet soft to the touch. If the dough is not soft to the touch but is very firm, add 1 tablespoon of water at a time, and process until the dough is smooth yet soft to the touch. Cover the work bowl, and let the dough rise until doubled, about 1 hour. Or remove the dough to a lightly greased bowl, cover, and let rise until doubled, about 1 hour.

TO MIX THE DOUGH IN THE BREAD MACHINE Pour the potato water (at room temperature) into the pan. Add the remaining ingredients, in the order listed. Make an indentation in the center of the dry ingredients and add the yeast. Select *Dough,* and press *Start.* If the dough is wet and sticky, add more flour, 1 tablespoon at a time, until the dough is smooth yet soft to the touch. If the dough is not soft to the touch but is very firm, add 1 teaspoon of water at a time, until the dough is smooth yet soft to the touch. The machine will stop when the dough is ready to shape and bake.

TO MIX AND BAKE THE BREAD IN THE BREAD MACHINE Pour the potato water (at room temperature) into the pan. Add the remaining ingredients, in the order listed. Make an indentation in the center of the dry ingredients and add the yeast. Select the *Basic* or *Whole Wheat* cycle, set the crust on *Medium,* and press *Start.* During the mixing cycle, if the dough is wet and sticky, add more flour, 1 tablespoon at a time, until the dough is smooth yet soft to the touch. If the dough is not soft to the touch but is very firm, add 1 teaspoon of water at a time, until the dough is smooth yet soft to the touch.

TO SHAPE AND BAKE IN THE OVEN Lightly grease an 8 × 4-inch loaf pan or an 8- or 9-inch round cake pan. Turn the dough out onto a lightly floured board or lightly oiled surface. Punch the dough down, and shape it into an oblong or round loaf. Place the loaf, with the smooth side up, into the pan. Cover and let rise in a warm place until almost doubled, 45 to 60 minutes. Preheat the oven to 375°F. Bake 35 to 40 minutes, until the loaf is golden and a wooden skewer inserted into the loaf comes out clean and dry. Brush the top of the loaf while it's still hot with melted butter, if desired. Remove from the pan and cool on a wire rack.

COOKING POTATOES

Place peeled russet potatoes into a saucepan and cover with water. Simmer for 15 to 20 minutes, until the potatoes can be easily pierced with a skewer. Drain immediately and thoroughly, reserving the liquid, and allow the potatoes to cool. This liquid is referred to as "potato water" in the recipe. Press the potatoes through a ricer or mash with a fork (it is okay to leave small lumps). To measure, pack the mashed potatoes level into cups intended for measuring dry ingredients.

Wild Mushroom Pudding

Because of my love for fresh bread and because normally I bake every day, I end up with a lot of day-old slices—you know, bits and ends. I've taken to cutting these bits and ends into cubes, packaging them in a resealable plastic bag and freezing them. When I've collected enough, I make a savory pudding; this is one of my favorites. I use the wild mushrooms that grow in our woods; but commercially cultivated "wild" mushrooms, such as shiitake, portobello, and crimini, are also incredibly tasty, and ordinary button mushrooms aren't that bad, either!

6 SERVINGS

1/2 pound fresh mushrooms, cleaned and thinly sliced

4 tablespoons butter

6 cups bread cubes, cut 1/2 inch, made from Potato Wheat Bread (page 196) or other whole grain bread, toasted

1/2 cup chopped sweet onion

1/2 cup chopped celery

1 cup half-and-half or milk

1/2 cup whipping cream

1 teaspoon salt

1/2 teaspoon freshly ground pepper

1/2 teaspoon crushed dried tarragon, if desired

2 eggs

1 cup shredded sharp Cheddar cheese

Lightly butter a 1 1/2-quart casserole. In a large skillet, cook the mushrooms in 3 tablespoons of the butter over medium-high heat about 2 minutes, until slightly soft. Layer half of the bread cubes in the bottom of the casserole. Arrange the mushrooms over the cubes. Melt the remaining 1 tablespoon butter in the skillet. Add the onions and celery. Cook over medium-high heat about 2 minutes, until the celery and onions are tender. Spread the onion mixture over the mushrooms and top with the remaining bread cubes.

Blend the half-and-half, cream, salt, pepper, tarragon, and eggs in a medium bowl. Pour over the ingredients in the baking dish. Sprinkle the cheese over the top. Cover and refrigerate several hours or overnight or let stand at room temperature until the bread absorbs the creamy mixture, about 30 minutes.

Preheat the oven to 325°F. Bake the pudding 45 to 60 minutes, until golden and a knife inserted in the center comes out clean. Serve hot.

RYE AND SAUERKRAUT BREAD

Sauerkraut worked into rye bread dough is a favorite of German immigrant bakers. The bread has a heartiness and country quality that makes it a perfect accompaniment to a rustic bean and sausage soup. It's intended to be made into a fat round loaf; if you want to bake it in the bread machine, you'll need to add the sauerkraut as if you were adding fruit or nuts: put it into the pan when the machine signals to add ingredients, or 20 to 25 minutes into the cycle. The sauerkraut must be drained very well. Measure and chop it; then drain on paper towels about 10 minutes, until it is no longer wet.

Sampler Loaf	Regular Loaf	Large Loaf
2/3 cup water	1 cup water	1 1/3 cups water
1 tablespoon dark molasses	2 tablespoons dark molasses	3 tablespoons dark molasses
1 tablespoon vegetable oil	2 tablespoons vegetable oil	3 tablespoons vegetable oil
1 teaspoon salt	1 teaspoon salt	2 teaspoons salt
1 teaspoon caraway seeds	1 1/2 teaspoons caraway seeds	2 teaspoons caraway seeds
1/2 cup dark rye flour	3/4 cup dark rye flour	1 cup dark rye flour
1 1/2 cups bread flour	2 1/4 cups bread flour	3 cups bread flour
1 teaspoon rapid-rising or active dry yeast	1 1/2 teaspoons rapid-rising or active dry yeast	2 teaspoons rapid-rising or active dry yeast
1/3 cup sauerkraut, chop coarsely and drain very well	1/2 cup sauerkraut, chop coarsely and drain very well	3/4 cup sauerkraut, chop coarsely and drain very well

TO MIX THE DOUGH BY HAND Heat the water until warm, between 105° and 115°F; pour it into a large, warmed bowl, and add the yeast and molasses. Let stand 5 minutes, until the yeast begins to bubble. Stir in the oil, salt, caraway seeds, and rye flour. Cover, and let stand 15 minutes. Add sauerkraut to dough after it has stood for 15 minutes. Slowly add the bread flour, and beat until a smooth dough forms. Turn the dough out onto a very lightly floured board, and knead, adding flour if necessary, until smooth and springy, about 5 minutes. Wash the bowl and grease it; place the dough back in the bowl, and turn it over to grease the top. Cover, and let rise until doubled, about 1 hour.

TO MIX THE DOUGH WITH A HEAVY-DUTY MIXER Heat the water until warm, between 105° and 115°F; pour it into the warmed mixing bowl, and add the yeast and molasses. Let stand 5 minutes, until the yeast begins to bubble. Add the oil, salt, caraway seeds, and rye flour. Cover, and let stand 15 minutes. Add sauerkraut to dough after it has stood for 15 minutes. Slowly add the bread flour, and beat until a smooth dough forms. Knead the dough in the mixer with the dough hook, on medium to high speed, adding flour as necessary, until the dough pulls away from the sides of the bowl and is smooth and springy but still soft to the touch. Remove the dough hook, cover the bowl, and let the dough rise until doubled, about 1 hour.

TO MIX THE DOUGH IN THE FOOD PROCESSOR Place the plastic dough blade into the work bowl. Heat the water until very warm, between 120° and 130°F; stir in the molasses and oil, and set aside. Place the remaining ingredients, except the sauerkraut, into the work bowl. Turn the processor on, and slowly pour the water through the feed tube, processing until the dough is smooth and pulls away from the sides of the bowl. If the dough is wet and sticky, add more flour, 1 tablespoon at a time, until the dough is smooth yet soft to the touch. If the dough is not soft to the touch but is very firm, add 1 tablespoon of water at a time, and process until the dough is smooth yet soft to the touch. Add sauerkraut to dough just before you cover the work bowl and let dough rise. Cover the work bowl, and let the dough rise until doubled, about 1 hour. Or remove the dough to a lightly greased bowl, cover, and let rise until doubled, about 1 hour.

TO MIX THE DOUGH IN THE BREAD MACHINE Pour the water (at room temperature) into the pan, and add the remaining ingredients, except the yeast and sauerkraut. Make a small indentation in the dry ingredients, and add the yeast. Select *Dough,* and press *Start.* If the dough is wet and sticky, add more flour, 1 table-

spoon at a time, until the dough is smooth yet soft to the touch. If the dough is not soft to the touch but is very firm, add 1 teaspoon of water at a time, until the dough is smooth yet soft to the touch. Add the sauerkraut when the machine signals it's time to add ingredients or when the cycle ends. The machine will stop when the dough is ready to shape and bake.

TO MIX AND BAKE THE BREAD IN THE BREAD MACHINE Pour the water (at room temperature) into the pan, and add the remaining ingredients, except the yeast. Make a small indentation in the dry ingredients, and add the yeast. Select the *Fruit and Nut, Basic,* or *Whole Wheat* cycle; set the crust on *Medium;* and press *Start.* During the mixing cycle, if the dough is wet and sticky, add more flour, 1 tablespoon at a time, until the dough is smooth yet soft to the touch. If the dough is not soft to the touch but is very firm, add 1 teaspoon of water at a time, until the dough is smooth yet soft to the touch. Add the sauerkraut when the machine signals it's time to add ingredients.

TO SHAPE AND BAKE IN THE OVEN Lightly grease an 8- or 9-inch round cake pan. Turn the dough out onto a lightly floured board or lightly oiled surface. Punch it down, and knead in the sauerkraut (if you mixed the dough by hand, heavy-duty mixer, or food processor). Shape the dough into a round loaf, and place it, with the smooth side up, into the pan. Cover and let rise in a warm place until almost doubled, 45 to 60 minutes. Preheat the oven to 375°F. Bake 30 to 35 minutes, until the loaf is golden and a wooden skewer inserted into the loaf comes out clean and dry. Remove from the pan and cool on a wire rack.

SPINACH-FETA
WHOLE WHEAT BREAD

This bread is the very best and most predictable when shaped into a round loaf and baked conventionally.
When you knead the cheese and spinach into the dough by hand, they are identifiable in the baked loaf.
Be sure to dry the spinach very well before adding it to the bread, as liquid clinging to the leaves can make
a huge difference in the success of the bread.

Sampler Loaf

2/3 cup water

1 1/2 teaspoons sugar

1 tablespoon extra-virgin olive oil

1/2 teaspoon salt

1 teaspoon dried oregano

1 cup whole wheat flour

1 cup bread flour

1 teaspoon yeast

1 teaspoon whole wheat flour

4 ounces crumbled feta cheese

3/4 cup coarsely chopped fresh
  spinach

Regular Loaf

1 cup water

2 teaspoons sugar

1 1/2 tablespoons extra-virgin
  olive oil

1 teaspoon salt

1 1/2 teaspoons dried oregano

1 1/2 cups whole wheat flour

1 1/2 cups bread flour

1 1/2 teaspoons yeast

2 teaspoons whole wheat flour

6 ounces crumbled feta cheese

1 cup coarsely chopped
  fresh spinach

Large Loaf

1 1/3 cups water

1 tablespoon sugar

2 tablespoons extra-virgin
  olive oil

1 1/2 teaspoons salt

2 teaspoons dried oregano

2 cups whole wheat flour

2 cups bread flour

2 teaspoons yeast

1 tablespoon whole wheat flour

8 ounces crumbled feta cheese

1 1/2 cups coarsely chopped
  fresh spinach

GLAZE FOR BREAD BAKED CONVENTIONALLY
1 egg, beaten

TO MIX THE DOUGH BY HAND Heat the water until warm, between 105° and 115°F; pour it along with the sugar into a large, warmed bowl, and add the yeast. Let stand 5 minutes, until the yeast begins to bubble. Stir in the oil, salt, oregano, and 1 cup whole wheat flour. Beat until a smooth dough forms. Cover, and let stand 15 minutes. Slowly add the bread flour, and beat until a stiff, but soft, dough forms. Turn the dough out onto a very lightly floured board, and knead, adding flour if necessary, until smooth and springy, about 5 minutes. Toss the 1 teaspoon of whole wheat flour with the feta cheese. Knead in the cheese and spinach. Wash the bowl and grease it; place the dough back in the bowl, and turn it over to grease the top. Cover, and let rise until doubled, about 1 hour.

TO MIX THE DOUGH WITH A HEAVY-DUTY MIXER Heat the water until warm, between 105° and 115°F; pour it along with the sugar into the warmed mixing bowl, and add the yeast. Let stand 5 minutes, until the yeast begins to bubble. Add the oil salt, oregano, and 1 cup of whole wheat flour. Beat until smooth. Cover, and let stand 15 minutes. Slowly add the bread flour, and beat until a stiff, but soft, dough forms. Knead the dough in the mixer with the dough hook, on medium to high speed, adding flour as necessary, until the dough pulls away from the sides of the bowl and is smooth and springy but still soft to the touch. Toss the 1 teaspoon of whole wheat flour with the feta cheese. Knead in the cheese and spinach. Remove the dough hook, cover the bowl, and let the dough rise until doubled, about 1 hour.

TO MIX THE DOUGH IN THE FOOD PROCESSOR Place the plastic dough blade into the work bowl. Heat the water until very warm, between 120° and 130°F; set aside. Place the sugar, oil, slat, oregano, 1 cup whole wheat flour, and bread flour into the work bowl. Turn the processor on, and slowly pour the water through the feed tube, processing until the dough is smooth and pulls away from the sides of the bowl. If the dough is wet and sticky, add more flour, 1 tablespoon at a time, until the dough is smooth yet soft to the touch. If the dough is not soft to the touch but is very firm, add 1 tablespoon of water at a time, and process until the dough is smooth yet soft to the touch. Toss the 1 teaspoon of whole wheat

flour with the feta cheese. Mix in the cheese and spinach. Cover the work bowl, and let the dough rise until doubled, about 1 hour. Or remove the dough to a lightly greased bowl, cover, and let rise until doubled, about 1 hour.

TO MIX THE DOUGH IN THE BREAD MACHINE Pour the water (at room temperature) into the pan. Add the remaining ingredients, except the 1 teaspoon whole wheat flour, feta, and spinach, in the order listed. Make an indentation in the center of the dry ingredients and add the yeast. Select *Dough,* and press *Start.* If the dough is wet and sticky, add more flour, 1 tablespoon at a time, until the dough is smooth yet soft to the touch. If the dough is not soft to the touch but is very firm, add 1 teaspoon of water at a time, until the dough is smooth yet soft to the touch. The machine will stop when the dough is ready to shape and bake. Toss the 1 teaspoon of whole wheat flour with the feta cheese. Knead in the cheese and spinach.

TO MIX AND BAKE THE BREAD IN THE BREAD MACHINE Pour the water (at room temperature) into the pan. Add the remaining ingredients, except the 1 teaspoon whole wheat flour, feta, and spinach, in the order listed. Make an indentation in the center of the dry ingredients and add the yeast. Select the *Basic* or *Whole Wheat* cycle, set the crust on *Medium,* and press *Start.* During the mixing cycle, if the dough is wet and sticky, add more flour, 1 tablespoon at a time, until the dough is smooth yet soft to the touch. If the dough is not soft to the touch but is very firm, add 1 teaspoon of water at a time, until the dough is smooth yet soft to the touch. Toss the 1 teaspoon of whole wheat flour with the feta cheese. At the end of the kneading cycle, without turning off the machine, remove the dough from the pan. Knead in the cheese and spinach, and return the dough to the machine. Allow the machine to complete the bread.

TO SHAPE AND BAKE IN THE OVEN Lightly grease a baking sheet or cover it with parchment paper. Turn the dough out onto a lightly floured board or lightly oiled surface. Punch the dough down, and shape it into a fat round loaf. Place the loaf, with the smooth side up, onto the baking sheet. Cover and let rise in a warm place until almost doubled, 45 to 60 minutes. Preheat the oven to 375°F. To glaze, brush the loaf with the beaten egg. Bake 35 to 45 minutes, until the loaf sounds hollow when tapped and a wooden skewer inserted into the loaf comes out clean and dry. Remove from the pan and cool on a wire rack.

SUN-DRIED TOMATO
AND PESTO BREAD

This bread has the flavor and aroma of basil with a bite of pepper. It's perfect with minestrone or a pasta salad.

Sampler Loaf (1 baguette)

1 large egg plus water to equal
  $2/3$ cup

$1/4$ cup prepared pesto sauce

$1^1/2$ teaspoons sugar

$3/4$ teaspoon salt

$3/4$ teaspoon freshly ground
  coarse pepper

$1/4$ cup whole wheat flour

$1^3/4$ cups bread flour

1 teaspoon rapid-rising or active
  dry yeast

$1/4$ cup oil-packed, julienne-cut
  sun-dried tomatoes,
  well drained

Regular Loaf (2 baguettes)

1 large egg plus water to equal
  1 cup

$1/3$ cup prepared pesto sauce

2 teaspoons sugar

1 teaspoon salt

1 teaspoon freshly ground
  coarse pepper

$1/2$ cup whole wheat flour

$2^1/2$ cups bread flour

$1^1/2$ teaspoons rapid-rising or
  active dry yeast

$1/3$ cup oil-packed, julienne-cut
  sun-dried tomatoes,
  well drained

Large Loaf (2 baguettes)

1 large egg plus water to equal
  $1^1/3$ cups

$1/2$ cup prepared pesto sauce

1 tablespoon sugar

$1^1/2$ teaspoons salt

$1^1/2$ teaspoons freshly ground
  coarse pepper

$3/4$ cup whole wheat flour

$3^1/4$ cup bread flour

2 teaspoons rapid-rising or active
  dry yeast

$1/2$ cup oil-packed, julienne-cut
  sun-dried tomatoes,
  well drained

TO MIX THE DOUGH BY HAND Warm the egg under hot tap water, and crack into a measuring cup. Heat the water until warm, between 105° and 115°F, and add it to the egg. Pour the mixture into a large, warmed bowl, and add the yeast and sugar. Let stand 5 minutes, until the yeast begins to bubble. Stir in the pesto, tomatoes, salt, pepper, whole wheat flour, and 1 cup of the bread flour. Beat well. Cover, and let stand 15 minutes. Slowly add the remaining bread flour, and beat until a soft dough forms. Turn the dough out onto a very lightly floured board,

and knead, adding flour if necessary, until smooth and springy, about 5 minutes. Wash the bowl and grease it; place the dough back in the bowl, and turn it over to grease the top. Cover, and let rise until doubled, about 1 hour.

TO MIX THE DOUGH WITH A HEAVY-DUTY MIXER Warm the egg under hot tap water, and crack into a measuring cup. Heat the water until warm, between 105° and 115°F, and add it to the egg. Pour the mixture into a large, warmed bowl, and add the yeast and sugar. Let stand 5 minutes, until the yeast begins to bubble. Add the pesto, tomatoes, salt, pepper, whole wheat flour, and 1 cup of the bread flour. Beat well. Cover, and let stand 15 minutes. Slowly add the remaining bread flour, and beat until a soft dough forms. Knead the dough in the mixer with the dough hook, on medium to high speed, adding flour as necessary, until the dough pulls away from the sides of the bowl and is smooth and springy but still soft to the touch. Remove the dough hook, cover the bowl, and let the dough rise until doubled, about 1 hour.

TO MIX THE DOUGH IN THE FOOD PROCESSOR Place the plastic dough blade into the work bowl. Warm the egg under hot tap water, and crack into a measuring cup. Heat the water until very warm, between 120° and 130°F, and add it to the egg; set aside. Place the remaining ingredients into the work bowl. Turn the processor on, and slowly pour the water mixture through the feed tube, processing until the dough is smooth and pulls away from the sides of the bowl. If the dough is wet and sticky, add more flour, 1 tablespoon at a time, until the dough is smooth yet soft to the touch. If the dough is not soft to the touch but is very firm, add 1 tablespoon of water at a time, and process until the dough is smooth yet soft to the touch. Cover the work bowl, and let the dough rise until doubled, about 1 hour. Or remove the dough to a lightly greased bowl, cover, and let rise until doubled, about 1 hour.

TO MIX THE DOUGH IN THE BREAD MACHINE Warm the eggs under hot tap water, and crack into a measuring cup. Add water (at room temperature) to the eggs; pour

the mixture into the pan. Add the remaining ingredients, except the tomatoes, in the order listed. Make an indentation in the center of the dry ingredients and add the yeast. Select *Dough*, and press *Start*. If the dough is wet and sticky, add more flour, 1 tablespoon at a time, until the dough is smooth yet soft to the touch. If the dough is not soft to the touch but is very firm, add 1 teaspoon of water at a time, until the dough is smooth yet soft to the touch. Add the tomatoes when the machine signals it's time to add ingredients or when the cycle ends. The machine will stop when the dough is ready to shape and bake.

TO MIX AND BAKE THE BREAD IN THE BREAD MACHINE Warm the eggs under hot tap water, and crack into a measuring cup. Add water (at room temperature) to the eggs; pour the mixture into the pan. Add the remaining ingredients, except the tomatoes, in the order listed. Make an indentation in the center of the dry ingredients and add the yeast. Select the *Fruit and Nut, Basic,* or *Whole Wheat* cycle; set the crust on *Medium;* and press *Start*. During the mixing cycle, if the dough is wet and sticky, add more flour, 1 tablespoon at a time, until the dough is smooth yet soft to the touch. If the dough is not soft to the touch but is very firm, add 1 teaspoon of water at a time, until the dough is smooth yet soft to the touch. Add the tomatoes when the machine signals it's time to add ingredients.

TO SHAPE AND BAKE IN THE OVEN Lightly grease a baking sheet or cover it with parchment paper. Turn the dough out onto a lightly floured board or lightly oiled surface. Punch the dough down, and shape it into a round loaf. Place the loaf, with the smooth side up, into the pan. Let rise in a warm place until almost doubled, 45 minutes. Preheat the oven to 375°F. Using a sharp knife or razor, slash the top of the loaf. Bake 30 to 35 minutes, until the loaf is golden. Remove from the pan and cool on a wire rack.

To bake on baking tiles Leave the loaves, with the smooth side up, on the board, and let rise in a warm place until almost doubled, 45 minutes. Place baking tiles or a pizza tile on the top rack in the oven, and place a heavy, shallow pan on the bottom rack. Preheat the oven to 450°F. Using a sharp knife or a razor, slash the loaves; place the loaves onto the preheated tiles. Immediately pour 1 cup water into the pan on the bottom rack. Bake 15 to 20 minutes, until the loaves are golden. Remove from the oven and cool on a wire rack.

To bake in a pan Lightly grease a baking sheet. Place the loaves, with the smooth side up, onto the baking sheet. Cover and let rise in a warm place until almost doubled, 45 minutes. Preheat the oven to 375°F. Using a sharp knife or a razor, slash the top of the loaves. Bake 25 to 30 minutes, until the loaves are golden. Remove from the oven and cool on a wire rack.

SUN-DRIED TOMATO AND PARMESAN WHEAT BREAD

If the sun-dried tomatoes you have are paper dry, soak them in warm water for 10 minutes, then drain very well before adding them to the bread dough. Oil-packed, julienne-cut sun-dried tomatoes are also a good choice for this bread, but the bread will be a little richer. Be sure to drain them well before adding.

Sampler Loaf (1 baguette)

2/3 cup water

1 1/2 teaspoons sugar

1 tablespoon extra-virgin olive oil

1 teaspoon dried basil

3/4 teaspoon minced garlic

3/4 teaspoon salt

1/4 cup cornmeal

1/4 cup whole wheat flour

1 1/3 cups bread flour

1 teaspoon rapid-rising or active dry yeast

2 tablespoons chopped sun-dried tomatoes

2 tablespoons shredded Parmesan cheese

Regular Loaf (2 baguettes)

1 cup water

2 teaspoons sugar

1 1/2 tablespoons extra-virgin olive oil

1 1/2 teaspoon dried basil

1 teaspoon minced garlic

1 teaspoon salt

1/3 cup cornmeal

1/3 cup whole wheat flour

2 1/4 cups bread flour

1 1/2 teaspoons rapid-rising or active dry yeast

1/4 cup chopped sun-dried tomatoes

1/4 cup shredded Parmesan cheese

Large Loaf (2 baguettes)

1 1/3 cup water

1 tablespoon sugar

2 tablespoons olive oil

2 teaspoons dried basil

1 1/2 teaspoons minced garlic

1 1/2 teaspoons salt

1/2 cup cornmeal

1/2 cup whole wheat flour

2 3/4 cups bread flour

2 teaspoons rapid-rising or active dry yeast

1/3 cup chopped sun-dried tomatoes

1/3 cup shredded Parmesan cheese

TO MIX THE DOUGH BY HAND Heat the water until warm, between 105° and 115°F; pour it along with the sugar into a large, warmed bowl, and add the yeast. Let stand 5 minutes, until the yeast begins to bubble. Stir in the oil, basil, garlic, salt, cornmeal, and whole wheat flour. Beat until smooth. Cover, and let stand 15 minutes. Slowly add the bread flour, and beat until a soft dough forms. Turn the dough out onto a very lightly floured board, and knead, adding flour if necessary, until smooth and springy, about 5 minutes. Knead in the tomatoes and cheese. Wash the bowl and grease it; place the dough back in the bowl, and turn it over to grease the top. Cover, and let rise until doubled, about 1 hour.

TO MIX THE DOUGH WITH A HEAVY-DUTY MIXER Heat the water until warm, between 105° and 115°F; pour it along with the sugar into the warmed mixing bowl, and add the yeast. Let stand 5 minutes, until the yeast begins to bubble. Add the oil, basil, garlic, salt, cornmeal, and whole wheat flour. Beat until smooth. Cover, and let stand 15 minutes. Slowly add the bread flour, and beat until a soft dough forms. Knead the dough in the mixer with the dough hook, on medium to high speed, adding flour as necessary, until the dough pulls away from the sides of the bowl and is smooth and springy but still soft to the touch. Knead in the tomatoes and cheese. Remove the dough hook, cover the bowl, and let the dough rise until doubled, about 1 hour.

TO MIX THE DOUGH IN THE FOOD PROCESSOR
Place the plastic dough blade into the work bowl. Heat the water until very warm, between 120° and 130°F; set aside. Place the remaining ingredients, except the tomatoes, into the work bowl. Turn the processor on, and slowly pour the water through the feed tube, processing until the dough is smooth and pulls away from the sides of the bowl. If the dough is wet and sticky, add more flour, 1 tablespoon at a time, until the dough is smooth yet soft to the touch. If the dough is not soft to the touch but is very firm, add 1 tablespoon of water at a time, and process until the dough is smooth yet soft to the touch. Mix in the tomatoes. Cover the work bowl, and let the dough rise until doubled, about 1 hour. Or remove the dough to a lightly greased bowl, cover, and let rise until doubled, about 1 hour.

TO MIX THE DOUGH IN THE BREAD MACHINE Pour the water (at room temperature) into the pan. Add the remaining ingredients, except the tomatoes and cheese, in the order listed. Make an indentation in the center of the dry ingredients and add the yeast. Select *Dough,* and press *Start.* If the dough is wet and

sticky, add more flour, 1 tablespoon at a time, until the dough is smooth yet soft to the touch. If the dough is not soft to the touch but is very firm, add 1 teaspoon of water at a time, until the dough is smooth yet soft to the touch. Add the tomatoes and cheese when the machine signals it's time to add ingredients or when the cycle ends. The machine will stop when the dough is ready to shape and bake.

TO MIX AND BAKE THE BREAD IN THE BREAD MACHINE Pour the water (at room temperature) into the pan. Add the remaining ingredients, except the tomatoes and cheese, in the order listed. Make an indentation in the center of the dry ingredients and add the yeast. Select the *Basic* or *Whole Wheat* cycle; set the crust on *Medium;* and press *Start.* During the mixing cycle, if the dough is wet and sticky, add more flour, 1 tablespoon at a time, until the dough is smooth yet soft to the touch. If the dough is not soft to the touch but is very firm, add 1 teaspoon of water at a time, until the dough is smooth yet soft to the touch. Add the tomatoes and cheese when the machine signals it's time to add ingredients.

TO SHAPE AND BAKE IN THE OVEN Lightly grease a baking sheet. Turn the dough out onto a lightly floured board or lightly oiled surface. Punch the dough down, and divide the regular or large-size doughs into 2 parts. Shape each part into a baguette. Place the loaves, with the smooth side up, onto the baking sheet. Cover and let rise in a warm place until almost doubled, 45 minutes. Preheat the oven to 375°F. Using a sharp knife or a razor, slash the top of the loaves. Bake 30 to 35 minutes, until the loaves are golden. Remove from the pan and cool on a wire rack.

TOMATO-BASIL
SEMOLINA BAGUETTES

Little bites of sun-dried tomatoes makes this a delightful bread. Semolina flour is a hard-wheat flour that is often used for pasta; but because it is very high in protein, it's great for bread baking, too.

Sampler Loaf (1 baguette)

2/3 cup water

1 teaspoon freshly squeezed lemon juice

1 teaspoon sugar

1 teaspoon extra-virgin olive oil

1 teaspoon dried basil

1 teaspoon minced garlic

1 teaspoon salt

1/4 cup whole wheat flour

1/4 cup semolina flour

1 1/2 cups bread flour

1 teaspoon rapid-rising or active dry yeast

2 tablespoons oil-packed, julienne-cut sun-dried tomatoes, well drained

Regular Loaf (2 baguettes)

1 cup water

1 1/2 teaspoons freshly squeezed lemon juice

1 1/2 tablespoons sugar

1 1/2 teaspoons extra-virgin olive oil

1 1/2 teaspoons dried basil

1 1/2 teaspoons minced garlic

1 1/2 teaspoons salt

1/2 cup whole wheat flour

1/2 cup semolina flour

2 cups bread flour

1 1/2 teaspoons rapid-rising or active dry yeast

3 tablespoons oil-packed, julienne-cut sun-dried tomatoes, well drained

Large Loaf (2 baguettes)

1 1/3 cup water

2 teaspoons freshly squeezed lemon juice

1 tablespoon sugar

2 teaspoons extra-virgin olive oil

2 teaspoons dried basil

2 teaspoons minced garlic

2 teaspoons salt

3/4 cup whole wheat flour

3/4 cup semolina flour

2 1/2 cups bread flour

2 teaspoons rapid-rising or active dry yeast

1/4 cup oil-packed, julienne-cut sun-dried tomatoes, well drained

TO MIX THE DOUGH BY HAND Heat the water until warm, between 105° and 115°F; pour it along with the lemon juice and sugar into a large, warmed bowl, and add the yeast. Let stand 5 minutes, until the yeast begins to bubble. Stir in the oil, basil, garlic, salt, whole wheat flour, and semolina four. Beat until smooth. Slowly add half of the bread flour, and beat until a soft dough forms. Cover, and let stand 15 minutes. Turn the dough out onto a very lightly floured board, and knead, adding the remaining flour as necessary, until smooth and springy, about 5 minutes. Knead in the tomatoes. Wash the bowl and grease it; place the dough back in the bowl, and turn it over to grease the top. Cover, and let rise until doubled, about 1 hour.

TO MIX THE DOUGH WITH A HEAVY-DUTY MIXER Heat the water until warm, between 105° and 115°F; pour it along with the lemon juice and sugar into the warmed mixing bowl, and add the yeast. Let stand 5 minutes, until the yeast begins to bubble. Add the oil, basil, garlic, salt, whole wheat flour, and semolina flour. Beat until smooth. Slowly add half of the bread flour, and beat until a soft dough forms. Cover, and let stand 15 minutes. Knead the dough in the mixer with the dough hook, on medium to high speed, adding the remaining flour as necessary, until the dough pulls away from the sides of the bowl and is smooth and springy but still soft to the touch. Knead in the tomatoes. Remove the dough hook, cover the bowl, and let the dough rise until doubled, about 1 hour.

TO MIX THE DOUGH IN THE FOOD PROCESSOR Place the plastic dough blade into the work bowl. Heat the water until very warm, between 120° and 130°F; set aside. Add the lemon juice to the water. Place the remaining ingredients, except the tomatoes, into the work bowl. Turn the processor on, and slowly pour the water through the feed tube, processing until the dough is smooth and pulls away from the sides of the bowl. If the dough is wet and sticky, add more flour, 1 tablespoon at a time, until the dough is smooth yet soft to the touch. If the dough is not soft to the touch but is very firm, add 1 tablespoon of water at a time, and process until the dough is smooth yet soft to the touch. Mix in the tomatoes. Cover the work bowl, and let the dough rise until doubled, about 1 hour. Or remove the dough to a lightly greased bowl, cover, and let rise until doubled, about 1 hour.

TO MIX THE DOUGH IN THE BREAD MACHINE Pour the water (at room temperature) into the pan, and add the remaining ingredients, except the tomatoes. Place the tomatoes into the corners of the pan. Make an indentation in the dry ingredients and add the yeast. Select *Dough,* and press *Start.* If the dough is wet and sticky, add more flour, 1 tablespoon at a time, until the dough is smooth yet soft to the touch. If the dough is not soft to the touch but is very firm, add 1 teaspoon of water at a time, until the dough is smooth yet soft to the touch. The machine will stop when the dough is ready to shape and bake.

TO MIX AND BAKE THE BREAD IN THE BREAD MACHINE Pour the water (at room temperature) into the pan, and add the remaining ingredients, except the tomatoes. Place the tomatoes into the corners of the pan. Make an indentation in the dry ingredients and add the yeast. Select the *Basic* cycle, set the crust on *Medium,* and press *Start.* During the mixing cycle, if the dough is wet and sticky, add more flour, 1 tablespoon at a time, until the dough is smooth yet soft to the touch. If the dough is not soft to the touch but is very firm, add 1 teaspoon of water at a time, until the dough is smooth yet soft to the touch.

TO SHAPE AND BAKE IN THE OVEN Turn the dough out onto a lightly floured board; punch it down. Divide the regular or large size dough into 2 parts, and shape each into a baguette.

To bake on baking tiles Place the loaf, with the smooth side up, on a bread board, or rimless cookie sheet, sprinkled with flour or cornmeal and let rise in a warm place until doubled, 45 to 60 minutes. Place baking tiles or a pizza stone on a rack in the center of the oven. Fill a rimmed, shallow baking pan with stones or river rock no larger than $1^1/2$ inches in diameter and place it on the bottom rack of the oven. Preheat the oven to 450°F for at least 30 minutes. (Rocks should be hot enough to sizzle when water is dropped on them.) Using a sharp knife or a razor, slash the risen loaf lengthwise to a depth of about $1/4$ inch. Transfer the loaf onto the preheated baking tiles or pizza stone in the oven. (This is best done by gently easing the loaf onto the baking tile with the assistance of a straight-edged tool such as a bench scraper.) Immediately pour 1 cup water into the pan of rocks on the bottom rack of the oven. (This is most easily done by squirting water from a sport bottle onto the rocks.) Bake for 15 to 20 minutes, until loaf is golden brown. Remove from the oven and cool on a wire rack.

To bake in a pan   Lightly grease a baking sheet. Place the loaves, with the smooth side up, onto the baking sheet. Cover and let rise in a warm place until almost doubled, 45 minutes. Preheat the oven to 375°F. Using a sharp knife or a razor, slash the top of the loaves. Bake 25 to 30 minutes, until the loaves are golden. Remove from the oven and cool on a wire rack.

Herbed Garlic Butter

Not only is this butter delicious with Tomato-Basil Semolina Bread (page 210), either fresh or made into croutons, it's wonderful on steamed vegetables, poached fish, chicken breasts, and a simple baked potato.

ABOUT ³/₄ CUP

1 large garlic clove
¹/₄ cup (¹/₂ stick) butter, softened
¹/₂ cup parsley or watercress, firmly packed
2 tablespoons chopped fresh chives or 2 green
    onions, cut into 1-inch slices

1 teaspoon coarse (kosher) salt
Freshly ground coarse pepper, to taste

Turn on the food processor fitted with the steel blade, and add the garlic through the feed tube. While the machine is running add the remaining ingredients through the feed tube. Process until the mixture is smooth with dark green flecks. Or mince the garlic and place in a small bowl. Add the butter, and beat with a hand mixer until light and fluffy. Finely mince the parsley and chives; beat into the butter mixture. Add the salt and pepper; mix well.

TOMATO WHEAT BAGUETTES
WITH GARLIC AND ROSEMARY

Of course, if you bake this bread on the *French Bread* cycle in your bread machine, you won't have baguettes; but you will have lots of crunchy crust. Loaves baked on a baking sheet instead of on tiles will not have a classic crunchy crust, but they'll still be delicious.

Sampler Loaf (1 baguette)

²/3 cup tomato juice

¹/8 teaspoon salt

1 teaspoon extra-virgin olive oil

1 teaspoon dried rosemary

1 teaspoon minced garlic

¹/2 cup whole wheat flour

1¹/2 cups bread flour

1 teaspoon rapid-rising or active dry yeast

¹/4 cup chopped sun-dried tomatoes

Regular Loaf (2 baguettes)

1 cup tomato juice

¹/4 teaspoon salt

1¹/2 teaspoons extra-virgin olive oil

1¹/2 teaspoons dried rosemary

1¹/2 teaspoons minced garlic

³/4 cup whole wheat flour

2¹/4 cups bread flour

1¹/2 teaspoons rapid-rising or active dry yeast

¹/3 cup chopped sun-dried tomatoes

Large Loaf (2 baguettes)

1¹/3 cup tomato juice

¹/2 teaspoon salt

2 teaspoons extra-virgin olive oil

2 teaspoons dried rosemary

2 teaspoons minced garlic

1 cup whole wheat flour

3 cups bread flour

2 teaspoons rapid-rising or active dry yeast

¹/2 cup chopped sun-dried tomatoes

TO MIX THE DOUGH BY HAND Heat the tomato juice until warm, between 105° and 115°F; pour it into a large, warmed bowl, and add the yeast. Let stand 5 minutes, until the yeast begins to bubble. Stir in the salt, oil, rosemary, garlic, and whole wheat flour. Beat until smooth. Slowly add half of the bread flour, and beat until a soft dough forms. Cover, and let stand 15 minutes. Turn the dough out onto a very lightly floured board, and knead, adding the remaining flour as necessary, until smooth and springy,

about 5 minutes. Knead in the tomatoes. Wash the bowl and grease it; place the dough back in the bowl, and turn it over to grease the top. Cover, and let rise until doubled, about 1 hour.

TO MIX THE DOUGH WITH A HEAVY-DUTY MIXER Heat the tomato juice until warm, between 105° and 115°F; pour it into the warmed mixing bowl, and add the yeast and sugar. Let stand 5 minutes, until the yeast begins to bubble. Add the salt, oil, rosemary, garlic, and whole wheat flour. Beat until smooth. Slowly add half of the bread flour, and beat until a soft dough forms. Cover, and let stand 15 minutes. Knead the dough in the mixer with the dough hook, on medium to high speed, adding the remaining flour as necessary, until the dough pulls away from the sides of the bowl and is smooth and springy but still soft to the touch. Knead in the tomatoes. Remove the dough hook, cover the bowl, and let the dough rise until doubled, about 1 hour.

TO MIX THE DOUGH IN THE FOOD PROCESSOR

Place the plastic dough blade into the work bowl. Heat the tomato juice until very warm, between 120° and 130°F; set aside. Place the remaining ingredients into the work bowl. Turn the processor on, and slowly pour the tomato juice through the feed tube, processing until the dough is smooth and pulls away from the sides of the bowl. If the dough is wet and sticky, add more flour, 1 tablespoon at a time, until the dough is smooth yet soft to the touch. If the dough is not soft to the touch but is very firm, add 1 tablespoon of water at a time, and process until the dough is smooth yet soft to the touch. Cover the work bowl, and let the dough rise until doubled, about 1 hour. Or remove the dough to a lightly greased bowl, cover, and let rise until doubled, about 1 hour.

TO MIX THE DOUGH IN THE BREAD MACHINE

Pour the tomato juice (at room temperature) into the pan. Add the remaining ingredients, in the order listed. Make an indentation in the dry ingredients and add the yeast. Select *Dough,* and press *Start.* If the dough is wet

and sticky, add more flour, 1 tablespoon at a time, until the dough is smooth yet soft to the touch. If the dough is not soft to the touch but is very firm, add 1 teaspoon of water at a time, until the dough is smooth yet soft to the touch. The machine will stop when the dough is ready to shape and bake.

TO MIX AND BAKE THE BREAD IN THE BREAD MACHINE

Pour the tomato juice (at room temperature) into the pan. Add the remaining ingredients, in the order listed. Make an indentation in the dry ingredients and add the yeast. Select the *Basic* or *French Bread* cycle, set the crust on *Medium* or *Dark,* and press *Start.* During the mixing cycle, if the dough is wet and sticky, add more flour, 1 tablespoon at a time, until the dough is smooth yet soft to the touch. If the dough is not soft to the touch but is very firm, add 1 teaspoon of water at a time, until the dough is smooth yet soft to the touch.

TO SHAPE AND BAKE IN THE OVEN

Turn the dough out onto a lightly floured board; punch it down. Divide the regular or large size dough into 2 parts, and shape each into a baguette.

To bake on baking tiles Place the loaf, with the smooth side up, on a bread board, or rimless cookie sheet, sprinkled with flour or cornmeal and let rise in a warm place until doubled, 45 to 60 minutes. Place baking tiles or a pizza stone on a rack in the center of the oven. Fill a rimmed, shallow baking pan with stones or river rock no larger than $1^{1}/2$ inches in diameter and place it on the bottom rack of the oven. Preheat the oven to 450°F for at least 30 minutes. (Rocks should be hot enough to sizzle when water is dropped on them.) Using a sharp knife or a razor, slash the risen loaf lengthwise to a depth of about $1/4$ inch. Transfer the loaf onto the preheated baking tiles or pizza stone in the oven. (This is best done by gently easing the loaf onto the baking tile with the assistance of a straight-edged tool such as a bench scraper.) Immediately pour 1 cup water into the pan of rocks on the bottom rack of the oven. (This is most easily done by squirting water from a sport bottle onto the rocks.) Bake for 15 to 20 minutes, until loaf is golden brown. Remove from the oven and cool on a wire rack.

To bake in a pan Lightly grease a baking pan. Place the loaves, with the smooth side up, into the pan. Cover and let rise in a warm place until almost doubled, 45 minutes. Preheat the oven to 375°F. Using a sharp knife or a razor, slash the top of the loaves, and brush them with water. Bake 25 to 30 minutes, until the loaves are golden. Remove from the oven and cool on a wire rack.

Tomato Basil Crostini

Tomato Wheat Baguettes with Garlic and Rosemary (page 214) make a great appetizer when baked into crisp toasts, or crostini, and topped with a simple fresh tomato mixture.

24 APPETIZERS

1 loaf Tomato Wheat with Garlic and Rosemary
   bread, preferably day-old
Olive oil for brushing
6 Italian (Roma) tomatoes, chopped

3 garlic cloves, minced or pressed
3 tablespoons minced fresh basil
1/4 cup freshly grated Parmesan or Asiago cheese, or
   1/2 cup crumbled feta cheese

Preheat the oven to 300°F. Cut the bread into 1/4-inch slices on the diagonal (you will need 24 slices), and spread them in a single layer on a cookie sheet. Brush each slice with olive oil. Bake 30 to 45 minutes, without turning, until dry and crisp. Remove from the oven and allow to cool on the baking pan. Raise the oven to 400°F.

Mix the tomatoes, garlic, and basil in a medium bowl. Spread a spoonful on top of each piece of toasted bread. Sprinkle with the Parmesan cheese. *You can do this much ahead.* Just before serving, bake 2 to 3 minutes, until the topping is warm.

Buttermilk–Fennel Seed Rye

Caraway Rye Bread

Buttered Fennel Seed Croutons

Breakfast Bread Pudding with Chilies and Cheese

Chili Masa Cheddar Cheese Bread

Cinnamon-Honey Whole Wheat Bread

Danish Pumpernickel Bread

Danish Smorrebrod with Onion Jam and Pâté

Fennel-Rye Black Bread

Baked Ham on Rye Breakfast Sandwich

Herb and Onion Bread

Country Vegetable Chowder

Italian Herb Bread

Garden Fresh Vegetable Bake

Millet, Wheat, and Six-Seed High-Fiber Bread

Oatmeal Seed Bread

Orange Rye and Wheat Bread

Pecan and Caraway Bread

Rosemary Wheat Focaccia

Rustic Grains Bread

Spiced Scandinavian Limpa

five

WHOLE GRAIN BREADS
WITH HERBS, SPICES,
AND SEEDS

*I*n European and Scandinavian traditions, whole grain breads are made festive by the addition of seeds and spices. Fennel seed in a buttermilk rye, caraway in a molasses rye bread, cinnamon in whole wheat bread, and chili peppers in a cornmeal bread are all based on very natural flavor affinities. Poppy, sesame, and sunflower seeds not only add mild flavor but also are visually attractive and make handsome toppings for breads.

The breads themselves are delicious and basic. The addition of seeds and spices simply embellishes what already is very good. I like to turn to the breads in this chapter when I want an attractive, yet delicious loaf go to with a buffet meal or a soup supper. Bread on a board with a sharp serrated knife, so guests can cut their own slices, next to a hunk of some good cheese is often the appetizer course as people gather at our house. Here are many wonderful breads for you to choose from.

BUTTERMILK-FENNEL SEED RYE

The licorice flavor of fennel is pleasant in this Scandinavian-style rye bread.

Sampler Loaf

2/3 cup buttermilk

1 teaspoon packed brown sugar

2 teaspoons butter

1 teaspoon fennel seeds

1 teaspoon salt

1/4 cup dark rye flour

13/4 cups bread flour

1 teaspoon rapid-rising or active
    dry yeast

Regular Loaf

1 cup buttermilk

2 teaspoons packed brown sugar

1 tablespoon butter

2 teaspoons fennel seeds

11/2 teaspoons salt

1/2 cup dark rye flour

21/2 cups bread flour

11/2 teaspoons rapid-rising or
    active dry yeast

Large Loaf

11/3 cups buttermilk

1 tablespoon packed brown sugar

11/2 tablespoons butter

1 tablespoon fennel seeds

2 teaspoons salt

1 cup dark rye flour

3 cups bread flour

2 teaspoons rapid-rising or active
    dry yeast

TO MIX THE DOUGH BY HAND Heat the buttermilk, brown sugar, and butter, until the butter melts; cool until warm, between 105° and 115°F. Pour the mixture into a large, warmed bowl, and add the yeast. Let stand 5 minutes, until the yeast begins to bubble. Stir in the fennel seeds, salt, and rye flour. Beat well. Slowly add half of the bread flour and beat until a smooth dough forms. Cover, and let stand 15 minutes. Turn the dough out onto a very lightly floured board, and knead, adding the remaining flour as necessary, until smooth and springy, about 5 minutes. Wash the bowl and grease it; place the dough back in the bowl, and turn it over to grease the top. Cover, and let rise until doubled, about 1 hour.

TO MIX THE DOUGH WITH A HEAVY-DUTY MIXER Heat the buttermilk, brown sugar, and butter, until the butter melts; cool until warm, between 105° and 115°F. Pour the mixture into the warmed mixing bowl, and add the yeast. Let stand 5 minutes, until the yeast begins to bubble. Add the fennel seeds, salt, and rye flour. Beat well. Slowly add half of the bread flour and beat until a smooth dough forms. Cover, and let stand 15 minutes. Knead the dough in the mixer with the dough hook, on medium to high speed, adding the remaining flour as necessary, until the dough pulls away from the sides of the bowl and is smooth and springy but still soft to the touch. Remove the dough hook, cover the bowl, and let the dough rise until doubled, about 1 hour.

TO MIX THE DOUGH IN THE FOOD PROCESSOR Place the plastic dough blade into the work bowl. Heat the buttermilk, brown sugar, and butter, until the butter melts; cool until very warm, between 120° and 130°F; set aside. Place the remaining ingredients into the work bowl. Turn the processor on, and slowly pour the buttermilk mixture through the feed tube, processing until the dough is smooth and pulls away from the sides of the bowl. If the dough is wet and sticky, add more flour, 1 tablespoon at a time, until the dough is smooth yet soft to the touch. If the dough is not soft to the touch but is very firm, add 1 tablespoon of water at a time, and process until the dough is smooth yet soft to the touch. Cover the work bowl, and let the dough rise until doubled, about 1 hour. Or remove the dough to a lightly greased bowl, cover, and let rise until doubled, about 1 hour.

TO MIX THE DOUGH IN THE BREAD MACHINE Pour the buttermilk (at room temperature) into the pan. Add the remaining ingredients, in the order listed. Make an indentation in the dry ingredients and add the yeast. Select *Dough,* and press *Start.* If the dough is wet and sticky, add more flour, 1 tablespoon at a time, until the dough is smooth yet soft to the touch. If the dough is not soft to the touch but is very firm, add 1 teaspoon of water at a time, until the dough is smooth yet soft to the touch. The machine will stop when the dough is ready to shape and bake.

TO MIX AND BAKE THE BREAD IN THE BREAD MACHINE Pour the buttermilk (at room temperature) into the pan. Add the remaining ingredients, in the order listed. Make an indentation in the dry ingredients and add the yeast. Select the *Basic* cycle, set the crust on *Medium,* and press *Start.* During the mixing cycle, if the dough is wet and sticky, add more flour, 1 tablespoon at a time, until the dough is smooth

yet soft to the touch. If the dough is not soft to the touch but is very firm, add 1 teaspoon of water at a time, until the dough is smooth yet soft to the touch.

TO SHAPE AND BAKE IN THE OVEN Lightly grease a baking sheet. Turn the dough out onto a lightly floured board or lightly oiled surface. Punch the dough down, and shape it into a round loaf. Place the loaf, with the smooth side up, onto the baking sheet. Cover and let rise in a warm place until almost doubled, 45 to 60 minutes. Preheat the oven to 375°F. Bake 35 to 40 minutes, until the loaf is golden and a wooden skewer inserted into the loaf comes out clean and dry. Brush the top of the loaf while it's still hot with melted butter, if desired. Remove from the pan and cool on a wire rack.

CARAWAY RYE BREAD

Rye flour itself doesn't darken a bread very much, so most bakeries add black bread coloring made from burned sugar. I rather like the paleness of the crumb and the mild molasses and caraway flavor of this loaf. Although the bread is great for sandwiches, I usually go for just a slathering of butter.

Sampler Loaf	Regular Loaf	Large Loaf
2/3 cup water	1 cup water	11/3 cups water
1 tablespoon dark molasses	2 tablespoons dark molasses	3 tablespoons dark molasses
2 teaspoons butter	1 tablespoon butter	11/2 tablespoons butter
3/4 teaspoon salt	1 teaspoon salt	11/2 teaspoons salt
1 teaspoon caraway seeds	2 teaspoons caraway seeds	1 tablespoon caraway seeds
1/2 cup pumpernickel rye flour	3/4 cup pumpernickel rye flour	1 cup pumpernickel rye flour
11/2 cups bread flour	21/4 cups bread flour	3 cups bread flour
1 teaspoon rapid-rising or active dry yeast	11/2 teaspoons rapid-rising or active dry yeast	2 teaspoons rapid-rising or active dry yeast

TO MIX THE DOUGH BY HAND Heat the water until warm, between 105° and 115°F; pour it into a large, warmed bowl, and add the yeast. Let stand 5 minutes, until the yeast begins to bubble. Stir in the molasses, butter, salt, caraway seed, and rye flour. Beat well. Cover, and let stand 15 minutes. Slowly add the bread flour, and beat until a smooth dough forms. Turn the dough out onto a very lightly floured board, and knead, adding flour if necessary, until smooth and springy, about 5 minutes. Wash the bowl and grease it; place the dough back in the bowl, and turn it over to grease the top. Cover, and let rise until doubled, about 1 hour.

TO MIX THE DOUGH WITH A HEAVY-DUTY MIXER Heat the water until warm, between 105° and 115°F; pour it into the warmed mixing bowl, and add the yeast. Let stand 5 minutes, until the yeast begins to bubble. Add the molasses, butter, salt, caraway seeds, and rye flour. Beat well. Cover, and let stand 15 minutes. Slowly add the bread flour, and beat until a smooth dough forms. Knead the dough in the mixer with the dough hook, on medium to high speed, adding flour as necessary, until the dough pulls away from the sides of the bowl and is smooth and springy but still soft to the touch. Remove the dough hook, cover the bowl, and let the dough rise until doubled, about 1 hour.

TO MIX THE DOUGH IN THE FOOD PROCESSOR Place the plastic dough blade into the work bowl. Heat the water until very warm, between 120° and 130°F; set aside. Place the remaining ingredients into the work bowl. Turn the processor on, and slowly pour the water through the feed tube, processing until the dough is smooth and pulls away from the sides of the bowl. If the dough is wet and sticky, add more flour, 1 tablespoon at a time, until the dough is smooth yet soft to the touch. If the dough is not soft to the touch but is very firm, add 1 tablespoon of water at a time, and process until the dough is smooth yet soft to the touch. Cover the work bowl, and let the dough rise until doubled, about 1 hour. Or remove the dough to a lightly greased bowl, cover, and let rise until doubled, about 1 hour.

TO MIX THE DOUGH IN THE BREAD MACHINE Pour the water (at room temperature) into the pan. Add the remaining ingredients, in the order listed. Make an indentation in the dry ingredients and add the yeast. Select *Dough,* and press *Start.* If the dough is wet and sticky, add more flour, 1 tablespoon at a time, until the dough is smooth yet soft to the touch. If the dough is not soft to the touch but is very firm, add 1 teaspoon of water at a time, until the dough is smooth yet soft to the touch. The machine will stop when the dough is ready to shape and bake.

TO MIX AND BAKE THE BREAD IN THE BREAD MACHINE Pour the water (at room temperature) into the pan. Add the remaining ingredients, in the order listed. Make an indentation in the dry ingredients and add the yeast. Select the *Basic* or *Whole Wheat* cycle, set the crust on *Medium,* and press *Start.* During the mixing cycle, if the dough is wet and sticky, add more flour, 1 tablespoon at a time, until the dough is smooth yet soft to the touch. If the dough is not soft to the touch but is very firm, add 1 teaspoon of water at a time, until the dough is smooth yet soft to the touch.

TO SHAPE AND BAKE IN THE OVEN Lightly grease an 8- or 9-inch round cake pan or baking sheet. Turn the dough out onto a lightly floured board or lightly oiled surface. Punch the dough down, and shape it into a round loaf. Place the loaf, with the smooth side up, into the pan. Cover and let rise in a warm place until almost doubled, 45 to 60 minutes. Preheat the oven to 375°F. Bake 35 to 40 minutes, until the loaf is golden and a wooden skewer inserted into the loaf comes out clean and dry. Brush the top of the loaf while it's still hot with melted butter, if desired. Remove from the pan and cool on a wire rack.

Buttered Fennel Seed Croutons

Any close-textured stale seeded or plain rye bread is good, but I especially like Buttermilk–Fennel Seed Rye Bread (page 220) this way, because the licoricey flavor is emphasized. The croutons are good as a snack as well as with a simple pea soup.

4 CUPS

4 cups bread cubes, cut ¹/₂ inch, made from
   Buttermilk–Fennel Seed Rye Bread

¹/₄ cup (¹/₂ stick) butter, melted

2 teaspoons fennel seeds

Preheat the oven to 350°F. In a large bowl, toss the bread cubes with the butter and fennel seeds until evenly mixed. Turn out onto a baking sheet. Bake 15 to 20 minutes until the cubes are toasted. Serve immediately or store in an airtight container in a cool place or in the freezer.

Breakfast Bread Pudding with Chilies and Cheese

For an easy Sunday breakfast, assemble this dish the night before. Cover, refrigerate overnight, and bake it the next morning.

4 SERVINGS

4 large eggs
1 1/2 cups half-and-half
1 teaspoon salt
1/8 teaspoon cayenne
1/2 teaspoon dried oregano

2 cups bread cubes, cut 1/2 inch, made from crusty whole grain bread
6 ounces Monterey Jack cheese, shredded or chopped
2 roasted poblano chilies, chopped

Preheat the oven to 350°F. Grease a 9-inch square baking dish. In a large bowl, whisk together the eggs, half-and-half, salt, cayenne, and oregano. Add the bread cubes, cheese, and chilies; fold together. Pour the mixture into the baking dish. Bake 30 to 40 minutes, until the custard is set. Serve warm.

ROASTING CHILIES

To roast chili peppers, preheat the oven to 500°F. Rub the chilies with olive oil. Place on a baking pan and roast 10 to 13 minutes, until the skins are bubbly with charred spots. Remove from the oven, and place into a brown paper bag; let steam 15 minutes. Pull off the skins, open the chilies, and remove the seeds. Poblano chilies vary from mild to slightly hot. If you have the hot chilies, you may want to wear gloves. Be sure not to touch your eyes after handling the seeds of hot chili peppers.

CHILI MASA
CHEDDAR CHEESE BREAD

Masa harina is a finely ground cornmeal, treated with lime, from which corn tortillas are made. It is widely available in the baking or Mexican foods sections of most markets and whole foods stores. This is a pale, almost white bread with the aroma of cornmeal, a bite of chili flakes, the crunch of toasted pepitas, and the richness of cheese. When mixing this dough in the bread machine, it may seem to be very dry and crumbly at first because the masa really sucks up the liquid; however, after the machine has mixed the dough for a few minutes, it softens. If the dough is still dry, add water according to the directions. When you bake this bread in the bread machine, the character of it changes. The cheese gets mixed into the dough so that it is not distinguishable.

Sampler Loaf

^{2}/3 cup water

1 teaspoon freshly squeezed
   lemon juice

1 tablespoon corn oil

^{3}/4 teaspoon salt

1 teaspoon sugar

^{1}/2 teaspoon red pepper flakes

^{1}/2 cup masa harina

1^1/2 cups bread flour

1 teaspoon rapid-rising or active
   dry yeast

^{1}/3 cup toasted pepitas*

^{1}/4 cup diced sharp
   Cheddar cheese

Regular Loaf

1 cup water

2 teaspoons freshly squeezed
   lemon juice

2 tablespoons corn oil

1 teaspoon salt

1^1/2 teaspoons sugar

1 teaspoon red pepper flakes

^{3}/4 cup masa harina

2^1/4 cups bread flour

1^1/2 teaspoons rapid-rising or
   active dry yeast

^{1}/2 cup toasted pepitas*

^{1}/3 cup diced sharp
   Cheddar cheese

Large Loaf

1^1/3 cups water

1 tablespoon freshly squeezed
   lemon juice

3 tablespoons corn oil

1^1/2 teaspoons salt

2 teaspoons sugar

1^1/2 teaspoons red pepper flakes

1 cup masa harina

3 cups bread flour

2 teaspoons rapid-rising or active
   dry yeast

^{3}/4 cup toasted pepitas*

^{1}/2 cup diced sharp
   Cheddar cheese

GLAZE FOR BREAD BAKED CONVENTIONALLY

1 egg

1 tablespoon water

TO MIX THE DOUGH BY HAND Heat the water until warm, between 105° and 115°F; pour it into a large, warmed bowl, and add the yeast. Let stand 5 minutes, until the yeast begins to bubble. Stir in the lemon juice, oil, salt, sugar, pepper flakes, and masa harina. Beat well. Cover, and let stand 15 minutes. Slowly add the bread flour, and beat until a smooth dough forms. Turn the dough out onto a very lightly floured board, and knead, adding flour if necessary, until smooth and springy, about 5 minutes. Knead in the pepitas and cheese. Wash the bowl and grease it; place the dough back in the bowl, and turn it over to grease the top. Cover, and let rise until doubled, about 1 hour.

TO MIX THE DOUGH WITH A HEAVY-DUTY MIXER Heat the water until warm, between 105° and 115°F; pour it into the warmed mixing bowl, and add the yeast. Let stand 5 minutes, until the yeast begins to bubble. Add the lemon juice, oil, salt, sugar, pepper flakes, and masa marina. Beat well. Cover, and let stand 15 minutes. Slowly add the bread flour, and beat until a smooth dough forms. Knead the dough in the mixer with the dough hook, on medium to high speed, adding flour as necessary, until the dough pulls away from the sides of the bowl and is smooth and springy but still soft to the touch. Knead in the pepitas and cheese. Remove the dough hook, cover the bowl, and let the dough rise until doubled, about 1 hour.

TO MIX THE DOUGH IN THE FOOD PROCESSOR Place the plastic dough blade into the work bowl. Heat the water until very warm, between 120° and 130°F; set aside. Place the remaining ingredients, except the pepitas and cheese, into the work bowl. Turn the processor on, and slowly pour the water through the feed tube, processing until the dough is smooth and pulls away from the sides of the bowl. If the dough is wet and sticky, add more flour, 1 tablespoon at a time, until the dough is smooth yet soft to the touch. If the dough is not soft to the touch but is very firm, add 1 tablespoon of water at a time, and process until the dough is smooth yet soft to the touch. Mix in the pepitas and cheese. Cover the work bowl, and let the dough rise until doubled, about 1 hour. Or remove the dough to a lightly greased bowl, cover, and let rise until doubled, about 1 hour.

TO MIX THE DOUGH IN THE BREAD MACHINE Pour the water (at room temperature) into the pan. Add the remaining ingredients, except the pepitas and cheese, in the order listed. Make an indentation in the dry ingredients and add the yeast. Select *Dough,* and press *Start.* If the dough is wet and sticky, add more flour, 1 tablespoon at a time, until the dough is smooth yet soft to the touch. If the dough is not soft to the touch but is very firm, add 1 teaspoon of water at a time, until the dough is smooth yet soft to the touch. Add the pepitas and cheese when the machine signals it's time to add ingredients or

*Note *Pepitas are toasted pumpkin seeds, widely used in Mexican cooking. They are sold salted, roasted, and raw and with or without hulls. Pepitas are sold in health food, whole foods, and Mexican markets. My local grocery chain sells them in the bulk foods section. Substitute toasted, salted sunflower seeds if pepitas are not available.*

when the cycle ends. The machine will stop when the dough is ready to shape and bake.

TO MIX AND BAKE THE BREAD IN THE BREAD MACHINE Pour the water (at room temperature) into the pan. Add the remaining ingredients, except the pepitas and cheese, in the order listed. Make an indentation in the dry ingredients and add the yeast. Select the *Fruit and Nut, Basic,* or *Whole Wheat* cycle; set the crust on *Medium;* and press *Start.* During the mixing cycle, if the dough is wet and sticky, add more flour, 1 tablespoon at a time, until the dough is smooth yet soft to the touch. If the dough is not soft to the touch but is very firm, add 1 teaspoon of water at a time, until the dough is smooth yet soft to the touch. Add the pepitas and cheese when the machine signals it's time to add ingredients.

TO SHAPE AND BAKE IN THE OVEN Lightly grease a baking sheet. Turn the dough out onto a lightly floured board or lightly oiled surface. Punch the dough down, and shape it into a round loaf. Place the loaf, with the smooth side up, onto the baking sheet. Cover and let rise in a warm place until almost doubled, 45 minutes. Preheat the oven to 375°F. To glaze, beat the egg with the water, and brush the mixture on the loaf in a tic-tac-toe design. Bake 25 to 35 minutes, until the loaf is golden and a wooden skewer inserted into the loaf comes out clean and dry. Remove from the pan and cool on a wire rack.

CINNAMON-HONEY WHOLE WHEAT BREAD

Cinnamon and honey work together to bring out the wheaty flavor of this bread.

Sampler loaf	Regular Loaf	Large Loaf
2/3 cup water	1 cup water	1 1/3 cup water
1 tablespoon honey	1 1/2 tablespoons honey	2 tablespoons honey
1 tablespoon butter or shortening	1 1/2 tablespoons butter or shortening	2 tablespoons butter or shortening
1 teaspoon salt	1 1/2 teaspoons salt	2 teaspoons salt
1/4 teaspoon cinnamon	1/2 teaspoon cinnamon	1 teaspoon cinnamon
1 cup whole wheat flour	1 1/2 cups whole wheat flour	2 cups whole wheat flour
1 cup bread flour	1 1/2 cups bread flour	2 cups bread flour
1 teaspoon dry yeast	1 1/2 teaspoons dry yeast	2 teaspoons dry yeast

TO MIX THE DOUGH BY HAND Heat the water until warm, between 105° and 115°F; pour it into a large, warmed bowl, and add the yeast. Let stand 5 minutes, until the yeast begins to bubble. Stir in the honey, butter, salt, cinnamon, and whole wheat flour. Beat well. Slowly add half of the bread flour, and beat until a smooth dough forms. Cover, and let stand 15 minutes. Turn the dough out onto a very lightly floured board, and knead, adding the remaining flour as necessary, until smooth and springy, about 5 minutes. Wash the bowl and grease it; place the dough back in the bowl, and turn it over to grease the top. Cover, and let rise until doubled, about 1 hour.

TO MIX THE DOUGH WITH A HEAVY-DUTY MIXER Heat the water until warm, between 105° and 115°F; pour it into the warmed mixing bowl, and add the yeast. Let stand 5 minutes, until the yeast begins to bubble. Add the honey, butter, salt, cinnamon, and the whole wheat flour. Beat well. Slowly add half of the bread flour, and beat until a smooth dough forms. Cover, and let stand 15 minutes. Knead the dough in the mixer with the dough hook, on medium to high speed, adding the remaining flour as necessary, until the dough pulls away from the sides of the bowl and is smooth and springy but still soft to the touch. Remove the dough hook, cover the bowl, and let the dough rise until doubled, about 1 hour.

TO MIX THE DOUGH IN THE FOOD PROCESSOR Place the plastic dough blade into the work bowl. Heat the water until very warm, between 120° and 130°F; set aside. Place the remaining ingredients into the work bowl. Turn the processor on, and slowly pour the water through the feed tube, processing until the dough is smooth and pulls away from the sides of the bowl. If the dough is wet and sticky, add more flour, 1 tablespoon at a time, until the dough is smooth yet soft to the touch. If the dough is not soft to the touch but is very firm, add 1 tablespoon of water at a time, and process until the dough is smooth yet soft to the touch. Cover the work bowl, and let the dough rise until doubled, about 1 hour. Or remove the dough to a lightly greased bowl, cover, and let rise until doubled, about 1 hour.

TO MIX THE DOUGH IN THE BREAD MACHINE Pour the water (at room temperature) into the pan. Add the remaining ingredients, in the order listed. Make an indentation in the dry ingredients and add the yeast. Select *Dough,* and press *Start.* If the dough is wet and sticky, add more flour, 1 tablespoon at a time, until the dough is smooth yet soft to the touch. If the dough is not soft to the touch but is very firm, add 1 teaspoon of water at a time, until the dough is smooth yet soft to the touch. The machine will stop when the dough is ready to shape and bake.

TO MIX AND BAKE THE BREAD IN THE BREAD MACHINE Pour the water (at room temperature) into the pan. Add the remaining ingredients, in the order listed. Make an indentation in the dry ingredients and add the yeast. Select the *Basic* or *Whole Wheat* cycle, set the crust on *Medium,* and press *Start.* During the mixing cycle, if the dough is wet and sticky, add more flour, 1 tablespoon at a time, until the dough is smooth yet soft to the touch. If the dough is not soft to the touch but is very firm, add 1 teaspoon of water at a time, until the dough is smooth yet soft to the touch.

TO SHAPE AND BAKE IN THE OVEN Lightly grease an 8- or 9-inch round cake pan or a baking sheet. Turn the dough out onto a lightly floured board or lightly oiled surface. Punch the dough down, and shape it into a round loaf. Place the loaf, with the smooth side up, into the pan. Cover and let rise in a warm place until almost doubled, 45 to 60 minutes. Preheat the oven to 375°F. Bake 35 to 40 minutes, until the loaf is golden and a wooden skewer inserted into the loaf comes out clean and dry. Brush the top of the loaf while it's still hot with melted butter, if desired. Remove from the pan and cool on a wire rack.

DANISH PUMPERNICKEL BREAD

This is a close-textured bread with a wonderfully rich, grainy, sweet molasses flavor. One of the key ingredients, seven-grain cereal, can be found in the hot cereals section of a supermarket, the bulk foods section of a health or whole foods store, and the specialty section of a well-stocked market. Cut the bread into thin slices to use as a base for open-faced sandwiches, as the Danes do, or enjoy it simply buttered or topped with a shaving of Havarti served along with thick pea soup.

Sampler Loaf	Regular Loaf	Large Loaf
$2/3$ cup water	1 cup water	$1^{1}/3$ cup water
2 tablespoons dark molasses	3 tablespoons dark molasses	$1/4$ cup dark molasses
1 tablespoon soft butter	2 tablespoons soft butter	3 tablespoons soft butter
1 teaspoon caraway seeds	2 teaspoons caraway seeds	1 tablespoon caraway seeds
1 teaspoon salt	$1^{1}/2$ teaspoons salt	2 teaspoons salt
1 tablespoon 7-grain cereal	2 tablespoons 7-grain cereal	3 tablespoons 7-grain cereal
$3/4$ cup pumpernickel or dark rye flour	1 cup pumpernickel or dark rye flour	$1^{1}/2$ cups pumpernickel or dark rye flour
1 teaspoon gluten	2 teaspoons gluten	1 tablespoon gluten
$1^{1}/4$ cups bread flour	2 cups bread flour	$2^{1}/2$ cups bread flour
1 teaspoon rapid-rising or active dry yeast	$1^{1}/2$ teaspoons rapid-rising or active dry yeast	2 teaspoons rapid-rising or active dry yeast

TO MIX THE DOUGH BY HAND Heat the water until warm, between 105° and 115°F; pour it into a large, warmed bowl, and add the yeast and molasses. Let stand 5 minutes, until the yeast begins to bubble. Stir in the butter, caraway seeds, salt, cereal, and rye flour. Beat well. Cover, and let stand 15 minutes. Slowly add the gluten and bread flour, and beat until a soft dough forms. Turn the dough out onto a very lightly floured board, and knead, adding flour if necessary, until smooth and springy, about 5 minutes. Wash the bowl and grease it; place the dough back in the bowl, and turn it over to grease the top. Cover, and let rise until doubled, about 1 hour.

TO MIX THE DOUGH WITH A HEAVY-DUTY MIXER Heat the water until warm, between 105° and 115°F; pour it into the warmed mixing bowl, and add the yeast and molasses. Let stand 5 minutes, until the yeast begins to bubble. Add the butter, caraway seeds, salt, cereal, and rye flour. Beat well. Cover, and let stand 15 minutes. Slowly add the gluten and bread flour, and beat until a soft dough forms. Knead the dough in the mixer with the dough hook, on medium to high speed, adding flour as necessary, until the dough pulls away from the sides of the bowl and is smooth and springy but still soft to the touch. Remove the dough hook, cover the bowl, and let the dough rise until doubled, about 1 hour.

TO MIX THE DOUGH IN THE FOOD PROCESSOR Place the plastic dough blade into the work bowl. Heat the water until very warm, between 120° and 130°F; set aside. Place the remaining ingredients into the work bowl. Turn the processor on, and slowly pour the water through the feed tube, processing until the dough is smooth and pulls away from the sides of the bowl. If the dough is wet and sticky, add more flour, 1 tablespoon at a time, until the dough is smooth yet soft to the touch. If the dough is not soft to the touch but is very firm, add 1 tablespoon of water at a time, and process until the dough is smooth yet soft to the touch. Cover the work bowl, and let the dough rise until doubled, about 1 hour. Or remove the dough to a lightly greased bowl, cover, and let rise until doubled, about 1 hour.

TO MIX THE DOUGH IN THE BREAD MACHINE Pour the water (at room temperature) into the pan. Add the remaining ingredients, in the order listed. Make an indentation in the dry ingredients and add the yeast. Select *Dough,* and press *Start.* If the dough is wet and sticky, add more flour, 1 tablespoon at a time, until the dough is smooth yet soft to the touch. If the dough is not soft to the touch but is very firm, add 1 teaspoon of water at a time, until the dough is smooth yet soft to the touch. The machine will stop when the dough is ready to shape and bake.

TO MIX AND BAKE THE BREAD IN THE BREAD MACHINE Pour the water (at room temperature) into the pan. Add the remaining ingredients, in the order listed. Make an indentation in the dry ingredients and add the yeast. Select the *Basic* cycle, set the crust on *Medium,* and press *Start.* During the mixing cycle, if the dough is wet and sticky, add more flour, 1 tablespoon at a time, until the dough is smooth yet soft to the touch. If the dough is not soft to the touch but is very firm, add 1 teaspoon of water at a time, until the dough is smooth yet soft to the touch.

TO SHAPE AND BAKE IN THE OVEN Lightly grease a 9 × 5-inch loaf pan or an 8- or 9-inch round cake pan. Turn the dough out onto a lightly floured board or lightly oiled surface. Punch the dough down, and shape it into an oblong or round loaf. Place the loaf, with the smooth side up, into the pan. Cover and let rise in a warm place until almost doubled, 45 to 60 minutes. Preheat the oven to 350°F. Bake 35 to 40 minutes, until the loaf is golden and a wooden skewer inserted into the loaf comes out clean and dry. Remove from the pan and cool on a wire rack.

Pumpernickel rye and dark rye flour are unsifted and contain the bran from the rye kernel. These flours are available from various mills and are sold under several brand names. Hodgson Mills, Homestead Mills, and King Arthur Flour are three of the brand names I have used.

Danish Smorrebrod with Onion Jam and Pâté

This is a variation of a sandwich I enjoyed at Ida Davidson's in Copenhagen, where the sandwich menu is a full meter long!

1 SANDWICH

1 thick slice Danish Pumpernickel Bread

1 to 2 teaspoons Whipped Anchovy Butter
  (recipe follows)

Several leaves of baby lettuce

1 to 2 tablespoons Onion Jam (recipe follows)

1 to 2 tablespoons Chicken Liver Pâté
  (recipe follows)

Chopped green onion

Toast the bread on both sides under the broiler until lightly browned. Spread with the Anchovy Butter, and top with the lettuce. Top the lettuce with the Onion Jam and Chicken Liver Pâté. Garnish with chopped green onion.

Whipped Anchovy Butter

ABOUT ³/₄ CUP

¹/₂ cup (1 stick) butter, softened
1 teaspoon anchovy paste
1 teaspoon freshly squeezed lemon juice

In a small bowl, with a hand mixer, whip the butter, anchovy paste, and lemon juice until smooth and fluffy. Use immediately, or cover and refrigerate until ready to use; return to room temperature for easy spreading.

Onion Jam

In addition to contributing to Danish smorrebrod, this is wonderful as the lone filling in a sandwich. I keep a pot of onion jam in the refrigerator for other uses, too. Top a burger or a baked potato with it, toss it with pasta, or stir a spoonful into a vegetable soup for extra flavor.

1 CUP

2 large yellow onions, peeled
1 tablespoon extra-virgin olive oil
1 teaspoon sugar
1/4 teaspoon salt

Cut the onions into halves, from the top to the stem. Lay 1 half, cut side down on a cutting board, and cut it again from the top to the stem. Cut into thin slices, making quarter circles. Repeat with the remaining 3 halves. Warm the oil in a heavy skillet over medium heat. Add the onions and sprinkle with the sugar and salt. Sauté, stirring often, about 20 minutes, until the onions begin to wilt. Reduce the heat to low, cook, stirring occasionally, until the onions "melt" down to a golden color. They shouldn't brown at all, but should become very soft and juicy. Remove from the heat, and invert into a serving bowl or a refrigerator jar. Use immediately or store, covered, in the refrigerator.

Chicken Liver Pâté

I like to have a bit of chicken liver pâté on hand, especially when I know we'll be having guests in. Spread on croutons or crackers by itself or topped with thin slices of crisp apple, it makes a nice snack or appetizer.

1 CUP

4 ounces chicken livers
1 cup water
3 tablespoons butter
1/2 small onion, chopped
1 garlic clove, minced or mashed
1 tablespoon cognac
1 tablespoon whipping cream or sour cream
1/4 cup finely chopped toasted filberts or almonds

Rinse the livers and pat dry. Cut out any dark spots, and remove the veins and membranes. Bring the water to a boil in a medium saucepan; add the livers, reduce the heat, cover, and simmer 5 minutes. Drain, and set aside. Melt the butter in a medium skillet over moderate heat; add the onion and garlic, and cook until the onions are soft. Add the livers and cook, stirring until the livers are cooked through. Remove from the heat and cool. Turn into a food processor fitted with the steel blade. Process, adding the cognac and cream through the feed tube. Add the nuts. Invert into serving bowl, cover, and refrigerate until chilled.

FENNEL-RYE BLACK BREAD

Rye bread by itself is relatively light colored. Commercial bakeries often darken rye bread by using a thick, syrupy substance called black bread coloring made of burned sugar. I'm not particularly fond of the idea of coloring a bread just for the sake of coloring it; however, in this recipe, the coffee and cocoa powder add color as well as depth of flavor.

Sampler Loaf

2/3 cup water

1 tablespoon dark molasses

1 tablespoon butter or canola oil

3/4 teaspoon salt

1 teaspoon coffee granules
   or powder

1 teaspoon cocoa powder

1 teaspoon crushed fennel seed

3/4 cup dark rye flour

1 1/4 cups bread flour

1 teaspoon rapid-rising or active
   dry yeast

Regular Loaf

1 cup water

2 tablespoons dark molasses

1 1/2 tablespoons butter or
   canola oil

1 teaspoon salt

2 teaspoons coffee granules
   or powder

2 teaspoons cocoa powder

1 1/2 teaspoons crushed
   fennel seed

1 cup dark rye flour

2 cups bread flour

1 1/2 teaspoons rapid-rising or
   active dry yeast

Large Loaf

1 1/3 cups water

3 tablespoons dark molasses

2 tablespoons butter or canola oil

1 1/2 teaspoons salt

1 tablespoon coffee granules
   or powder

1 tablespoon cocoa powder

2 teaspoons crushed fennel seed

1 1/2 cups dark rye flour

2 1/2 cups bread flour

2 teaspoons rapid-rising or active
   dry yeast

TO MIX THE DOUGH BY HAND Heat the water until warm, between 105° and 115°F; pour it into a large, warmed bowl, and add the yeast. Let stand 5 minutes, until the yeast begins to bubble. Stir in the molasses, butter, salt, coffee granules, cocoa, fennel seed, and rye flour. Slowly add half of the bread flour, and beat until a smooth dough forms. Cover, and let stand 15 minutes. Turn the dough out onto a very lightly floured board, and knead, adding the remaining flour as necessary, until smooth and springy, about 5 minutes. Wash the bowl and grease it; place the dough back in the bowl, and turn it over to grease the top. Cover, and let rise until doubled, about 1 hour.

TO MIX THE DOUGH WITH A HEAVY-DUTY MIXER Heat the water until warm, between 105° and 115°F; pour it into the warmed mixing bowl, and add the yeast. Let stand 5 minutes, until the yeast begins to bubble. Add the molasses, butter, salt, coffee granules, cocoa, fennel seed, and rye flour. Slowly add half of the bread flour, and beat until a soft dough forms. Cover, and let stand 15 minutes. Knead the dough in the mixer with the dough hook, on medium to high speed, adding the remaining flour as necessary, until the dough pulls away from the sides of the bowl and is smooth and springy but still soft to the touch. Remove the dough hook, cover the bowl, and let the dough rise until doubled, about 1 hour.

TO MIX THE DOUGH IN THE FOOD PROCESSOR Place the plastic dough blade into the work bowl. Heat the water until very warm, between 120° and 130°F; set aside. Place the remaining ingredients into the work bowl. Turn the processor on, and slowly pour the water through the feed tube, processing until the dough is smooth and pulls away from the sides of the bowl. If the dough is wet and sticky, add more flour, 1 tablespoon at a time, until the dough is smooth yet soft to the touch. If the dough is not soft to the touch but is very firm, add 1 tablespoon of water at a time, and process until the dough is smooth yet soft to the touch. Cover the work bowl, and let the dough rise until doubled, about 1 hour. Or remove the dough to a lightly greased bowl, cover, and let rise until doubled, about 1 hour.

TO MIX THE DOUGH IN THE BREAD MACHINE Pour the water (at room temperature) into the pan. Add the remaining ingredients, in the order listed. Make an indentation in the dry ingredients and add the yeast. Select *Dough*, and press *Start.* If the dough is wet and sticky, add more flour, 1 tablespoon at a time, until the dough is smooth yet soft to the touch. If the dough is not soft to the touch but is very firm, add 1 teaspoon of water at a time, until the

dough is smooth yet soft to the touch. The machine will stop when the dough is ready to shape and bake.

TO MIX AND BAKE THE BREAD IN THE BREAD MACHINE Pour the water (at room temperature) into the pan. Add the remaining ingredients, in the order listed. Make an indentation in the dry ingredients and add the yeast. Select the *Basic* or *Whole Wheat* cycle, set the crust on *Medium,* and press *Start.* During the mixing cycle, if the dough is wet and sticky, add more flour, 1 tablespoon at a time, until the dough is smooth yet soft to the touch. If the dough is not soft to the touch but is very firm, add 1 teaspoon of water at a time, until the dough is smooth yet soft to the touch.

TO SHAPE AND BAKE IN THE OVEN Lightly grease an 8- or 9-inch round cake pan or a baking sheet. Turn the dough out onto a lightly floured board or lightly oiled surface. Punch the dough down, and shape it into a round loaf. Place the loaf, with the smooth side up, into the pan. Cover and let rise in a warm place until almost doubled, 45 to 60 minutes. Preheat the oven to 375°F. Bake 35 to 40 minutes, until the loaf is golden and a wooden skewer inserted into the loaf comes out clean and dry. Brush the top of the loaf while it's still hot with melted butter, if desired. Remove from the pan and cool on a wire rack.

Baked Ham on Rye Breakfast Sandwich

Here's a breakfast for those planning an active day. It makes a great Sunday supper, too.

2 SERVINGS

2 slices toasted Fennel Rye Black Bread (page 238)

2 ounces Swiss cheese, thinly sliced

3 ounces shaved boiled ham

2 large eggs

1/2 cup low-sodium chicken broth

1/3 cup whipping cream

1 small red bell pepper, finely chopped

1/8 teaspoon dried tarragon

Salt and freshly ground pepper, to taste

Preheat the oven to 350°F. Lightly coat a shallow baking pan with nonstick spray. Place the toast into the pan, and top with the cheese. Scrunch the ham so that it makes a nest on top of the cheese, and crack one egg into each nest. Bake 15 minutes, just until the yolks are set.

While the eggs bake, put the chicken broth, whipping cream, and bell pepper into a small saucepan. Heat to boiling, and boil until reduced by half and the sauce is glossy looking. Season with the tarragon, salt, and pepper.

To serve, arrange the sandwiches on serving plates, and spoon the sauce around them.

HERB AND ONION BREAD

The topping of onion, sesame seeds, and poppy seeds, for loaves baked conventionally, makes this round loaf appealing.

Sampler Loaf

2/3 cup water

1/2 teaspoon salt

1/2 teaspoon dillweed

1 teaspoon sugar

1 teaspoon dried onion flakes

1 1/2 teaspoons freshly squeezed lemon juice

1 tablespoon canola oil

1 1/2 cups whole wheat flour

1/2 cup bread flour

1/2 tablespoon gluten

1 teaspoon rapid-rising or active dry yeast

Regular Loaf

1 cup water

1 teaspoon salt

1 teaspoon dillweed

2 teaspoons sugar

2 teaspoons dried onion flakes

1 tablespoon freshly squeezed lemon juice

2 tablespoons canola oil

2 cups whole wheat flour

1 cup bread flour

1 tablespoon gluten

1 1/2 teaspoons rapid-rising or active dry yeast

Large Loaf

1 1/3 cups water

1 1/2 teaspoons salt

1 1/2 teaspoons dillweed

1 tablespoon sugar

1 tablespoon dried onion flakes

1 1/2 tablespoons freshly squeezed lemon juice

3 tablespoons canola oil

3 cups whole wheat flour

1 cup bread flour

1 1/2 tablespoons gluten

2 teaspoons rapid-rising or active dry yeast

GLAZE FOR BREAD BAKED CONVENTIONALLY

1 large egg

1 tablespoon water or milk

1/4 to 3/4 teaspoon dried onion flakes

1/4 to 3/4 teaspoon sesame seeds

1/4 to 3/4 teaspoon poppy seeds

TO MIX THE DOUGH BY HAND Heat the water until warm, between 105° and 115°F; pour it into a large, warmed bowl, and add the yeast, salt, dill weed, and sugar. Let stand 5 minutes, until the yeast begins to bubble. Stir in the onion, lemon juice, oil, and whole wheat flour. Beat well until smooth. Cover, and let stand 15 minutes. Slowly add the bread flour and gluten, and beat until a soft dough forms. Turn the dough out onto a very lightly floured board, and knead, adding flour if necessary, until smooth and springy, about 5 minutes. Wash the bowl and grease it; place the dough back in the bowl, and turn it over to grease the top. Cover, and let rise until doubled, about 1 hour.

TO MIX THE DOUGH WITH A HEAVY-DUTY MIXER   Heat the water until warm, between 105° and 115°F; pour it into the warmed mixing bowl, and add the yeast, salt, dill weed, and sugar. Let stand 5 minutes, until the yeast begins to bubble. Add the onion, lemon juice, oil, and whole wheat flour. Beat until smooth. Cover, and let stand 15 minutes. Slowly add the bread flour and gluten, and beat until a soft dough forms. Knead the dough in the mixer with the dough hook, on medium to high speed, adding flour as necessary, until the dough pulls away from the sides of the bowl and is smooth and springy but still soft to the touch. Remove the dough hook, cover the bowl, and let the dough rise until doubled, about 1 hour.

TO MIX THE DOUGH IN THE FOOD PROCESSOR   Place the plastic dough blade into the work bowl. Heat the water until very warm, between 120° and 130°F; set aside. Place the remaining ingredients into the work bowl. Turn the processor on, and slowly pour the water through the feed tube, processing until the dough is smooth and pulls away from the sides of the bowl. If the dough is wet and sticky, add more flour, 1 tablespoon at a time, until the dough is smooth yet soft to the touch. If the dough is not soft to the touch but is very firm, add 1 tablespoon of water at a time, and process until the dough is smooth yet soft to the touch. Cover the work bowl, and let the dough rise until doubled, about 1 hour. Or remove the dough to a lightly greased bowl, cover, and let rise until doubled, about 1 hour.

TO MIX THE DOUGH IN THE BREAD MACHINE   Pour the water (at room temperature) into the pan. Add the remaining ingredients, in the order listed. Make an indentation in the dry ingredients and add the yeast. Select *Dough,* and press *Start.* If the dough is wet and sticky, add more flour, 1 tablespoon at a time, until the dough is smooth yet soft to the touch. If the dough is not soft to the touch but is very firm, add 1 teaspoon of water at a time, until the dough is smooth yet soft to the touch. The machine will stop when the dough is ready to shape and bake.

TO MIX AND BAKE THE BREAD IN THE BREAD MACHINE   Pour the water (at room temperature) into the pan. Add the remaining ingredients, in the order listed. Make an indentation in the dry ingredients and add the yeast. Select the *Basic* or *Whole Wheat* cycle, set the crust on *Medium,* and press *Start.* During the mixing cycle, if the dough is wet and sticky, add more flour, 1 tablespoon at a time, until the dough is smooth yet soft to the touch. If the dough is not soft to the touch but is very firm, add 1 teaspoon of water at a time, until the dough is smooth yet soft to the touch.

TO SHAPE AND BAKE IN THE OVEN   Lightly grease a baking sheet. Turn the dough out onto a lightly floured board or lightly oiled surface. Punch the dough down, and shape it into a round loaf. Place the loaf, with the smooth side up, onto the baking sheet. Cover and let rise in a warm place until almost doubled, 45 to 60 minutes. Preheat the oven to 375°F. To glaze, beat the egg with the water, brush the mixture on the loaf, and sprinkle on the sesame and poppy seeds. Using a sharp knife or razor, slash the top of the loaf. Bake 30 to 35 minutes, until the loaf is golden. Remove from the pan and cool on a wire rack.

Country Vegetable Chowder

This hearty vegetable soup takes less than half an hour to make and is perfect for a cold winter day's supper. Served with Herbed Croutons or Herb and Garlic Croutons (page 249) it is very satisfying!

4 TO 6 SERVINGS

2 small leeks or 1 medium onion, sliced

2 tablespoons butter

2 tablespoons all-purpose flour

1/2 teaspoon dried thyme

1/2 teaspoon dried basil

2 cups vegetable or chicken broth

1 can (15 1/2 ounces) diced tomatoes with herbs

1 rib celery, finely diced

3 medium Yukon Gold potatoes, peeled and diced in 1/2-inch cubes

1 cup freshly cooked lima or fava beans or 1 can (13 to 15 ounces), drained

1 1/2 cups cream, half-and-half, or undiluted evaporated milk

Salt and freshly ground pepper, to taste

Herbed Croutons (to be added to taste by each guest—recipe follows)

In a large pot or Dutch oven, sauté the leeks in the butter over medium/low heat. Add the flour, herbs, broth, tomatoes, celery, and potatoes; bring to a boil. Reduce the heat, cover, and simmer 15 to 20 minutes over low heat, until the potatoes are tender. Stir in the beans and cream. Season with the salt and pepper. Top each serving with Herbed Croutons.

Herbed Croutons

Feel free to use whatever combination of herbs you like best.

2 CUPS

2 cups bread cubes, cut ¹/₂ inch, made from any leftover, non-sweet bread

3 tablespoons olive oil or butter

1 tablespoon mixed Italian herbs, or 1 teaspoon each of oregano, basil, and thyme

1 teaspoon coarse (kosher) salt

Preheat the oven to 375°F. Toss the bread cubes with the oil to coat lightly; sprinkle with the herbs and salt. Spread the cubes on an ungreased baking sheet, and bake until golden and crisp, about 20 minutes.

Crostini: Cut the bread in thin slices, and cut each slice into 2- to 3-inch squares. Brush each square with oil, and sprinkle with the herbs and salt. Continue with the recipe.

ITALIAN HERB BREAD

Just a bit of granular multigrain cereal adds texture to this herbed bread. Shape the dough into breadsticks or individual dinner rolls. It also makes a great pizza crust.

Sampler Loaf

2/3 cup water

1 tablespoon extra-virgin olive oil

1 teaspoon mixed Italian herbs*

2 teaspoons sugar

3/4 teaspoon salt

1 tablespoon 7-grain cereal

3 tablespoons prepared pesto sauce

1/4 cup whole wheat flour

1 3/4 cups bread flour

1 teaspoon rapid-rising or active dry yeast

Regular Loaf

1 cup water

1 1/2 tablespoon extra-virgin olive oil

2 teaspoons mixed Italian herbs*

1 tablespoon sugar

1 teaspoon salt

1 1/2 tablespoons 7-grain cereal

1/4 cup prepared pesto sauce

1/3 cup whole wheat flour

2 2/3 cups bread flour

1 1/2 teaspoons rapid-rising or active dry yeast

Large Loaf

1 1/3 cups water

2 tablespoons extra-virgin olive oil

1 tablespoon mixed Italian herbs*

1 1/2 tablespoons sugar

1 1/2 teaspoons salt

2 tablespoons 7-grain cereal

1/3 cup prepared pesto sauce

1/2 cup whole wheat flour

3 1/2 cups bread flour

2 teaspoons rapid-rising or active dry yeast

TO MIX THE DOUGH BY HAND Heat the water until warm, between 105° and 115°F; pour it into a large, warmed bowl, and add the yeast, herbs, sugar, salt, and cereal. Let stand 5 minutes, until the yeast begins to bubble. Stir in the oil, pesto, and whole wheat flour. Beat until smooth. Cover, and let stand 15 minutes. Slowly add the bread flour, and beat until a soft dough forms. Turn the dough out onto a very lightly floured board, and knead, adding flour if necessary, until smooth and springy, about 5 minutes. Wash the bowl and grease it; place the dough back in the bowl, and turn it over to grease the top. Cover, and let rise until doubled, about 1 hour.

TO MIX THE DOUGH WITH A HEAVY-DUTY MIXER Heat the water until warm, between 105° and 115°F; pour it into the warmed mixing

*Note   *Commercial mixtures include dried oregano, basil, rosemary, and savory and are available in the spice section of your local supermarket*

bowl, and add the yeast, herbs, sugar, salt, and cereal. Let stand 5 minutes, until the yeast begins to bubble. Add the oil, pesto, and whole wheat flour. Beat until smooth. Cover, and let stand 15. minutes. Slowly add the bread flour, and beat until a soft dough forms. Knead the dough in the mixer with the dough hook, on medium to high speed, adding flour as necessary, until the dough pulls away from the sides of the bowl and is smooth and springy but still soft to the touch. Remove the dough hook, cover the bowl, and let the dough rise until doubled, about 1 hour.

TO MIX THE DOUGH IN THE FOOD PROCESSOR

Place the plastic dough blade into the work bowl. Heat the water until very warm, between 120° and 130°F; set aside. Place the remaining ingredients into the work bowl. Turn the processor on, and slowly pour the water through the feed tube, processing until the dough is smooth and pulls away from the sides of the bowl. If the dough is wet and sticky, add more flour, 1 tablespoon at a time, until the dough is smooth yet soft to the touch. If the dough is not soft to the touch but is very firm, add 1 tablespoon of water at a time, and process until the dough is smooth yet soft to the touch. Cover the work bowl, and let the dough rise until doubled, about 1 hour. Or remove the dough to a lightly greased bowl, cover, and let rise until doubled, about 1 hour.

TO MIX THE DOUGH IN THE BREAD MACHINE

Pour the water (at room temperature) into the pan. Add the remaining ingredients, in the order listed. Make an indentation in the dry ingredients and add the yeast. Select *Dough,* and press *Start.* If the dough is wet and sticky, add more flour, 1 tablespoon at a time, until the dough is smooth yet soft to the touch. If the dough is not soft to the touch but is very firm, add 1 teaspoon of water at a time, until the dough is smooth yet soft to the touch. The machine will stop when the dough is ready to shape and bake.

TO MIX AND BAKE THE BREAD IN THE BREAD MACHINE

Pour the water (at room temperature) into the pan. Add the remaining ingredients, in the order listed. Make an indentation in the dry ingredients and add the yeast. Select the *Basic* or *Whole Wheat* cycle, set the crust on *Medium,* and press *Start.* During the mixing cycle, if the dough is wet and sticky, add more flour, 1 tablespoon at a time, until the dough is smooth yet soft to the touch. If the dough is not soft to the touch but is very firm, add 1 teaspoon of water at a time, until the dough is smooth yet soft to the touch.

TO SHAPE AND BAKE IN THE OVEN

Turn the dough out onto a lightly floured board or lightly oiled surface. Punch the dough down, and shape it into a baguette or round loaf.

To bake on baking tiles   Leave the loaf, with the smooth side up, on the board. Cover and let rise in a warm place until almost doubled, 45 to 60 minutes. Place baking tiles or a pizza tile on the top rack in the oven, and place a heavy, shallow pan on the bottom rack. Preheat the oven to 450°F. Using a sharp knife or a razor, slash the loaf; place the loaf onto the preheated tiles.

Immediately pour 1 cup water into the pan on the bottom rack. Bake 15 to 20 minutes, until the loaf is golden. Remove from the oven and cool on a wire rack.

To bake in a pan Lightly grease a baking sheet or cover it with parchment paper. Place the loaf, with the smooth side up, onto the baking sheet. Cover and let rise in a warm place until almost doubled, 45 to 60 minutes. Preheat the oven to 375°F. Using a sharp knife or a razor, slash the top of the loaf, and brush it with water. Bake 25 to 30 minutes, until the loaf is golden. Remove from the oven and cool on a wire rack.

Garden Fresh Vegetable Bake

This is a colorful, make-ahead vegetable dish that goes with almost any kind of buffet menu. I love it when the baby carrots are fresh from the garden, but I also use the tiny carved carrots available from the produce counter. In a pinch, I will cut large carrots into $1 \times 1/4$-inch strips.

6 SERVINGS

2 cups baby carrots

3 small zucchini, cut into 1/4-inch slices

1 cup cherry tomatoes, washed and stemmed

1 cup Herb and Garlic Croutons (recipe follows)

2 tablespoons cornstarch

$1^1/2$ cups half-and-half or milk

2 tablespoons butter

1 teaspoon salt

1 teaspoon dried basil

1/4 teaspoon freshly ground pepper

Preheat the oven to 350°F. Grease a 1- or $1^1/2$-quart casserole or baking dish. Place the carrots in a small saucepan. Add just enough water to cover. Bring to a boil over high heat; reduce the heat, and simmer about 5 minutes, until the carrots are crisp-tender. Drain. Put them into the bottom of the casserole. Top the carrots with the zucchini, tomatoes, and croutons.

In a medium saucepan, blend the cornstarch and half-and-half. Bring to a boil over medium heat, stirring constantly. Boil, stirring, about 1 minute, until thickened and smooth. Remove from the heat, and stir in the butter and seasonings. Pour over the vegetable mixture. Bake 20 to 30 minutes, until the sauce bubbles around the edges and the zucchini is crisp-tender. Serve hot.

Herb and Garlic Croutons

These are perfect served as snacks, to top off vegetables, or sprinkled on a salad or soup.

4 CUPS

3 tablespoons extra-virgin olive oil

1 teaspoon mixed Italian herbs or crushed rosemary

1 large garlic clove, minced or pressed

1/2 teaspoon coarse (kosher) salt

4 cups bread cubes, cut 1/2 inch, made from Italian Herb Bread (page 245) or any whole grain bread that has no fruit

Preheat the oven to 350°F. In a large bowl, combine the oil, herbs, garlic, and salt. Add the bread cubes, and toss until evenly coated. Spread in a single layer on a cookie sheet. Bake 10 to 15 minutes, until crisp; cool. Store in an airtight container in a cool place or freeze.

MILLET, WHEAT, AND SIX-SEED HIGH-FIBER BREAD

Great flavor and texture! This is one of my favorite breads. Anise and fennel add an aromatic sweet quality to the bread, while the sunflower and sesame seeds add crunch. Millet has a sweet, nutty flavor. You can buy the flour in health foods and whole food markets and through mail-order catalogs.

Sampler Loaf	Regular Loaf	Large Loaf
2/3 cup water	1 cup water	1 1/3 cups water
1 tablespoon honey	2 tablespoons honey	3 tablespoons honey
1 tablespoon canola oil	1 1/2 tablespoons canola oil	2 tablespoons canola oil
3/4 teaspoon salt	1 teaspoon salt	1 1/2 teaspoons salt
1 tablespoon sunflower seeds	2 tablespoons sunflower seeds	3 tablespoons sunflower seeds
1 teaspoon sesame seeds	1 1/2 teaspoons sesame seeds	2 teaspoons sesame seeds
1 teaspoon poppy seeds	1 1/2 teaspoons poppy seeds	2 teaspoons poppy seeds
1 teaspoon caraway seeds	1 1/2 teaspoons caraway seeds	2 teaspoons caraway seeds
1 teaspoon anise seeds	1 1/2 teaspoons anise seeds	2 teaspoons anise seeds
1 teaspoon fennel seeds	1 1/2 teaspoons fennel seeds	2 teaspoons fennel seeds
1 tablespoon unprocessed wheat bran	2 tablespoons unprocessed wheat bran	3 tablespoons unprocessed wheat bran
1/4 cup millet flour	1/3 cup millet flour	1/2 cup millet flour
3/4 cup whole wheat flour	1 1/2 cups whole wheat flour	1 3/4 cups whole wheat flour
1 cup bread flour	1 1/2 cups bread flour	2 cups bread flour
1 teaspoon rapid-rising or active dry yeast	1 1/2 teaspoons rapid-rising or active dry yeast	2 teaspoons rapid-rising or active dry yeast

GLAZE FOR BREAD BAKED CONVENTIONALLY

1 large egg

1 tablespoon water

TO MIX THE DOUGH BY HAND Heat the water until warm, between 105° and 115°F; pour it into a large, warmed bowl, and add the yeast and honey. Let stand 5 minutes, until the yeast begins to bubble. Stir in the oil, salt, seeds, wheat bran, millet flour, and whole wheat flour. Beat until smooth. Cover, and let stand 15 minutes. Slowly add the bread flour, and beat until a soft dough forms. Turn the dough out onto a very lightly floured board, and knead, adding flour if necessary, until smooth and springy, about 5 minutes. Wash the bowl and grease it; place the dough back in the bowl, and turn it over to grease the top. Cover, and let rise until doubled, about 1 hour.

TO MIX THE DOUGH WITH A HEAVY-DUTY MIXER

Heat the water until warm, between 105° and 115°F; pour it into the warmed mixing bowl, and add the yeast and honey. Let stand 5 minutes, until the yeast begins to bubble. Add the oil, salt, seeds, wheat bran, millet flour, and whole wheat flour. Beat until smooth. Cover, and let stand 15 minutes. Slowly add the bread flour, and beat until a soft dough forms. Knead the dough in the mixer with the dough hook, on medium to high speed, adding flour as necessary, until the dough pulls away from the sides of the bowl and is smooth and springy but still soft to the touch. Remove the dough hook, cover the bowl, and let the dough rise until doubled, about 1 hour.

TO MIX THE DOUGH IN THE FOOD PROCESSOR

Place the plastic dough blade into the work bowl. Heat the water until very warm, between 115° and 120°F; set aside. Place the remaining ingredients into the work bowl. Turn the processor on, and slowly pour the water through the feed tube, processing until the dough is smooth and pulls away from the sides of the bowl. If the dough is wet and sticky, add more flour, 1 tablespoon at a time, until the dough is smooth yet soft to the touch. If the dough is not soft to the touch but is very firm, add 1 tablespoon of water at a time, and process until the dough is smooth yet soft to the touch. Cover the work bowl, and let the dough rise until doubled, about 1 hour. Or remove the dough to a lightly greased bowl, cover, and let rise until doubled, about 1 hour.

TO MIX THE DOUGH IN THE BREAD MACHINE

Pour the water (at room temperature) into the pan. Add the remaining ingredients, in the order listed. Make an indentation in the dry ingredients and add the yeast. Select *Dough*, and press *Start*. If the dough is wet and sticky, add more flour, 1 tablespoon at a time, until the dough is smooth yet soft to the touch. If the dough is not soft to the touch but is very firm, add 1 teaspoon of water at a time, until the dough is smooth yet soft to the touch. The machine will stop when the dough is ready to shape and bake.

TO MIX AND BAKE THE BREAD IN THE BREAD MACHINE

Pour the water (at room temperature) into the pan. Add the remaining ingredients, in the order listed. Make an indentation in the dry ingredients and add the yeast. Select the *Basic* or *Whole Wheat* cycle, set the crust on *Medium*, and press *Start*. During the mixing cycle, if the dough is wet and sticky, add more flour, 1 tablespoon at a time, until the dough is smooth yet soft to the touch. If the dough is not soft to the touch but is very firm, add 1 teaspoon of water at a time, until the dough is smooth yet soft to the touch.

TO SHAPE AND BAKE IN THE OVEN

Lightly grease a baking sheet. Turn the dough out onto a lightly floured board or lightly oiled surface. Punch the dough down, and shape it into a round loaf. Place the loaf, with the smooth side up, onto the baking sheet. Cover and let rise in a warm place until almost doubled, 45 to 60 minutes. Preheat the oven to 375°F. To glaze, beat the egg with the water, and brush the mixture on the loaf. Bake 25 to 30 minutes, until the loaf is golden. Remove from the pan and cool on a wire rack.

OATMEAL SEED BREAD

This bread is worth a trip to the local whole foods market! You can get all of the seeds and the thick rolled oats there.

Sampler Loaf

$2/3$ cup water

1 tablespoon canola oil

$3/4$ teaspoon salt

1 tablespoon sugar

1 teaspoon flax seeds

1 teaspoon sesame seeds

1 teaspoon poppy seeds

2 tablespoons toasted sunflower seeds

1 tablespoon yellow cornmeal

$1/4$ cup thick old-fashioned rolled oats

$1/2$ cup whole wheat flour

$1^{1}/4$ cups bread flour

1 teaspoon rapid-rising or active dry yeast

Regular Loaf

1 cup water

$1^{1}/2$ tablespoon canola oil

1 teaspoon salt

$1^{1}/2$ tablespoon sugar

$1^{1}/2$ teaspoons flax seeds

$1^{1}/2$ teaspoons sesame seeds

$1^{1}/2$ teaspoons poppy seeds

3 tablespoons toasted sunflower seeds

$1^{1}/2$ tablespoons yellow cornmeal

$1/3$ cup thick old-fashioned rolled oats

$2/3$ cup whole wheat flour

$1^{1}/2$ cups bread flour

$1^{1}/2$ teaspoon rapid-rising or active dry yeast

Large Loaf

$1^{1}/3$ cups water

2 tablespoons canola oil

$1^{1}/2$ teaspoons salt

2 tablespoons sugar

2 teaspoons flax seeds

2 teaspoons sesame seeds

2 teaspoons poppy seeds

$1/4$ cup toasted sunflower seeds

2 tablespoons yellow cornmeal

$1/2$ cup thick old-fashioned rolled oats

1 cup whole wheat flour

$2^{1}/3$ cups bread flour

2 teaspoons rapid-rising or active dry yeast

GLAZE FOR BREAD BAKED CONVENTIONALLY

1 large egg

1 tablespoon water

1 to 2 tablespoons thick old-fashioned rolled oats

TO MIX THE DOUGH BY HAND Heat the water until warm, between 105° and 115°F; pour it into a large, warmed bowl, and add the yeast and sugar. Let stand 5 minutes, until the yeast begins to bubble. Stir in the oil, salt, seeds, cornmeal, rolled oats, and whole wheat flour. Beat well. Cover, and let stand 15 minutes. Slowly add the bread flour, and beat until a soft dough forms. Turn the dough out onto a very lightly floured board, and knead, adding flour if necessary, until smooth and springy, about 5 minutes. Wash the bowl and grease it; place the dough back in the bowl, and turn it over to grease the top. Cover, and let rise until doubled, about 1 hour.

TO MIX THE DOUGH WITH A HEAVY-DUTY MIXER Heat the water until warm, between 105° and 115°F; pour it into the warmed mixing bowl, and add the yeast and sugar. Let stand 5 minutes, until the yeast begins to bubble. Add the oil, salt, seeds, cornmeal, rolled oats, and whole wheat flour. Beat well. Cover, and let stand 15 minutes. Slowly add the bread flour, and beat until a soft dough forms. Knead the dough in the mixer with the dough hook, on medium to high speed, adding flour as necessary, until the dough pulls away from the sides of the bowl and is smooth and springy but still soft to the touch. Remove the dough hook, cover the bowl, and let the dough rise until doubled, about 1 hour.

TO MIX THE DOUGH IN THE FOOD PROCESSOR Place the plastic dough blade into the work bowl. Heat the water until very warm, between 120° and 130°F; set aside. Place the remaining ingredients into the work bowl. Turn the processor on, and slowly pour the water through the feed tube, processing until the dough is smooth and pulls away from the sides of the bowl. If the dough is wet and sticky, add more flour, 1 tablespoon at a time, until the dough is smooth yet soft to the touch. If the dough is not soft to the touch but is very firm, add 1 tablespoon of water at a time, and process until the dough is smooth yet soft to the touch. Cover the work bowl, and let the dough rise until doubled, about 1 hour. Or remove the dough to a lightly greased bowl, cover, and let rise until doubled, about 1 hour.

TO MIX THE DOUGH IN THE BREAD MACHINE Pour the water (at room temperature) into the pan. Add the remaining ingredients, in the order listed. Make an indentation in the dry ingredients and add the yeast. Select *Dough,* and press *Start.* If the dough is wet and sticky, add more flour, 1 tablespoon at a time, until the dough is smooth yet soft to the touch. If the dough is not soft to the touch but is very firm, add 1 teaspoon of water at a time, until the dough is smooth yet soft to the touch. The machine will stop when the dough is ready to shape and bake.

TO MIX AND BAKE THE BREAD IN THE BREAD MACHINE Pour the water (at room temperature) into the pan. Add the remaining ingredients, in the order listed. Make an indentation in the dry ingredients and add the yeast. Select the *Basic* or *Whole Wheat* cycle, set the crust on *Medium,* and press *Start.* During the mixing cycle, if the dough is wet and sticky, add more flour, 1 tablespoon at a time, until the dough is smooth yet soft to the touch. If the dough is not soft to the touch but is very firm, add 1 teaspoon of water at a time, until the dough is smooth yet soft to the touch.

TO SHAPE AND BAKE IN THE OVEN Lightly grease a baking sheet. Turn the dough out onto a lightly floured board or lightly oiled surface. Punch the dough down, and shape it into a round loaf. Place the loaf, with the smooth side up, onto the baking sheet. Cover and let rise in a warm place until almost doubled, 45 to 60 minutes. Preheat the oven to 375°F. To glaze, beat the egg with the water, brush the mixture on the loaf, and sprinkle on the rolled oats. Bake 25 to 30 minutes, until the loaf is golden and a wooden skewer inserted into the loaf comes out clean and dry. Remove from the pan and cool on a wire rack.

ORANGE RYE AND WHEAT BREAD

For the best flavor, the caraway seeds should be ground in this bread. To grind, place the seeds into a coffee mill, and grind until not quite powdery.

Sampler Loaf

2/3 cup buttermilk*

1 tablespoon dark molasses

1 teaspoon salt

1 teaspoon grated orange zest

1 teaspoon ground caraway seeds

1/4 cup medium rye flour

1/4 cup whole wheat flour

1 1/2 cups bread flour

1 teaspoon rapid-rising or active
   dry yeast

Regular Loaf

1 cup buttermilk*

2 tablespoons dark molasses

1 1/2 teaspoons salt

2 teaspoons grated orange zest

2 teaspoons ground caraway seeds

1/2 cup medium rye flour

1/2 cup whole wheat flour

2 cups bread flour

1 1/2 teaspoons rapid-rising or
   active dry yeast

Large Loaf

1 1/3 cups buttermilk*

3 tablespoons dark molasses

2 teaspoons salt

1 tablespoon grated orange zest

1 tablespoon ground
   caraway seeds

3/4 cup medium rye flour

3/4 cup whole wheat flour

2 1/2 cups bread flour

2 teaspoons rapid-rising or active
   dry yeast

GLAZE FOR BREAD BAKED CONVENTIONALLY
1 to 2 tablespoons warmed molasses for brushing loaves

TO MIX THE DOUGH BY HAND Heat the buttermilk until warm, between 105° and 115°F; pour it into a large, warmed bowl, and add the yeast and molasses. Let stand 5 minutes, until the yeast begins to bubble. Stir in the salt, orange zest, caraway seeds, rye flour, and whole wheat flour. Beat well. Slowly add half of the bread flour, and beat until a smooth dough forms. Cover, and let stand 15 minutes. Turn the dough out onto a very lightly floured board, and knead, adding the remaining flour as necessary, until smooth and springy, about 5 minutes. Wash the bowl and grease it; place the dough back in the bowl, and turn it over to grease the top. Cover, and let rise until doubled, about 1 hour.

TO MIX THE DOUGH WITH A HEAVY-DUTY MIXER Heat the buttermilk until warm, between 105° and 115°F; pour it into the warmed mixing bowl, and add the yeast and molasses. Let stand 5 minutes, until the yeast begins to bubble. Add the salt, orange zest,

Note   *You can substitute water plus buttermilk powder, mixed according to the package directions.*

caraway seeds, rye flour and whole wheat flour. Beat well. Slowly add half of the bread flour, and beat until a smooth dough forms. Cover, and let stand 15 minutes. Knead the dough in the mixer with the dough hook, on medium to high speed, adding the remaining flour as necessary, until the dough pulls away from the sides of the bowl and is smooth and springy but still soft to the touch. Remove the dough hook, cover the bowl, and let the dough rise until doubled, about 1 hour.

TO MIX THE DOUGH IN THE FOOD PROCESSOR Place the plastic dough blade into the work bowl. Heat the buttermilk until very warm, between 120° and 130°F; set aside. Place the remaining ingredients into the work bowl. Turn the processor on, and slowly pour the buttermilk through the feed tube, processing until the dough is smooth and pulls away from the sides of the bowl. If the dough is wet and sticky, add more flour, 1 tablespoon at a time, until the dough is smooth yet soft to the touch. If the dough is not soft to the touch but is very firm, add 1 tablespoon of water at a time, and process until the dough is smooth yet soft to the touch. Cover the work bowl, and let the dough rise until doubled, about 1 hour. Or remove the dough to a lightly greased bowl, cover, and let rise until doubled, about 1 hour.

TO MIX THE DOUGH IN THE BREAD MACHINE Pour the buttermilk (at room temperature) into the pan. Add the remaining ingredients, in the order listed. Make an indentation in the dry ingredients and add the yeast. Select *Dough,* and press *Start.* If the dough is wet and sticky, add more flour, 1 tablespoon at a time,

until the dough is smooth yet soft to the touch. If the dough is not soft to the touch but is very firm, add 1 teaspoon of water at a time, until the dough is smooth yet soft to the touch. The machine will stop when the dough is ready to shape and bake.

TO MIX AND BAKE THE BREAD IN THE BREAD MACHINE Pour the buttermilk (at room temperature) into the pan. Add the remaining ingredients, in the order listed. Make an indentation in the dry ingredients and add the yeast. Select the *Basic* or *Whole Wheat* cycle, set the crust on *Medium,* and press *Start.* During the mixing cycle, if the dough is wet and sticky, add more flour, 1 tablespoon at a time, until the dough is smooth yet soft to the touch. If the dough is not soft to the touch but is very firm, add 1 teaspoon of water at a time, until the dough is smooth yet soft to the touch.

TO SHAPE AND BAKE IN THE OVEN Lightly grease an 8- or 9-inch round cake pan or baking sheet. Turn the dough out onto a lightly floured board or lightly oiled surface. Punch the dough down, and shape it into a round loaf. Place the loaf, with the smooth side up, into the pan. Cover and let rise in a warm place until almost doubled, 45 to 60 minutes. Preheat the oven to 375°F. Bake 35 to 40 minutes, until the loaf is golden and a wooden skewer inserted into the loaf comes out clean and dry. Brush the top of the loaf while it's still hot with warm molasses, if desired. Remove from the pan and cool on a wire rack.

PECAN AND CARAWAY BREAD

Oat flour and pecans work together to bring out the nutty flavor in this almost-white bread. Caraway seeds throw a twist into the flavor combination, making this a great bread for ham sandwiches.

Sampler Loaf	Regular Loaf	Large Loaf
$2/3$ cup water	1 cup water	$1^1/3$ cups water
1 tablespoon sugar	2 tablespoons sugar	3 tablespoons sugar
1 tablespoon butter	$1^1/2$ tablespoons butter	2 tablespoons butter
$3/4$ teaspoon salt	$1^1/2$ teaspoons salt	2 teaspoons salt
1 teaspoon caraway seeds	2 teaspoons caraway seeds	1 tablespoon caraway seeds
$1/4$ cup oat flour*	$1/2$ cup oat flour*	$3/4$ cup oat flour*
$1^3/4$ cups bread flour	$2^1/2$ cups bread flour	$3^1/4$ cups bread flour
1 teaspoon rapid-rising or active dry yeast	$1^1/2$ teaspoons rapid-rising or active dry yeast	2 teaspoons rapid-rising or active dry yeast
$1/2$ cup chopped pecans	1 cup chopped pecans	$1^1/2$ cups chopped pecans

TO MIX THE DOUGH BY HAND Heat the water until warm, between 105° and 115°F; pour it into a large, warmed bowl, and add the yeast. Let stand 5 minutes, until the yeast begins to bubble. Stir in the sugar, butter, salt, caraway seeds, oat flour, and $1/2$ cup of the bread flour. Beat well. Cover, and let stand 15 minutes. Slowly add the remaining bread flour, and beat until a smooth dough forms. Turn the dough out onto a very lightly floured board, and knead, adding flour if necessary, until smooth and springy, about 5 minutes. Knead in the pecans.

Wash the bowl and grease it; place the dough back in the bowl, and turn it over to grease the top. Cover, and let rise until doubled, about 1 hour.

TO MIX THE DOUGH WITH A HEAVY-DUTY MIXER Heat the water until warm, between 105° and 115°F; pour it into the warmed mixing bowl, and add the yeast. Let stand 5 minutes, until the yeast begins to bubble. Add the sugar, butter, salt, caraway seeds, oat flour, and $1/2$ cup of the bread flour. Beat well. Cover, and let stand

*Note   Oat flour is available in health food and whole foods markets. As a substitute, process rolled oats (either quick or old-fashioned) in a blender or food processor fitted with the steel blade until finely ground.

15 minutes. Slowly add the remaining bread flour, and beat until a smooth dough forms. Knead the dough in the mixer with the dough hook, on medium to high speed, adding flour as necessary, until the dough pulls away from the sides of the bowl and is smooth and springy but still soft to the touch. Knead in the pecans. Remove the dough hook, cover the bowl, and let the dough rise until doubled, about 1 hour.

TO MIX THE DOUGH IN THE FOOD PROCESSOR
Place the plastic dough blade into the work bowl. Heat the water until very warm, between 120° and 130°F; set aside. Place the remaining ingredients, except the pecans, into the work bowl. Turn the processor on, and slowly pour the water through the feed tube, processing until the dough is smooth and pulls away from the sides of the bowl. If the dough is wet and sticky, add more flour, 1 tablespoon at a time, until the dough is smooth yet soft to the touch. If the dough is not soft to the touch but is very firm, add 1 tablespoon of water at a time, and process until the dough is smooth yet soft to the touch. Mix in the pecans. Cover the work bowl, and let the dough rise until doubled, about 1 hour. Or remove the dough to a lightly greased bowl, cover, and let rise until doubled, about 1 hour.

TO MIX THE DOUGH IN THE BREAD MACHINE Pour the water (at room temperature) into the pan. Add the remaining ingredients, except the pecans, in the order listed. Make an indentation in the dry ingredients and add the yeast. Select *Dough,* and press *Start.* If the dough is wet and sticky, add more flour, 1 tablespoon at a time, until the dough is smooth yet soft to the touch. If the dough is not soft to the touch but is very firm, add 1 teaspoon of water at a time, until

the dough is smooth yet soft to the touch. Add the pecans when the machine signals it's time to add ingredients or when the cycle ends. The machine will stop when the dough is ready to shape and bake.

TO MIX AND BAKE THE BREAD IN THE BREAD MACHINE Pour the water (at room temperature) into the pan. Add the remaining ingredients, except the pecans, in the order listed. Make an indentation in the dry ingredients and add the yeast. Select the *Basic* or *Whole Wheat* cycle; set the crust on *Medium;* and press *Start.* During the mixing cycle, if the dough is wet and sticky, add more flour, 1 tablespoon at a time, until the dough is smooth yet soft to the touch. If the dough is not soft to the touch but is very firm, add 1 teaspoon of water at a time, until the dough is smooth yet soft to the touch. Add the pecans when the machine signals it's time to add ingredients.

TO SHAPE AND BAKE IN THE OVEN Lightly grease an 8- or 9-inch round cake pan or a baking sheet. Turn the dough out onto a lightly floured board or lightly oiled surface. Punch the dough down, and shape it into a round loaf. Place the loaf, with the smooth side up, into the pan. Cover and let rise in a warm place until almost doubled, 45 to 60 minutes. Preheat the oven to 375°F. Bake 35 to 40 minutes, until the loaf is golden and a wooden skewer inserted into the loaf comes out clean and dry. Brush the top of the loaf while it's still hot with melted butter, if desired. Remove from the pan and cool on a wire rack.

ROSEMARY WHEAT FOCACCIA

Although the tastiest shape for this bread is a rather flattish, freeform, round loaf, it's excellent baked right in the bread machine pan, too. Try it toasted with olive oil drizzled over, alongside a spinach salad or a hearty minestrone.

Sampler Loaf

2/3 cup water

1 1/2 teaspoons dried rosemary

1 teaspoon salt

1 1/2 teaspoons sugar

1 tablespoon extra-virgin olive oil

1 tablespoon freshly grated
    Parmesan cheese

1 cup whole wheat flour

1 cup bread flour

1 teaspoon rapid-rising or active
    dry yeast

Regular Loaf

1 cup water

2 teaspoons dried rosemary

1 1/2 teaspoons salt

2 teaspoons sugar

1 1/2 tablespoons extra-virgin
    olive oil

2 tablespoons freshly grated
    Parmesan cheese

1 1/2 cups whole wheat flour

1 1/2 cups bread flour

1 1/2 teaspoons rapid-rising or
    active dry yeast

Large Loaf

1 1/3 cups water

1 tablespoon dried rosemary

2 teaspoons salt

1 tablespoon sugar

2 tablespoons extra-virgin
    olive oil

3 tablespoons freshly grated
    Parmesan cheese

2 cups whole wheat flour

2 cups bread flour

2 teaspoons rapid-rising or active
    dry yeast

TOPPINGS FOR BREAD BAKED CONVENTIONALLY

1 to 3 tablespoons extra-virgin olive oil

2 to 4 teaspoons dried rosemary

2 to 3 tablespoons freshly grated Parmesan cheese

TO MIX THE DOUGH BY HAND Heat the water until warm, between 105° and 115°F; pour it into a large, warmed bowl, and add the yeast, rosemary, salt, and sugar. Let stand 5 minutes, until the yeast begins to bubble. Stir in the oil and whole wheat flour. Beat until smooth. Cover, and let stand 15 minutes. Slowly add the bread flour, and beat until a soft dough forms. Turn the dough out onto a very lightly floured board,

and knead, adding flour if necessary, until smooth and springy, about 5 minutes. Wash the bowl and grease it; place the dough back in the bowl, and turn it over to grease the top. Cover, and let rise until doubled, about 1 hour.

TO MIX THE DOUGH WITH A HEAVY-DUTY MIXER Heat the water until warm, between 105° and 115°F; pour it into the warmed mixing

bowl, and add the yeast, rosemary, salt, and sugar. Let stand 5 minutes, until the yeast begins to bubble. Add the oil and whole wheat flour. Beat until smooth. Cover, and let stand 15 minutes. Slowly add the bread flour, and beat until a soft dough forms. Knead the dough in the mixer with the dough hook, on medium to high speed, adding flour as necessary, until the dough pulls away from the sides of the bowl and is smooth and springy but still soft to the touch. Remove the dough hook, cover the bowl, and let the dough rise until doubled, about 1 hour.

TO MIX THE DOUGH IN THE FOOD PROCESSOR Place the plastic dough blade into the work bowl. Heat the water until very warm, between 120° and 130°F; set aside. Place the remaining ingredients into the work bowl. Turn the processor on, and slowly pour the water through the feed tube, processing until the dough is smooth and pulls away from the sides of the bowl. If the dough is wet and sticky, add more flour, 1 tablespoon at a time, until the dough is smooth yet soft to the touch. If the dough is not soft to the touch but is very firm, add 1 tablespoon of water at a time, and process until the dough is smooth yet soft to the touch. Cover the work bowl, and let the dough rise until doubled, about 1 hour. Or remove the dough to a lightly greased bowl, cover, and let rise until doubled, about 1 hour.

TO MIX THE DOUGH IN THE BREAD MACHINE Pour the water (at room temperature) into the pan. Add the remaining ingredients, in the order listed. Make an indentation in the dry ingredients and add the yeast. Select *Dough*, and press *Start*. If the dough is wet and sticky, add more flour, 1 tablespoon at a time, until the dough is smooth yet soft to the touch. If

the dough is not soft to the touch but is very firm, add 1 teaspoon of water at a time, until the dough is smooth yet soft to the touch. The machine will stop when the dough is ready to shape and bake.

TO MIX AND BAKE THE BREAD IN THE BREAD MACHINE Pour the water (at room temperature) into the pan. Add the remaining ingredients, in the order listed. Make an indentation in the dry ingredients and add the yeast. Select the *Basic* or *Whole Wheat* cycle, set the crust on *Medium,* and press *Start*. During the mixing cycle, if the dough is wet and sticky, add more flour, 1 tablespoon at a time, until the dough is smooth yet soft to the touch. If the dough is not soft to the touch but is very firm, add 1 teaspoon of water at a time, until the dough is smooth yet soft to the touch.

TO SHAPE AND BAKE IN THE OVEN Lightly grease a baking sheet. Turn the dough out onto a lightly floured board or lightly oiled surface. Punch the dough down, and shape it into a flat round (8 inches in diameter for the sampler-size dough, 12 inches for the regular-size dough, and 16 inches for the large-size dough). Place the round, with the smooth side up, onto the baking sheet. Cover and let rise in a warm place until almost doubled, 45 to 60 minutes. Preheat the oven to 375°F. With your fingertips, punch depressions into the round all over the top. Sprinkle with oil, rosemary, and cheese. Bake 25 to 30 minutes, until golden. Remove from the pan and cool on a wire rack.

RUSTIC GRAINS BREAD

Whole oat groats, wheat flakes, rye flakes, sunflower seeds, sesame seeds, whole millet, poppy seeds and whole flax are the ingredients in the special Harvest Grains Blend from King Arthur Flour. My Rustic Grains Mixture (page 147) makes a good substitute.

Sampler Loaf	**Regular Loaf**	**Large Loaf**
2/3 cup water	1 cup water	1 1/3 cups water
3/4 teaspoon salt	1 teaspoon salt	1 1/2 teaspoons salt
1 tablespoon canola oil	1 1/2 tablespoons canola oil	2 tablespoons canola oil
1 tablespoon sugar	1 1/2 tablespoons sugar	2 tablespoons sugar
2 tablespoons yellow cornmeal	3 tablespoons yellow cornmeal	1/4 cup yellow cornmeal
1/3 cup Rustic Grains Mixture	1/2 cup Rustic Grains Mixture	2/3 cup Rustic Grains Mixture
1/2 cup whole wheat flour	2/3 cup whole wheat flour	1 cup whole wheat flour
1 cup bread flour	1 2/3 cups bread flour	2 cups bread flour
1 teaspoon rapid-rising or active dry yeast	1 1/2 teaspoons rapid-rising or active dry yeast	2 teaspoons rapid-rising or active dry yeast

GLAZE FOR BREAD BAKED CONVENTIONALLY

1 egg

1 to 2 tablespoons Rustic Grains Mixture

TO MIX THE DOUGH BY HAND Heat the water until warm, between 105°F and 115°F; pour it into a large, warmed bowl. Add the yeast, salt, oil, sugar, cornmeal, Rustic Grains Mixture and the whole wheat flour. Slowly add half of the bread flour and beat until a smooth dough forms. Cover, and let stand 15 minutes. Turn the dough out onto a very lightly floured board, and knead, adding the remaining flour as necessary, until smooth and springy, about 5 minutes. Wash the bowl and grease it; place the dough back in the bowl, and turn it over to grease the top. Cover, and let rise until doubled, about 1 hour.

TO MIX THE DOUGH WITH A HEAVY-DUTY MIXER Heat the water until warm, between 105° and 115°F; pour it into the warmed mixing bowl. Add the yeast, salt, oil, sugar, cornmeal, Rustic Grains Mixture, and whole wheat flour. Let stand 5 minutes until yeast bubbles. Slowly add half of the bread flour, and beat until a smooth dough forms. Cover, and let stand 15 minutes. Knead the dough in the mixer with the dough hook, on medium to high speed, adding the remaining flour as necessary, until the dough pulls away from the sides of the bowl and is smooth and springy but still soft to the touch. Remove the dough hook, cover the bowl, and let the dough rise until doubled, about 1 hour.

TO MIX THE DOUGH IN THE FOOD PROCESSOR Place the plastic dough blade into the work bowl. Heat the water until very warm, between 120° and 130°F; set aside. Place the remaining ingredients into the work bowl. Turn the processor on, and slowly pour the water through the feed tube, processing until the dough is smooth and pulls away from the sides of the bowl. If the dough is wet and sticky, add more flour, 1 tablespoon at a time, until the dough is smooth yet soft to the touch. If the dough is not soft to the touch but is very firm, add 1 tablespoon of water at a time, and process until the dough is smooth yet soft to the touch. Cover the work bowl, and let the dough rise until doubled, about 1 hour. Or remove the dough to a lightly greased bowl, cover, and let rise until doubled, about 1 hour.

TO MIX THE DOUGH IN THE BREAD MACHINE Pour the water (at room temperature) into the pan. Add the remaining ingredients, in the order listed. Make an indentation in the dry ingredients and add the yeast. Select *Dough,* and press *Start.* If the dough is wet and sticky, add more flour, 1 tablespoon at a time, until the dough is smooth yet soft to the touch. If the dough is not soft to the touch but is very firm, add 1 teaspoon of water at a time, until the

dough is smooth yet soft to the touch. The machine will stop when the dough is ready to shape and bake.

TO MIX AND BAKE THE BREAD IN THE BREAD MACHINE Pour the water (at room temperature) into the pan. Add the remaining ingredients, in the order listed. Make an indentation in the dry ingredients and add the yeast. Select the *Basic* or *Whole Wheat* cycle, set the crust on *Medium,* and press *Start.* During the mixing cycle, if the dough is wet and sticky, add more flour, 1 tablespoon at a time, until the dough is smooth yet soft to the touch. If the dough is not soft to the touch but is very firm, add 1 teaspoon of water at a time, until the dough is smooth yet soft to the touch.

TO SHAPE AND BAKE IN THE OVEN Lightly grease a 9 × 5-inch loaf pan or an 8- or 9-inch round cake pan. Turn the dough out onto a lightly floured board or lightly oiled surface. Punch the dough down, and shape it into an oblong or round loaf. Place the loaf, with the smooth side up, into the pan. Cover and let rise in a warm place until almost doubled, 45 minutes. Preheat the oven to 375°F. To glaze, beat the egg with the water, brush the mixture on the loaf, and sprinkle on the Rustic Grain Mixture. Bake 25 to 35 minutes, until the loaf is golden. Remove from the pan and cool on a wire rack.

SPICED SCANDINAVIAN LIMPA

The combination of fennel, caraway, and orange gives Swedish limpa its characteristic flavor. *Limpa* is simply the Swedish word for "loaf." Soy sauce in a Scandinavian bread recipe might seem a little incongruous, but I got the original recipe, including the soy sauce, from a Scandinavian baker and then adapted it to a single-loaf size for conventional and bread machine baking.

Sampler Loaf

2/3 cup water

1 tablespoon soy sauce

1 teaspoon fennel seeds

1 teaspoon caraway seeds

1 teaspoon grated orange zest

1/2 teaspoon salt

1 tablespoon sugar

1 tablespoon butter

1 cup light rye flour

1 cup bread flour

1 tablespoon gluten

1 teaspoon rapid-rising or active
   dry yeast

Regular Loaf

1 cup water

1 1/2 tablespoons soy sauce

1 1/2 teaspoons fennel seeds

1 1/2 teaspoons caraway seeds

1 1/2 teaspoons grated orange zest

3/4 teaspoon salt

1 1/2 tablespoons sugar

1 1/2 tablespoons butter

1 1/2 cups light rye flour

1 1/2 cups bread flour

2 tablespoons gluten

1 1/2 teaspoons rapid-rising or
   active dry yeast

Large Loaf

1 1/3 cups water

2 tablespoons soy sauce

2 teaspoons fennel seeds

2 teaspoons caraway seeds

2 teaspoons grated orange zest

1 teaspoon salt

2 tablespoons sugar

2 tablespoons butter

2 cups light rye flour

2 cups bread flour

3 tablespoons gluten

2 teaspoons rapid-rising or active
   dry yeast

GLAZE FOR BREAD BAKED CONVENTIONALLY

1 teaspoon molasses

1 teaspoon water

TO MIX THE DOUGH BY HAND Heat the water until warm, between 105° and 115°F; pour it into a large, warmed bowl, and add the yeast. Let stand 5 minutes, until the yeast begins to bubble. Stir in the soy sauce, seeds, orange zest, salt, sugar, butter, and rye flour. Cover, and let stand 15 minutes. Slowly add the bread flour and gluten and beat until a smooth dough forms. Turn the dough out onto a very lightly floured board, and knead, adding flour if necessary, until smooth and springy, about 5 minutes. Wash the bowl and grease it; place the dough back in the bowl, and turn it over to grease the top. Cover, and let rise until doubled, about 1 hour.

TO MIX THE DOUGH WITH A HEAVY-DUTY MIXER Heat the water until warm, between 105° and 115°F; pour it into the warmed mixing bowl, and add the yeast. Let stand 5 minutes, until the yeast begins to bubble. Add the soy sauce, seeds, orange zest, salt, sugar, butter, and rye flour. Cover, and let stand 15 minutes. Slowly add the bread flour and gluten, and beat until a smooth dough forms.Knead the dough in the mixer with the dough hook, on medium to high speed, adding flour as necessary, until the dough pulls away from the sides of the bowl and is smooth and springy but still soft to the touch. Remove the dough hook, cover the bowl, and let the dough rise until doubled, about 1 hour.

TO MIX THE DOUGH IN THE FOOD PROCESSOR Place the plastic dough blade into the work bowl. Heat the water until very warm, between 120° and 130°F; set aside. Place the remaining ingredients into the work bowl. Turn the processor on, and slowly pour the water through the feed tube, processing until the dough is smooth and pulls away from the sides of the bowl. If the dough is wet and sticky, add more flour, 1 tablespoon at a time, until the dough is smooth yet soft to the touch. If the dough is not soft to the touch but is very firm, add 1 tablespoon of water at a time, and process until the dough is smooth yet soft to the touch. Cover the work bowl, and let the dough rise until doubled, about 1 hour. Or remove the dough to a lightly greased bowl, cover, and let rise until doubled, about 1 hour.

TO MIX THE DOUGH IN THE BREAD MACHINE Pour the water (at room temperature) into the pan. Add the remaining ingredients, in the order listed. Make an indentation in the dry ingredients and add the yeast. Select *Dough,* and press *Start.* If the dough is wet and sticky, add more flour, 1 tablespoon at a time, until the dough is smooth yet soft to the touch. If the dough is not soft to the touch but is very firm, add 1 teaspoon of water at a time, until the dough is smooth yet soft to the touch. The machine will stop when the dough is ready to shape and bake.

TO MIX AND BAKE THE BREAD IN THE BREAD MACHINE Pour the water (at room temperature) into the pan. Add the remaining ingredients, in the order listed. Make an indentation in the dry ingredients and add the yeast. Select the *Basic* cycle, set the crust on *Medium,* and press *Start.* During the mixing cycle, if the dough is wet and sticky, add more flour, 1 tablespoon at a time, until the dough is smooth yet soft to the touch. If the dough is not soft to the touch but is very firm, add 1 teaspoon of water at a time, until the dough is smooth yet soft to the touch.

TO SHAPE AND BAKE IN THE OVEN Lightly grease an 8- or 9-inch round cake pan. Turn the dough out onto a lightly floured or lightly oiled surface. Punch the dough down, and shape it into a round loaf. Place the loaf, with the smooth side up, into the pan. Cover and let rise in a warm place until almost doubled, 1 hour. Preheat the oven to 375°F. In a small bowl mix the molasses with the water, and brush on the loaf. Bake 35 to 40 minutes, until a wooden skewer inserted into the loaf comes out clean and dry. Remove from the pan and cool on a wire rack.

Country Sourdough Bread

Baba Ganoush (Eggplant Spread)

Finnish Sour Rye Bread

Oatmeal Sourdough Bread

Sourdough Currant Rye Bread

Sourdough Pumpernickel Rye Bread

Wheat Sourdough French Bread

Grilled Portobello Mushroom and Goat Cheese Sandwich

Whole Wheat Sourdough Raisin Bread

six

SOURDOUGH BREAD AND SOURDOUGH STARTERS

When the pioneers trudged westward in their covered wagons, many of them carried along a pouch of sourdough starter. Today, sourdough bread has become a symbol of the American West.

Over the years, I've kept a starter going, which I began by setting a bowl of milk out in the open to "catch" wild yeast. Then I mixed in flour, and let it stand until it became bubbly. This method is chancy; but when I finally got a good starter, it made fabulous bread. The classic way in which the starter is saved is to mix it into a fresh batch of bread dough, and then save back about a cupful for use as yeast in the next baking.

An active sourdough starter needs to be replenished after each use. To do that, add equal parts of water and unbleached all-purpose flour, rye flour, or whole wheat flour to the starter pot, let it bubble up again, and then refrigerate it. An active starter usually takes just a couple of hours to get bubbly. It can be refrigerated, covered, but you need to "feed" the starter with fresh water and flour every three or four days so that it will not spoil. You can add a pinch of regular active dry yeast or cake yeast to boost the starter's activity.

When making sourdough bread in the bread machine using this pot starter, half the measure counts as liquid in the recipe, which is important to know because the balance of liquid to flour is critical.

You can use sourdough starter made with regular all-purpose white flour to make sourdough rye bread, sourdough wheat bread, or multigrain bread. Sourdough starter made with rye or whole wheat flour quickly develops an intense sour flavor, and you need to use or refresh it every day by removing part of the starter and replacing it with fresh water and flour to keep the starter fresh.

To make your own starter for sourdough bread, there are four choices: (1) Use the catch method I described above, (2) make a sourdough starter using regular active dry yeast, (3) purchase a package of sourdough yeast starter, and (4) obtain a small amount of starter from a friend. Commercial sourdough starter is often labeled "San Francisco" sourdough yeast starter. To use, follow the directions on the package. Such starters are available in specialty food shops and through mail-order catalogs. If you have a friend who has a sourdough starter, ask for $^1/2$ to 1 cup of it. Build up your own pot starter by mixing it with equal amounts of water and flour, using $^1/2$ to 1 cup each.

Why include all this in a book designed to make breads by hand *and* by machine? Because of the influence of temperature and humidity. The automatic bread machine is a faithful assistant, especially in the cold climate in which I live, because it keeps the dough at the perfect warm temperature for the sourdough to do its work and to develop its full flavor. Sometimes I program the machine to make dough, and after a rest period, I program it to make dough again without removing the dough from the machine, so that a full sourdough flavor can develop. The bread machine is a tool not the boss in the kitchen, and I use it for its attributes!

ABOUT REFRIGERATING DOUGHS

To make any dough that you refrigerate, be sure to use regular active dry yeast and not quick-rising, rapid-rising, or bread machine yeast, because they are not designed for cool temperatures.

Sourdough Pot Starter Using Active Dry Yeast

When you use this starter in a bread machine recipe, figure that half of it counts as liquid in the recipe.

ABOUT 2 CUPS

1 cup warm water, 105° to 115°F
1 cup unbleached all-purpose flour, whole wheat flour, or medium rye flour
1/8 teaspoon active dry yeast

In a large nonreactive bowl or crock (preferably one with a tight-fitting lid), mix the water, flour, and yeast. Cover, and let stand 24 to 36 hours, until the starter is bubbly and has a sweet-sour aroma. Cover and refrigerate for storage.

Replenish after each use with a mixture of half water and half flour. Let stand at room temperature 1 to 2 hours, until bubbly. Cover and refrigerate.

COUNTRY SOURDOUGH BREAD

Plain nonfat yogurt enhances the sourdough flavor in this bread. Use sourdough starter made with white, rye, or whole wheat flour. The addition of dry yeast boosts the rising power of the dough. For a thick, crusty crust, bake this loaf on a preheated tile with steam as directed.

Sampler Loaf

2 tablespoons water

1/2 cup sourdough starter (page 267)

1/3 cup nonfat plain yogurt

1 teaspoon salt

1/2 cup dark rye flour

1/2 cup whole wheat flour

1 cup bread flour

1 tablespoon gluten

1 teaspoon rapid-rising or active dry yeast

Regular Loaf

3 tablespoons water

3/4 cup sourdough starter (page 267)

1/2 cup nonfat plain yogurt

1 1/2 teaspoons salt

3/4 cup dark rye flour

3/4 cup whole wheat flour

1 1/2 cups bread flour

4 teaspoons gluten

1 1/2 teaspoons rapid-rising or active dry yeast

Large Loaf

1/4 cup water

2/3 cup sourdough starter (page 267)

1/4 cup nonfat plain yogurt

2 teaspoons salt

1 cup dark rye flour

1 cup whole wheat flour

2 cups bread flour

2 tablespoon gluten

1 teaspoons rapid-rising or active dry yeast

TO MIX THE DOUGH BY HAND Heat the water until warm, between 105° and 115°F; pour it into a large, warmed bowl. Add the sourdough starter (at room temperature) and the yeast. Let stand 5 minutes, until the yeast begins to bubble. Stir in the salt, rye flour, and whole wheat flour. Beat until smooth. Cover, and let stand 15 minutes. Slowly add the bread flour and gluten, and beat until a smooth dough forms. Turn the dough out onto a very lightly floured board, and knead, adding flour if necessary, until smooth and springy, about 5 minutes. Wash the bowl and grease it; place the dough back in the bowl, and turn it over to grease the top. Cover, and let rise until doubled, about 1 hour.

TO MIX THE DOUGH WITH A HEAVY-DUTY MIXER Heat the water until warm, between 105° and 115°F; pour it into the warmed mixing bowl. Add the sourdough starter (at room temperature) and the yeast. Let stand 5 minutes, until the yeast begins to bubble. Add the salt, rye flour, and whole wheat flour. Beat until smooth. Cover, and let stand 15 minutes. Slowly add the bread flour and gluten, and beat until a smooth dough forms. Knead the dough in the mixer with the dough hook, on medium to high speed, adding flour as necessary, until the dough pulls away from the sides of the bowl and is smooth and springy but still soft to the touch. Remove the dough hook, cover the bowl, and let the dough rise until doubled, about 1 hour.

TO MIX THE DOUGH IN THE FOOD PROCESSOR
Place the plastic dough blade into the work bowl. Heat the water until very warm, between 120° and 130°F; set aside. Place the remaining ingredients into the work bowl, putting the sourdough starter in last. Pour the water on top. Process until the dough is smooth and pulls away from the sides of the bowl. If the dough is wet and sticky, add more flour, 1 tablespoon at a time, until the dough is smooth yet soft to the touch. If the dough is not soft to the touch but is very firm, add 1 tablespoon of water at a time, and process until the dough is smooth yet soft to the touch. Cover the work bowl, and let the dough rise until doubled, about 1 hour. Or remove the dough to a lightly greased bowl, cover, and let rise until doubled, about 1 hour.

TO MIX THE DOUGH IN THE BREAD MACHINE   Pour the water (at room temperature) into the pan. Add the remaining ingredients, in the order listed. Make an indentation in the dry ingredients and add the yeast. Select *Dough,* and press *Start.* If the dough is wet and sticky, add more flour, 1 tablespoon at a time, until the dough is smooth yet soft to the touch. If the dough is not soft to the touch but is very firm, add 1 teaspoon of water at a time, until the dough is smooth yet soft to the touch. The machine will stop when the dough is ready to shape and bake.

TO MIX AND BAKE THE BREAD IN THE BREAD MACHINE   Pour the water (at room temperature) into the pan. Add the remaining ingredients, in the order listed. Make an indentation in the dry ingredients and add the yeast. Select the *Basic* or *French Bread* cycle, set the crust on *Medium,* and press *Start.* During the mixing cycle, if the dough is wet and sticky, add more flour, 1 tablespoon at a time, until the dough is smooth yet soft to the touch. If the dough is not soft to the touch but is very firm, add 1 teaspoon of water at a time, until the dough is smooth yet soft to the touch.

TO SHAPE AND BAKE IN THE OVEN   Turn the dough out onto a lightly floured board or lightly oiled surface. Punch the dough down, and shape it into a round loaf.

To bake on baking tiles   Leave the loaf, with the smooth side up, on the board, cover, and let rise in a warm place until almost doubled, 45 to 60 minutes. Place baking tiles or a pizza tile on the top rack in the oven, and place a heavy, shallow pan on the bottom rack. Preheat the oven to 450°F. Using a sharp knife or a razor, slash the loaf in a tic-tac-toe design, and brush with water; place the loaf onto the preheated tiles. Immediately pour 1 cup water into the pan on the bottom rack. Bake 25 minutes, until the loaf is evenly golden. Remove from the oven and cool on a wire rack.

To bake in a pan   Lightly grease a baking sheet. Place the loaf, with the smooth side up, onto the baking sheet. Cover, and let rise in a warm place until almost doubled, 45 to 60 minutes. Preheat the oven to 400°F. Using a sharp knife or a razor, slash the top of the loaf in a tic-tac-toe design, and brush it with water. Bake 45 minutes, until the loaf is golden. Remove from the oven and cool on a wire rack.

Baba Ganoush (Eggplant Spread)

Baba Ganoush is basically cooked eggplant, finely chopped and flavored with garlic, herbs, and spices. This is one of my favorite make-ahead spreads for a party, because it goes with all kinds of breads, especially with Country Sourdough Bread (page 268). When I'm in a hurry, I cook the eggplant in the microwave oven, 12 minutes per pound. Otherwise, my favorite way to cook it is on the grill, since it picks up a great smoky taste. You can make this spread a couple of days ahead. Keep it covered and refrigerated; allow it to return to room temperature for about 20 minutes before serving.

ABOUT 2 CUPS

1 eggplant, about 1 pound

2 tablespoons extra-virgin olive oil

1 red bell pepper, cut into 1/8-inch dice

1 small onion, minced

2 garlic cloves, minced or pressed

1 large fresh tomato, peeled, seeded, and cut into
   1/8-inch dice

3 tablespoons freshly squeezed lemon juice

Salt and freshly ground black pepper, to taste

2 tablespoons minced fresh chives

2 tablespoons chopped parsley or cilantro

Pierce the eggplant all over with a fork and rub with 1 tablespoon oil. Preheat oven to 400°F. Place eggplant on baking sheet and roast for 50 to 60 minutes, uncovered, until very soft. Cool until you can handle the eggplant with bare hands.

In a nonstick medium skillet heat the remaining oil over medium heat and add the bell pepper, onion, and garlic. Cook, stirring occasionally, about 6 minutes, until soft but not browned. Cool.

With a spoon, scrape the flesh from the cooled eggplant skin. Chop it, and add it to the onion-garlic mixture. Turn the mixture into a medium a bowl, and add the tomato, lemon juice, salt, and black pepper. Cover, and refrigerate until ready to serve. Just before serving, stir in the chives and parsley.

FINNISH SOUR RYE BREAD

This is a classic of northern Europe, especially in Finland where bakers produce sourdough rye loaves in many different shapes, much as French bakers do with their classic loaves. Finns believe that the flavor of the bread depends on its shape. Basically, there are two favorite shapes: a plain round loaf and a loaf created by flattening the round loaf to about 1 inch thickness, with a hole in the center. This shape dates back to days when loaves were strung on poles and dried.

Sampler Loaf	Regular Loaf	Large Loaf
1/3 cup water	1/2 cup water	2/3 cup water
2/3 cup sourdough starter (page 267)	1 cup sourdough starter (page 267)	1 1/3 cups sourdough starter (page 267)
1 teaspoon salt	1 1/2 teaspoons salt	2 teaspoons salt
1 1/4 cups dark rye flour	2 1/4 cups dark rye flour	3 cups dark rye flour
1/2 cup bread flour	3/4 cup bread flour	1 cup bread flour
1 tablespoon gluten	4 teaspoons gluten	2 tablespoons gluten
1 teaspoon active dry yeast*	1 1/2 teaspoons active dry yeast*	2 teaspoons active dry yeast*

TO MIX THE DOUGH BY HAND Heat the water until warm, between 105° and 115°F; pour it into a large, warmed bowl. Add the sourdough starter (at room temperature) and the yeast. Let stand 5 minutes, until the yeast begins to bubble. Stir in the salt and rye flour. Beat until smooth. Cover, and let stand 15 minutes. Slowly add the bread flour and gluten, and beat until a smooth dough forms. Turn the dough out onto a very lightly floured board, and knead, adding flour if necessary, until smooth and springy, about 5 minutes. Wash the bowl and grease it; place the dough back in the bowl, and turn it over to grease the top. Cover, and let rise until doubled, about 1 hour. For a more intense sourdough flavor, place the dough in a plastic bag, and refrigerate overnight.

TO MIX THE DOUGH WITH A HEAVY-DUTY MIXER Heat the water until warm, between

*Note   *If you are baking the bread in the bread machine, use rapid-rising yeast. Do not use rapid-rising yeast if you plan to refrigerate the dough.*

105° and 115°F; pour it into the warmed mixing bowl. Add the sourdough starter (at room temperature) and the yeast. Let stand 5 minutes, until the yeast begins to bubble. Add the salt and rye flour. Beat until smooth. Cover, and let stand 15 minutes. Slowly add the bread flour and gluten, and beat until a smooth dough forms. Knead the dough in the mixer with the dough hook, on medium to high speed, adding flour as necessary, until the dough pulls away from the sides of the bowl and is smooth and springy but still soft to the touch. Remove the dough hook, cover the bowl, and let the dough rise until doubled, about 1 hour. For a more intense sourdough flavor, place the dough in a plastic bag, and refrigerate overnight.

TO MIX THE DOUGH IN THE FOOD PROCESSOR

Place the plastic dough blade into the work bowl. Heat the water until very warm, between 120° and 130°F; set aside. Place the remaining ingredients into the work bowl, putting the sourdough starter in last. Turn the processor on, and slowly pour the water through the feed tube, processing until the dough is smooth and pulls away from the sides of the bowl. If the dough is wet and sticky, add more flour, 1 tablespoon at a time, until the dough is smooth yet soft to the touch. If the dough is not soft to the touch but is very firm, add 1 tablespoon of water at a time, and process until the dough is smooth yet soft to the touch. Cover the work bowl, and let the dough rise until doubled, about 1 hour. Or remove the dough to a lightly greased bowl, cover, and let rise until doubled, about 1 hour. For a more intense sourdough flavor, place the dough in a plastic bag, and refrigerate overnight.

TO MIX THE DOUGH IN THE BREAD MACHINE

Pour the water (at room temperature) into the pan. Add the remaining ingredients, in the order listed. Make an indentation in the dry ingredients and add the yeast. Select *Dough,* and press *Start.* If the dough is wet and sticky, add more flour, 1 tablespoon at a time, until the dough is smooth yet soft to the touch. If the dough is not soft to the touch but is very firm, add 1 teaspoon of water at a time, until the dough is smooth yet soft to the touch. The machine will stop when the dough is ready to shape and bake. For a more intense sourdough flavor, place the dough in a plastic bag, and refrigerate overnight.

TO MIX AND BAKE THE BREAD IN THE BREAD MACHINE

Pour the water (at room temperature) into the pan. Add the remaining ingredients, in the order listed. Make an indentation in the dry ingredients and add the yeast. Select the *Basic* or *French Bread* cycle, set the crust on *Medium,* and press *Start.* During the mixing cycle, if the dough is wet and sticky, add more flour, 1 tablespoon at a time, until the dough is smooth yet soft to the touch. If the dough is not soft to the touch but is very firm, add 1 teaspoon of water at a time, until the dough is smooth yet soft to the touch.

TO SHAPE AND BAKE IN THE OVEN

If the dough was refrigerated, allow it to come to room temperature; as it does so, it will rise again. Turn the dough out onto a lightly floured board or lightly oiled surface. Punch the dough down, and shape it into a smooth round loaf. To make the Finnish-style country loaf with a hole in the center, flatten the dough to about 12 inches in diameter. With floured fingers, make a hole in the center of the loaf, then stretch and pull that hole to about 3 inches in diameter. It will fill in a little as the loaf rises and bakes. After rising and before baking, pierce the loaf with a fork. (Illustrated on the front cover of the book).

To bake on baking tiles   Place the loaf, with the smooth side up, on a bread board, or rimless cookie sheet, sprinkled with flour or cornmeal and let rise in a warm place until doubled, 45 to 60 minutes. Or, cover a cookie sheet with a piece of foil and lightly oil it. Place loaf onto the foil. Place baking tiles or a pizza stone on a rack in the center of the oven. Fill a rimmed, shallow baking pan with stones or river rock no larger than $1^1/2$ inches in diameter and place it on the bottom rack of the oven. Preheat the oven to 450°F for at least 30 minutes. (Rocks should be hot enough to sizzle when water is dropped on them.) Using a sharp knife or a razor, slash the risen loaf lengthwise to a depth of about $^1/4$ inch. Transfer the loaf onto the preheated baking tiles or pizza stone in the oven. (This is best done by gently easing the loaf onto the baking tile with the assistance of a straight-edged tool such as a bench scraper. For the large loaf with a hole in the center, transfer is easier if you shape the loaf on a piece of greased foil as it is shaped, then transfer the loaf, foil, and all onto the baking stone. Foil is easy to remove from the bottom of the loaf after baking.) Immediately pour 1 cup water into the pan of rocks on the bottom rack of the oven. (This is most easily done by squirting water from a sport bottle onto the rocks.) Bake for 15 to 20 minutes, until loaf is golden brown. Remove from the oven and cool on a wire rack.

To bake in a pan   Lightly grease a baking pan. Place the loaf, with the smooth side up, into the pan. Cover, and let rise in a warm place until almost doubled, 45 to 60 minutes. Preheat the oven to 375°F. Using a sharp knife or a razor, slash the top of the loaf in a crosshatch, and brush it with water. Bake 30 to 35 minutes, until the loaf is golden brown. Remove from the oven and cool on a wire rack.

OATMEAL SOURDOUGH BREAD

Typical of most whole grains, rolled oats help to develop a rich flavor in this bread.

Sampler Loaf

$^1/_3$ cup warm water

$^2/_3$ cup sourdough starter*
(page 267)

1 teaspoon salt

$^1/_2$ cup regular or old-fashioned
rolled oats

$1^1/_2$ cups bread flour

1 teaspoon dry yeast

Regular Loaf

$^1/_2$ cup warm water

1 cup sourdough starter*
(page 267)

$1^1/_2$ teaspoons salt

1 cup regular or old-fashioned
rolled oats

2 cups bread flour

$1^1/_2$ teaspoons dry yeast

Large Loaf

$^2/_3$ cups warm water

$1^1/_3$ cups sourdough starter*
(page 267)

2 teaspoons salt

$1^1/_2$ cups regular or old-fashioned
rolled oats

$2^1/_2$ cups bread flour

2 teaspoons dry yeast

TO MIX DOUGH BY HAND Heat the water until warm, between 105°F and 115°F. Pour it in a large warmed bowl. Add the sourdough starter (at room temperature), and add the yeast. Let stand for 5 minutes until yeast begins to bubble. Stir in the salt, rolled oats, and half of the bread flour. Beat until smooth. Cover, and let stand for 15 minutes. Slowly add the remaining bread flour and beat unti a smooth dough forms. Turn the dough out onto a very lightly floured board, and knead, adding flour as necessary, until smooth and springy, about 5 minutes. Wash the bowl, grease it, place the dough back in the bowl, and turn it over to grease the top. Cover, and let rise until doubled, about 1 hour.

TO MIX THE DOUGH WITH A HEAVY-DUTY MIXER Heat the water until warm, between 105°F and 115°F. Pour it into the warmed mixing bowl. Add the sourdough starter (at room temperature), and add the yeast. Let stand for 5 minutes. Stir in the salt, rolled oats, and half of the bread flour. Cover, and let stand 15 minutes. Slowly add the remaining bread flour and beat until a smooth dough forms. Knead the dough in the mixer with the dough hook on medium to high speed, adding flour as necessary, until the dough pulls away from the sides of the bowl and is smooth and springy but still soft to the touch. Remove the dough hook, cover the bowl, and let the dough rise until doubled, about 1 hour.

TO MIX THE DOUGH IN THE FOOD PROCESSOR Place the plastic dough blade into the work bowl. Heat the water until very warm, between 120°F and 130°F; set aside. Place the remaining ingredients into the work bowl, putting the sourdough starter in last. Turn the processor on, and slowly

*Note   Sourdough starter that is made with equal measure of flour and liquid.

pour the water through the feed tube, processing until the dough is smooth and pulls away from the sides of the bowl. If the dough is wet and sticky, add more flour, 1 tablespoon at a time, until the dough is smooth yet soft to the touch. If the dough is not soft to the touch but is very firm, add 1 tablespoon of water at a time, and process until the dough is smooth yet soft to the touch. Cover the work bowl, and let the dough rise until doubled, about 1 hour. Or remove the dough to a lightly greased bowl, cover, and let rise until doubled, about 1 hour.

TO MIX THE DOUGH IN THE AUTOMATIC BREAD MACHINE

Pour the water (at room temperature) into the pan. Add the remaining ingredients, in the order listed. Make an indentation in the dry ingredients and add the yeast. Select *Dough* and press *Start*. If the dough is wet and sticky, add more flour, 1 tablespoon at a time, until the dough is smooth and soft to the touch. If the dough is not soft to the touch but very firm, add 1 teaspoon of water at a time until the dough is smooth and soft to the touch. The machine will stop when the dough is ready to shape and bake.

TO MIX AND SHAPE THE BREAD IN THE BREAD MACHINE

Pour the water (at room temperature) into the pan. Add the remaining ingredients in the order listed. Make an indentation in the dry ingredients and add the yeast. Select *Basic* or *French Bread* cycle, set the crust on *Medium* and press *Start*. During the mixing cycle, if the dough is wet and sticky, add more flour, 1 tablespoon at a time, until the dough is smooth yet soft to the touch. If the dough is not soft to the touch but is very firm, and 1 teaspoon of water at a time, until the dough is smooth yet soft to the touch.

TO SHAPE AND BAKE DOUGH IN THE OVEN

Turn the dough out onto a lightly floured board or lightly oiled surface. Punch the dough down, and shape it into a round loaf.

To bake on tiles   Place the loaf, with the smooth side up, on a bread board, or rimless cookie sheet, sprinkled with flour or cornmeal and let rise in a warm place until doubled, 45 to 60 minutes. Place baking tiles or a pizza stone on a rack in the center of the oven. Fill a rimmed, shallow baking pan with stones or river rock no larger than $1 1/2$ inches in diameter and place it on the bottom rack of the oven. Preheat the oven to 450°F for at least 30 minutes. (Rocks should be hot enough to sizzle when water is dropped on them.) Using a sharp knife or a razor, slash the risen loaf lengthwise to a depth of about $1/4$ inch. Transfer the loaf onto the preheated baking tiles or pizza stone in the oven. (This is best done by gently easing the loaf onto the baking tile with the assistance of a straight-edged tool such as a bench scraper.) Immediately pour 1 cup water into the pan of rocks on the bottom rack of the oven. (This is most easily done by squirting water from a sport bottle onto the rocks.) Bake for 15 to 20 minutes, until loaf is golden brown. Remove from the oven and cool on a wire rack.

To bake in pan   Lightly grease a baking pan or cookie sheet. Place the loaf with the smooth side up onto the pan. Cover and let rise in a warm place until almost doubled in size, $1 1/2$ to 2 hours. Preheat oven to 375°F. Using a sharp knife or a razor, slash the top of the loaf, and spritz or brush with water. Bake 30 to 35 minutes or until the loaf is golden brown. Remove from the oven and cool on a wire rack.

SOURDOUGH CURRANT RYE BREAD

This is a dense, small, dark rye bread that's loaded with lots of dried currants, which sweeten the loaf. It's a wonderful addition to a cheese board and served thinly sliced with sweet butter. If the currants are very dry, soak them in warm water to cover for 10 minutes; then drain thoroughly.

Sampler Loaf

$^1/_3$ cup water

$^2/_3$ cup rye sourdough starter (page 281)

1 teaspoon salt

$^1/_2$ cup dark rye flour

$1^1/_2$ cups bread flour

$1^1/_4$ teaspoons rapid-rising or active dry yeast

$^1/_2$ cup currants

Regular Loaf

$^1/_2$ cup water

1 cup rye sourdough starter (page 281)

$1^1/_2$ teaspoons salt

$^3/_4$ cup dark rye flour

$2^1/_4$ cups bread flour

$1^1/_2$ teaspoons rapid-rising or active dry yeast

1 cup currants

Large Loaf

$^2/_3$ cup water

$1^1/_3$ cups rye sourdough starter (page 281)

2 teaspoons salt

$1^1/_2$ cups dark rye flour

$2^1/_2$ cups bread flour

2 teaspoons rapid-rising or active dry yeast

$1^1/_2$ cups currants

TO MIX THE DOUGH BY HAND Heat the water until warm, between 105° and 115°F; pour it into a large, warmed bowl. Add the sourdough starter (at room temperature) and the yeast. Let stand 5 minutes, until the yeast begins to bubble. Stir in the salt and rye flour. Beat until smooth. Cover, and let stand 15 minutes. Slowly add the bread flour, and beat until a smooth dough forms. Turn the dough out onto a very lightly floured board, and knead, adding flour if necessary, until smooth and springy, about 5 minutes. Knead in the currants. Wash the bowl and grease it; place the dough back in the bowl, and turn it over to grease the top. Cover, and let rise until doubled, about 1 hour.

TO MIX THE DOUGH WITH A HEAVY-DUTY MIXER Heat the water until warm, between 105° and 115°F; pour it into the warmed mixing bowl. Add the sourdough starter (at room temperature) and the yeast. Let stand 5 minutes, until the yeast begins to bubble. Add the salt and rye flour. Beat until smooth. Cover, and let stand 15 minutes. Slowly add the bread flour, and beat until a smooth dough forms. Knead the dough in the mixer with the dough hook, on medium to high speed, adding flour as necessary, until the dough pulls away from the sides of the bowl and is smooth and springy but still soft to the touch. Knead in the currants. Remove the dough hook, cover the bowl, and let the dough rise until doubled, about 1 hour.

TO MIX THE DOUGH IN THE FOOD PROCESSOR
Place the plastic dough blade into the work bowl. Heat the water until very warm, between 120° and 130°F; set aside. Place the remaining ingredients, except the currants, into the work bowl, putting the sourdough starter in last. Turn the processor on, and slowly pour the water through the feed tube, processing until the dough is smooth and pulls away from the sides of the bowl. If the dough is wet and sticky, add more flour, 1 tablespoon at a time, until the dough is smooth yet soft to the touch. If the dough is not soft to the touch but is very firm, add 1 tablespoon of water at a time, and process until the dough is smooth yet soft to the touch. Mix in the currants. Cover the work bowl, and let the dough rise until doubled, about 1 hour. Or remove the dough to a lightly greased bowl, cover, and let rise until doubled, about 1 hour.

TO MIX THE DOUGH IN THE BREAD MACHINE Pour the water (at room temperature) into the pan. Add the remaining ingredients, except the currants, in the order listed. Make an indentation in the dry ingredients and add the yeast. Select *Dough,* and press *Start.* If the dough is wet and sticky, add more flour, 1 tablespoon at a time, until the dough is smooth yet soft to the touch. If the dough is not soft to the touch but is very firm, add 1 teaspoon of water at a time, until the dough is smooth yet soft to the touch. Add the currants when the machine signals it's time to add ingredients or when the cycle ends. The machine will stop when the dough is ready to shape and bake.

TO MIX AND BAKE THE BREAD IN THE BREAD MACHINE Pour the water (at room temperature) into the pan. Add the remaining ingredients, except the currants, in the order listed. Make an indentation in the dry ingredients and add the yeast. Select the *Fruit and Nut* or *Basic* cycle, set the crust on *Medium,* and press *Start.* During the mixing cycle, if the dough is wet and sticky, add more flour, 1 tablespoon at a time, until the dough is smooth yet soft to the touch. If the dough is not soft to the touch but is very firm, add 1 teaspoon of water at a time, until the dough is smooth yet soft to the touch. Add the currants when the machine signals it's time to add ingredients.

TO SHAPE AND BAKE IN THE OVEN Lightly grease an 8- or 9-inch round cake pan or pie plate. Turn the dough out onto a lightly floured board or lightly oiled board. Punch the dough down, and shape it into a round loaf. Place the loaf, with the smooth side up, into the pan. Cover, and let rise in a warm place until almost doubled, 45 to 60 minutes. Preheat the oven to 350°F. Using a sharp knife or a razor slash the top of the loaf in a crosshatch; brush on water. Bake 45 minutes, until a wooden skewer inserted into the loaf comes out clean and dry. Remove from the pan and cool on a wire rack.

SOURDOUGH PUMPERNICKEL
RYE BREAD

Scandinavians begin to crave their heavy, rye sourdough bread when they visit the United States for any length of time. I've tried to duplicate the dense, grainy bread that they can get so easily in their bakeries. American rye flour has less gluten in it than does the Finnish rye flour. It is also milled a little differently, so I compensate by adding vital gluten. I use organic stone-ground rye flour, which has a course texture. Because rye flour makes a sourdough starter quickly, I've devised a way to make sourdough rye breads by adding rye flour to my regular wheat starter. That way I don't have to keep many different kinds of sourdough starters on hand. Remember to mix the starter 24 hours before you want to make the bread. The espresso powder darkens the loaf and can be left out if you don't mind a lighter colored bread.

Regular Loaf

1 batch Rye Sourdough Starter
    (recipe follows)

1/2 cup lukewarm water

2 teaspoons salt

1 tablespoon barley malt,
    sorghum molasses, or honey

1 tablespoon ground caraway
    seeds* (optional)

2 tablespoons espresso powder

1 cup stone-ground or
    dark rye flour

3 tablespoons gluten

1 cup bread flour

*Note   *To grind the caraway seeds, place them in a coffee mill or spice grinder, and process until fine.*

TO MIX THE DOUGH BY HAND   Make the Rye Sourdough Starter in a large bowl. The next day, add the remaining ingredients, except the bread flour. Add half of the bread flour, and beat until a smooth, stiff dough forms. Turn the dough out onto a very lightly floured board, and knead, adding the remaining flour as necessary, until smooth and springy, about 5 minutes. Wash the bowl and grease it; place the dough back in the bowl, and turn it over to grease the top. Cover, and let rise until doubled, about 1 hour. For a more intense sourdough flavor, place the dough in a plastic bag, and refrigerate overnight.

TO MIX THE DOUGH WITH A HEAVY-DUTY MIXER   Make the Rye Sourdough Starter in the mixing bowl. The next day, add the remaining ingredients, except the bread flour. Add half of the bread flour, and beat until a smooth, stiff dough forms. Knead the dough in the mixer with the dough hook, on medium to high speed, adding the remaining flour as necessary, until the dough pulls away from the sides of the bowl and is smooth and springy but still soft to the touch. Remove the dough hook, cover the bowl, and let the dough rise until doubled, about 1 hour. For a more intense sourdough flavor, place the dough in a plastic bag, and refrigerate overnight.

TO MIX THE DOUGH IN THE FOOD PROCESSOR   Make the Rye Sourdough Starter in a large bowl. The next day, place the plastic dough blade into the work bowl. Place the starter in the work bowl, and add the remaining ingredients, except the water. Turn the processor on, and slowly pour the water through the feed tube, processing until the dough is smooth and pulls away from the sides of the bowl. If the dough is wet and sticky, add more flour, 1 tablespoon at a time, until the dough is smooth yet soft to the touch. If the dough is not soft to the touch but is very firm, add 1 tablespoon of water at a time, and process until the dough is smooth yet soft to the touch. Cover the work bowl, and let the dough rise until doubled, about 1 hour. Or remove the dough to a lightly greased bowl, cover, and let rise until doubled, about 1 hour. For a more intense sourdough flavor, place the dough in a plastic bag, and refrigerate overnight.

TO MIX THE DOUGH IN THE BREAD MACHINE   Make the Rye Sourdough Starter in the bread pan. The next day, add the remaining ingredients. Select *Dough,* and press *Start.* If the dough is wet and sticky, add more flour, 1 tablespoon at a time, until the dough is smooth yet soft to the touch. If the dough is not soft to the touch but is very firm, add 1 teaspoon of water at a time, until the dough is smooth yet soft to the touch. The machine will stop when the dough is ready to shape and bake. For a more intense sourdough flavor, place the dough in a plastic bag, and refrigerate overnight.

TO MIX AND BAKE THE BREAD IN THE BREAD MACHINE   Make the Rye Sourdough Starter in the bread pan. The next day, add the remaining ingredients. Select the *Basic* or *Whole Wheat* cycle, set the crust on *Medium,* and press *Start.* During the mixing cycle, if the dough is wet and sticky, add more flour, 1 tablespoon at a time, until the dough is smooth yet soft to the touch. If the dough is not soft to the touch but is very firm, add 1 teaspoon of water at a time, until the dough is smooth yet soft to the touch.

TO SHAPE AND BAKE IN THE OVEN Lightly grease a baking sheet. If the dough was refrigerated, allow it to come to room temperature; as it does so, it will rise again. Turn the dough out onto a lightly floured board or lightly oiled surface. Punch the dough down, and shape it into a round loaf. Place the loaf, with the smooth side up, into the pan. Cover with a towel, and let rise in a warm place until almost doubled, 45 to 60 minutes. Preheat the oven to 375°F. Using a sharp knife or a razor, slash the loaf in a tic-tac-toe design; brush it with water. Bake 40 to 45 minutes, until a wooden skewer inserted into the loaf comes out clean and dry. Remove from the pan and cool on a wire rack.

Rye Sourdough Starter

2 CUPS

1/2 cup sourdough starter (page 267)
1/2 cup lukewarm water
1 cup stone-ground or dark rye flour
1/4 teaspoon active dry yeast

To mix by hand: Combine all the ingredients in a large bowl. Mix until smooth. Cover and let stand 24 hours at room temperature.

To mix in the bread machine: Place all the ingredients in the bread pan. Select *Dough* and press *Start.* When the cycle ends, leave the starter in the machine for 24 hours.

WHEAT SOURDOUGH FRENCH BREAD

A small amount of whole wheat flour in the bread dough results in a creamy crumb and a delicious sour flavor in this bread. This is a perfect, basic recipe to use for designing your favorite flavored bread, adding the many suggested combinations which follow this recipe. I like to make round or oblong loaves, although you can shape the dough into baguettes. For baguettes, the sampler loaf makes just one loaf, while the regular and large sized batches of dough can each be divided into two baguettes.

Sampler loaf

1/3 cup warm water

2/3 cup sourdough starter*
   (page 267)

1 teaspoon salt

1/2 cup whole wheat flour

1 to 1 1/2 cups bread flour

Regular loaf

1/2 cup water

1 cup sourdough starter*
   (page 267)

1 1/2 teaspoons salt

1 cup whole wheat flour

2 cups bread flour

1 1/2 teaspoons dry yeast

Large loaf

2/3 cups warm water

1 1/3 cups sourdough starter*
   (page 267)

2 teaspoons salt

1 1/2 cups whole wheat flour

2 1/2 cups bread flour

2 teaspoons dry yeast

TO MIX DOUGH BY HAND   Heat the water until warm, between 105°F and 115°F. Pour into a large warmed bowl. Add the sourdough starter (at room temperature), and add the yeast. Let stand for 5 minutes until the yeast begins to bubble. Stir in the salt, whole wheat flour, and half the bread flour. Beat until smooth. Cover, and let stand for 15 minutes. Slowly add the remaining bread flour and beat until a smooth dough forms. Turn the dough out onto a very lightly floured board and knead, adding flour as necessary, until smooth and springy, about 5 minutes. Wash the bowl, grease it, place the dough back in the bowl, and turn it over to grease top. Cover, and let rise until doubled, about 1 hour.

TO MIX DOUGH WITH A HEAVY-DUTY MIXER
Heat the water until warm, between 105°F and 115°F. Pour into the warm mixing bowl. Add the sourdough starter (at room temperature) and the yeast. Let stand 5 minutes. Add the salt, whole wheat flour, and half the bread flour. Beat until smooth. Cover, and let stand 15 minutes. Slowly add the remaining half of the bread flour, and beat until a smooth dough forms. Knead the dough in the mixer with the dough hook on medium to high speed, adding flour as necessary, until the dough pulls away from the sides of the bowl and is smooth and springy but still soft to the touch. Remove the dough hook, cover the bowl, and let the dough rise until doubled, about 1 hour.

*Note   *Sourdough starter that is made with equal measure of flour and liquid*

TO MIX THE DOUGH IN THE FOOD PROCESSOR Place the plastic dough blade into the work bowl. Heat the water until very warm, between 120°F and 130°F. Set aside. Place the remaining ingredients into the work bowl, putting the sourdough starter in last. Turn the processor on, and slowly pour in the water through the feed tube, processing until the dough is smooth and pulls away from the sides of the bowl. If the dough is wet and sticky, add more flour, 1 tablespoon at a time, until the dough is smooth yet soft to the touch. If the dough is not soft to the touch but is very firm, add 1 tablespoon of water at a time, and process until the dough is smooth yet soft to the touch. Cover the work bowl, and let the dough rise until doubled, about 1 hour. Or remove the dough to a lightly greased bowl, cover, and let rise until doubled, about 1 hour.

TO MIX THE DOUGH IN THE BREAD MACHINE Pour the water (at room temperature) into the pan. Add the remaining ingredients. Make an indentation in the dry ingredients and add the yeast. Select *Dough,* and press *Start.* If the dough is wet and sticky, add more flour, 1 tablespoon at a time, until the dough is smooth yet soft to the touch. If the dough is not soft to the touch but is very firm, add 1 teaspoon of water at a time, until the dough is smooth yet soft to the touch. The machine will stop when the dough is ready to shape and bake.

TO MIX AND BAKE THE BREAD IN THE BREAD MACHINE Pour the water (at room temperature) into the pan. Add the remaining ingredients. Make an indentation in the dry ingredients and add the yeast. Select the *Basic* or *French Bread* cycle, set the crust on *Medium,* and press *Start.* During the mixing cycle, if the dough is wet and sticky, add more flour, 1 tablespoon at a time, until the dough is smooth yet soft to the touch. If

the dough is not soft to the touch but is very firm, add 1 teaspoon of water at a time, until the dough is smooth yet soft to the touch.

TO SHAPE AND BAKE IN THE OVEN Turn the dough out onto a lightly floured board or lightly oiled surface. Punch the dough down, and shape it into a round loaf.

To bake on tiles Place the loaf, with the smooth side up, on a bread board, or rimless cookie sheet, sprinkled with flour or cornmeal and let rise in a warm place until doubled, 45 to 60 minutes. Place baking tiles or a pizza stone on a rack in the center of the oven. Fill a rimmed, shallow baking pan with stones or river rock no larger than 1 1/2 inches in diameter and place it on the bottom rack of the oven. Preheat the oven to 450°F for at least 30 minutes. (Rocks should be hot enough to sizzle when water is dropped on them.) Using a sharp knife or a razor, slash the risen loaf lengthwise to a depth of about 1/4 inch. Transfer the loaf onto the preheated baking tiles or pizza stone in the oven. (This is best done by gently easing the loaf onto the baking tile with the assistance of a straight-edged tool such as a bench scraper.) Immediately pour 1 cup water into the pan of rocks on the bottom rack of the oven. (This is most easily done by squirting water from a sport bottle onto the rocks.) Bake for 15 to 20 minutes, until loaf is golden brown. Remove from the oven and cool on a wire rack.

To bake in pan Lightly grease a baking pan or cookie sheet. Place the loaf with the smooth side up onto the pan. Cover and let rise in a warm place until almost doubled in size, 1 1/2 to 2 hours. Preheat oven to 375°F. Using a sharp knife, slash the top of the loaf, and spritz or brush with water. Bake 30 to 35 minutes or until the loaf is golden brown. Remove from the oven and cool on a wire rack.

Grilled Portobello Mushroom and Goat Cheese Sandwich

The meaty flavor of portobello mushrooms, combined with the tart flavor of goat cheese and balanced off with aromatic herbs, makes a great sandwich topping for thick slices of pan-grilled bread. In the final broiling, the juices from the mushroom soak into the bread. Roast the garlic while the bread is baking, so you'll be ready to put together this sandwich.

2 SERVINGS

2 portobello mushrooms
About 3 tablespoons extra-virgin olive oil
Salt and freshly ground pepper, to taste
2 garlic cloves, roasted
Fresh basil leaves

Fresh thyme leaves
Fresh parsley
3 to 4 ounces Montrachet cheese
2 thick slices whole wheat bread

Preheat the broiler. Trim the stems from the mushrooms. Brush with some of the olive oil, and season with salt and pepper.

In a food processor fitted with the steel blade, process the garlic and herbs until finely chopped. Add the cheese and process just until mixed; do not overprocess. Fill the hollow side of each mushroom with half of the cheese mixture.

Brush the bread slices with the remaining olive oil. Grill or broil until browned on both sides, about 1 minute on each side. Place one filled mushroom, cheese side up, on each slice of bread. Broil until the cheese mixture turns very light brown.

WHOLE WHEAT
SOURDOUGH RAISIN BREAD

The bread has a chewy crust and a hearty flavor. The raisins add a pleasantly sweet flavor to the bread.

Sampler Loaf	Regular Loaf	Large Loaf
1/3 cup water	1/2 cup water	2/3 cup water
2/3 cup sourdough starter (page 267)	1 cup sourdough starter (page 267)	1 1/3 cups sourdough starter (page 267)
1 teaspoon salt	1 1/2 teaspoons salt	2 teaspoons salt
1/2 cup whole wheat flour	1 cup whole wheat flour	1 1/2 cups whole wheat flour
1 1/2 cups bread flour	2 cups bread flour	2 1/2 cups bread flour
1 teaspoon rapid-rising or active dry yeast	1 1/2 teaspoons rapid-rising or active dry yeast	2 teaspoons rapid-rising or active dry yeast
1/3 cup raisins	1/2 cup raisins	2/3 cup raisins

TO MIX THE DOUGH BY HAND Heat the water until warm, between 105° and 115°F; pour it into a large, warmed bowl. Add the sourdough starter (at room temperature) and the yeast. Let stand 5 minutes, until the yeast begins to bubble. Stir in the salt and, whole wheat flour, and half of the bread flour. Beat until smooth. Cover, and let stand 15 minutes. Slowly add the remaining bread flour, and beat until a smooth dough forms. Turn the dough out onto a very lightly floured board, and knead, adding flour if necessary, until smooth and springy, about 5 minutes. Knead in the raisins. Wash the bowl and grease it; place the dough back in the bowl, and turn it over to grease the top. Cover, and let rise until doubled, about 1 hour.

TO MIX THE DOUGH WITH A HEAVY-DUTY MIXER Heat the water until warm, between 105° and 115°F; pour into the warmed mixing bowl. Add the sourdough starter (at room temperature) and the yeast. Let stand 5 minutes, until the yeast begins to bubble. Add the salt, whole wheat flour, and half of the bread flour. Beat until smooth. Cover, and let stand 15 minutes. Slowly add the remaining bread flour, and beat until a smooth dough forms. Knead the dough in the mixer with the dough hook, on medium to high speed, adding flour as necessary, until the dough pulls away from the sides of the bowl and is smooth and springy but still soft to the touch. Knead in the raisins. Remove the dough hook, cover the bowl, and let the dough rise until doubled, about 1 hour.

TO MIX THE DOUGH IN THE FOOD PROCESSOR
Place the plastic dough blade into the work bowl.
Heat the water until very warm, between 120°
and 130°F; set aside. Place the remaining ingredients into the work bowl, putting the sourdough
starter in last. Turn the processor on, and slowly
pour the water through the feed tube, processing
until the dough is smooth and pulls away from
the sides of the bowl. If the dough is wet and
sticky, add more flour, 1 tablespoon at a time,
until the dough is smooth yet soft to the touch. If
the dough is not soft to the touch but is very
firm, add 1 tablespoon of water at a time, and
process until the dough is smooth yet soft to the
touch. Mix in the raisins. Cover the work bowl,
and let the dough rise until doubled, about 1
hour. Or remove the dough to a lightly greased
bowl, cover, and let rise until doubled, about 1
hour.

**TO MIX THE DOUGH IN THE BREAD
MACHINE** Pour the water (at room temperature) into the pan. Add the remaining ingredients, except the raisins, in the order listed. Make
an indentation in the dry ingredients and add the
yeast. Select *Dough,* and press *Start.* If the dough is
wet and sticky, add more flour, 1 tablespoon at a
time, until the dough is smooth yet soft to the
touch. If the dough is not soft to the touch but is
very firm, add 1 teaspoon of water at a time, until
the dough is smooth yet soft to the touch. Add
the raisins when the machine signals it's time to
add ingredients or when the cycle ends. The
machine will stop when the dough is ready to
shape and bake.

**TO MIX AND BAKE THE BREAD IN THE
BREAD MACHINE** Pour the water (at room
temperature) into the pan. Add the remaining

ingredients, except the raisins, in the order listed.
Make an indentation in the dry ingredients and
add the yeast. Select the *Basic* or *French Bread*
cycle, set the crust on *Medium,* and press *Start.*
During the mixing cycle, if the dough is wet and
sticky, add more flour, 1 tablespoon at a time,
until the dough is smooth yet soft to the touch. If
the dough is not soft to the touch but is very
firm, add 1 teaspoon of water at a time, until the
dough is smooth yet soft to the touch. Add the
raisins when the machine signals it's time to add
ingredients.

TO SHAPE AND BAKE IN THE OVEN Turn
the dough out onto a lightly floured board or
lightly oiled surface. Punch the dough down, and
shape it into around loaf.

To bake on baking tiles Leave the loaf, with
the smooth side up, on the board, cover with a
towel, and let rise in a warm place until almost
doubled, 1 1/2 to 2 hours. Place baking tiles or a
pizza tile on the top rack in the center of the
oven, and place a heavy, shallow pan on the bottom rack. Preheat the oven to 450°F. Using a
sharp knife or a razor, slash the loaf, and brush
with water; place the loaf onto the preheated
tiles. Immediately pour 1 cup water into the pan
on the bottom rack. Bake 15 to 20 minutes, until
the loaf is golden brown. Remove from the oven
and cool on a wire rack.

To bake in a pan Lightly grease a baking sheet.
Place the loaf, with the smooth side up, onto the
baking sheet. Cover and let rise in a warm place
until almost doubled, 1 1/2 to 2 hours. Preheat the
oven to 375°F. Using a sharp knife or a razor, slash
the top of the loaf, and brush it with water. Bake
30 to 35 minutes, until the loaf is golden brown.
Remove from the oven and cool on a wire rack.

DESIGNING FLAVORED SOURDOUGH BREAD

To create breads with a variety of flavors, start with a basic sourdough bread and mix in one or a combination of the following ingredients after the first knead, or when the machine signals it's time to add ingredients. For sampler loaves, add a total of 1/3 to 1/2 cup additional ingredients; for regular loaves, add 1/2 to 3/4 cup; and for large loaves, add 3/4 to 1 cup.

Sun-dried tomatoes, not packed in oil, chopped fine

Kalamata olives, well drained, pitted, chopped

Sharp Cheddar cheese, cut into 1/2-inch cubes

Nuts (walnuts, pecans, filberts), coarsely chopped and toasted

Dried fruit (raisins, cranberries, cherries, figs)

Red bell pepper, cut into strips

Spinach, dried completely and shredded

Here are some good combinations:

Walnuts and figs

Cheese and nuts

Rosemary, olive, and bell peppers

Shredded carrots and tarragon

Dried cranberries and grated orange zest

Old-Fashioned Caraway Rye Baguette

Light Wheat Berry Bread

Old-Fashioned Rye Bread

Oven Ratatouille

The Very Best French Bread Made at Home

Parmesan Croutons

Garlic Croutons

Herbed Croutons

Crouton Toast Slices

Whole Wheat Berry Bread

Tapenade

Whole Wheat French Bread

Roasted Red Peppers

seven

BREADS MADE
WITH SPONGES

This chapter focuses on the ancient method of baking dough that is based on first making a "sponge," and then completing the dough 6 to 12 hours later. The sponge method of preparing bread dough takes several hours, but most of it is unattended time. The effort is no more than is necessary to make bread in the bread machine, but you will need to plan a day or so ahead whenever using this method. To make bread from a sponge, a very small amount of yeast is added to water and flour. The mixture is allowed to ferment for several hours, often up to a whole day, to give the yeast time to grow and develop. During this time, the dough develops a mild sourdough flavor and aroma, giving a chewy texture to the bread.

The bread machine works beautifully for making sponges, and when you use a whole grain flour for the sponge you get a sour flavor quickly. You simply process the sponge ingredients in the machine on the *Dough* cycle. When you're ready to bake the bread, you simply add the remaining ingredients and restart the machine. Although I prefer to shape and bake these breads in the conventional oven, you can bake them in the bread machine.

A Note about Loaf Size

All the recipes in this chapter include measurements for just one size loaf: the regular (1-pound) loaf.

A Note about Yeast

The yeast used in sponge-based breads is regular active dry yeast. Do not use bread machine, quick-rising, or rapid-rising yeast.

OLD-FASHIONED
CARAWAY RYE BAGUETTE

The bubbly sponge is the secret to this loaf's crusty crust and open, soft interior.

1 REGULAR-SIZE LOAF

FOR THE SPONGE
1¹/₂ cups bread flour
1/4 cup stone-ground rye flour
³/₄ teaspoon active dry yeast
³/₄ cup water

TO FINISH THE DOUGH
¹/₂ cup water
1¹/₂ cups bread flour
1/4 cup stone-ground rye flour
2 teaspoons salt
1 teaspoon ground caraway seeds*

TO MIX THE DOUGH BY HAND First make the sponge by placing the bread flour, rye four, and yeast into a warm large nonreactive bowl. Heat the water until warm, between 105° and 115°F; pour it into the bowl, and blend until well mixed. Cover, and let stand 12 to 24 hours, until the sponge is bubbly and has a sweet and lightly sour aroma. To finish the dough, stir the sponge down. Heat the water until warm, between 105° and 115°F. Add the water, bread flour, rye flour, salt, and caraways seeds to the sponge, and beat until a dough forms. Turn the dough out onto a very lightly floured board, and knead, adding flour if necessary, until smooth and springy, about 5 minutes. Wash the bowl and grease it;

place the dough back in the bowl, and turn it over to grease the top. Cover, and let rise until doubled, about 1 hour.

TO MIX THE DOUGH WITH A HEAVY-DUTY MIXER First make the sponge by placing the bread flour, rye four, and yeast into a warm large nonreactive bowl. Heat the water until warm, between 105° and 115°F; pour it into the bowl, and blend until well mixed. Cover, and let stand 12 to 24 hours, until the sponge is bubbly and has a sweet and lightly sour aroma. To finish the dough, stir the sponge down, and pour it into the warmed mixing bowl. Heat the water until warm, between 105° and 115°F. Add the water, bread

*Note   To grind the caraway seeds, place them in a coffee mill or spice grinder, and process until fine.

flour, rye flour, salt, and caraway seeds to the sponge, and beat until a dough forms. Knead the dough in the mixer with the dough hook, on medium to high speed, adding flour as necessary, until the dough pulls away from the sides of the bowl and is smooth and springy but still soft to the touch. Remove the dough hook, cover the bowl, and let the dough rise until doubled, about 1 hour.

TO MIX THE DOUGH IN THE FOOD PROCESSOR First make the sponge by placing the bread flour, rye flour and yeast into a warm large nonreactive bowl. Heat the water until warm, between 105° and 115°F; pour it into the bowl, and blend until well mixed. Cover, and let stand 12 to 24 hours, until the sponge is bubbly and has a sweet and lightly sour aroma. To finish the dough, stir the sponge down, and pour it into the work bowl fitted with the plastic dough blade. Heat the water until warm, between 105° and 115°F. Add the water, bread flour, rye flour, salt, and caraway seeds to the sponge, and process until the dough is smooth and pulls away from the sides of the bowl. If the dough is wet and sticky, add more flour, 1 tablespoon at a time, until the dough is smooth yet soft to the touch. If the dough is not soft to the touch but is very firm, add 1 tablespoon of water at a time, and process until the dough is smooth yet soft to the touch. Cover the work bowl, and let the dough rise until doubled, about 1 hour. Or remove the dough to a lightly greased bowl, cover, and let rise until doubled, about 1 hour.

TO MIX THE DOUGH IN THE BREAD MACHINE First make the sponge by placing the sponge ingredients (at room temperature) into the pan. Select *Dough,* and press *Start.* When the cycle ends, unplug the machine and let the sponge stand 12 to 24 hours, until it is bubbly and has a sweet and lightly sour aroma. To finish the dough, add the dough ingredients (at room temperature) to the pan. Select *Dough,* and press *Start.* If the dough is wet and sticky, add more flour, 1 tablespoon at a time, until the dough is smooth yet soft to the touch. If the dough is not soft to the touch but is very firm, add 1 teaspoon of water at a time, until the dough is smooth yet soft to the touch. The machine will stop when the dough is ready to shape and bake.

TO MIX AND BAKE THE BREAD IN THE BREAD MACHINE First make the sponge by placing the sponge ingredients (at room temperature) into the pan. Select *Dough,* and press *Start.* When the cycle ends, unplug the machine and let the sponge stand 12 to 24 hours, until it is bubbly and has a sweet and lightly sour aroma. To finish the dough, add the dough ingredients (at room temperature) to the pan. Select the *Basic* or *French Bread* cycle, set the crust on *Medium,* and press *Start.* During the mixing cycle, if the dough is wet and sticky, add more flour, 1 tablespoon at a time, until the dough is smooth yet soft to the touch. If the dough is not soft to the touch but is very firm, add 1 teaspoon of water at a time, until the dough is smooth yet soft to the touch.

TO SHAPE AND BAKE IN THE OVEN Turn the dough out onto a lightly floured board or lightly oiled surface. Punch the dough down, and shape it into a baguette, about 12 inches long.

To bake on baking tiles Leave the loaf, with the smooth side up, on the board, or place on a lightly oiled surface. Cover, and let rise in a warm place until almost doubled, 45 minutes. Place baking tiles or a pizza tile on the top rack in the oven, and place a heavy, shallow pan on the bottom rack. Preheat the oven to 450°F. Using a sharp knife or a razor, slash the loaf; place the loaf onto the preheated tiles. Immediately pour 1 cup water into the pan on the bottom rack, and spritz the loaf with water. Bake 10 minutes; reduce the heat to 400°F, and bake 15 to 20 minutes longer, until the loaf is golden brown and crusty. Remove from the oven and cool on a wire rack.

To bake in a pan Lightly grease a baking sheet. Place the loaf, with the smooth side up, onto the baking sheet. Cover and let rise in a warm place until almost doubled, 45 minutes. Preheat the oven to 375°F. Using a sharp knife or a razor, slash the top of the loaf, and spritz it with water. Bake 30 to 35 minutes, until the loaf is golden brown. Remove from the oven and cool on a wire rack.

LIGHT WHEAT BERRY BREAD

This is a pale wheat bread with the texture of cooked whole wheat kernels throughout. There are no directions for baking Light Wheat Berry Bread in the bread machine, because the whole wheat berries add too much moisture to the dough. It is absolutely wonderful baked in the oven, with its crispy crust and light interior.

1 REGULAR-SIZE LOAF

FOR THE SPONGE
1 1/2 cups bread flour
3/4 teaspoon active dry yeast
3/4 cup water

TO FINISH THE DOUGH
1 cup cooked whole wheat berries, very well
   drained (page 164)
1/2 cup water
2 cups bread flour
1 1/2 teaspoons salt

TO MIX THE DOUGH BY HAND First make the sponge by placing the flour and yeast into a warm large nonreactive bowl. Heat the water until warm, between 105° and 115°F; pour it into the bowl, and blend until well mixed. Cover, and let stand 12 to 24 hours, until the sponge is bubbly and has a sweet and lightly sour aroma. To finish the dough, stir the sponge down. Heat the water until warm, between 105° and 115°F. Add the wheat berries, water, flour, and salt to the sponge, and beat until a dough forms. Turn the dough out onto a very lightly floured board, and knead, adding flour if necessary, until smooth and springy, about 5 minutes. Wash the

bowl and grease it; place the dough back in the bowl, and turn it over to grease the top. Cover, and let rise until doubled, about 1 hour.

TO MIX THE DOUGH WITH A HEAVY-DUTY MIXER First make the sponge by placing the flour and yeast into a warm large nonreactive bowl. Heat the water until warm, between 105° and 115°F; pour it into the bowl, and blend until well mixed. Cover, and let stand 12 to 24 hours, until the sponge is bubbly and has a sweet and lightly sour aroma. To finish the dough, stir the sponge down, and pour it into the warm mixing bowl. Heat the water until warm, between 105°

and 115°F. Add the wheat berries, water, flour, and salt to the sponge, and beat until a dough forms. Knead the dough in the mixer with the dough hook, on medium to high speed, adding flour as necessary, until the dough pulls away from the sides of the bowl and is smooth and springy but still soft to the touch. Remove the dough hook, cover the bowl, and let the dough rise until doubled, about 1 hour.

TO MIX THE DOUGH IN THE FOOD PROCESSOR

First make the sponge by placing the flour and yeast into a warm large nonreactive bowl. Heat the water until warm, between 105° and 115°F; pour it into the bowl, and blend until well mixed. Cover, and let stand 12 to 24 hours, until the sponge is bubbly and has a sweet and lightly sour aroma. To finish the dough, stir the sponge down, and pour into the work bowl fitted with the plastic dough blade. Heat the water until warm, between 105° and 115°F. Add the wheat berries, flour, and salt to the sponge, and process, adding the water gradually through the feed tube, until the dough is smooth and pulls away from the sides of the bowl. If the dough is wet and sticky, add more flour, 1 tablespoon at a time, until the dough is smooth yet soft to the touch. If the dough is not soft to the touch but is very firm, add 1 tablespoon of water at a time, and process until the dough is smooth yet soft to the touch. Cover the work bowl, and let the dough rise until doubled, about 1 hour. Or remove the dough to a lightly greased bowl, cover, and let rise until doubled, about 1 hour.

TO MIX THE DOUGH IN THE BREAD MACHINE

First make the sponge by placing the sponge ingredients (at room temperature) into the pan. Select the *Dough* cycle, and press *Start*. When the cycle is finished, unplug the machine, and let the sponge stand 12 to 24 hours, until it is bubbly and has a sweet and slightly sour aroma. To finish the dough, add the remaining dough ingredients (at room temperature) to the sponge. Select *Dough,* and press *Start.* If the dough is wet and sticky, add more flour, 1 tablespoon at a time, until the dough is smooth yet soft to the touch. If the dough is not soft to the touch but is very firm, add 1 teaspoon of water at a time, until the dough is smooth yet soft to the touch. The machine will stop when the dough is ready to shape and bake.

TO SHAPE AND BAKE IN THE OVEN

Preheat the oven to 375°F. Lightly sprinkle a baking sheet with cornmeal. Turn the dough out onto a lightly floured board or lightly oiled surface. Punch the dough down, and shape it into a round loaf. Place the loaf, with the smooth side up, onto the baking sheet. Cover and let rise 45 minutes until almost doubled. Using a sharp knife or razor, slash the top of the loaf, and spritz with water. Bake 25 to 30 minutes, until the loaf is golden brown and crusty. Remove from the pan and cool on a wire rack.

OLD-FASHIONED RYE BREAD

This is the bread my Finnish grandmother and mother made. When I asked my mom about this method she replied "Oh, that's how we've always made bread—to save on yeast, you know." This yeast-saving method to me is the better method. The bread is crusty, the interior porous and moist.

1 REGULAR-SIZE LOAF

FOR THE SPONGE
1¹/₂ cups bread flour
¹/₄ cup stone-ground rye flour
³/₄ teaspoon active dry yeast
³/₄ cup water

TO FINISH THE DOUGH
¹/₂ cup water
1¹/₂ cups bread flour
¹/₄ cup stone-ground rye flour
2 teaspoons salt

TO MIX THE DOUGH BY HAND First make the sponge by placing the bread flour, rye flour, and yeast into a warm large nonreactive bowl. Heat the water until warm, between 105° and 115°F; pour it into the bowl, and blend until well mixed. Cover, and let stand 12 to 24 hours, until the sponge is bubbly and has a sweet and lightly sour aroma. To finish the dough, stir the sponge down. Heat the water until warm, between 105° and 115°F. Add the water, bread flour, rye flour, and salt to the sponge, and beat until a dough forms. Turn the dough out onto a very lightly floured board, and knead, adding flour if necessary, until smooth and springy, about 5 minutes. Wash the bowl and grease it; place the dough back in the bowl, and turn it over to grease the top. Cover, and let rise until doubled, about 1 hour.

TO MIX THE DOUGH WITH A HEAVY-DUTY MIXER First make the sponge by placing the bread flour, rye flour, and yeast into a warm large nonreactive bowl. Heat the water until warm, between 105° and 115°F; pour it into the bowl, and blend until well mixed. Cover, and let stand 12 to 24 hours, until the sponge is bubbly and has a sweet and lightly sour aroma. To finish the dough, stir the sponge down, and pour into the warmed mixing bowl. Heat the water until warm, between 105° and 115°F. Add the water, bread flour, rye flour, and salt to the sponge, and beat until a dough forms. Knead the dough in the mixer with the dough hook, on medium to high speed, adding flour as necessary, until the dough pulls away from the sides of the bowl and is smooth and springy but still soft to the touch.

Remove the dough hook, cover the bowl, and let the dough rise until doubled, about 1 hour.

TO MIX THE DOUGH IN THE FOOD PROCESSOR

First make the sponge by placing the bread flour, rye flour, and yeast into a warm large nonreactive bowl. Heat the water until warm, between 105° and 115°F; pour it into the bowl, and blend until well mixed. Cover, and let stand 12 to 24 hours, until the sponge is bubbly and has a sweet and lightly sour aroma. To finish the dough, stir the sponge down, and pour it into the work bowl fitted with the plastic dough blade. Heat the water until warm, between 105° and 115°F. Add the water, bread flour, rye flour, and salt to the sponge, and process until the dough is smooth and pulls away from the sides of the bowl. If the dough is wet and sticky, add more flour, 1 tablespoon at a time, until the dough is smooth yet soft to the touch. If the dough is not soft to the touch but is very firm, add 1 tablespoon of water at a time, and process until the dough is smooth yet soft to the touch. Cover the work bowl, and let the dough rise until doubled, about 1 hour. Or remove the dough to a lightly greased bowl, cover, and let rise until doubled, about 1 hour.

TO MIX THE DOUGH IN THE BREAD MACHINE

First make the sponge by placing the sponge ingredients (at room temperature) into the pan. Select *Dough,* and press *Start.* When the cycle ends, unplug the machine and let the sponge stand 12 to 24 hours, until it is bubbly and has a sweet and lightly sour aroma. To finish the dough, add the dough ingredients (at room temperature) to the pan. Select *Dough,* and press *Start.* If the dough is wet and sticky, add more flour, 1 tablespoon at a time, until the dough is smooth yet soft to the touch. If the dough is not soft to the touch but is very firm, add 1 teaspoon of water at a time, until the dough is smooth yet soft to the touch. The machine will stop when the dough is ready to shape and bake.

TO MIX AND BAKE THE BREAD IN THE BREAD MACHINE

First make the sponge by placing the sponge ingredients (at room temperature) into the pan. Select *Dough,* and press *Start.* When the cycle ends, unplug the machine and let the sponge stand 12 to 24 hours, until it is bubbly and has a sweet and lightly sour aroma. To finish the dough, add the dough ingredients (at room temperature) to the pan. Select the *Basic* or *French Bread* cycle, set the crust on *Medium,* and press *Start.* During the mixing cycle, if the dough is wet and sticky, add more flour, 1 tablespoon at a time, until the dough is smooth yet soft to the touch. If the dough is not soft to the touch but is very firm, add 1 teaspoon of water at a time, until the dough is smooth yet soft to the touch.

TO SHAPE AND BAKE IN THE OVEN

Turn the dough out onto a lightly floured board or lightly oiled surface. Punch the dough down, and shape it into a round loaf.

To bake on baking tiles Place the loaf, with the smooth side up, on a bread board, or rimless cookie sheet, sprinkled with flour or cornmeal and let rise in a warm place until doubled, 45 to 60 minutes. Place baking tiles or a pizza stone on a rack in the center of the oven. Fill a rimmed, shallow baking pan with stones or river rock no larger than 1 1/2 inches in diameter and place it on the bottom rack of the oven. Preheat the oven to 450°F for at least 30 minutes. (Rocks should be hot enough to sizzle when water is dropped on them.) Using a sharp knife or a razor, slash the risen loaf lengthwise to a depth of about 1/4 inch. Transfer the loaf onto the preheated baking tiles or pizza stone in the oven. (This is best done by gently easing the loaf onto the baking tile with the assistance of a straight-edged tool such as a bench scraper.) Immediately pour 1 cup water into the pan of rocks on the bottom rack of the oven. (This is most easily done by squirting water from a sport bottle onto the rocks.) Bake for 15 to 20 minutes, until loaf is golden brown. Remove from the oven and cool on a wire rack.

To bake in a pan Lightly grease a baking sheet. Place the loaf, with the smooth side up, onto the baking sheet. Cover and let rise in a warm place until almost doubled, 45 minutes. Preheat the oven to 375°F. Using a sharp knife or a razor, slash the top of the loaf, and brush it with water. Bake 30 to 35 minutes, until the loaf is golden brown and crusty. Remove from the oven and cool on a wire rack.

Oven Ratatouille

This is a great appetizer or snack for a large group of people. It is very easy to make: just pile all the ingredients into a big casserole and bake it long and slow. It's best made ahead, and tastes just as good cold as hot. Best of all, it's fresh tasting and there's hardly any fat in it. I like to surround a pot of ratatouille with slices of various kinds of bread, which makes a pretty presentation.

6 TO 8 CUPS

2 large onions, sliced

6 large garlic cloves, minced or mashed

1 medium unpeeled eggplant, cut into
    1/2-inch cubes

6 medium zucchini, thickly sliced

2 green or red bell peppers, seeded and cut
    into chunks

4 tablespoons extra-virgin olive oil

2 teaspoons salt

1 teaspoon dried basil

1/2 cup minced parsley

GARNISH

4 large tomatoes, cut into 1-inch chunks

1/2 cup sliced fresh basil leaves

FOR SERVING

1 to 2 loaves whole wheat, rye, or Tuscan
    Bread (page 32), sliced

Freshly grated Parmesan cheese (optional)

Preheat the oven to 350°F. Layer the onions, garlic, eggplant, zucchini, and bell peppers in a lightly greased 6-quart casserole. Press the vegetables down firmly and drizzle with the olive oil. Sprinkle with the salt, cover, and bake 3 hours. Uncover occasionally and press the vegetables down, basting any that look dry with some of the accumulated liquid. Uncover during the last hour if the mixture is getting soupy. Serve immediately; or cool and chill, if serving as an appetizer spread.

Before serving, garnish the ratatouille with the tomatoes, basil, and parsley. To serve, surround the casserole with slices of bread with a dish of Parmesan cheese.

THE VERY BEST FRENCH BREAD
MADE AT HOME

Even though this bread does not include a large amount of whole grain flour, I decided to include it in this book because I have had so many requests for the recipe. A small amount of barley and rye flour adds creaminess to the texture and boosts the sourdough flavor. This sponge method French bread has a crunchy crust and porous but tender interior. The long, slow fermentation of a small amount of yeast accounts for the wonderful texture and flavor. Even the bread baked in the machine has the right texture, if not the right shape. And when I bake the bread in the oven, I always do it on the preheated tiles with steam.

1 REGULAR-SIZE LOAF

FOR THE SPONGE
$^1/_2$ cup whole wheat flour or all-purpose flour
$1^1/_4$ cups bread flour
$^3/_4$ teaspoon active dry yeast
$^3/_4$ cup water

TO FINISH THE DOUGH
$^1/_2$ cup water
$2^1/_2$ cups bread flour
$1^1/_2$ teaspoons salt

TO MIX THE DOUGH BY HAND First make the sponge by placing the whole wheat or all-purpose flour, bread flour, and yeast into a warm large nonreactive bowl. Heat the water until warm, between 105° and 115°F; pour it into the bowl, and blend until well mixed. Cover, and let stand 12 to 24 hours, until the sponge is bubbly and has a sweet and lightly sour aroma. To finish the dough, stir the sponge down. Heat the water until warm, between 105° and 115°F. Add the water, flour, and salt to the sponge, and beat until a dough forms. Turn the dough out onto a very lightly floured board, and knead, adding flour if necessary, until smooth and springy, about 5 minutes. Wash the bowl and grease it; place the dough back in the bowl, and turn it over to grease the top. Cover, and let rise until doubled, about 1 hour.

TO MIX THE DOUGH WITH A HEAVY-DUTY MIXER First make the sponge by placing the whole wheat or all-purpose flour, bread flour, and yeast into a warm large nonreactive bowl. Heat the water until warm, between 105° and

115°F; pour it into the bowl, and blend until well mixed. Cover, and let stand 12 to 24 hours, until the sponge is bubbly and has a sweet and lightly sour aroma. To finish the dough, stir the sponge down, and pour into the warmed mixing bowl. Heat the water until warm, between 105° and 115°F. Add the water, flour, and salt to the sponge, and beat until a dough forms. Knead the dough in the mixer with the dough hook, on medium to high speed, adding flour as necessary, until the dough pulls away from the sides of the bowl and is smooth and springy but still soft to the touch. Remove the dough hook, cover the bowl, and let the dough rise until doubled, about 1 hour.

TO MIX THE DOUGH IN THE FOOD PROCESSOR

First make the sponge by placing the barley, rye and bread flour and yeast into a warm large nonreactive bowl. Heat the water until warm, between 105° and 115°F; pour it into the bowl, and blend until well mixed. Cover, and let stand 12 to 24 hours, until the sponge is bubbly and has a sweet and lightly sour aroma. To finish the dough, stir the sponge down, and pour it into the work bowl fitted with the plastic dough blade. Heat the water until warm, between 105° and 115°F. Add the water, flour, and salt to the sponge, and process until the dough is smooth and pulls away from the sides of the bowl. If the dough is wet and sticky, add more flour, 1 tablespoon at a time, until the dough is smooth yet soft to the touch. If the dough is not soft to the touch but is very firm, add 1 tablespoon of water at a time, and process until the dough is smooth yet soft to the touch. Cover the work bowl, and let the dough rise until doubled, about 1 hour. Or remove the dough to a lightly greased bowl, cover, and let rise until doubled, about 1 hour.

TO MIX THE DOUGH IN THE BREAD MACHINE

First make the sponge by placing the sponge ingredients (at room temperature) into the pan. Select *Dough,* and press *Start.* When the cycle ends, unplug the machine and let the sponge stand 12 to 24 hours, until it is bubbly and has a sweet and lightly sour aroma. To finish the dough, add the dough ingredients (at room temperature) to the pan. Select *Dough,* and press *Start.* If the dough is wet and sticky, add more flour, 1 tablespoon at a time, until the dough is smooth yet soft to the touch. If the dough is not soft to the touch but is very firm, add 1 teaspoon of water at a time, until the dough is smooth yet soft to the touch. The machine will stop when the dough is ready to shape and bake.

TO MIX AND BAKE THE BREAD IN THE BREAD MACHINE

First make the sponge by placing the sponge ingredients (at room temperature) into the pan. Select *Dough,* and press *Start.* When the cycle ends, unplug the machine and let the sponge stand 12 to 24 hours, until it is bubbly and has a sweet and lightly sour aroma. To finish the dough, add the dough ingredients (at room temperature) to the pan. Select the *Basic* or *French Bread* cycle, set the crust on *Medium,* and press *Start.* During the mixing cycle, if the dough is wet and sticky, add more flour, 1 tablespoon at a time, until the dough is smooth yet soft to the touch. If the dough is not soft to the touch but is very firm, add 1 teaspoon of water at a time, until the dough is smooth yet soft to the touch.

TO SHAPE AND BAKE IN THE OVEN Turn the dough out onto a lightly floured board or lightly oiled surface. Punch the dough down, and shape it into round loaf or long baguette.

To bake on baking tiles Place the loaf, with the smooth side up, on a bread board, or rimless cookie sheet, sprinkled with flour or cornmeal and let rise in a warm place until doubled, 45 to 60 minutes. Place baking tiles or a pizza stone on a rack in the center of the oven. Fill a rimmed, shallow baking pan with stones or river rock no larger than 1 1/2 inches in diameter and place it on the bottom rack of the oven. Preheat the oven to 450°F for at least 30 minutes. (Rocks should be hot enough to sizzle when water is dropped on them.) Using a sharp knife or a razor, slash the risen loaf lengthwise to a depth of about 1/4 inch. Transfer the loaf onto the preheated baking tiles or pizza stone in the oven. (This is best done by gently easing the loaf onto the baking tile with the assistance of a straight-edged tool such as a bench scraper.) Immediately pour 1 cup water into the pan of rocks on the bottom rack of the oven. (This is most easily done by squirting water from a sport bottle onto the rocks.) Bake for 15 to 20 minutes, until loaf is golden brown. Remove from the oven and cool on a wire rack.

To bake in a pan Lightly grease a baking pan. Place the loaf, with the smooth side up, into the pan. Cover, and let rise in a warm place until almost doubled, 45 minutes. Preheat the oven to 375°F. Using a sharp knife or a razor, slash the top of the loaf, and brush it with water. Bake 30 to 35 minutes, until the loaf is golden. Remove from the oven and cool on a wire rack.

Parmesan Croutons

Use any nonsweet bread to make delicious, crunchy croutons to top soups, salads, or serve as a snack. See variations below.

4 CUPS

4 cups bread cubes, preferably from day-old bread
   cut in 1/2 inch squares (do not remove crusts)

3 tablespoons olive, canola, or corn oil
1/4 cup shredded Parmesan cheese

Preheat the oven to 350°F. In a bowl, toss the bread cubes with the oil and cheese. Spread on an ungreased cookie sheet in a single layer so that the cubes are all slightly separated. Bake for 15 to 20 minutes, checking the cubes often, until croutons are dry and crisp. Stir if necessary, once or twice.

Garlic Croutons

Add 1 or 2 cloves of crushed fresh garlic to the olive oil before adding to the bread. Parmesan cheese is optional.

Herbed Croutons

Sprinkle 1 teaspoon each dried basil, thyme, rosemary, and oregano over the cubes after adding the oil. Parmesan cheese is optional.

Crouton Toast Slices

I like to have a jar of plain, thinly sliced toasted bread on hand, especially in summertime. They keep well at room temperature, provided they are out of direct sunlight and in an airtight jar or tin and are great for snacking just as they are. They also are wonderful when used as a base for quick appetizers or hors d'oeuvres.

You can use any day-old loaf of bread to make crouton toast slices. (Day-old bread slices the best). If the loaf was baked in a bread machine, cut it into two parts from top to bottom, for easier handling. Then, place the loaf with its cut side down on a board, and with a sharp, preferably serrated knife, cut into 1/4 inch slices. Lay the slices in a single layer on a cookie sheet. Preheat the oven to 250°F and bake for 45 minutes. Turn the oven off, and leave the toasts in the oven for 15 minutes longer or until dry and crisp. There is no need to turn the slices over because they are cut so thin. Remove from the cookie sheet and store immediately in an airtight container.

WHOLE WHEAT BERRY BREAD

This is a 100% whole wheat bread with a dense, heavy crumb that's full of wonderful whole wheat flavor. Top it with Tapenade (page 307), Hummus (page 173), or Oven Ratatouille (page 299) for a quick snack. Because the wheat berries add a lot of moisture to the dough, this bread should not be baked in the bread machine.

1 REGULAR-SIZE LOAF

FOR THE SPONGE
1 1/2 cups whole wheat flour
3/4 teaspoon active dry yeast
3/4 cup water

TO FINISH THE DOUGH
1 cup cooked whole wheat berries, very well drained (page 164)
1/2 cup water
2 cups whole wheat flour
1 1/2 teaspoons salt

TO MIX THE DOUGH BY HAND First make the sponge by placing the whole wheat flour and yeast into a warm large nonreactive bowl. Heat the water until warm, between 105° and 115°F; pour it into the bowl, and blend until well mixed. Cover, and let stand 12 to 24 hours, until the sponge is bubbly and has a sweet and lightly sour aroma. To finish the dough, stir the sponge down. Heat the water until warm, between 105° and 115°F. Add the wheat berries, water, whole wheat flour, and salt to the sponge, and beat until a dough forms. Turn the dough out onto a very lightly floured board, and knead, adding flour if necessary, until smooth and springy, about 5 minutes. Wash the bowl and grease it;

place the dough back in the bowl, and turn it over to grease the top. Cover, and let rise until doubled, about 1 hour.

TO MIX THE DOUGH WITH A HEAVY-DUTY MIXER First make the sponge by placing the whole wheat flour and yeast into a warm large nonreactive bowl. Heat the water until warm, between 105° and 115°F; pour it into the bowl, and blend until well mixed. Cover, and let stand 12 to 24 hours, until the sponge is bubbly and has a sweet and lightly sour aroma. To finish the dough, stir the sponge down, and pour into the warmed mixing bowl. Heat the water until warm, between 105° and 115°F. Add the wheat berries, water, whole wheat flour, and salt to the sponge, and beat until a dough forms. Knead the dough in the mixer with the dough hook, on medium to high speed, adding flour as necessary, until the dough pulls away from the sides of the bowl and is smooth and springy but still soft to the touch. Remove the dough hook, cover the bowl, and let the dough rise until doubled, about 1 hour.

TO MIX THE DOUGH IN THE FOOD PROCESSOR First make the sponge by placing the whole wheat flour and yeast into a warm large nonreactive bowl. Heat the water until warm, between 105° and 115°F; pour it into the bowl, and blend until well mixed. Cover, and let stand 12 to 24 hours, until the sponge is bubbly and has a sweet and lightly sour aroma. To finish the dough, stir the sponge down, and pour it into the work bowl fitted with the plastic dough blade. Heat the water until warm, between 105° and 115°F. Add the wheat berries, water, whole wheat flour, and salt to the sponge, and beat until a dough forms. processing until the dough is smooth and pulls away from the sides of the bowl. If the dough is wet and sticky, add more flour, 1 tablespoon at a time, until the dough is smooth yet soft to the touch. If the dough is not soft to the touch but is very firm, add 1 tablespoon of water at a time, and process until the dough is smooth yet soft to the touch. Cover the work bowl, and let the dough rise until doubled, about 1 hour. Or remove the dough to a lightly greased bowl, cover, and let rise until doubled, about 1 hour.

TO MIX THE DOUGH IN THE BREAD MACHINE First make the sponge by placing the sponge ingredients (at room temperature) into the pan. Select *Dough,* and press *Start.* When the cycle ends, unplug the machine and let the sponge stand 12 to 24 hours, until it is bubbly and has a sweet and lightly sour aroma. To finish the dough, add the remaining dough ingredients (at room temperature) to the pan. Select *Dough,* and press *Start.* If the dough is wet and sticky, add more flour, 1 tablespoon at a time, until the dough is smooth yet soft to the touch. If the dough is not soft to the touch but is very firm, add 1 teaspoon of water at a time, until the dough is smooth yet soft to the touch. The machine will stop when the dough is ready to shape and bake.

TO SHAPE AND BAKE IN THE OVEN Lightly grease a baking sheet. Turn the dough out onto a lightly floured board or lightly oiled surface. Punch the dough down, and shape it into a round loaf. Place the loaf, with the smooth side up, onto the baking sheet. Cover, and let rise in a warm place until almost doubled, 45 minutes. Preheat the oven to 350°F. Using a sharp knife or a razor, slash the top the loaf. Bake 30 to 35 minutes, until the loaf is brown. Remove from the pan and cool on a wire rack.

Tapenade

Tapenade is a spread that has its roots in the Mediterranean countries. It can be made with French niçoise, Italian gaeta, Greek kalamata, or even supermarket olives, depending on your taste and what's available. Here's a basic recipe that you can vary as you wish. Experiment a bit. I don't like my spreads to be too salty, but I do love the lusty flavor of olive oil. Use the fresh herbs that are available to you in the summertime from the market or your own herb garden. For a simple appetizer, spread the tapenade on toasted Wheat Sourdough French Bread (page 282), Whole Wheat Berry Bread page (page 305) or Whole Wheat French Bread (page 308).

1 CUP

1 cup pitted French, Italian, or Greek olives
1 to 2 garlic cloves, peeled
1 teaspoon capers, drained
3 tablespoons extra-virgin olive oil
1 teaspoon freshly squeezed lemon juice

2 tablespoons mixed fresh herb leaves (cilantro, oregano, flat-leaf parsley)
Freshly ground pepper, to taste
Anchovies, to taste (optional)

Combine all of the ingredients in the work bowl of a food processor fitted with the steel blade. Process only until finely chopped, not smoothly puréed. Serve at room temperature.

WHOLE WHEAT FRENCH BREAD

This makes a tasty bread, with a satisfying whole wheat flavor that is just mildly sour. I provide directions for baking the bread in the bread machine; however, I prefer to bake it in the oven, because I like the traditional shape.

1 REGULAR-SIZE LOAF

FOR THE SPONGE
1 cup bread flour
$^{1}/_{2}$ cup stone-ground whole wheat flour
$^{3}/_{4}$ teaspoon active dry yeast
$^{3}/_{4}$ cup water

TO FINISH THE DOUGH
$^{1}/_{2}$ cup water
2 cups stone-ground whole wheat flour
$1^{1}/_{2}$ teaspoons salt

TO MIX THE DOUGH BY HAND First make the sponge by placing the bread flour, whole wheat flour, and yeast into a warm large nonreactive bowl. Heat the water until warm, between 105° and 115°F; pour it into the bowl, and blend until well mixed. Cover, and let stand 12 to 24 hours, until the sponge is bubbly and has a sweet and lightly sour aroma. To finish the dough, stir the sponge down. Heat the water until warm, between 105° and 115°F. Add the water, whole wheat flour, and salt to the sponge, and beat until a dough forms. Turn the dough out onto a very lightly floured board, and knead, adding flour if necessary, until smooth and springy, about 5 minutes. Wash the bowl and grease it; place the dough back in the bowl, and turn it over to grease the top. Cover, and let rise until doubled, about 1 hour.

TO MIX THE DOUGH WITH A HEAVY-DUTY MIXER First make the sponge by placing the bread flour, whole wheat flour, and yeast into a warm large nonreactive bowl. Heat the water until warm, between 105° and 115°F; pour it into the bowl, and blend until well mixed. Cover, and

let stand 12 to 24 hours, until the sponge is bubbly and has a sweet and lightly sour aroma. To finish the dough, stir the sponge down, and pour into the warmed mixing bowl. Heat the water until warm, between 105° and 115°F. Add the water, whole wheat flour, and salt to the sponge, and beat until a dough forms. Knead the dough in the mixer with the dough hook, on medium to high speed, adding flour as necessary, until the dough pulls away from the sides of the bowl and is smooth and springy but still soft to the touch. Remove the dough hook, cover the bowl, and let the dough rise until doubled, about 1 hour.

TO MIX THE DOUGH IN THE FOOD PROCESSOR First make the sponge by placing the bread flour, whole wheat flour, and yeast into a warm large nonreactive bowl. Heat the water until warm, between 105° and 115°F; pour it into the bowl, and blend until well mixed. Cover, and let stand 12 to 24 hours, until the sponge is bubbly and has a sweet and lightly sour aroma. To finish the dough, stir the sponge down, and pour it into the work bowl fitted with the plastic dough blade.

Heat the water until warm, between 105° and 115°F. Add the water, whole wheat flour, and salt to the sponge, and process until the dough is smooth and pulls away from the sides of the bowl. If the dough is wet and sticky, add more flour, 1 tablespoon at a time, until the dough is smooth yet soft to the touch. If the dough is not soft to the touch but is very firm, add 1 tablespoon of water at a time, and process until the dough is smooth yet soft to the touch. Cover the work bowl, and let the dough rise until doubled, about 1 hour.

TO MIX THE DOUGH IN THE BREAD MACHINE   First make the sponge by placing the sponge ingredients (at room temperature) into the pan. Select *Dough,* and press *Start.* When the cycle ends, unplug the machine and let the sponge stand 12 to 24 hours, until it is bubbly and has a sweet and lightly sour aroma. To finish the dough, add the dough ingredients (at room temperature) to the pan. Select *Dough,* and press *Start.* If the dough is wet and sticky, add more flour, 1 tablespoon at a time, until the dough is smooth yet soft to the touch. If the dough is not soft to the touch but is very firm, add 1 teaspoon of water at a time, until the dough is smooth yet soft to the touch. The machine will stop when the dough is ready.

TO MIX AND BAKE THE BREAD IN THE BREAD MACHINE   First make the sponge by placing the sponge ingredients (at room temperature) into the pan. Select *Dough,* and press *Start.* When the cycle ends, unplug the machine and let the sponge stand 12 to 24 hours, until it is bubbly and has a sweet and lightly sour aroma. To finish the dough, add the dough ingredients (at room temperature) to the pan. Select the *Basic* or *French Bread* cycle, set the crust on *Medium,* and press *Start.* During the mixing cycle, if the dough is wet and sticky, add more flour, 1 tablespoon at a time,

until the dough is smooth yet soft to the touch. If the dough is not soft to the touch but is very firm, add 1 teaspoon of water at a time, until the dough is smooth yet soft to the touch.

TO SHAPE AND BAKE IN THE OVEN   Turn the dough out onto a lightly floured board or lightly oiled surface. Punch the dough down, and shape it into 1 large baguette or 2 smaller baguettes.

To bake on baking tiles   Place the loaf, with the smooth side up, on a bread board, or rimless cookie sheet, sprinkled with flour or cornmeal and let rise in a warm place until doubled, 45 to 60 minutes. Place baking tiles or a pizza stone on a rack in the center of the oven. Fill a shallow baking pan with stones or river rock no larger than $1^{1}/2$ inches in diameter and place it on the bottom rack of the oven. Preheat the oven to 450°F for at least 30 minutes. (Rocks should be hot enough to sizzle when water is dropped on them.) Using a sharp knife or a razor, slash the risen loaf lengthwise to a depth of about $1/4$ inch. Transfer the loaf onto the preheated baking tiles or pizza stone in the oven. (This is best done by gently easing the loaf onto the baking tile with the assistance of a straight-edged tool such as a bench scraper.) Immediately pour 1 cup water into the pan of rocks on the bottom rack of the oven. (This is most easily done by squirting water from a sport bottle onto the rocks.) Bake for 15 to 20 minutes, until loaf is golden brown. Remove from the oven and cool on a wire rack.

To bake in a pan   Lightly grease a baking sheet. Place the loaf, with the smooth side up, onto the baking sheet. Cover and let rise in a warm place until almost doubled, 45 to 60 minutes. Preheat the oven to 375°F. Using a sharp knife or a razor, slash the top of the loaf $1/4$ inch deep, and brush it with water. Bake 30 to 35 minutes, until the loaf is golden. Remove from the oven and cool on a wire rack.

Roasted Red Peppers

Several years ago, in Spain, I was introduced to freshly roasted red bell peppers, which were served as a topping for thick slices of bread, along with spoonfuls of olive oil. I've been roasting peppers ever since. Here they are roasted in a conventional oven. You can, however, roast peppers over a charcoal or gas grill, which provides a wonderful flavor. If you have a gas stovetop and you want to roast just 1 or 2 peppers, it may be quicker to pierce each pepper on a fork and hold it over a flame until the skin starts to blacken, turning it so it scorches evenly all over.

ABOUT 2 CUPS

6 large red bell peppers
1 tablespoon extra-virgin olive oil

Preheat the oven to 450°F. Place the bell peppers on an ungreased baking sheet and roast them for 20 to 30 minutes or until they scorch and the skin blisters and puffs up with blackened spots. Immediately put them into a paper bag and close the top. Let the bell peppers cool in the bag for 15 to 30 minutes.

After the bell peppers have cooled, peel off the skins, cut in half, and remove the seeds. Do not rinse them or you'll lose a lot of the flavor. This is a slightly messy job, but don't worry about getting every last bit of skin off. The bell peppers will be juicy and delicious. Cut them into strips and serve them covered with olive oil.

Red Pepper Butter

Use this purée alone on bread or in sandwiches.

ABOUT 2 CUPS

6 roasted red peppers
1 tablespoon extra-virgin olive oil
Pinch cayenne
Salt, to taste

Drain the roasted and peeled bell peppers and put them into the work bowl of a food processor fitted with a steel blade. Process until puréed. Place the oil into a wide skillet over medium heat. Add the bell pepper purée and cook, stirring constantly, until all the watery liquid has evaporated. Season with the cayenne and salt. Serve immediately or turn into a covered container and refrigerate for up to 2 weeks.

Almond Raisin Monkey Bread

Coffee-Glazed Cinnamon Butterfly Rolls

Cinnamon-Walnut Twists

Dutch Easter Bread

Fruit and Nut–Filled Christmas Wreath

French Toast with Fruit and Whipped Cream

Cranberry Pecan Spread

Golden Oat Saffron Bread

Hot Cross Buns

Maple-Cinnamon Sticky Buns

Julekage

Raisin Pecan Spread

Panettone

Portuguese Sweet Bread

Mango Butter

Pulla (Finnish Cardamom Coffee Braid)

Orange Butter

Poor Knights

Cinnamon Toast

Italian Rosemary and Raisin Buns

Swedish Tea Ring

Swedish Beer Rye Bread

Sweet Orange Bread

Orange Toasts

Whole Wheat Stollen

eight

HOLIDAY AND COFFEE BREADS

*W*hole grains have a natural nuttiness and richness that nicely complement spices, fruits and nuts. With a little more sugar and fat than their savory counterparts, these breads are tender, moist, and delectable, making them perennial favorites. All of these breads—buttery coffee cakes, sweet rolls, and traditional loaves for the holidays—are a little less sweet and rich than their "all-white" versions. Look for some new flavors in time-honored classics, such as whole wheat flour in Finnish Cardamom Coffee Braid, and oatmeal added to Golden Oat Saffron Bread.

A bread machine that does the mixing and proofing of sweet doughs has never been more welcome. It takes just minutes to gather and measure ingredients into the pan and the push of a button. When the dough is ready for shaping and baking it is silky, smooth, and at the perfect temperature for further rising. See Chapter 3 (page 93) for detailed information about adding ingredients to doughs made in the bread machine.

Unlike the majority of the recipes in this book, most of these breads are not baked in the machine. Instead, they're shaped by hand into a fantastic array of shapes and sizes, and because the dough is so easy to work with, the big challenges to the beginning baker are much less.

If the dough seems too soft to be easily handled, try covering and refrigerating it until it is firm enough to shape. This can take just a few minutes, and can be a convenience when schedules get hectic. You can refrigerate the dough as long as overnight. However, if you plan ahead to refrigerate the dough, I suggest that you use regular active dry yeast instead of quick rising yeast for the best results. If you refrigerate the dough for just a short time—an hour or two, don't worry about the type of yeast you use.

ALMOND RAISIN MONKEY BREAD

Monkey bread is a loaf that is made by arranging clumps of dough dipped in butter in a baking pan and baked in a conventional oven. To serve, unmold the loaf onto a plate; guests pull apart the irregular pieces of baked bread.

Sampler Loaf

1 large egg plus undiluted evaporated milk to equal $2/3$ cup

$3/4$ teaspoon salt

$1/3$ cup sugar

4 tablespoons ($1/2$ stick) butter

$1/4$ cup whole wheat flour

$13/4$ cups bread flour

1 teaspoon rapid-rising or active dry yeast

$1/4$ cup raisins

$1/4$ cup slivered almonds

Regular Loaf

1 large egg plus undiluted evaporated milk to equal 1 cup

1 teaspoon salt

$1/2$ cup sugar

5 tablespoons butter

$1/3$ cup whole wheat flour

$22/3$ cups bread flour

$11/2$ teaspoons rapid-rising or active dry yeast

$1/3$ cup raisins

$1/3$ cup slivered almonds

Large Loaf

2 large eggs plus undiluted evaporated milk to equal $11/3$ cups

$11/2$ teaspoons salt

$2/3$ cup sugar

8 tablespoons (1 stick) butter

$1/2$ cup whole wheat flour

$31/2$ cups bread flour

2 teaspoons rapid-rising or active dry yeast

$1/2$ cup raisins

$1/2$ cup slivered almonds

FOR COATING PIECES OF BREAD DOUGH

2 to 4 tablespoons sugar

1 to 2 teaspoons cinnamon

2 to 4 tablespoons melted butter

TO MIX THE DOUGH BY HAND Warm the eggs under hot tap water, and crack into a measuring cup. Heat the milk until warm, between 105° and 115°F, and add it to the eggs. Pour the mixture into a large, warmed bowl, and add the yeast. Let stand 5 minutes, until the yeast begins to bubble. Stir in the salt, sugar, butter, whole wheat flour, and half of the bread flour. Beat well. Cover, and let stand 15 minutes. Slowly add the remaining bread flour, and beat well. Turn the dough out onto a very lightly floured board, and knead, adding flour if necessary, until smooth and springy, about 5 minutes. Knead in the raisins and almonds. Wash the bowl and grease it; place the dough back in the bowl, and turn it over to grease the top. Cover, and let rise until doubled, about 1 hour.

TO MIX THE DOUGH WITH A HEAVY-DUTY MIXER Warm the eggs under hot tap water, and crack into a measuring cup. Heat the milk until warm, between 105° and 115°F, and add it to the eggs. Pour the mixture into the warmed mixing bowl, and add the yeast. Let stand 5 minutes, until the yeast begins to bubble. Add the salt, sugar, butter, whole wheat flour, and half of the bread flour. Beat well. Cover, and let stand 15 minutes. Slowly add the remaining bread flour, and beat well. Knead the dough in the mixer with the dough hook, on medium to high speed, adding flour as necessary, until the dough pulls away from the sides of the bowl and is smooth and springy but still soft to the touch. Knead in the raisins and almonds. Remove the dough hook, cover the bowl, and let the dough rise until doubled, about 1 hour.

TO MIX THE DOUGH IN THE FOOD PROCESSOR Place the plastic dough blade into the work bowl. Warm the eggs under hot tap water, and crack into a measuring cup. Heat the milk until very warm, between 120° and 130°F, and add it to the eggs; set aside. Place the remaining ingredients, except the raisins and almonds, into the work bowl. Turn the processor on, and slowly pour the milk mixture through the feed tube, processing until the dough is smooth and pulls away from the sides of the bowl. If the dough is wet and sticky, add more flour, 1 tablespoon at a time,

until the dough is smooth yet soft to the touch. If the dough is not soft to the touch but is very firm, add 1 tablespoon of water at a time, and process until the dough is smooth yet soft to the touch. Mix in the raisins and almonds. Cover the work bowl, and let the dough rise until doubled, about 1 hour. Or remove the dough to a lightly greased bowl, cover, and let rise until doubled, about 1 hour.

TO MIX THE DOUGH IN THE BREAD MACHINE Warm the eggs under hot tap water, and crack into a measuring cup. Add the milk (at room temperature) to the eggs; pour the mixture into the pan. Add the remaining ingredients, except the raisins and almonds, in the order listed. Make an indentation in the dry ingredients and add the yeast. Select *Dough,* and press *Start.* If the dough is wet and sticky, add more flour, 1 tablespoon at a time, until the dough is smooth yet soft to the touch. If the dough is not soft to the touch but is very firm, add 1 teaspoon of water at a time, until the dough is smooth yet soft to the touch. Add the raisins and almonds when the machine signals it's time to add ingredients or when the cycle ends. The machine will stop when the dough is ready to shape and bake.

TO SHAPE AND BAKE IN THE OVEN Generously grease an 8-inch ring pan (sampler-size dough) or a 10- to 12-inch straight-sided or fluted tube pan (regular- and large-size dough). In a small bowl, mix the sugar and cinnamon for coating the dough. Turn the dough out onto a lightly floured board or lightly oiled surface. Punch the dough down, and divide it into small parts; you should get 16 pieces from the sampler-size dough, 32 pieces from the regular-size dough, and 48 pieces from the large-size dough. Dip each piece in melted butter, then roll in the cinnamon-sugar, and place in the pan. Cover and let rise in a warm place until almost doubled, 45 to 60 minutes. Preheat the oven to 375°F. Bake 30 to 35 minutes, until the loaf is golden and a wooden skewer inserted into the loaf comes out clean and dry. Allow to cool 10 minutes in the pan and then invert the bread onto a serving plate or basket.

COFFEE-GLAZED
CINNAMON BUTTERFLY ROLLS

※

In Finland these delicate, buttery, rolls with a nutty filling and coffee-flavored glaze are known by the name of korvapuustit, or "cinnamon ears." A special but simple technique produces the butterfly shape.

Sampler size (8 rolls)

FOR THE DOUGH

1 large egg plus milk to equal
   2/3 cup

1 teaspoon vanilla

3/4 teaspoon salt

2 tablespoons sugar

4 tablespoons (1/2 stick) butter

1/4 teaspoon freshly grated nutmeg

1/2 teaspoon cinnamon

1/2 teaspoon ground cardamom

3/4 cup whole wheat flour

11/4 cups bread flour

11/4 teaspoons rapid-rising or
   active dry yeast

FOR THE FILLING

3 tablespoons butter, softened

3/4 cup sugar

2 teaspoons cinnamon

1/2 cup chopped toasted filberts
   or almonds

GLAZE

1 egg beaten with 1 tablespoon milk

1/4 cup pearl sugar*

ICING

1 cup powdered sugar

1 to 2 tablespoons cooled brewed coffee

Regular size (12 rolls)

FOR THE DOUGH

2 large eggs plus milk to equal
   1 cup

11/2 teaspoons vanilla

1 teaspoon salt

3 tablespoons sugar

6 tablespoons butter

1/2 teaspoon freshly grated nutmeg

3/4 teaspoon cinnamon

3/4 teaspoon ground cardamom

1 cup whole wheat flour

2 cups bread flour

2 teaspoons rapid-rising or active
   dry yeast

FOR THE FILLING

4 tablespoons (1/2 stick) butter,
   softened

1 cup sugar

1 tablespoons cinnamon

3/4 cup chopped toasted filberts
   or almonds

Large size (16 rolls)

FOR THE DOUGH

3 large eggs plus milk to equal
   11/3 cups

2 teaspoons vanilla

11/2 teaspoons salt

1/4 cup sugar

8 tablespoons (1 stick) butter

3/4 teaspoon freshly grated nutmeg

1 teaspoon cinnamon

1 teaspoon ground cardamom

11/2 cups whole wheat flour

21/2 cups bread flour

21/2 teaspoons rapid-rising or
   active dry yeast

FOR THE FILLING

6 tablespoons butter, softened

11/2 cups sugar

4 teaspoons cinnamon

1 cup chopped toasted filberts or
   almonds

Note   *See Mail-Order Sources (p. 387)
for Scandinavian ingredients.*

TO MIX THE DOUGH BY HAND First make the dough. Warm the eggs under hot tap water, and crack into a measuring cup. Heat the milk until warm, between 105° and 115°F, and add it to the eggs. Pour the mixture into a large, warmed bowl, and add the yeast. Let stand 5 minutes, until the yeast begins to bubble. Stir in the vanilla, salt, sugar, butter, nutmeg, cinnamon, cardamom, whole wheat flour, and half of the bread flour. Beat well. Cover, and let stand 15 minutes. Slowly add the remaining bread flour, and beat well. Turn the dough out onto a very lightly floured board, and knead, adding flour if necessary, until smooth and springy, about 5 minutes. Wash the bowl and grease it; place the dough back in the bowl, and turn it over to grease the top. Cover, and let rise until doubled, about 1 hour.

TO MIX THE DOUGH WITH A HEAVY-DUTY MIXER First make the dough. Warm the eggs under hot tap water, and crack into a measuring cup. Heat the milk until warm, between 105° and 115°F, and add it to the eggs. Pour the mixture into a the warmed mixing bowl, and add the yeast. Let stand 5 minutes, until the yeast begins to bubble. Add the vanilla, salt, sugar, butter, nutmeg, cinnamon, cardamom, whole wheat flour, and half of the bread flour. Beat well. Cover, and let stand 15 minutes. Slowly add the remaining bread flour, and beat until a soft dough forms. Knead the dough in the mixer with the dough hook, on medium to high speed, adding flour as necessary, until the dough pulls away from the sides of the bowl and is smooth and springy but still soft to the touch. Remove the dough hook, cover the bowl, and let the dough rise until doubled, about 1 hour.

TO MIX THE DOUGH IN THE FOOD PROCESSOR First make the dough. Place the plastic dough blade in the work bowl. Warm the eggs under hot tap water, and crack into a measuring cup. Heat the milk until very warm, between 120° and 130°F, and add it to the eggs; set aside. Place the remaining ingredients into the work bowl. Turn the processor on, and slowly pour the milk mixture through the feed tube, processing until the dough is smooth and pulls away from the sides of the bowl. If the dough is wet and sticky, add more flour, 1 tablespoon at a time, until the dough is smooth yet soft to the touch. If the dough is not soft to the touch but is very firm, add 1 tablespoon of water at a time, and process until the dough is smooth yet soft to the touch. Cover the work bowl, and let the dough rise until doubled, about 1 hour. Or remove the dough to a lightly greased bowl, cover, and let rise until doubled, about 1 hour.

TO MIX THE DOUGH IN THE BREAD MACHINE First make the dough. Warm the eggs under hot tap water, and crack into a measuring cup. Add the milk (at room temperature) to the eggs; pour the mixture into the pan. Add the remaining ingredients. Make an indentation in the dry ingredients and add the yeast. Select *Dough,* and press *Start.* If the dough is wet and sticky, add more flour, 1 tablespoon at a time, until the dough is smooth yet soft to the touch. If the dough is not soft to the touch but is very firm, add 1 teaspoon of water at a time, until the dough is smooth yet soft to the touch. The machine will stop when the dough is ready to shape and bake.

TO SHAPE, FILL, AND BAKE IN THE OVEN
Make the filling. In a small bowl, mix the butter, sugar, and cinnamon to make a paste. Lightly grease 1 or 2 baking sheets or cover them with parchment paper.

Turn the dough out onto a lightly floured board or lightly oiled surface. Punch the dough down, and roll it into a rectangle, 8 inches wide and 12 inches (sampler size), 16 inches (regular size), or 20 inches (large size) long. Spread the rectangle with the filling and the nuts. Starting at the long edge, roll up the dough, jelly roll style.

Cut the dough into equal pieces; you should get 8 rolls from the sampler-size dough, 12 from the regular-size dough, and 16 from the large-size dough. Place the rolls so that the cut sides are to the left and right. Then, with your thumbs, press the center of the roll. In so doing, the spiral edges pop outward.

Place the rolls onto the baking sheet. Cover and let rise in a warm place until puffy, 45 minutes. Preheat the oven to 400°F. Beat the egg with the milk, brush the mixture on the rolls, and sprinkle on the pearl sugar. Bake 10 to 12 minutes, until just golden.

While the rolls bake, mix the powdered sugar with the coffee to make a thin icing. Drizzle the icing over the warm rolls.

CINNAMON-WALNUT TWISTS

These are irresistible cinnamon-sugar crusted, buttery walnut-filled twists that are baked in the conventional oven, not the bread machine. They freeze well and taste delicious when reheated.

Sampler size (6 twists)

FOR THE DOUGH

1 egg plus milk (scalded and cooled*) to equal 2/3 cup

3 tablespoons butter, softened

1/2 teaspoon salt

1/4 teaspoon cinnamon

1/2 teaspoon freshly grated nutmeg

1/4 teaspoon ground cardamom

1/4 cup sugar

1/4 cup barley flour

1/4 cup whole wheat flour

1 1/4 cups bread flour

1 teaspoon rapid-rising or active dry yeast

FILLING AND TOPPING

1 cup sugar

1 tablespoon cinnamon

1/3 cup ground walnuts

4 tablespoons (1/2 stick) butter, softened

Regular size (10 twists)

FOR THE DOUGH

2 eggs plus milk (scalded and cooled*) to equal 1 cup

6 tablespoons butter, softened

1 teaspoon salt

1 teaspoon cinnamon

1 teaspoon freshly grated nutmeg

1/2 teaspoon ground cardamom

1/3 cup sugar

1/3 cup barley flour

1/3 cup whole wheat flour

2 1/4 cups bread flour

1 1/2 teaspoons rapid-rising or active dry yeast

FILLING AND TOPPING

1 1/2 cups sugar

2 tablespoons cinnamon

3/4 cup ground walnuts

6 tablespoons butter, softened

Large size (18 twists)

FOR THE DOUGH

3 eggs plus milk (scalded and cooled*) to equal 1 1/3 cups

9 tablespoons butter, softened

1 1/2 teaspoons salt

2 teaspoons cinnamon

2 teaspoons freshly grated nutmeg

1 teaspoon ground cardamom

1/2 cup sugar

1/2 cup barley flour

1/2 cup whole wheat flour

3 cups bread flour

2 teaspoons rapid-rising or active dry yeast

FILLING AND TOPPING

2 cups sugar

2 tablespoons cinnamon

1 cup ground walnuts

8 tablespoons (1 stick) butter, softened

*Note: *The milk needs to be scalded and cooled to remove a natural enzyme that may affect the dough. It sometimes causes the flour to break down and the dough gets stringy and wet.*

TO MIX THE DOUGH BY HAND First make the dough. Warm the eggs under hot tap water, and crack into a measuring cup. Heat the milk until warm, between 105° and 115°F, and add it to the eggs. Pour the mixture into a large, warmed bowl, and add the yeast. Let stand 5 minutes, until the yeast begins to bubble. Stir in the butter, salt, cinnamon, nutmeg, cardamom, sugar, barley flour, and whole wheat flour. Beat well. Cover, and let stand 15 minutes. Slowly add the bread flour, and beat until a smooth dough forms. Cover, and let stand 15 minutes. Turn the dough out onto a very lightly floured board, and knead, adding flour if necessary, until smooth and springy, about 5 minutes. Wash the bowl and grease it; place the dough back in the bowl, and turn it over to grease the top. Cover, and let rise until doubled, about 1 hour.

TO MIX THE DOUGH WITH A HEAVY-DUTY MIXER First make the dough. Warm the eggs under hot tap water, and crack into a measuring cup. Heat the cooled milk until warm, between 105° and 115°F, and add it to the eggs. Pour the mixture into the warmed mixing bowl, and add the yeast. Let stand 5 minutes, until the yeast begins to bubble. Add the butter, salt, cinnamon, nutmeg, cardamom, sugar, barley flour, and whole wheat flour. Beat well. Cover, and let stand 15 minutes. Slowly add the bread flour, and beat until a smooth dough forms. Knead the dough in the mixer with the dough hook, on medium to high speed, adding flour as necessary, until the dough pulls away from the sides of the bowl and is smooth and springy but still soft to the touch. Remove the dough hook, cover the bowl, and let the dough rise until doubled, about 1 hour.

TO MIX THE DOUGH IN THE FOOD PROCESSOR First make the dough. Place the plastic dough blade into the work bowl. Warm the eggs under hot tap water, and crack into a measuring cup. Heat the cooled milk until very warm, between 120° and 130°F; set aside. Place the remaining ingredients into the work bowl. Turn the processor on, and slowly pour the milk mixture through the feed tube, processing until the dough is smooth and pulls away from the sides of the bowl. If the dough is wet and sticky, add more flour, 1 tablespoon at a time, until the dough is smooth yet soft to the touch. If the dough is not soft to the touch but is very firm, add 1 tablespoon of water at a time, and process until the dough is smooth yet soft to the touch. Cover the work bowl, and let the dough rise until doubled, about 1 hour. Or remove the dough to a lightly greased bowl, cover, and let rise until doubled, about 1 hour.

TO MIX THE DOUGH IN THE BREAD MACHINE First make the dough. Warm the eggs under hot tap water, and crack into a measuring cup. Add the milk (cooled to room temperature) to the eggs; pour the mixture into the pan. Add the remaining ingredients. Make an indentation in the dry ingredients and add the yeast. Select *Dough,* and press *Start.* If the dough is wet and sticky, add more flour, 1 tablespoon at a time, until the dough is smooth yet soft to the touch. If the dough is not soft to the touch but is very firm, add 1 teaspoon of water at a time, until the dough is smooth yet soft to the touch. The machine will stop when the dough is ready to shape and bake.

TO SHAPE, FILL, AND BAKE IN THE OVEN
Lightly grease 1 or 2 baking sheets or cover them with parchment paper. Make the filling and topping. In a medium bowl, mix the cinnamon and sugar. Remove half of the cinnamon-sugar to a small bowl; stir in the walnuts. Melt half of the butter in a shallow pan, such as a pie or cake pan. Reserve the remaining softened butter.

Turn the dough out onto a lightly floured board or lightly oiled surface. Punch the dough down, and roll it into an 8-inch (sampler-size dough), 14-inch (regular-size dough), or 20-inch (large-size dough) square. Spread the dough with the reserved softened butter, and sprinkle the walnut mixture evenly on top. Carefully fold the dough in half, pressing to seal the edges. With a sharp straight-edged knife or a pizza wheel, cut the dough from the fold to the seal into 6, 12, or 18 equal strips, depending on the size dough you made.

Dip each strip into the melted butter, and then into the cinnamon-sugar. Twist each strip into a corkscrew and place on the baking sheet. Cover the pans with plastic wrap, and let rise in a warm place until almost doubled, about 40 minutes. Preheat the oven to 375°F. Bake the twists for 25 minutes, until golden. Cool on a wire rack.

DUTCH EASTER BREAD

This is pretty when shaped into a round loaf and glazed with a sugar icing. Whole wheat flour adds nutti-ness to the flavor of this bread. It is the best when baked in a conventional oven on a baking sheet, so I've not included instructions for bread machine baking. This makes the most authentic loaf. You can mix the dough in the bread machine, but then bake the bread in the oven.

Sampler Loaf

1 large egg beaten with scalded-then-cooled milk to measure ²/3 cups

2 tablespoons butter

¹/4 cup sugar

1 teaspoon grated lemon zest

³/4 teaspoon salt

¹/4 cup whole wheat flour

1³/4 cups bread flour

1 teaspoon rapid-rising or active dry yeast

¹/4 cup mixed candied fruit

¹/4 cup slivered almonds

GLAZE

1 egg

1 tablespoon milk

ICING AND DECORATION*

1 cup powdered sugar

2 to 3 tablespoons milk or cream

¹/2 teaspoon almond extract

Additional fruits, for decoration

Regular Loaf

1 large egg beaten with scalded-then-cooled milk to measure 1 cup

3 tablespoons butter

¹/3 cup sugar

1¹/2 teaspoons grated lemon zest

1 teaspoon salt

¹/3 cup whole wheat flour

2²/3 cups bread flour

1¹/2 teaspoons rapid-rising or active dry yeast

¹/3 cup mixed candied fruit

¹/3 cup slivered almonds

Large Loaf

1 large egg beaten with scalded-then-cooled milk to measure 1¹/3 cups

¹/4 cup (¹/2 stick) butter

¹/2 cup sugar

2 teaspoons grated lemon zest

1¹/2 teaspoons salt

¹/2 cup whole wheat flour

3¹/2 cups bread flour

2 teaspoons rapid-rising or active dry yeast

¹/2 cup mixed candied fruit

¹/2 cup slivered almonds

Note: *If you are going to freeze this bread, do not ice or decorate the loaf. Wrap the bread in plastic or put into an airtight bag, and freeze. To thaw, place the wrapped loaf on the counter or unwrap and warm in the microwave on high, 1 to 2 minutes, or in the oven at 300°F, about 15 minutes. Let the bread cool; then ice and decorate as directed.*

TO MIX THE DOUGH BY HAND Warm the egg under hot tap water, and crack into a measuring cup. Heat the milk until warm, between 105° and 115°F, and add it to the egg. Pour the mixture into a large, warmed bowl, and add the yeast. Let stand 5 minutes, until the yeast begins to bubble. Stir in the butter, sugar, lemon zest, salt, whole wheat flour, and half of the bread flour. Beat well. Cover, and let stand 15 minutes. Slowly add the remaining bread flour, and beat well. Turn the dough out onto a very lightly floured board, and knead, adding flour if necessary, until smooth and springy, about 5 minutes. Knead in the fruit and almonds. Wash the bowl and grease it; place the dough back in the bowl, and turn it over to grease the top. Cover, and let rise until doubled, about 1 hour.

TO MIX THE DOUGH WITH A HEAVY-DUTY MIXER Warm the egg under hot tap water, and crack into a measuring cup. Heat the milk until warm, between 105° and 115°F, and add it to the egg. Pour the mixture into the warmed mixing bowl, and add the yeast. Let stand 5 minutes, until the yeast begins to bubble. Add the butter, sugar, lemon zest, salt, whole wheat flour, and half of the bread flour. Beat well. Cover, and let stand 15 minutes. Mix in the fruit and almonds. Slowly add the remaining bread flour, and beat well. Knead the dough in the mixer with the dough hook, on medium to high speed, adding flour as necessary, until the dough pulls away from the sides of the bowl and is smooth and springy but still soft to the touch. Remove the dough hook, cover the bowl, and let the dough rise until doubled, about 1 hour.

TO MIX THE DOUGH IN THE FOOD PROCESSOR Place the plastic dough blade into the work bowl. Warm the egg under hot tap water, and crack into a measuring cup. Heat the milk until very warm, between 120° and 130°F, and add it to the egg; set aside. Place the remaining ingredients, except the fruit and almonds, into the work bowl. Turn the processor on, and slowly pour the milk mixture through the feed tube, processing until the dough is smooth and pulls away from the sides of the bowl. If the dough is wet and sticky, add more flour, 1 tablespoon at a time, until the dough is smooth yet soft to the touch. If the dough is not soft to the touch but is very firm, add 1 tablespoon of water at a time, and process until the dough is smooth yet soft to the touch. Cover the work bowl, and let the dough rise until doubled, about 1 hour. Or remove the dough to a lightly greased bowl, cover, and let rise until doubled, about 1 hour.

TO MIX THE DOUGH IN THE BREAD MACHINE Warm the egg under hot tap water, and add it along with the milk (at room temperature) into the pan. Add the remaining ingredients, except the fruit, in the order listed. Make an indentation in the dry ingredients and add the yeast. Select *Dough,* and press *Start.* If the dough is wet and sticky, add more flour, 1 tablespoon at a time, until the dough is smooth yet soft to the touch. If the dough is not soft to the touch but is very firm, add 1 teaspoon of water at a time, until the dough is smooth yet soft to the touch. Add the fruit when the machine signals it's time to add ingredients or when the cycle ends. The machine will stop when the dough is ready to shape and bake.

TO SHAPE AND BAKE IN THE OVEN Lightly grease a baking sheet. Turn the dough out onto a lightly floured board or lightly oiled surface. Punch the dough down, and shape it into a round loaf. Place the loaf, with the smooth side up, onto the baking sheet. Cover and let rise in a warm place until almost doubled, 45 to 50 minutes. Preheat the oven to 350°F. To glaze, beat the egg with the milk, and brush the mixture on the loaf. Bake 40 to 45 minutes, until the loaf is golden and a wooden skewer inserted into the loaf comes out clean and dry. Remove from the pan and cool on a wire rack.

To make the icing, combine the powdered sugar, milk, and almond extract in a small bowl; mix until smooth. Drizzle or spread on the cooled loaf. Arrange additional candied fruits on top to decorated, if desired.

FRUIT AND NUT-FILLED CHRISTMAS WREATH

This is a very pretty bread to serve. Obviously, it cannot be baked in a bread machine if you are going for this shape. You can mix the dough in the bread machine, but then bake the bread in the oven. The dough is rolled out to make a large rectangle, sprinkled with filling, and rolled up like a jelly roll. The roll is cut in half lengthwise to expose the filling, and twisted together into a wreath shape.

Sampler Size

FOR THE DOUGH

1 egg plus water to equal $2/3$ cup
$1/2$ teaspoon salt
$1/2$ teaspoon ground cardamom
$1/4$ teaspoon freshly grated nutmeg
$1/4$ cup sugar
$1/4$ cup ($1/2$ stick) butter, softened
$1/2$ cup whole wheat flour
$1^1/2$ cups bread flour
$1/4$ cup nonfat dry milk
$1^1/4$ teaspoons rapid-rising or
 active dry yeast
2 tablespoons chopped almonds

FOR THE FILLING

$1/2$ cup chopped nuts*
3 tablespoons all-purpose flour
$1/3$ cup chopped candied cherries
3 tablespoons butter, softened
3 tablespoons packed
 brown sugar
$1/4$ teaspoon almond extract

ICING

1 cup powdered sugar
2 to 3 tablespoons cream or milk
$1/4$ teaspoon almond extract

Regular Size

FOR THE DOUGH

2 eggs plus water to equal 1 cup
$3/4$ teaspoon salt
$3/4$ teaspoon ground cardamom
$1/2$ teaspoon freshly grated nutmeg
$1/3$ cup sugar
$1/3$ cup butter, softened
$3/4$ cup whole wheat flour
$2^1/4$ cups bread flour
$1/3$ cup nonfat dry milk
$1^3/4$ teaspoons rapid-rising or
 active dry yeast
3 tablespoons chopped almonds

FOR THE FILLING

$3/4$ cup chopped nuts*
$1/4$ cup all-purpose flour
$1/2$ cup chopped candied cherries
$1/4$ cup butter, softened
$1/4$ cup packed brown sugar
$1/2$ teaspoon almond extract

Large Size

FOR THE DOUGH

3 eggs plus water to equal
 $1^1/3$ cups
1 teaspoon salt
1 teaspoon ground cardamom
$3/4$ teaspoon freshly grated nutmeg
$1/2$ cup sugar
$1/2$ cup (1 stick) butter, softened
1 cup whole wheat flour
3 cups bread flour
$1/2$ cup nonfat dry milk
2 teaspoons rapid-rising or active
 dry yeast
$1/4$ cup chopped almonds

FOR THE FILLING

1 cup chopped nuts*
6 tablespoons all-purpose flour
$3/4$ cup chopped candied cherries
6 tablespoons butter, softened
6 tablespoons packed brown sugar
$3/4$ teaspoon almond extract

*Note   *Use almonds, filberts, walnuts, or pecans.*

TO MIX THE DOUGH BY HAND First make the dough. Warm the eggs under hot tap water, and crack into a measuring cup. Heat the water until warm, between 105° and 115°F, and add it to the eggs. Pour the mixture into a large, warmed bowl, and add the yeast. Let stand 5 minutes, until the yeast begins to bubble. Stir in the salt, cardamom, nutmeg, sugar, butter, whole wheat flour, half of the bread flour, and the dry milk. Beat well. Cover, and let stand 15 minutes. Slowly add the remaining bread flour, and beat well. Turn the dough out onto a very lightly floured board, and knead, adding flour if necessary, until smooth and springy, about 5 minutes. Knead in the almonds. Wash the bowl and grease it; place the dough back in the bowl, and turn it over to grease the top. Cover, and let rise until doubled, about 1 hour.

TO MIX THE DOUGH WITH A HEAVY-DUTY MIXER First make the dough. Warm the eggs under hot tap water, and crack into a measuring cup. Heat the water until warm, between 105° and 115°F, and add it to the eggs. Pour the mixture into the warmed mixing bowl, and add the yeast. Let stand 5 minutes, until the yeast begins to bubble. Add the salt, cardamom, nutmeg, sugar, butter, whole wheat flour, half of the bread flour, and the dry milk. Beat well. Cover, and let stand 15 minutes. Slowly add the remaining bread flour, and beat well. Knead the dough in the mixer with the dough hook, on medium to high speed, adding flour as necessary, until the dough pulls away from the sides of the bowl and is smooth and springy but still soft to the touch. Knead in the almonds. Remove the dough hook, cover the bowl, and let the dough rise until doubled, about 1 hour.

TO MIX THE DOUGH IN THE FOOD PROCESSOR First make the dough. Warm the eggs under hot tap water, and crack into a measuring cup. Heat the water until very warm, between 120° and 130°F, and add it to the eggs; set aside. Place the remaining ingredients, except the almonds, into the work bowl. Turn the processor on, and slowly pour the water mixture through the feed tube, processing until the dough is smooth and pulls away from the sides of the bowl. If the dough is wet and sticky, add more flour, 1 tablespoon at a time, until the dough is smooth yet soft to the touch. If the dough is not soft to the touch but is very firm, add 1 tablespoon of water at a time, and process until the dough is smooth yet soft to the touch. Cover the work bowl, and let the dough rise until doubled, about 1 hour. Or remove the dough to a lightly greased bowl, cover, and let rise until doubled, about 1 hour.

TO MIX THE DOUGH IN THE BREAD MACHINE First make the dough. Warm the eggs under hot tap water, and crack into a measuring cup. Add the water (at room temperature) to the eggs; pour the mixture into the pan. Add the remaining ingredients, except the almonds, in the order listed. Make an indentation in the dry ingredients and add the yeast. Select *Dough,* and press *Start.* If the dough is wet and sticky, add more flour, 1 tablespoon at a time, until the dough is smooth yet soft to the touch. If the dough is not soft to the touch but is very firm, add 1 teaspoon of water at a time, until the dough is smooth yet soft to the touch. Add the almonds when the machine signals it's time to add ingredients or when the cycle ends. The machine will stop when the dough is ready to shape and bake.

TO SHAPE, FILL, AND BAKE IN THE OVEN
To make the filling, combine all the ingredients in a medium bowl. Lightly grease a baking sheet or cover it with parchment. Turn the dough out onto a lightly floured board or lightly oiled surface. Punch the dough down, and roll it into a rectangle, 8 × 16 inches (sampler size), 9 × 24 inches (regular size), or 9 × 30 inches (large size). Sprinkle the filling onto the dough, leaving a 1-inch margin around the edges. Starting from the long end, carefully roll up the dough, jelly roll style. Pinch the seam to seal.

Using a sharp knife, cut the roll in half lengthwise; turn the cut sides up. Carefully twist the halves together, keeping the cut sides up, to expose the filling. Place the twisted dough on the baking sheet and form it into a wreath. Pinch the ends to seal. Cover, and let rise in a warm place until almost doubled, 45 minutes.

Preheat the oven to 375°F. Bake 20 minutes, until the loaf is evenly browned. Meanwhile, make the icing. Combine the powdered sugar, milk, and almond extract in a small bowl. Mix until smooth. Drizzle the icing over the warm bread. Remove from the pan and cool on a wire rack.

French Toast with Fruit and Whipped Cream

During the holidays when we sometimes have eggnog on hand, I'll use it instead of the milk; and because eggnog already has nutmeg in it, I'll eliminate the spice from the recipe. This is a great way to use day-old Fruit and Nut–Filled Christmas Wreath (page 327), cut in thick, irregular slices. Or try it with day-old cinnamon rolls!

4 SERVINGS

4 large eggs

$^1/_8$ teaspoon salt

$^1/_4$ cup sugar

1 cup milk

$^1/_4$ teaspoon freshly grated nutmeg

4 thick slices of any kind of firm, day-old bread

Powdered sugar in a shaker (about 1 teaspoon)

$^1/_2$ cup butter

Fresh fruit (about 2 cups)*

Lightly whipped cream, for garnish

In a large bowl, beat the eggs with the salt, sugar, milk, and nutmeg, until the eggs are no longer stringy. Dip the bread into the mixture on both sides, and remove to a platter. Let stand 10 minutes, and dip the bread in the egg mixture again, turning it so it soaks up the liquid. You can do this much ahead (even the night before); put the dipped bread onto a platter in a single layer, cover with plastic wrap, and refrigerate.

Heat the butter in a large heavy skillet over medium heat until foamy. Brown the bread 3 to 5 minutes on each side. Shake powdered sugar over each piece before serving. Serve with fruit and whipped cream.

*Note: *Try sliced peaches, berries, or sliced poached pears or apples.*

Cranberry Pecan Spread

This is perfect served with almost any sweet holiday bread.

2 CUPS

1 package (8 ounces) cream cheese

1 tablespoon freshly squeezed orange juice

1 teaspoon grated orange zest

$^{1}/_{2}$ cup finely chopped pecans

$^{1}/_{2}$ cup cranberries

    In a medium-sized bowl, beat the cheese until fluffy using a hand-held electric mixer. Mix in the remaining ingredients. Turn into a serving dish. Keep refrigerated until ready to use.

GOLDEN OAT SAFFRON BREAD

This braided bread, flavored with golden saffron, is baked for St. Lucia's Day in Sweden. Oat flour gives it a nutty flavor. The bread machine makes easy work of mixing and kneading the dough. Although you can bake this bread in the machine, it is traditionally braided and baked in the oven. Unfortunately, there is no good substitute for saffron to get the same flavor. If you can't find saffron, just leave it out.

Sampler Loaf

1 egg plus scalded milk to equal
⅔ cup

½ teaspoon salt

¼ cup sugar

1/16 teaspoon pulverized saffron
(a piece the size of a grain of
rice)

½ cup oat flour*

1½ cups bread flour

1 teaspoon rapid-rising or active
dry yeast

¼ cup (½ stick) butter, softened

Regular Loaf

1 egg plus scalded milk to equal
1 cup

¾ teaspoon salt

⅓ cup sugar

⅛ teaspoon pulverized saffron

¾ cup oat flour*

2¼ cups bread flour

1½ teaspoons rapid-rising or
active dry yeast

6 tablespoons butter, softened

Large Loaf

2 eggs plus scalded milk to
1⅓ cups

1 teaspoon salt

½ cup sugar

¼ teaspoon pulverized saffron

1 cup oat flour*

3 cups bread flour

2 teaspoons rapid-rising or active
dry yeast

½ cup (1 stick) butter, softened

GLAZE FOR BREAD BAKED CONVENTIONALLY

1 egg

1 tablespoon milk

Pearl sugar** and/or sliced almonds

Note

Oat flour is available in whole foods markets, but you can make it by pulverizing quick-cooking rolled oats in the blender or food processor.

**See Mail-Order Sources (p. 387) for Scandinavian ingredients*

TO MIX THE DOUGH BY HAND Warm the eggs under hot tap water, and crack into a measuring cup. Cool the milk until warm, between 105° and 115°F, and add it to the eggs. Pour the mixture into a large, warmed bowl, and add the yeast. Let stand 5 minutes, until the yeast begins to bubble. Stir in the salt, sugar, saffron, oat flour, and half of the bread flour. Beat well. Cover, and let stand 15 minutes. Slowly add the remaining bread flour, and beat well. Turn the dough out onto a very lightly floured board, and knead, adding flour if necessary, until smooth and springy, about 5 minutes. Wash the bowl and grease it; place the dough back in the bowl, and turn it over to grease the top. Cover, and let rise until doubled, about 1 hour.

TO MIX THE DOUGH WITH A HEAVY-DUTY MIXER Warm the eggs under hot tap water, and crack into a measuring cup. Cool the milk until warm, between 105° and 115°F, and add it to the eggs. Pour the mixture into the warmed mixing bowl, and add the yeast. Let stand 5 minutes, until the yeast begins to bubble. Add the salt, sugar, saffron, butter, oat flour, and half of the bread flour. Beat well. Cover, and let stand 15 minutes. Slowly add the remaining bread flour, and beat well. Knead the dough in the mixer with the dough hook, on medium to high speed, adding flour as necessary, until the dough pulls away from the sides of the bowl and is smooth and springy but still soft to the touch. Remove the dough hook, cover the bowl, and let the dough rise until doubled, about 1 hour.

TO MIX THE DOUGH IN THE FOOD PROCESSOR Place the plastic dough blade into the work bowl. Warm the eggs under hot tap water, and crack into a measuring cup. Cool the milk until very warm, between 120° and 130°, and add it to the eggs; set aside. Place the remaining ingredients into the work bowl. Turn the processor on, and slowly pour the milk mixture through the feed tube, processing until the dough is smooth and pulls away from the sides of the bowl. If the dough is wet and sticky, add more flour, 1 tablespoon at a time, until the dough is smooth yet soft to the touch. If the dough is not soft to the touch but is very firm, add 1 tablespoon of water at a time, and process until the dough is smooth yet soft to the touch. Cover the work bowl, and let the dough rise until doubled, about 1 hour. Or remove the dough to a lightly greased bowl, cover, and let rise until doubled, about 1 hour.

TO MIX THE DOUGH IN THE BREAD MACHINE Warm the eggs under hot tap water, and crack into a measuring cup. Cool the milk to room temperature, and add it to the eggs. Pour the mixture into the pan. Add the remaining ingredients, except the butter, in the order listed. Make an indentation in the dry ingredients and add the yeast. Select *Dough,* and press *Start.* Add the butter about 10 minutes into the cycle. If the dough is wet and sticky, add more flour, 1 tablespoon at a time, until the dough is smooth yet soft to the touch. If the dough is not soft to the touch but is very firm, add 1 teaspoon of water at a time, until the dough is smooth yet soft to the touch. The machine will stop when the dough is ready to shape and bake.

TO MIX AND BAKE THE BREAD IN THE BREAD MACHINE Warm the eggs under hot tap water, and crack into a measuring cup. Cool the milk to room temperature, and add it to the eggs. Pour the mixture into the pan. Add the remaining ingredients, except the butter. Make an indentation in the dry ingredients and add the yeast. Select the *Basic* or *Sweet Bread* cycle, set the crust on *Medium,* and press *Start.* Add the butter about 10 minutes into the cycle. During the mixing cycle, if the dough is wet and sticky, add more flour, 1 tablespoon at a time, until the dough is smooth yet soft to the touch. If the dough is not soft to the touch but is very firm, add 1 teaspoon of water at a time, until the dough is smooth yet soft to the touch.

TO SHAPE AND BAKE IN THE OVEN   Cover a baking sheet with parchment paper. Turn the dough out onto a lightly oiled surface. Punch the dough down, and cut it into thirds. Shape each third into a rope by rolling it between the palms of your hands and the oiled surface, until the rope is about 1 inch in diameter. Braid the strands, pinching the ends to seal. Place the loaf, with the smooth side up, onto the baking sheet. Cover and let rise in a warm place until almost doubled, 45 to 60 minutes. Preheat the oven to 375°F. To glaze, beat the egg with the milk, brush the mixture on the loaf, and sprinkle on sugar and/or almonds. Bake 15 to 25 minutes, until the loaf is golden and a wooden skewer inserted into the loaf comes out clean and dry. Remove from the pan and cool on a wire rack.

HOT CROSS BUNS

How about some fresh hot cross buns? Usually, it would be more trouble than it's worth to make only a half dozen buns. But using the smallest batch of dough, that's what you can do and have fresh buns with little effort when you have the bread machine mix the dough for you. Of course, you'll need to shape and bake them conventionally.

Sampler size (6 buns)

1 egg plus scalded and cooled
    milk to equal 2/3 cup

1/2 teaspoon salt

1/4 teaspoon freshly grated nutmeg

2 tablespoons sugar

2 tablespoons butter, softened

1/4 cup whole wheat flour

11/4 cups bread flour

2 tablespoons nonfat dry milk

1 teaspoon active rapid-rising or
    active dry yeast

2 tablespoons currants

Regular size (12 buns)

2 eggs plus scalded and cooled
    milk to equal 1 cup

3/4 teaspoon salt

1/2 teaspoon freshly grated nutmeg

1/4 cup sugar

1/2 cup (1 stick) butter, softened

1/2 cup whole wheat flour

21/2 cups bread flour

1/4 cup nonfat dry milk

11/2 teaspoons active rapid-rising
    or active dry yeast

1/4 cup currants

Large size (18 buns)

3 eggs plus scalded and cooled
    milk to equal 11/3 cups

1 teaspoon salt

3/4 teaspoon freshly grated nutmeg

6 tablespoons sugar

6 tablespoons butter, softened

11/4 cups whole wheat flour

3 cups bread flour

1/2 cup nonfat dry milk

2 teaspoons active rapid-rising or
    active dry yeast

1/2 cup currants

ICING

1/2 cup powdered sugar

1 tablespoon cream or milk

1/8 teaspoon almond extract

TO MIX THE DOUGH BY HAND   Warm the eggs under hot tap water, and crack into a measuring cup. Heat the milk until warm, between 105° and 115°F, and add it to the eggs. Pour the mixture into a large, warmed bowl, and add the yeast. Let stand 5 minutes, until the yeast begins to bubble. Stir in the salt, nutmeg, sugar, butter, whole wheat flour, half of the bread flour, and the dry milk. Beat until smooth. Cover, and let stand 15 minutes. Slowly add the remaining bread flour, and beat until a soft dough forms. Turn the dough out onto a very lightly floured board, and knead, adding flour if necessary, until smooth and springy, about 5 minutes. Knead in the currants. Wash the bowl and grease it; place the dough back in the bowl, and turn it over to grease the top. Cover, and let rise until doubled, about 1 hour.

TO MIX THE DOUGH WITH A HEAVY-DUTY MIXER Warm the eggs under hot tap water, and crack into a measuring cup. Heat the milk until warm, between 105° and 115°F, and add it to the eggs. Pour the mixture into the warmed mixing bowl, and add the yeast. Let stand 5 minutes, until the yeast begins to bubble. Add the salt, nutmeg, sugar, butter, whole wheat flour, half of the bread flour, and the dry milk. Beat until smooth. Cover, and let stand 15 minutes. Slowly add the remaining bread flour, and beat until a soft dough forms. Knead the dough in the mixer with the dough hook, on medium to high speed, adding flour as necessary, until the dough pulls away from the sides of the bowl and is smooth and springy but still soft to the touch. Knead in the currants. Remove the dough hook, cover the bowl, and let the dough rise until doubled, about 1 hour.

TO MIX THE DOUGH IN THE FOOD PROCESSOR Place the plastic dough blade in the work bowl. Warm the eggs under hot tap water, and crack into a measuring cup. Heat the water until very warm, between 120° and 130°F, and add it to the eggs; set aside. Place the remaining ingredients, except the currants, into the work bowl. Turn the processor on, and slowly pour the milk mixture through the feed tube, processing until the dough is smooth and pulls away from the sides of the bowl. If the dough is wet and sticky, add more flour, 1 tablespoon at a time, until the dough is smooth yet soft to the touch. If the dough is not soft to the touch but is very firm, add 1 tablespoon of water at a time, and process until the dough is smooth yet soft to the touch. Mix in the currants. Cover the work bowl, and let the dough rise until doubled, about 1 hour. Or remove the dough to a lightly greased bowl, cover, and let rise until doubled, about 1 hour.

TO MIX THE DOUGH IN THE BREAD MACHINE Warm the eggs under hot tap water, and crack into a measuring cup. Add the milk (at room temperature) to the eggs; pour the mixture into the pan. Add the remaining ingredients, except the currants, in the order listed. Make an indentation in the dry ingredients and add the yeast. Select *Dough,* and press *Start.* If the dough is wet and sticky, add more flour, 1 tablespoon at a time, until the dough is smooth yet soft to the touch. If the dough is not soft to the touch but is very firm, add 1 teaspoon of water at a time, until the dough is smooth yet soft to the touch. Add the currants when the machine signals it's time to add ingredients or when the cycle ends. The machine will stop when the dough is ready to shape and bake.

TO SHAPE AND BAKE IN THE OVEN Lightly grease a baking sheet or cover it with parchment paper. Turn the dough out onto a lightly floured board or lightly oiled surface. Punch the dough down, and divide it into small parts; you should get 6 pieces from the sampler-size dough, 12 pieces from the regular-size dough, and 18 pieces from the large-size dough. Shape each piece into a smooth ball. Place onto the baking sheet, with the smooth side up, and brush each piece with oil. Cover, and let rise in a warm place until almost doubled, 45 minutes. Preheat the oven to 375°F. Bake 15 to 20 minutes, until the buns are golden. Remove from the pan and cool on a wire rack.

Make the icing by combining all the ingredients in a medium bowl; mix until smooth. Put the icing into a small, heavy duty plastic bag and cut off the corner, then squeeze the icing out to make the crosses on the buns.

I usually coat the countertop with nonstick spray when shaping breads—that way, there is very little to clean up.

MAPLE-CINNAMON STICKY BUNS

I like to make sticky buns on the weekends to go with late-morning coffee. Often I set my bread machine to make dough using the *Delay-Start* cycle. In the morning, the dough is warm and ready for shaping. Although I love egg-rich doughs, when I use the *Delay-Start* cycle, I omit the eggs. Be sure to add the dry milk to the top of the flour so that it will not reconstitute until the machine begins mixing.

Sampler size (8 buns)

FOR THE DOUGH

2/3 cup water

3/4 teaspoon salt

2 tablespoons sugar

1/4 cup (1/2 stick) butter

1/4 cup barley flour or
   all-purpose flour

3/4 cup whole wheat flour

1 cup bread flour

1/4 cup nonfat dry milk

1 1/4 teaspoons rapid-rising or
   active dry yeast

FOR THE STICKY
BUN SYRUP

3 tablespoons butter, melted

1/4 cup pure maple syrup

1/2 teaspoon cinnamon

FOR THE FILLING

3 tablespoons butter, softened

3/4 cup sugar

2 teaspoons cinnamon

Regular size (12 buns)

FOR THE DOUGH

1 cup water

1 teaspoon salt

3 tablespoons sugar

6 tablespoons butter

1/3 cup barley flour or
   all-purpose flour

1 cup whole wheat flour

1 2/3 cups bread flour

1/3 cup nonfat dry milk

1 1/4 teaspoons rapid-rising or
   active dry yeast

FOR THE STICKY
BUN SYRUP

1/4 cup (1/2 stick) butter, melted

1/3 cup pure maple syrup

3/4 teaspoon cinnamon

FOR THE FILLING

1/4 cup (1/2 stick) butter, softened

1 cup sugar

1 tablespoon cinnamon

Large size (12 buns)

FOR THE DOUGH

1 1/3 cups water

1 1/2 teaspoons salt

1/4 cup sugar

1/2 cup (1 stick) butter

1/2 cup barley flour or
   all-purpose flour

1 1/2 cups whole wheat flour

2 cups bread flour

1/2 cup nonfat dry milk

2 1/2 teaspoons rapid-rising or
   active dry yeast

FOR THE STICKY
BUN SYRUP

6 tablespoons butter, melted

1/2 cup pure maple syrup

1 teaspoon cinnamon

FOR THE FILLING

6 tablespoons butter, softened

1 1/2 cup sugar

4 teaspoons cinnamon

TO MIX THE DOUGH BY HAND First make the dough. Heat the water until warm, between 105° and 115°F; pour it into a large, warmed bowl, and add the yeast. Let stand 5 minutes, until the yeast begins to bubble. Stir in the salt, sugar, butter, barley flour, whole wheat flour, half of the bread flour, and the dry milk. Beat well. Cover, and let stand 15 minutes. Slowly add the remaining bread flour, and beat well. Turn the dough out onto a very lightly floured board, and knead, adding flour if necessary, until smooth and springy, about 5 minutes. Wash the bowl and grease it; place the dough back in the bowl, and turn it over to grease the top. Cover, and let rise until doubled, about 1 hour.

TO MIX THE DOUGH WITH A HEAVY-DUTY MIXER First make the dough. Heat the water until warm, between 105° and 115°F; pour it into the warmed mixing bowl, and add the yeast. Let stand 5 minutes, until the yeast begins to bubble. Add the salt, sugar, butter, barley flour, whole wheat flour, half of the bread flour, and the dry milk. Beat well. Cover, and let stand 15 minutes. Slowly add the remaining bread flour, and beat until a soft dough forms. Knead the dough in the mixer with the dough hook, on medium to high speed, adding flour as necessary, until the dough pulls away from the sides of the bowl and is smooth and springy but still soft to the touch. Remove the dough hook, cover the bowl, and let the dough rise until doubled, about 1 hour.

TO MIX THE DOUGH IN THE FOOD PROCESSOR First make the dough. Place the plastic dough blade into the work bowl. Heat the water until very warm, between 120° and 130°F; set aside. Place the remaining ingredients into the work bowl. Turn the processor on, and slowly pour the water through the feed tube, processing until the dough is smooth and pulls away from the sides of the bowl. If the dough is wet and sticky, add more flour, 1 tablespoon at a time, until the dough is smooth yet soft to the touch. If the dough is not soft to the touch but is very firm, add 1 tablespoon of water at a time, and process until the dough is smooth yet soft to the touch. Cover the work bowl, and let the dough rise until doubled, about 1 hour. Or remove the dough to a lightly greased bowl, cover, and let rise until doubled, about 1 hour.

TO MIX THE DOUGH IN THE BREAD MACHINE First make the dough. Pour the water (at room temperature) into the pan. Add the remaining ingredients, in the order listed. Make an indentation in the dry ingredients and add the yeast. Select *Dough,* and press *Start.* You may wish to program the machine to "delay start" following the instructions on your machine. If the dough is wet and sticky, add more flour, 1 tablespoon at a time, until the dough is smooth yet soft to the touch. If the dough is not soft to the touch but is very firm, add 1 teaspoon of water at a time, until the dough is smooth yet soft to the touch. The machine will stop when the dough is ready to shape and bake.

TO SHAPE, FILL, AND BAKE IN THE OVEN Lightly grease an 8- or 9-inch round cake pan (sampler-size dough), a 9-inch square cake pan (regular-size dough), or a 9 × 13-inch baking pan (large-size dough). Make the sticky bun syrup by spreading the melted butter in the bottom of the pan. Pour the maple syrup evenly over the butter, and sprinkle with the cinnamon; set aside. Make the filling. In a medium bowl, combine the butter, sugar, and cinnamon, until a paste forms.

Turn the dough out onto a lightly floured board or lightly oiled surface. Punch the dough down, and pat and roll it into a rectangle, 8 inches wide and 12 inches (sampler size), 16 inches (regular size), or 20 inches (large size) long. Spread the filling evenly over the dough. Starting on the long side, carefully roll the dough, jelly roll style; pinch the edge to seal. Cut the roll into equal pieces; you should get 8 pieces from the sampler-size dough, 12 pieces from the regular-size dough, and 16 pieces from the large-size dough.

Place the pieces, cut side up, into the prepared pan. Cover and let rise in a warm place until puffy, 45 minutes. Preheat the oven to 375°F. Bake 20 to 25 minutes, until the buns are golden. Immediately invert onto a plate or platter to cool.

JULEKAGE

This is the classic fruited Christmas bread in Sweden and Norway, although there are many variations (from baker to baker). Julekage works well in the bread machine, which is a great convenience if you are busy with many things. The small amount of whole wheat flour gives the bread a slightly nutty flavor and a creamy colored crumb. I prefer to bake this bread in the oven instead of the bread machine, because it is so pretty with the glaze and icing.

Sampler Loaf

1 egg plus scalded milk to equal 2/3 cup

1/2 teaspoon salt

1/2 teaspoon ground cardamom

2 tablespoons sugar

2 tablespoons butter

1/4 cup whole wheat flour

1 1/2 cups bread flour

1 teaspoon rapid-rising or active dry yeast

2 tablespoons raisins

2 tablespoons glacé cherries

2 tablespoons slivered almonds

Regular Loaf

2 eggs plus scalded milk to equal 1 cup

1 teaspoon salt

1 teaspoon ground cardamom

1/4 cup sugar

1/4 cup (1/2 stick) butter

1/2 cup whole wheat flour

2 1/2 cups bread flour

1 1/2 teaspoons rapid-rising or active dry yeast

1/4 cup raisins

1/4 cup glacé cherries, halved

1/4 cup slivered almonds

Large Loaf

3 egg plus scalded milk to equal 1 1/3 cups

1 1/2 teaspoons salt

1 1/2 teaspoons ground cardamom

1/2 cup sugar

1/2 cup (1 stick) butter

3/4 cup whole wheat flour

3 cups bread flour

2 teaspoons rapid-rising or active dry yeast

1/2 cup raisins

1/2 cup glacé cherries, halved

1/2 cup slivered almonds

GLAZE FOR BREAD BAKED CONVENTIONALLY

1 egg

1 tablespoon milk

ICING

1 cup powdered sugar

2 to 3 tablespoons cream or milk

TO MIX THE DOUGH BY HAND Warm the eggs under hot tap water, and crack into a measuring cup. Cool the milk until warm, between 105° and 115°F, and add it to the eggs. Pour the mixture into a large, warmed bowl, and add the yeast. Let stand 5 minutes, until the yeast begins to bubble. Stir in the salt, cardamom, sugar, butter, whole wheat flour, and half of the bread flour. Beat well. Cover, and let stand 15 minutes. Slowly add the remaining bread flour, and beat well. Turn the dough out onto a very lightly floured board, and knead, adding flour if necessary, until smooth and springy, about 5 minutes. Knead in the fruit and almonds. Wash the bowl and grease it; place the dough back in the bowl, and turn it over to grease the top. Cover, and let rise until doubled, about 1 hour.

TO MIX THE DOUGH WITH A HEAVY-DUTY MIXER Warm the eggs under hot tap water, and crack into a measuring cup. Cool the milk until warm, between 105° and 115°F, and add it to the eggs. Pour the mixture into the warmed mixing bowl, and add the yeast. Let stand 5 minutes, until the yeast begins to bubble. Add the salt, cardamom, sugar, butter, whole wheat flour, and half of the bread flour. Beat well. Cover, and let stand 15 minutes. Slowly add the remaining bread flour, and beat well. Knead the dough in the mixer with the dough hook, on medium to high speed, adding flour as necessary, until the dough pulls away from the sides of the bowl and is smooth and springy but still soft to the touch. Knead in the fruit and almonds. Remove the dough hook, cover the bowl, and let the dough rise until doubled, about 1 hour.

TO MIX THE DOUGH IN THE FOOD PROCESSOR Place the plastic dough blade into the work bowl. Warm the eggs under hot tap water, and crack into a measuring cup. Cool the milk until very warm, between 120° and 130°F, and add it to the eggs; set aside. Place the remaining ingredients, except the raisins, cherries, and almonds, into the work bowl. Turn the processor on, and slowly pour the milk mixture through the feed tube, processing until the dough is smooth and pulls away from the sides of the bowl. If the dough is wet and sticky, add more flour, 1 tablespoon at a time, until the dough is smooth yet soft to the touch. If the dough is not soft to the touch but is very firm, add 1 tablespoon of water at a time, and process until the dough is smooth yet soft to the touch. Mix in the fruit and almond. Cover the work bowl, and let the dough rise until doubled, about 1 hour. Or remove the dough to a lightly greased bowl, cover, and let rise until doubled, about 1 hour.

TO MIX THE DOUGH IN THE BREAD MACHINE Warm the eggs under hot tap water, and crack into a measuring cup. Cool the milk to room temperature, add it to the eggs; pour the mixture into the pan. Add the remaining ingredients, except the raisins, cherries, and almonds, in the order listed. Make an indentation in the dry ingredients and add the yeast. Select *Dough,* and press *Start.* If the dough is wet and sticky, add more flour, 1 tablespoon at a time, until the dough is smooth yet soft to the touch. If the dough is not soft to the touch but is very firm, add 1 teaspoon of water at a time, until the dough is smooth yet soft to the touch. Add the fruit and almonds when the machine signals it's time to add ingredients or when the cycle ends. The machine will stop when the dough is ready to shape and bake.

TO MIX AND BAKE THE BREAD IN THE BREAD MACHINE Warm the eggs under hot tap water, and crack into a measuring cup. Cool the milk to room temperature, add it to the eggs; pour the mixture into the pan. Add the remaining ingredients, except the raisins, cherries, and almonds, in the order listed. Make an indentation in the dry ingredients and add the yeast. Select the *Fruit and Nut, Basic,* or *Sweet Bread* cycle; set the crust on *Medium;* and press *Start.* During the mixing cycle, if the dough is wet and sticky, add more flour, 1 tablespoon at a time, until the dough is smooth yet soft to the touch. If the dough is not soft to the touch but is very firm, add 1 teaspoon of water at a time, until the dough is smooth yet soft to the touch. Add the fruit and almonds when the machine signals it's time to add ingredients.

TO SHAPE AND BAKE IN THE OVEN Lightly grease a baking sheet or cover it with parchment paper. Turn the dough out onto a lightly floured board or lightly oiled surface. Punch the dough down, and shape it into a round loaf. Place the loaf, with the smooth side up, onto the baking sheet. Cover and let rise in a warm place until almost doubled, 45 minutes. Preheat the oven to 350°F. To glaze, beat the egg with the milk, and brush the mixture on the loaf. Bake 35 to 40 minutes, until the loaf is evenly browned. Remove from the pan and cool on a wire rack.

Make the icing by combining the powdered sugar with the cream in a small bowl; mix until smooth. Drizzle or spread over the cooled bread.

Raisin Pecan Spread

Have a pot of this crunchy, slightly sweet cream cheese spread on hand during the holiday season to serve with Julekage (page 341), Pulla (page 351), or almost any other sweet yeast bread.

ABOUT 1 CUP

$1/2$ cup raisins

$1/3$ cup freshly squeezed orange juice

$1/4$ cup pecans, lightly toasted

1 package (3 ounces) cream cheese

Thin slices of Julekage or other sweet yeast bread

Combine the raisins and orange juice in a small saucepan, and bring to a simmer over medium heat. Cook, stirring occasionally, until the liquid has reduced to 1 tablespoon. Transfer the mixture to a food processor fitted with the steel blade. Add the pecans and cream cheese. Process until the mixture is very finely chopped, but not quite puréed, adding 1 tablespoon more orange juice, if necessary.

PANETTONE

This delicate, porous sweet bread—studded with raisins, citron, and orange—originated in Milan, Italy. It is now a favorite throughout Italy and the United States, and you can find it almost any time of year. It's wonderful with a cup of cappuccino for breakfast. It is attractive when baked in the tall, traditional panettone pan, but the shape of the bread machine's pan is very similar. You can also bake this bread into a round loaf on a cookie sheet.

Sampler Loaf

1 egg plus 1 egg yolk plus scalded milk to equal 2/3 cup

1/4 teaspoon salt

2 tablespoons sugar

3/4 teaspoon anise seed

3/4 teaspoon grated lemon zest

2 tablespoons butter

1/4 cup whole wheat flour

1 1/4 cups bread flour

1 teaspoon rapid-rising or active dry yeast

2 tablespoon golden raisins

2 tablespoons chopped citrons

2 tablespoons chopped candied orange peel

2 tablespoons pine nuts

Regular Loaf

1 egg plus 2 egg yolks plus scalded milk to equal 1 cup

1/2 teaspoon salt

1/4 cup sugar

1 teaspoon anise seed

1 teaspoon grated lemon zest

1/4 cup (1/2 stick) butter

1/2 cup whole wheat flour

2 1/3 cups bread flour

1 1/2 teaspoons rapid-rising or active dry yeast

1/4 cup golden raisins

1/4 cup chopped citrons

1/4 cup chopped candied orange peel

1/4 cup pine nuts

Large Loaf

2 eggs plus 3 egg yolks plus scalded milk to equal 1 1/3 cups

1 teaspoon salt

3/4 cup sugar

1 1/2 teaspoons anise seed

1 1/2 teaspoons lemon zest

1/2 cup (1 stick) butter

3/4 cup whole wheat flour

3 1/4 cups bread flour

2 teaspoons rapid-rising or active dry yeast

1/2 cup golden raisins

1/2 cup chopped citrons

1/2 cup chopped candied orange peel

1/2 cup pine nuts

GLAZE FOR BREAD BAKED CONVENTIONALLY

1 egg

1 tablespoon milk

TO MIX THE DOUGH BY HAND Warm the eggs under hot tap water, and crack into a measuring cup. Cool the milk until warm, between 105° and 115°F, and add it to the eggs. Pour the mixture into a large, warmed bowl, and add the yeast. Let stand 5 minutes, until the yeast begins to bubble. Stir in the salt sugar, anise seed, lemon zest, butter, whole wheat flour, and half of the bread flour. Beat well. Cover, and let stand 15 minutes. Slowly add the remaining bread flour, and beat well. Turn the dough out onto a very lightly floured board, and knead, adding flour if necessary, until smooth and springy, about 5 minutes. Knead in the fruits, orange peel, and pine nuts. Wash the bowl and grease it; place the dough back in the bowl, and turn it over to grease the top. Cover, and let rise until doubled, about 1 hour.

TO MIX THE DOUGH WITH A HEAVY-DUTY MIXER Warm the eggs under hot tap water, and crack into a measuring cup. Add the egg yolks to the egg. Cool the milk until warm, between 105° and 115°F, and add it to the eggs. Pour the mixture into the warmed mixing bowl, and add the yeast. Let stand 5 minutes, until the yeast begins to bubble. Add the salt, sugar, anise seed, lemon zest, butter, whole wheat flour, and half of the bread flour. Beat well. Cover, and let stand 15 minutes. Slowly add the remaining bread flour, and beat well. Knead the dough in the mixer with the dough hook, on medium to high speed, adding flour as necessary, until the dough pulls away from the sides of the bowl and is smooth and springy but still soft to the touch. Knead in the fruits, orange peel, and pine nuts. Remove the dough hook, cover the bowl, and let the dough rise until doubled, about 1 hour.

TO MIX THE DOUGH IN THE FOOD PROCESSOR Place the plastic dough blade into the work bowl. Warm the eggs under hot tap water, and crack into a measuring cup. Cool the milk until very warm, between 120° and 130°F, and add it to the eggs and egg yolks; set aside. Place the remaining ingredients, except the raisins, citrons, orange peel, and pine nuts, into the work bowl. Turn the processor on, and slowly pour the milk mixture through the feed tube, processing until the dough is smooth and pulls away from the sides of the bowl. If the dough is wet and sticky, add more flour, 1 tablespoon at a time, until the dough is smooth yet soft to the touch. If the dough is not soft to the touch but is very firm, add 1 tablespoon of water at a time, and process until the dough is smooth yet soft to the touch. Mix in the fruit, orange peel, and pine nuts. Cover the work bowl, and let the dough rise until doubled, about 1 hour. Or remove the dough to a lightly greased bowl, cover, and let rise until doubled, about 1 hour.

TO MIX THE DOUGH IN THE BREAD MACHINE Warm the eggs under hot tap water, and crack into a measuring cup and add the egg yolks. Cool the milk to room temperature, and add it to the eggs; pour the mixture into the pan. Add the remaining ingredients, except the raisins, citrons, orange peel, and pine nuts, in the order listed. Make an indentation in the dry ingredients and add the yeast. Select *Dough,* and press *Start.* If the dough is wet and sticky, add more flour, 1 tablespoon at a time, until the dough is smooth yet soft to the touch. If the dough is not soft to the touch but is very firm, add 1 teaspoon of water at a time, until the dough is smooth yet soft to the touch. Add the fruit, orange peel, and pine nuts when the machine signals it's time to add ingredients or when the cycle ends. The machine will stop when the dough is ready to shape and bake.

TO MIX AND BAKE THE BREAD IN THE BREAD MACHINE Warm the eggs under hot tap water, and crack into a measuring cup. Add theegg yoks. Cool the milk to room temperature, and add it to the eggs; pour the mixture into the pan. Add the remaining ingredients, except the raisins, citrons, orange peel, and pine nuts, in the order listed. Make an indentation in the dry ingredients and add the yeast. Select the *Fruit and Nut, Basic,* or *Sweet Bread* cycle; set the crust on *Medium;* and press *Start.* During the mixing cycle, if the dough is wet and sticky, add more flour, 1 tablespoon at a time, until the dough is smooth yet soft to the touch. If the dough is not soft to the touch but is very firm, add 1 teaspoon of water at a time, until the dough is smooth yet soft to the touch. Add the fruit, orange peel, and pine nuts when the machine signals it's time to add ingredients.

TO SHAPE AND BAKE IN THE OVEN Lightly grease a tall panettone pan or a baking sheet or cover it with parchment paper. Turn the dough out onto a lightly floured board or lightly oiled surface. Punch the dough down, and shape it into a round loaf. Place the loaf, with the smooth side up, into the pan. Cover and let rise in a warm place until almost doubled, 45 minutes. Preheat the oven to 350°F. Using a sharp knife or razor, cut a cross, about $1/2$ inch deep, on the top of the loaf. To glaze, beat the egg with the milk, brush the mixture on the loaf, and sprinkle on the pearl sugar and/or almonds. Bake 35 to 40 minutes, until the loaf is evenly browned. Remove from the pan and cool on a wire rack.

PORTUGUESE SWEET BREAD

Sometimes called Hawaiian sweet bread, this delicate, golden loaf owes part of its tenderness to cooked potato. The Portuguese brought this bread to Hawaii in the late 1800s. Because potatoes vary in the amount of water they contain, if you choose to bake the bread in the bread machine, be careful that the dough isn't too moist or too dry. When potato is added to any mixture, it tends to make the dough soft. It is much easier to get a good loaf when you bake the bread in the oven rather than in the bread machine.

Sampler Loaf	Regular Loaf	Large Loaf
2 tablespoons water	3 tablespoons water	1/4 cup water
1/2 cup warm, cooked, finely diced potato (page 198)	2/3 cup warm, cooked, finely diced potato (page 198)	1 cup warm, cooked, finely diced potato (page 198)
2 eggs, warmed	3 eggs, warmed	4 eggs, warmed
1/2 teaspoon salt	1 teaspoon salt	1 1/2 teaspoons salt
1/4 cup sugar	6 tablespoons sugar	1/2 cup sugar
1/4 cup nonfat dry milk	6 tablespoons nonfat dry milk	1/2 cup nonfat dry milk
1/4 cup (1/2 stick) butter, softened	6 tablespoons butter, softened	1/2 cup (1 stick) butter, softened
1/2 cup whole wheat flour	2/3 cup whole wheat flour	1 cup whole wheat flour
1 1/2 cups bread flour	2 1/3 cups bread flour	3 cups bread flour
1 1/2 teaspoons rapid-rising or active dry yeast	2 teaspoons rapid-rising or active dry yeast	3 teaspoons rapid-rising or active dry yeast

GLAZE FOR BREAD BAKED CONVENTIONALLY
1 egg, beaten
Sugar

TO MIX THE DOUGH BY HAND Put the potato into a large, warmed mixing bowl. Heat the water until warm, between 105° and 115°F; pour it along with the eggs into the mixing bowl. Beat until well blended. Add the yeast, stir until dissolved, cover, and let stand 5 minutes, until the yeast begins to bubble. Stir in the salt, sugar, dry milk, butter, and whole wheat flour. Beat until smooth. Cover, and let stand 15 minutes. Slowly add the bread flour, and beat well. Turn the dough out onto a very lightly floured board, and knead, adding flour if necessary, until smooth and springy, about 5 minutes. Wash the bowl and grease it; place the dough back in the bowl, and turn it over to grease the top. Cover, and let rise until doubled, about 1 hour.

TO MIX THE DOUGH WITH A HEAVY-DUTY MIXER Put the potato into the warmed mixing bowl. Heat the water until warm, between 105° and 115°F; pour it along with the eggs into the mixing bowl. Beat until well blended. Add the yeast, stir until dissolved; cover, and let stand 5 minutes, until the yeast begins to bubble. Stir in the salt, sugar, dry milk, butter, and whole wheat flour. Beat until smooth. Cover, and let stand 15 minutes. Slowly add the bread flour, and beat well. Knead the dough in the mixer with the dough hook, on medium to high speed, adding flour as necessary, until the dough pulls away from the sides of the bowl and is smooth and springy but still soft to the touch. Remove the dough hook, cover the bowl, and let the dough rise until doubled, about 1 hour.

TO MIX THE DOUGH IN THE FOOD PROCESSOR Place the potato into the work bowl fitted with the plastic dough blade. Heat the water until very warm, between 120° and 130°F, mix in the eggs, and set aside. Place the remaining ingredients into the work bowl, and process until blended. Turn the processor on, and slowly pour the water mixture through the feed tube, processing until the dough is smooth and pulls away from the sides of the bowl. If the dough is wet and sticky, add more flour, 1 tablespoon at a time, until the dough is smooth yet soft to the touch. If the

dough is not soft to the touch but is very firm, add 1 tablespoon of water at a time, and process until the dough is smooth yet soft to the touch. Cover the work bowl, and let the dough rise until doubled, about 1 hour. Or remove the dough to a lightly greased bowl, cover, and let rise until doubled, about 1 hour.

TO MIX THE DOUGH IN THE BREAD MACHINE Pour the water (at room temperature) into the pan. Add the remaining ingredients, in the order listed. Make an indentation in the dry ingredients and add the yeast. Select *Dough*, and press *Start*. If the dough is wet and sticky, add more flour, 1 tablespoon at a time, until the dough is smooth yet soft to the touch. If the dough is not soft to the touch but is very firm, add 1 teaspoon of water at a time, until the dough is smooth yet soft to the touch. The machine will stop when the dough is ready to shape and bake.

TO SHAPE AND BAKE IN THE OVEN Line a baking sheet with parchment paper. Turn the dough out onto a lightly floured board or lightly oiled surface. Punch the dough down, and shape it into a round loaf. Place the loaf, with the smooth side up, onto the baking sheet. Cover and let rise in a warm place until almost doubled, 30 to 45 minutes. Preheat the oven to 350°F. To glaze, beat the egg, and brush on the loaf; sprinkle with sugar. Bake 50 to 60 minutes, until the loaf is golden and a wooden skewer inserted into the loaf comes out clean and dry. Remove from the pan and cool on a wire rack.

Mango Butter

The easiest way to cook the mango purée is in the microwave oven. The idea is to evaporate any extra liquid. The result is a delicious, smooth, golden spread with a concentrated mango flavor. It is a perfect spread for almost any coffee bread.

ABOUT 4 CUPS

4 cups puréed fresh mango (about 3 large mangoes)
1 1/2 cups sugar
1/4 cup freshly squeezed lime juice

Press the mango purée through a strainer in to a 3-quart heatproof glass bowl; add the sugar and lime juice. Cook in the microwave oven on high power for 30 to 40 minutes, stirring occasionally, until the mixture is thick, jam-like, and reduced to about 4 cups.

Meanwhile, place four 8-ounce canning jars into a pot of boiling water, and boil, along with jar lids, for 20 minutes. Bring another large pot of water to boil. Spoon the hot mango mixture into the jars. Be sure that the rims of the jars are absolutely clean before placing the lids on. Process in a boiling water bath for 20 minutes to seal the lids, if desired. Refrigerate up to 2 months if not sealed.

Banana Butter: Substitute 4 cups mashed ripe bananas for the mango purée and freshly squeezed lemon juice for the lime juice. Proceed with the recipe.

PULLA (FINNISH CARDAMOM COFFEE BRAID)

Whenever I bake Pulla, my family comes running! The aroma of cardamom makes the house smell like Christmas. I can't think of a more appealing potpourri. For the best flavor, I always use freshly ground cardamom. Although you can bake this loaf in the bread machine, you'd miss out on the lovely braid.

Sampler Loaf

1 egg plus scalded milk to equal ²/3 cup

¹/4 teaspoon salt

2 tablespoons sugar

¹/2 teaspoon freshly ground cardamom

¹/2 cup whole wheat flour

1¹/2 cups bread flour

1 teaspoon rapid-rising or active dry yeast

¹/4 cup (¹/2 stick) butter

Regular Loaf

1 egg plus scalded milk to equal 1 cup

¹/2 teaspoon salt

¹/4 cup sugar

1 teaspoon freshly ground cardamom

³/4 cup whole wheat flour

2¹/4 cups bread flour

1¹/2 teaspoons rapid-rising or active dry yeast

¹/3 cup butter

Large Loaf

2 eggs plus scalded milk to equal 1¹/3 cups

1 teaspoon salt

³/4 cup sugar

1¹/2 teaspoons freshly ground cardamom

1 cup whole wheat flour

3 cups bread flour

2 teaspoons rapid-rising or active dry yeast

¹/2 cup (1 stick) butter

GLAZE FOR BREAD BAKED CONVENTIONALLY

1 egg

1 tablespoon milk

Pearl sugar and/or sliced almonds

TO MIX THE DOUGH BY HAND Warm the eggs under hot tap water, and crack into a measuring cup. Cool the milk until warm, between 105° and 115°F, and add it to the eggs. Pour the mixture into a large, warmed bowl, and add the yeast. Let stand 5 minutes, until the yeast begins to bubble. Stir in the salt sugar, cardamom, whole wheat flour, and half of the bread flour. Beat well. Cover, and let stand 15 minutes. Slowly add the butter and remaining bread flour, and beat well. Turn the dough out onto a very lightly floured board, and knead, adding flour if necessary, until smooth and springy, about 5 minutes. Wash the bowl and grease it; place the dough back in the bowl, and turn it over to grease the top. Cover, and let rise until doubled, about 1 hour.

TO MIX THE DOUGH WITH A HEAVY-DUTY MIXER

Warm the eggs under hot tap water, and crack into a measuring cup. Cool the milk until warm, between 105° and 115°F, and add it to the eggs. Pour the mixture into the warmed mixing bowl, and add the yeast. Let stand 5 minutes, until the yeast begins to bubble. Add the salt, sugar, cardamom, whole wheat flour, and half of the bread flour. Beat well. Cover, and let stand 15 minutes. Slowly add the butter and remaining bread flour, and beat well. Knead the dough in the mixer with the dough hook, on medium to high speed, adding flour as necessary, until the dough pulls away from the sides of the bowl and is smooth and springy but still soft to the touch. Remove the dough hook, cover the bowl, and let the dough rise until doubled, about 1 hour.

TO MIX THE DOUGH IN THE FOOD PROCESSOR

Place the plastic dough blade into the work bowl. Warm the eggs under hot tap water, and crack into a measuring cup. Cool the milk until very warm, between 120° and 130°F, and add it to the eggs; set aside. Place the remaining ingredients into the work bowl. Turn the processor on, and slowly pour the milk mixture through the feed tube, processing until the dough is smooth and pulls away from the sides of the bowl. If the dough is wet and sticky, add more flour, 1 table-spoon at a time, until the dough is smooth yet soft to the touch. If the dough is not soft to the touch but is very firm, add 1 tablespoon of water at a time, and process until the dough is smooth yet soft to the touch. Cover the work bowl, and let the dough rise until doubled, about 1 hour. Or remove the dough to a lightly greased bowl, cover, and let rise until doubled, about 1 hour.

TO MIX THE DOUGH IN THE BREAD MACHINE

Warm the eggs under hot tap water, and crack into a measuring cup. Cool the milk to room temperature, and add it to the eggs; pour the mixture into the pan. Add the remaining ingredients, except the butter, in the order listed. Make an indentation in the dry ingredients and add the yeast. Select *Dough,* and press *Start.* Add the butter about 10 minutes into the cycle. If the dough is wet and sticky, add more flour, 1 table-spoon at a time, until the dough is smooth yet soft to the touch. If the dough is not soft to the touch but is very firm, add 1 teaspoon of water at a time, until the dough is smooth yet soft to the touch. The machine will stop when the dough is ready to shape and bake.

TO MIX AND BAKE THE BREAD IN THE BREAD MACHINE

Warm the eggs under hot tap water, and crack into a measuring cup. Cool the milk to room temperature, and add it to the eggs; pour the mixture into the pan. Add the remaining ingredients, except the butter, in the order listed. Make an indentation in the dry ingredients and add the yeast. Select the *Basic* or *Sweet Bread* cycle, set the crust on *Medium,* and press *Start.* Add the butter about 10 minutes into the cycle. During the mixing cycle, if the dough is wet and sticky, add more flour, 1 table-spoon at a time, until the dough is smooth yet soft to the touch. If the dough is not soft to the touch but is very firm, add 1 teaspoon of water at a time, until the dough is smooth yet soft to the touch.

TO SHAPE AND BAKE IN THE OVEN

Line a baking sheet with parchment paper. Turn the dough out onto a lightly oiled surface. Punch the dough down, and divide it into 3 pieces. Shape each piece into a rope by rolling it between your palms and the oiled surface, until the strand is about 1 inch in diameter. Braid the strands, pinching the ends to seal. Place the loaf onto the baking sheet. Cover and let rise in a warm place until almost doubled, 45 to 60 minutes. Preheat the oven to 375°F. To glaze, beat the egg with the milk, brush the mixture on the loaf, and sprinkle on the pearl sugar and/or almonds. Bake 15 to 25 minutes, until the loaf is golden and a wooden skewer inserted into the loaf comes out clean and dry. Remove from the pan and cool on a wire rack.

Orange Butter

This is a delicious spread for Pulla (page 351) or almost any other sweet yeast bread.

3/4 CUP

1/2 cup (1 stick) unsalted butter, softened

2 tablespoons frozen orange juice
    concentrate, thawed

2 tablespoons powdered sugar

1 tablespoon grated orange zest

In a small bowl, beat the butter until light and fluffy using a hand mixer. Gradually add the orange juice concentrate, powdered sugar, and orange zest; beat until well blended.

Poor Knights

This old Scandinavian classic is nothing more than buttered, grilled bread, served with fresh berries or fruit, powdered sugar, and whipped cream. It's great made from Pulla (page 351).

(page 351)

1 SERVING

1 large, thick slice Pulla	Powdered sugar
2 teaspoons butter	Fresh berries or fruit
1 teaspoon sugar	Lightly whipped cream

Spread the bread with butter on both sides, and sprinkle with sugar on both sides. Place a skillet over medium heat. When the skillet is hot enough to bounce a drop of water, add the bread. Grill about 1 minute per side, until brown. Serve immediately, dusted with powdered sugar, and topped with fruit and whipped cream.

Cinnamon Toast

We used to buy "cinnamon korppua" from the local grocery store in Floodwood, Minnesota, when I was a young girl. It was made in a bakery in nearby Cromwell. We would butter it, and dunk it in our coffee as an after-school snack. (Yes, we drank coffee!) If our weekly supply of Pulla (page 351), which we baked on Saturday, wasn't used up at the end of the week, we'd make the korppua ourselves. This old-time bread was often made partly with a whole grain flour to save on the wheat flour mixed with the white. In the old days it was made with barley, oat, or light rye flour as well. When we made our own korppua, this is how we did it. Although the toast was flavored with cinnamon, the bread we used was flavored with cardamom.

12 TOASTS

12 slices Pulla, cut 1/2 inch thick

3 tablespoons melted butter

6 tablespoons sugar

1 tablespoon cinnamon

Preheat the oven to 350°F. Slice the bread into 1/2 to 3/4-inch pieces. Lay on a cookie sheet in a single layer. Brush each piece lightly with the melted butter. Mix the sugar and cinnamon together, and sprinkle over the bread slices. Bake 10 to 15 minutes, until completely dry and firm. Store in an airtight container, away from direct sunlight in a cool place.

ITALIAN ROSEMARY AND RAISIN BUNS

Pan de Ramerino is eaten in Tuscany on the Thursday before Easter (Maundy Thursday). Typical of the Easter breads of many Christian countries, these buns are rich with eggs. Untypical of most Easter breads, though, they are rich with olive oil rather than butter. Olive oil in the bread gives a beautiful texture to the crust. The oil, balanced with the flavors of rosemary and golden raisins, makes these buns something to look forward to all year. But they're a treat too delicious not to enjoy anytime!

Sampler size (4 buns)

1 large egg plus one egg yolk plus water to equal 2/3 cup

2 tablespoons extra-virgin olive oil

1 tablespoon sugar

3/4 teaspoon salt

1 teaspoon chopped fresh rosemary

1/4 cup whole wheat flour

1 3/4 cups bread flour

1 teaspoon rapid-rising or active dry yeast

1/2 cup golden raisins

Regular size (8 buns)

2 large eggs plus 2 egg yolks plus water to equal 1 cup

3 tablespoons extra-virgin olive oil

3 tablespoons sugar

1 teaspoon salt

2 teaspoons chopped fresh rosemary

1/2 cup whole wheat flour

2 1/4 cups bread flour

1 1/2 teaspoons rapid-rising or active dry yeast

2/3 cup golden raisins

Large size (12 buns)

2 large eggs plus 3 egg yolks plus water to equal 1 1/3 cups

1/4 cup extra-virgin olive oil

3 tablespoons sugar

1 1/2 teaspoon salt

1 tablespoon chopped fresh rosemary

3/4 cup whole wheat flour

3 cups bread flour

2 teaspoons rapid-rising or active dry yeast

3/4 cup golden raisins

TOPPING FOR BREAD BAKED CONVENTIONALLY

Olive oil

Rosemary leaves

TO MIX THE DOUGH BY HAND Heat the water until warm, between 105° and 115°F. Place egg and egg yolk into the measuring cup and add water to measure. Pour it along with the sugar into a large, warmed bowl, and add the yeast. Let stand 5 minutes, until the yeast begins to bubble. Stir in the eggs, egg yolk, oil, sugar, salt, rosemary, whole wheat flour, and half of the bread flour. Beat until smooth. Cover, and let stand 15 minutes. Slowly add the remaining bread flour, and beat until a soft dough forms. Turn the dough out onto a very lightly floured board, and knead, adding flour if necessary, until smooth and springy, about 5 minutes. Knead in the raisins. Wash the bowl and grease it; place the dough back in the bowl, and turn it over to grease the top. Cover, and let rise until doubled, about 1 hour.

TO MIX THE DOUGH WITH A HEAVY-DUTY MIXER   Heat the water until warm, between 105° and 115°F. Place egg and egg yolk into the measuring cup and add water to measure. Pour it along with the sugar into the warmed mixing bowl, and add the yeast. Let stand 5 minutes, until the yeast begins to bubble. Add the eggs, egg yolk, oil, sugar, salt, rosemary, whole wheat flour, and half of the bread four. Beat until smooth. Cover, and let stand 15 minutes. Slowly add the remaining bread flour, and beat until a soft dough forms. Knead the dough in the mixer with the dough hook, on medium to high speed, adding flour as necessary, until the dough pulls away from the sides of the bowl and is smooth and springy but still soft to the touch. Knead in the raisins. Remove the dough hook, cover the bowl, and let the dough rise until doubled, about 1 hour.

TO MIX THE DOUGH IN THE FOOD PROCESSOR Place the plastic dough blade into the work bowl. Heat the water until very warm, between 120° and 130°F; set aside. Place egg and egg yolk into the measuring cup and add water to measure. Place the remaining ingredients, except the raisins, into the work bowl. Turn the processor on, and slowly pour the water through the feed tube, processing until the dough is smooth and pulls away from the sides of the bowl. If the dough is wet and sticky, add more flour, 1 tablespoon at a time, until the dough is smooth yet soft to the touch. If the dough is not soft to the touch but is very firm,

add 1 tablespoon of water at a time, and process until the dough is smooth yet soft to the touch. Mix in the raisins. Cover the work bowl, and let the dough rise until doubled, about 1 hour. Or remove the dough to a lightly greased bowl, cover, and let rise until doubled, about 1 hour.

TO MIX THE DOUGH IN THE BREAD MACHINE   Place egg and egg yolk into the measuring cup and add water to measure, then pour into the pan. Add the remaining ingredients, except the raisins, in the order listed. Make an indentation in the dry ingredients and add the yeast. Select *Dough,* and press *Start.* If the dough is wet and sticky, add more flour, 1 tablespoon at a time, until the dough is smooth yet soft to the touch. If the dough is not soft to the touch but is very firm, add 1 teaspoon of water at a time, until the dough is smooth yet soft to the touch. Add the raisins when the machine signals it's time to add ingredients or when the cycle ends. The machine will stop when the dough is ready to shape and bake.

TO SHAPE AND BAKE IN THE OVEN   Lightly grease a baking sheet or cover it with parchment paper. Turn the dough out onto a lightly floured board or lightly oiled surface. Punch the dough down, and divide it into equal parts; you should get 4 pieces from the sampler-size dough, 8 pieces from the regular-size dough, and 12 pieces from the large-size dough. Shape each part into a ball, and place the buns onto the baking sheet. Let rise in a warm place until almost doubled, 45 to 60 minutes. Preheat the oven to 375°F. Flatten each ball with your hand, and brush the tops with olive oil. Sprinkle with rosemary. Using a sharp knife or razor, slash each bun deeply in a tic-tac-toe design. Bake 15 to 20 minutes, until the buns are golden. Remove from the pan and cool on a wire rack.

SWEDISH TEA RING

Ever since I was a young girl, we made something we called Swedish Tea Ring during the holidays and for special occasions. This bread, obviously, cannot be baked in the bread machine, but the machine does a great job preparing the dough. If you'd like, frost the cooled tea ring with a simple powdered sugar and milk icing.

Sampler Ring

FOR THE DOUGH

1 egg plus undiluted evaporated
    milk to equal $2/3$ cup

$1/2$ teaspoon salt

2 tablespoons sugar

3 tablespoons butter

$1/4$ cup whole wheat flour

$13/4$ cups bread flour

1 teaspoon rapid-rising or active
    dry yeast

FOR THE FILLING

2 tablespoons butter, softened

$1/3$ cup sugar

$1/2$ teaspoon cinnamon

$1/3$ cup golden raisins

$1/3$ cup chopped walnuts
    or pecans

Regular Ring

FOR THE DOUGH

2 eggs plus undiluted evaporated
    milk to equal 1 cup

1 teaspoon salt

2 tablespoons sugar

$1/4$ cup ($1/2$ stick) butter

$1/2$ cup whole wheat flour

$21/2$ cups bread flour

$11/2$ teaspoons rapid-rising or
    active dry yeast

FOR THE FILLING

3 tablespoons butter, softened

$1/2$ cup sugar

$3/4$ teaspoon cinnamon

$1/3$ cup golden raisins

$1/2$ cup chopped walnuts
    or pecans

Large Ring

FOR THE DOUGH

3 eggs plus undiluted evaporated
    milk to equal $11/3$ cup

$11/2$ teaspoons salt

$1/4$ cup sugar

6 tablespoons butter

$3/4$ cup whole wheat flour

$31/4$ cups bread flour

2 teaspoons rapid-rising or active
    dry yeast

FOR THE FILLING

$1/4$ cup butter, softened

$3/4$ cup sugar

1 teaspoon cinnamon

$3/4$ cup golden raisins

$3/4$ cup chopped walnuts
    or pecans

TO MIX THE DOUGH BY HAND First make the dough. Warm the eggs under hot tap water, and crack into a measuring cup. Heat the milk until warm, between 105° and 115°F, and add it to the eggs. Pour the mixture into a large, warmed bowl, and add the yeast. Let stand 5 minutes, until the yeast begins to bubble. Stir in the salt, sugar, butter, whole wheat flour, and half of the bread flour. Beat well. Cover, and let stand 15 minutes. Slowly add the remaining bread flour, and beat well. Turn the dough out onto a very lightly floured board, and knead, adding flour if necessary, until smooth and springy, about 5 minutes. Wash the bowl and grease it;

place the dough back in the bowl, and turn it over to grease the top. Cover, and let rise until doubled, about 1 hour.

TO MIX THE DOUGH WITH A HEAVY-DUTY MIXER

First make the dough. Warm the eggs under hot tap water, and crack into a measuring cup. Heat the milk until warm, between 105° and 115°F, and add it to the eggs. Pour the mixture into the warmed mixing bowl, and add the yeast. Let stand 5 minutes, until the yeast begins to bubble. Add the salt, sugar, butter, whole wheat flour, and half of the bread flour. Beat well. Cover, and let stand 15 minutes. Slowly add the remaining bread flour, and beat well. Knead the dough in the mixer with the dough hook, on medium to high speed, adding flour as necessary, until the dough pulls away from the sides of the bowl and is smooth and springy but still soft to the touch. Remove the dough hook, cover the bowl, and let the dough rise until doubled, about 1 hour.

TO MIX THE DOUGH IN THE FOOD PROCESSOR

First make the dough. Place the plastic dough blade into the work bowl. Warm the eggs under hot tap water, and crack into a measuring cup. Heat the milk until very warm, between 120° and 130°F, and add it to the eggs; set aside. Place the remaining ingredients into the work bowl. Turn the processor on, and slowly pour the milk mixture through the feed tube, processing until the dough is smooth and pulls away from the sides of the bowl. If the dough is wet and sticky, add more flour, 1 tablespoon at a time, until the dough is smooth yet soft to the touch. If the

dough is not soft to the touch but is very firm, add 1 tablespoon of water at a time, and process until the dough is smooth yet soft to the touch. Cover the work bowl, and let the dough rise until doubled, about 1 hour. Or remove the dough to a lightly greased bowl, cover, and let rise until doubled, about 1 hour.

TO MIX THE DOUGH IN THE BREAD MACHINE

First make the dough. Warm the eggs under hot tap water, and crack into a measuring cup. add the milk (at room temperature) to the eggs. Pour the mixture into the pan. Add the remaining ingredients, in the order listed. Make an indentation in the dry ingredients and add the yeast. Select *Dough,* and press *Start.* If the dough is wet and sticky, add more flour, 1 tablespoon at a time, until the dough is smooth yet soft to the touch. If the dough is not soft to the touch but is very firm, add 1 teaspoon of water at a time, until the dough is smooth yet soft to the touch. The machine will stop when the dough is ready to shape and bake.

TO SHAPE, FILL, AND BAKE IN THE OVEN

Lightly grease a baking sheet. Prepare the filling ingredients, and in a small bowl, combine the sugar and cinnamon.

Turn the dough out onto a lightly floured board or lightly oiled surface. Punch the dough down, and pat and roll it out into a rectangle, 12 inches wide and 16 inches (sampler size), 20 inches (regular size), or 24 inches (large size) long. Spread the dough with the softened butter. Sprinkle on the sugar and cinnamon, the raisins, and the nuts. Starting on the long side, carefully roll up the dough, jelly roll style, pinching the edge to seal.

Place the roll, with the smooth side up, onto the baking sheet. Form it into a ring, pinching the ends to seal. With a pair of sharp scissors, make cuts almost all the way through the roll, from the outside toward the center, every $1/2$ inch. Pull the cut dough slices outward and lay them down with a cut side up. Cover and let rise in a warm place until puffy, 45 to 60 minutes. Preheat the oven to 375°F. Bake 16 to 20 minutes, until the ring is golden. Remove from the pan and cool on a wire rack.

SWEDISH BEER RYE BREAD

Vörtbröd ("beer bread")—made with beer and flavored with orange rind and aniseed—was a bread reserved for special occasions in the olden days of Sweden. This recipe is adapted from a holiday bread that was baked and decorated during Advent and used as a centerpiece on the table. When the Christmas season was over, the bread was buried in the seed bin in the granary, to be removed on the first day of sowing in the spring. The loaf was soaked in beer, and distributed among all the members of the household. Even the horse got a piece of the bread! This was done as a blessing to acknowledge the carryover of life from one season to the next. This tradition is no longer practiced, but this delicious bread is still enjoyed during the holiday season at festive meals. I love to add raisins too, but they are optional. This fancy loaf is decorated with a curled-dough cross on top.

Sampler Loaf	**Regular Loaf**	**Large Loaf**
2/3 cup dark beer	1 cup dark beer	1 1/3 cups dark beer
1 tablespoon packed brown sugar	2 tablespoons packed brown sugar	3 tablespoons packed brown sugar
1/2 teaspoon aniseed	3/4 teaspoon aniseed	1 teaspoon aniseed
1/2 teaspoon grated orange zest	3/4 teaspoon grated orange zest	1 teaspoon grated orange zest
1 teaspoon salt	1 1/2 teaspoons salt	2 teaspoons salt
1 tablespoon butter or oil	2 tablespoons butter or oil	3 tablespoons butter or oil
1/2 cup light rye flour	3/4 cup light rye flour	1 cup light rye flour
1 1/2 cups bread flour	2 1/4 cups bread flour	3 cups bread flour
1 tablespoon gluten	1 1/2 tablespoons gluten	2 tablespoons gluten
1 teaspoon rapid-rising or active dry yeast	1 1/2 teaspoons rapid-rising or active dry yeast	2 teaspoons rapid-rising or active dry yeast
1/4 cup raisins (optional)	1/3 cup raisins (optional)	1/3 cup raisins (optional)

GLAZE FOR BREAD BAKED CONVENTIONALLY
1 tablespoon dark molasses
1 tablespoon water

TO MIX THE DOUGH BY HAND Heat the beer until warm, between 105° and 115°F; pour it into a large, warmed bowl, and add the yeast and brown sugar. Let stand 5 minutes, until the yeast begins to bubble. Stir in the aniseed, orange zest, salt, butter, and rye bread. Cover, and let stand 15 minutes. Slowly add the bread flour and gluten, and beat until a smooth dough forms. Turn the dough out onto a very lightly floured board, and knead, adding flour if necessary, until smooth and springy, about 5 minutes. Knead in the raisins. Wash the bowl and grease it; place the dough back in the bowl, and turn it over to grease the top. Cover, and let rise until doubled, about 1 hour.

TO MIX THE DOUGH WITH A HEAVY-DUTY MIXER Heat the beer until warm, between 105° and 115°F; pour it into the warmed mixing bowl, and add the yeast and brown sugar. Let stand 5 minutes, until the yeast begins to bubble. Add the aniseed, orange zest, salt, butter, and rye flour. Cover, and let stand 15 minutes. Slowly add the bread flour and gluten, and beat until a smooth dough forms. Knead the dough in the mixer with the dough hook, on medium to high speed, adding flour as necessary, until the dough pulls away from the sides of the bowl and is smooth and springy but still soft to the touch. Knead in the raisins. Remove the dough hook, cover the bowl, and let the dough rise until doubled, about 1 hour.

TO MIX THE DOUGH IN THE FOOD PROCESSOR Place the plastic dough blade into the work bowl. Heat the beer until very warm, between 120° and 130°F; set aside. Place the remaining ingredients, except the raisins, into the work bowl. Turn the processor on, and slowly pour the beer through the feed tube, processing until the dough is smooth and pulls away from the sides of the bowl. If the dough is wet and sticky, add more flour, 1 tablespoon at a time, until the dough is smooth yet soft to the touch. If the dough is not soft to the touch but is very firm, add 1 tablespoon of water at a time, and process until the dough is smooth yet soft to the touch. Mix in the raisins. Cover the work bowl, and let the dough rise until doubled, about 1 hour. Or remove the dough to a lightly greased bowl, cover, and let rise until doubled, about 1 hour.

TO MIX THE DOUGH IN THE BREAD MACHINE Pour the beer (at room temperature) into the pan. Add the remaining ingredients, except the raisins, in the order listed. Make an indentation in the dry ingredients and add the yeast. Select *Dough*, and press *Start*. If the dough is wet and sticky, add more flour, 1 tablespoon at a time, until the dough is smooth yet soft to the touch. If the dough is not soft to the touch but is very firm, add 1 teaspoon of water at a time, until the dough is smooth yet soft to the touch. Add the raisins when the machine signals it's time to add ingredients or when the cycle ends. The machine will stop when the dough is ready to shape and bake.

TO MIX AND BAKE THE BREAD IN THE BREAD MACHINE Pour the beer (at room temperature) into the pan. Add the remaining ingredients, except the raisins, in the order listed. Make an indentation in the dry ingredients and add the yeast. Select the *Fruit and Nut, Basic,* or *Whole Wheat* cycle; set the crust on *Medium;* and press *Start.* During the mixing cycle, if the dough is wet and sticky, add more flour, 1 tablespoon at a time, until the dough is smooth yet soft to the touch. If the dough is not soft to the touch but is very firm, add 1 teaspoon of water at a time, until the dough is smooth yet soft to the touch. Add the raisins when the machine signals it's time to add ingredients.

TO SHAPE AND BAKE IN THE OVEN Lightly grease an 8- or 9-inch round cake pan. Turn the dough out onto a lightly floured board or lightly oiled surface. Punch the dough down, and remove a 1-cup piece of dough. Shape the remaining dough into a round loaf. Place the loaf, with the smooth side up, into the pan. Divide the reserved dough into 2 parts, and shape each part into a 10-inch-long rope. At each end of both ropes, cut a 4-inch vertical slit (leaving the center 2 inches of each rope uncut). Place the ropes in a cross on top of the loaf; roll the slit ends into curlicues. Cover and let rise in a warm place until almost doubled, 1 hour.

Preheat the oven to 375°F. Mix the molasses with the water; set aside. Bake 15 minutes. Brush the top of the loaf with half of the molasses mixture. Bake 15 to 20 minutes longer, until a wooden skewer inserted into the loaf comes out clean and dry. Remove from the pan and cool on a wire rack. Brush the top of the warm loaf with the remaining molasses mixture.

SWEET ORANGE BREAD

For fresh bread in the morning use the *Delay-Start* cycle on the machine, and replace the egg with ¼ cup additional water. Be sure to add the instant milk on top of the flour, to keep it out of the liquid. Alternately, you can shape the dough into rolls. The sampler-size dough makes a small round coffeecake, perfect for 2 or 3 people.

Sampler Loaf

1 egg

3 tablespoons frozen orange juice concentrate, thawed

Water to equal ²/₃ cup

¹/₂ teaspoon salt

1 teaspoon grated orange zest

3 tablespoons sugar

3 tablespoons nonfat dry milk

1¹/₂ tablespoons butter

¹/₂ cup whole wheat flour

1¹/₂ cups bread flour

1 teaspoon rapid-rising or active dry yeast

¹/₄ cup sliced or slivered almonds

Regular Loaf

1 egg

¹/₄ cup frozen orange juice concentrate, thawed

Water to equal 1 cup

1 teaspoon salt

2 teaspoons grated orange zest

¹/₄ cup sugar

¹/₄ cup nonfat dry milk

2 tablespoons butter

³/₄ cup whole wheat flour

2¹/₄ cups bread flour

1¹/₂ teaspoons rapid-rising or active dry yeast

¹/₂ cup sliced or slivered almonds

Large Loaf

2 eggs

6 tablespoons frozen orange juice concentrate, thawed

Water to equal 1¹/₂ cups

1¹/₂ teaspoon salt

1 tablespoon grated orange zest

6 tablespoons sugar

6 tablespoons nonfat dry milk

3 tablespoons butter

1 cup whole wheat flour

3 cups bread flour

2 teaspoons rapid-rising or active dry yeast

³/₄ cup sliced or slivered almonds

GLAZE FOR BREAD BAKED CONVENTIONALLY

1 egg, beaten

Pearl sugar* and/or sliced or slivered almonds

TO MIX THE DOUGH BY HAND Warm the eggs under hot tap water, and crack into a measuring cup; add the orange juice concentrate. Heat water until warm, between 105° and 115°F, and add it to the egg mixture. Pour the mixture into a large, warmed bowl, and add the yeast. Let stand 5 minutes, until the yeast begins to bubble. Stir in the salt, orange zest, sugar, dry milk,

*__Note__ *See Mail-Order Sources (p. 387) for Scandinavian ingredients.*

butter, and whole wheat flour. Beat well. Cover, and let stand 15 minutes. Slowly add the bread flour, and beat until a soft dough forms. Turn the dough out onto a very lightly floured board, and knead, adding flour if necessary, until smooth and springy, about 5 minutes. Knead in the almonds. Wash the bowl and grease it; place the dough back in the bowl, and turn it over to grease the top. Cover, and let rise until doubled, about 1 hour.

TO MIX THE DOUGH WITH A HEAVY-DUTY MIXER Warm the eggs under hot tap water, and crack into a measuring cup; add the orange juice concentrate. Heat water until warm, between 105° and 115°F, and add it to the egg mixture. Pour the mixture into the warmed mixing bowl, and add the yeast. Let stand 5 minutes, until the yeast begins to bubble. Add the salt, orange zest, sugar, dry milk, butter, and whole wheat flour. Beat well. Cover, and let stand 15 minutes. Slowly add the bread flour, and beat until a soft dough forms. Knead the dough in the mixer with the dough hook, on medium to high speed, adding flour as necessary, until the dough pulls away from the sides of the bowl and is smooth and springy but still soft to the touch. Knead in the almonds. Remove the dough hook, cover the bowl, and let the dough rise until doubled, about 1 hour.

TO MIX THE DOUGH IN THE FOOD PROCESSOR Warm the eggs under hot tap water, and crack into a measuring cup; add the orange juice concentrate. Heat the water until very warm, between 120° and 130°F, and add it to the egg mixture; set aside. Place the remaining ingredients, except the almonds, into the work bowl. Turn the processor on, and slowly pour the egg mixture through the feed tube, processing until the dough is smooth

and pulls away from the sides of the bowl. If the dough is wet and sticky, add more flour, 1 tablespoon at a time, until the dough is smooth yet soft to the touch. If the dough is not soft to the touch but is very firm, add 1 tablespoon of water at a time, and process until the dough is smooth yet soft to the touch. Cover the work bowl, and let the dough rise until doubled, about 1 hour. Or remove the dough to a lightly greased bowl, cover, and let rise until doubled, about 1 hour.

TO MIX THE DOUGH IN THE BREAD MACHINE Warm the eggs under hot tap water, and crack into a measuring cup; add the orange juice concentrate (at room temperature). Add water (at room temperature) to the egg mixture; pour it into the pan. Add the remaining ingredients in the order listed. Make an indentation in the dry ingredients and add the yeast. Select *Dough*, and press *Start*. If the dough is wet and sticky, add more flour, 1 tablespoon at a time, until the dough is smooth yet soft to the touch. If the dough is not soft to the touch but is very firm, add 1 teaspoon of water at a time, until the dough is smooth yet soft to the touch. Add the almods when the machine beeps. The machine will stop when the dough is ready to shape and bake.

TO MIX AND BAKE THE BREAD IN THE BREAD MACHINE Warm the eggs under hot tap water, and crack into a measuring cup; add the orange juice concentrate (at room temperature). Add water (at room temperature) to the egg mixture; pour it into the pan. Add the remaining ingredients in the order listed. Make an indentation in the dry ingredients and add the yeast. Select the *Basic* cycle, set the crust on *Medium*, and press *Start*. During the mixing cycle, if the dough is wet and sticky, add more flour, 1 tablespoon at a time, until the dough is smooth yet soft to the touch. If the dough is not soft to the touch but is very firm, add 1 teaspoon of water at a time, until the dough is smooth yet soft to the touch. Add almonds when the machine beeps.

TO SHAPE AND BAKE IN THE OVEN Lightly grease a baking sheet. Turn the dough out onto a lightly floured board or lightly oiled surface.

Punch the dough down, and shape it into a round loaf. Place the loaf, with the smooth side up, onto the baking sheet. Cover, and let rise in a warm place until almost doubled, 45 minutes. Preheat the oven to 350°F. To glaze, brush the beaten egg on the loaf, and sprinkle on pearl sugar and/or almonds. Bake 35 to 60 minutes, until the loaf is golden and a wooden skewer inserted into the loaf comes out clean and dry. Remove from the pan and cool on a wire rack.

Orange Toasts

Spread this orange butter on thin slices of Sweet Orange Bread (page 365), Pulla (page 351), or almost any other sweet or non-sweet bread. Baked until crisp it makes a delicious snack. I like to serve it with a fresh fruit salad or fruit compote for breakfast or lunch.

48 TOASTS

48 slices bread, approximately 2" × 4" cut 1/4 inch
    thick
1/2 cup (1 stick) butter, softened

1/2 cup sugar
1 tablespoon freshly grated orange zest

To prepare the bread slices, if you baked the bread in the bread machine, cut the loaf lengthwise (from top to bottom) into two parts. Then slice the bread crosswise into 1/4 inch slices. Place the slices in a single layer on an ungreased cookie sheet.

Preheat the oven to 250°F.

In a small bowl, whip the butter and sugar together until light and fluffy, then beat in the orange zest.

Spread about 1 teaspoonful of the whipped butter evenly over the top of each slice of bread. Bake for 45 minutes, then turn the oven off and leave the toast in the oven for 15 minutes more, or until dry and toasted (no need to turn over).

WHOLE WHEAT STOLLEN

Richly laden with brandy-soaked fruits and nuts, Dresden Stollen is a Christmas classic from Germany. There are many variations of this recipe; however, all are shaped like a large Parkerhouse roll. Stollen is traditionally "aged," which means that it can and should be made ahead, but just 24 hours is long enough to prevent crumbling: Wrap the completely cooled loaf in airtight plastic and then in foil; keep in a cool place (about 50°F) to develop the rich, fruity, buttery flavor. For longer storage, place in the freezer for up to 2 months. Because of the special shaping of stollen and all of the fruit in the dough, this bread cannot be baked in the machine.

Sampler Loaf	Regular Loaf	Large Loaf
FOR THE FRUIT AND NUT MIXTURE	**FOR THE FRUIT AND NUT MIXTURE**	**FOR THE FRUIT AND NUT MIXTURE**
1/3 cup golden raisins	1/2 cup golden raisins	3/4 cup golden raisins
1/3 cup dried cherries or cranberries	1/2 cup dried cherries or cranberries	3/4 cup dried cherries or cranberries
1/3 cup dried pineapple slices, diced	1/2 cup dried pineapple slices, diced	3/4 cup dried pineapple slices, diced
1/3 cup candied orange peel*	1/2 cup candied orange peel*	3/4 cup candied orange peel*
1/2 cup slivered or sliced almonds	3/4 cup slivered or sliced almonds	1 cup slivered or sliced almonds
1/2 cup brandy or rum	3/4 cup brandy or rum	1 cup brandy or rum
FOR THE DOUGH	**FOR THE DOUGH**	**FOR THE DOUGH**
1 egg plus milk to equal 2/3 cup	2 eggs plus milk to equal 1 cup	3 eggs plus milk to equal 1 1/3 cups
1/2 teaspoon salt	1 teaspoon salt	1 1/2 teaspoons salt
3 tablespoons sugar	1/4 cup sugar	1/3 cup sugar
1/4 cup (1/2 stick) butter	6 tablespoons butter	1/2 cup (1 stick) butter
1/4 cup whole wheat flour	1/2 cup whole wheat flour	3/4 cup whole wheat flour
1 3/4 cups bread flour	2 1/2 cups bread flour	3 1/4 cups bread flour
1 teaspoon rapid-rising or active dry yeast	1 1/2 teaspoons rapid-rising or active dry yeast	2 teaspoons rapid-rising or active dry yeast

FOR FINISHING

2 tablespoons butter, melted

3 tablespoons powdered sugar

FOR ALL MIXING METHODS First make the fruit and nut mixture. In a large bowl, combine the fruits, almonds, and brandy; mix well. The fruits should have absorbed all of the liquid. If not, drain and reserve extra and add, if necessary, to the dough. Cover, and set aside. Also, for all methods, scald and cool the milk.

TO MIX THE DOUGH BY HAND Next make the dough. Warm the eggs under hot tap water, and crack into a measuring cup. Heat the milk until warm, between 105° and 115°F, and add it to the eggs. Pour the mixture into a large, warmed bowl, and add the yeast. Let stand 5 minutes, until the yeast begins to bubble. Stir in the salt, sugar, butter, whole wheat flour, and half of the bread flour. Beat well. Cover, and let stand 15 minutes. Stir in the fruit and nut mixture. Slowly add the remaining bread flour, and beat well. Turn the dough out onto a very lightly floured board, and knead, adding flour if necessary, until smooth and springy, about 5 minutes. Knead in the fruits and nuts. Wash the bowl and grease it; place the dough back in the bowl, and turn it over to grease the top. Cover, and let rise until doubled, about 1 hour.

TO MIX THE DOUGH WITH A HEAVY-DUTY MIXER Next make the dough. Warm the eggs under hot tap water, and crack into a measuring cup. Heat the milk until warm, between 105° and 115°F, and add it to the eggs. Pour the mixture into the warmed mixing bowl, and add the yeast. Let stand 5 minutes, until the yeast begins to bubble. Add the salt, sugar, butter, whole wheat flour, and half of the bread flour. Beat well. Cover, and let stand 15 minutes. Mix in the fruit and nut mixture. Slowly add the remaining bread flour, and beat well. Knead the dough in the

mixer with the dough hook, on medium to high speed, adding flour as necessary, until the dough pulls away from the sides of the bowl and is smooth and springy but still soft to the touch. Knead in the fruit and nuts. Remove the dough hook, cover the bowl, and let the dough rise until doubled, about 1 hour.

TO MIX THE DOUGH IN THE FOOD PROCESSOR Next make the dough. Place the plastic dough blade into the work bowl. Warm the eggs under hot tap water, and crack into a measuring cup. Heat the milk until very warm, between 120° and 130°F, and add it to the eggs; set aside. Place the remaining ingredients, except the fruit and nuts, into the work bowl. Turn the processor on, and slowly pour the milk mixture through the feed tube, processing until the dough is smooth and pulls away from the sides of the bowl. If the dough is wet and sticky, add more flour, 1 tablespoon at a time, until the dough is smooth yet soft to the touch. If the dough is not soft to the touch but is very firm, add 1 tablespoon of water at a time, and process until the dough is smooth yet soft to the touch. Remove the dough to a lightly floured board, and knead in the fruit and nut mixture by hand. Place the dough in a greased bowl, cover, and let rise until doubled, about 1 hour.

TO MIX THE DOUGH IN THE BREAD MACHINE Next make the dough. Warm the eggs under hot tap water, and crack into a measuring cup. Add the milk (at room temperature to the eggs; pour the mixture into the pan, and add the remaining ingredients, except the fruit and nuts, ending with the yeast. Make an indentation in the dry ingredients and add the yeast. Select *Dough*, and press *Start*. If the dough is wet and sticky, add more flour, 1 tablespoon at a time, until the dough is smooth yet soft to the touch. If the dough is not soft to the touch but is very firm, add 1 teaspoon of water at a time, until the dough is smooth yet soft to the touch. The machine will stop when the dough is ready to shape and bake. Knead in the fruits and nuts at this point before shaping.

TO SHAPE AND BAKE IN THE OVEN Line a baking sheet with parchment paper. Turn the dough out onto a lightly floured board or lightly oiled surface. Punch the dough down, and shape it into a 7 × 9-inch oval. Brush the dough with 1 tablespoon of the melted butter. Make a crease in the dough lengthwise with the handle of a wooden spoon, just off center. Fold the dough lengthwise, bringing the smaller section over the larger one. Place the loaf onto the baking sheet. Cover loosely with a towel, and let rise in a warm place until almost doubled, 45 minutes. Preheat the oven to 350°F. Bake 25 to 35 minutes, until the loaf is golden and a wooden skewer inserted into the loaf comes out clean and dry. Brush the top of the loaf while it's still hot with the 1 tablespoon remaining melted butter, and sprinkle with powdered sugar. Remove from the pan and cool on a wire rack.

Brown Rice, Spelt, Pecan, and Raisin Bread

Buckwheat and Spelt Bread

Kamut Bread

Oatmeal Spelt Bread

Buckwheat Yeast Waffles

nine

NONWHEAT BREADS

*P*eople on special diets often must avoid wheat and wheat products. Our grandson must avoid not only wheat but also barley, oats, corn, rye, dairy products, eggs, and a host of other foods. This has become an interesting challenge for me. So, I've set out to try to make a yeast-raised bread that he can have. Yeast is okay, honey and maple syrup are okay, sugar is not. The challenge is to mix up a bread dough that has enough elasticity to capture the carbon dioxide produced by the yeast, so that the dough will rise sufficiently.

I've tried most of the following grains in salads, side dishes, main dishes, and various kinds of baked goods. Because these grains do not contain gluten, they work in cookies, biscuits, and pancakes. But in this book I'm concerned with yeast-raised breads, and I've tried a number of things. The most successful is spelt, if vegetable gums are added to the dough (they're available in whole foods markets). I've used most of the flours in baked goods other than yeast breads.

The following is a description of each of the grains that I have found ground into flour.

AMARANTH

First of all, what is amaranth? It's been known as a simple weed in the United States, but is now being acknowledged as a nutritious annual plant. The seeds of this purplish flower are ground into a flour used for bread. Amaranth flour originated with the Aztecs, who discovered its nutritional value centuries ago. It can be found in Caribbean and Asian markets. Amaranth is high in carbohydrates and is an unusually complete vegetable-grain protein. It is rich in calcium, iron, and phosphorus, yet contains little fat. It combines well with other flours to make delicious, smooth-textured breads, muffins, pancakes, cookies, cakes, and brownies. Although the protein content in amaranth flour is high, it isn't the same as gluten, the protein in wheat flour that makes the elastic meshwork, trapping the gas that makes bread rise.

ARROWROOT

Long used as a thickener in place cornstarch, arrowroot is snow white and flavorless. For baking, it can be used to lighten other wheat alternatives in wheat-free breads. It's best to buy arrowroot in bulk from health food stores, as otherwise it is very expensive. Keep it stored in a tightly covered container, because it absorbs moisture readily.

BROWN RICE FLOUR

Brown rice has been cultivated since at least 5000 B.C., and it can be ground into flour. Brown rice is the entire grain with only the inedible outer husk removed. The nutritious, high-fiber bran coating gives it a light tan color and nut-like flavor. The presence of the bran means that the rice can become rancid, so the shelf life is only about six months. Brown rice can be used in yeast breads, but it must be in combination with other grains, or the flavor will be too "ricey."

Breads baked with brown rice flour tend to be dry unless they contain other flours and/or ground nuts. Substitute ground nuts for 25 percent of the flour. Brown rice flour can substitute for wheat flour almost cup for cup; remove 2 tablespoons brown rice flour and add 2 tablespoons vegetable gum (such as guar gum or xanthan gum), which must be added because the brown rice flour has no gluten to enhance the rising properties of the bread. In addition, add 1/4 cup ground nuts (such as pecans) to reduce the dryness in the flour mixture. Dates, prunes, raisins, and other dried fruit will add flavor and moistness as well. Shredded vegetables, such as carrots and zucchini, will do the same. Canola, sunflower, safflower, and olive oil also increase the moistness in breads.

BUCKWHEAT FLOUR

Buckwheat has been used in northern climates (Finland and Russia) for centuries. The flavor is strong and not appealing to everybody. It is often blended with a milder white flour or starch to moderate the flavor. It has a dark grey color. Buckwheat flour is ground from toasted buckwheat groats. However, for a milder flavored flour, you can make the flour by grinding untoasted buckwheat groats yourself. Grind $1/2$ cup at a time in the blender, grain grinder, or coffee grinder; then sift it into a bowl. Buckwheat flour can be used in the same way as brown rice flour. Traditionally, it has been used for making pancakes and waffles. Buckwheat Yeast Waffles (page 386) are a favorite breakfast of mine.

CHICK-PEA (GARBANZO BEAN) FLOUR

Chick-pea flour has a mild "beany" flavor. When mixed with other flours (no more than 25 percent), it adds protein to baked goods, although it is not gluten. It can be used half and half with ground nuts. Chick-peas are readily available in supermarkets, but because they are so hard they're difficult to grind at home, it's best to buy already ground chick-pea flour. This is the flour that is used to make an instant hummus, a popular spread for bread (for a recipe that uses freshly cooked chick-peas, see page 173)

KAMUT

The word *kamut* comes from the ancient Egyptian word for "wheat." Some consider this to be the great-great-grandfather of grains. It is a variety of high-protein wheat that has never been hybridized. Thirty-six of the kernels were brought to Montana in the late 1940s, and the grain has been grown commercially in that state alone. The kernels are about three times the length of a kernel of wheat, have a nutty flavor, and are high in protein. Kamut is most readily available in health

food stores, but some supermarkets and mail-order catalogs are beginning to sell it. It is difficult to find in some parts of the country.

MILLET

Millet is an American cereal grass that, in its whole grain, resembles a mustard seed. It can be cooked like rice and, when ground into flour, can be added to a mixture of other grains. It has a bland flavor and works well in cookies and cakes. Millet that is included in bird seed mixtures is not suitable for human consumption.

OAT FLOUR

For those who can tolerate it, oat flour makes a suitable substitute for wheat in cookies and cakes. But because oat has no gluten, it needs assistance for yeast-risen breads in the form of a vegetable gum or a combination of guar gum, xanthan gum, and tapioca flour. Usually, it is best to combine flours for their flavor, texture, and moistness to produce the best possible results. You can make oat flour by grinding rolled oats into a fine powder. Sift the results and regrind larger particles into flour.

POTATO FLOUR

Do not confuse potato flour with potato starch, which is made in a different way. Potato flour can be used to substitute part of the wheat flour in a recipe, no more than about $1/2$ cup for each cup of wheat flour. It can be blended with brown rice flour, spelt, soy flour, and vegetable gums to make a yeast bread. Potato flour is made from cooked potatoes, whereas potato starch is made from raw potatoes and looks and feels like cornstarch.

QUINOA

A tiny grain, no larger than a mustard seed, once fed an ancient civilization that stretched from the seacoast of Chile to the peaks of the Peruvian Andes. The Incas called it quinoa, the "Mother Grain." Quinoa has a nutty flavor and is often blended with corn flour to make pastas and breads. It has more protein than most other grains, including wheat; and although the protein is not gluten it is nutritionally complete, supplying all the essential amino acids in a balanced pattern. It is delicious not only in a bread but in salads and hot dishes as well.

SOY FLOUR

Soy flour has a slightly "beany" flavor, which can be camouflaged by mixing it with other flours, fruit, spices, carob, or nuts. It can be successfully used to add protein to yeast breads, but no more than 25 percent of the total flour content. It mixes well with buckwheat, amaranth, ground nuts, potato flour, tapioca flour, and vegetable gums to make bread dough. Soy is commonly an allergen, so it should not be used more than once every four days or so, if a wheat-allergic person can tolerate it.

SPELT

Spelt is an Old World grain that has been a favorite of Europeans for centuries. It is high in protein, has the appearance of whole wheat flour, has a flavor similar to whole wheat, and can be used alone to make yeast breads. People who cannot eat wheat can often digest spelt. Spelt will produce a tasty yeast bread that will rise even more successfully when a vegetable gum is added to the dough.

TAPIOCA FLOUR

Tapioca flour, is taken from the root of the cassava plant. Pearl tapioca is available in most supermarkets, but the flour is usually found in health-food stores and Asian markets. Tapioca flour has a thickening property that, when used in combination with nonwheat flour, can help produce a lighter baked product than when it is not used.

TEFF

Teff is the smallest grain in the world: 150 grains of teff weigh as much as a single grain of wheat! Teff is high in minerals, calcium, and dietary fiber. It has been used for thousands of years to bake injera, a delicious Ethiopian flat bread. It is also used for wheat-free quick breads.

BAKING YEAST BREADS WITH NONWHEAT FLOURS

To make gluten-free or low-gluten yeast breads, you need to add something to the dough that will help trap the gas and strengthen the structure of the bread. Vegetable gums—guar gum and xanthan gum—work because they form a sticky, stringy gum when mixed with liquid. Tapioca flour also helps produce a stringy texture in bread dough. The bread machine aids in the formation of the structure of the bread because it kneads the dough so vigorously. This meshwork structure is not as strong as that formed by gluten, so if the dough rises too much or too quickly, your bread will fall during baking. I have found that using regular active dry yeast, rather than rapid-rising yeast, works better in low-gluten breads. This is probably because regular yeast doesn't bubble up as quickly and makes smaller pockets of gas in the meshwork of the bread.

Although the bread machine does an excellent job of mixing and proofing the bread dough, you get the finest loaf of nonwheat bread when it is shaped by hand and baked it in the conventional oven. This is probably because bread generally retains more of its moisture when it is baked conventionally; this is probably related to the baking time, which is shorter in the oven than in the machine. Here are a few nonwheat recipes to use as a base for your creativity. Check the introduction to Chapter 3 for information about adding ingredients to the bread machine.

BROWN RICE, SPELT, PECAN, AND RAISIN BREAD

Without the vegetable gum and tapioca flour, which hold in the moistness, this bread is very dry and crumbly. I prefer to mix the dough in a machine and shape it by hand and bake it in the oven. That way I can monitor the rising time better.

Sampler Loaf	Regular Loaf	Large Loaf
2/3 cup water	1 cup water	1 1/3 cups water
2 tablespoons honey	3 tablespoons honey	1/4 cup honey
1 tablespoon extra-virgin olive or canola oil	1 1/2 tablespoons extra-virgin olive or canola oil	2 tablespoons extra-virgin olive or canola oil
3/4 teaspoon salt	1 teaspoon salt	1 1/2 teaspoons salt
1/4 cup brown rice flour	1/3 cup brown rice flour	1/2 cup brown rice flour
1 3/4 cups spelt flour	2 2/3 cups spelt flour	3 1/2 cups spelt flour
1 tablespoon tapioca flour	1 1/2 tablespoons tapioca flour	2 tablespoons tapioca flour
1 tablespoon xanthan gum	1 1/2 tablespoons xanthan gum	2 tablespoons xanthan gum
2 teaspoons active dry yeast	3 teaspoons active dry yeast	4 teaspoons active dry yeast
1/4 cup raisins	1/3 cup raisins	1/2 cup raisins

TO MIX THE DOUGH BY HAND Heat the water until warm, between 105° and 115°F; pour it into a large, warmed bowl, and add the yeast. Let stand 5 minutes, until the yeast begins to bubble. Stir in the honey, oil, salt, rice flour, half of the spelt flour, the tapioca flour, and xanthan gum. Beat vigorously. Cover, and let stand 15 minutes. Mix in almost all of the remaining spelt flour. Turn the dough out onto a very lightly spelt-floured board, and knead, adding the remaining spelt flour if necessary, until smooth and springy, about 5 minutes. Knead in the raisins. Wash the bowl and grease it; place the dough back in the bowl, and turn it over to grease the top. Cover, and let rise until doubled, about 1 hour.

TO MIX THE DOUGH WITH A HEAVY-DUTY MIXER Heat the water until warm, between 105° and 115°F; pour it into the warmed mixing bowl, and add the yeast. Let stand 5 minutes, until the yeast begins to bubble. Add the honey, oil, salt, brown rice flour, half of the spelt flour, the tapioca flour, and the xanthan gum. Beat well. Cover, and let stand 15 minutes. Mix in most of the remaining spelt flour. Knead the dough in the mixer with the dough hook, on medium to high speed, adding spelt flour as necessary, until smooth and springy but still soft to the touch. Knead in the raisins. Remove the dough hook, cover the bowl, and let the dough rise until doubled, about 1 hour.

TO MIX THE DOUGH IN THE FOOD PROCESSOR Place the plastic dough blade into the work bowl. Heat the water until very warm, between 120° and 130°F; set aside. Place the remaining ingredients, except the raisins, into the work bowl. Turn the processor on, and slowly pour the water through the feed tube, processing until the dough is smooth and pulls away from the sides of the bowl. If the dough is wet and sticky, add more flour, 1 tablespoon at a time, until the dough is smooth yet soft to the touch. If the dough is not soft to the touch but is very firm, add 1 tablespoon of water at a time, and process until the dough is smooth yet soft to the touch. Mix in the raisins. Cover the work bowl, and let the dough rise until doubled, about 1 hour. Or remove the dough to a lightly greased bowl, cover, and let rise until doubled, about 1 hour.

TO MIX THE DOUGH IN THE BREAD MACHINE Pour the water (at room temperature) into the pan. Add the remaining ingredients, except the raisins, in the order listed. Make an indentation in the dry ingredients and add the yeast. Select *Dough,* and press *Start.* If the dough is wet and sticky, add more flour, 1 tablespoon at a time, until the dough is smooth yet soft to the touch. If the dough is not soft to the touch but is very firm, add 1 teaspoon of water at a time, until

the dough is smooth yet soft to the touch. Add the raisins when the machine signals it's time to add ingredients or when the cycle ends. The machine will stop when the dough is ready to shape and bake.

TO MIX AND BAKE THE BREAD IN THE BREAD MACHINE Pour the water (at room temperature) into the pan. Add the remaining ingredients, except the raisins, in the order listed. Make an indentation in the dry ingredients and add the yeast. Select the *Basic* or *Whole Wheat* cycle, set the crust on *Medium,* and press *Start.* During the mixing cycle, if the dough is wet and sticky, add more flour, 1 tablespoon at a time, until the dough is smooth yet soft to the touch. If the dough is not soft to the touch but is very firm, add 1 teaspoon of water at a time, until the dough is smooth yet soft to the touch. Add the raisins when the machine signals it's time to add ingredients.

TO SHAPE AND BAKE IN THE OVEN Lightly grease an 8 × 4 1/2-inch or 9 × 5-inch loaf pan. Turn the dough out onto a lightly spelt-floured board or lightly oiled surface. Punch the dough down, and shape it into an oblong loaf. Place the loaf, with the smooth side up, into the pan. Cover and let rise in a warm place until almost doubled, 45 to 60 minutes. Preheat the oven to 375°F. Bake 30 to 45 minutes, until the loaf is golden and a wooden skewer inserted into the loaf comes out clean and dry. Remove from the pan and cool on a wire rack.

BUCKWHEAT AND SPELT BREAD

Buckwheat flour adds its characteristic flavor and deep color to this wheat-free bread. This bread needs the extra kneading and extra rising time of the *Whole Wheat* cycle if you choose to bake the dough in the machine. Usually, I prefer to have the machine make the dough so that I can shape and bake it myself. Also, I have had better luck using active dry yeast rather than rapid-rising yeast. Expect any nonwheat bread to have a dense texture. Slice thinly to serve. Instead of maple syrup you can use honey or any other suitable liquid sweetener.

Sampler Loaf

2/3 cup water

3 tablespoons 100% pure maple syrup

1 tablespoon extra-virgin olive or canola oil

3/4 teaspoon salt

1/3 cup buckwheat flour

2 cups spelt flour

1 tablespoon tapioca flour

1 tablespoon xanthan gum

2 teaspoons active dry yeast

1/4 cup raisins (optional)

Regular Loaf

1 cup water

1/4 cup 100% pure maple syrup

1 1/2 tablespoons extra-virgin olive or canola oil

1 teaspoon salt

1/2 cup buckwheat flour

3 cups spelt flour

1 1/2 tablespoons tapioca flour

1 1/2 tablespoons xanthan gum

1 tablespoon active dry yeast

1/2 cup raisins (optional)

Large Loaf

1 1/3 cups water

1/3 cup 100% pure maple syrup

2 tablespoons extra-virgin olive or canola oil

1 1/2 teaspoons salt

2/3 cup buckwheat flour

4 cups spelt flour

2 tablespoons tapioca flour

2 tablespoons xanthan gum

1 1/2 tablespoons active dry yeast

3/4 cup raisins (optional)

TO MIX THE DOUGH BY HAND Heat the water until warm, between 105° and 115°F; pour it into a large, warmed bowl, and add the yeast. Let stand 5 minutes, until the yeast begins to bubble. Stir in the syrup, oil, salt, buckwheat flour, half of the spelt flour, the tapioca flour, and xanthan gum. Beat vigorously. Cover, and let stand 15 minutes. Mix in most of the remaining spelt flour. Turn the dough out onto a very lightly spelt-floured board, and knead, adding the remaining spelt flour if necessary, until smooth and springy, about 5 minutes. Knead in the raisins. Wash the bowl and grease it; place the dough back in the bowl, and turn it over to grease the top. Cover, and let rise until doubled, about 1 hour.

TO MIX THE DOUGH WITH A HEAVY-DUTY MIXER Heat the water until warm, between 105° and 115°F; pour it into the warmed mixing

bowl, and add the yeast. Let stand 5 minutes, until the yeast begins to bubble. Add the syrup, oil, salt, buckwheat flour, half of the spelt flour, the tapioca flour and xanthan gum. Beat well. Cover, and let stand 15 minutes. Mix in most of the remaining spelt flour. Knead the dough in the mixer with the dough hook, on medium to high speed, adding spelt flour as necessary, until the dough pulls away from the sides of the bowl and is smooth and springy but still soft to the touch. Knead in the raisins. Remove the dough hook, cover the bowl, and let the dough rise until doubled, about 1 hour.

TO MIX THE DOUGH IN THE FOOD PROCESSOR

Place the plastic dough blade into the work bowl. Heat the water until very warm, between 120° and 130°F; set aside. Place the remaining ingredients, except the raisins, into the work bowl. Turn the processor on, and slowly pour the water through the feed tube, processing until the dough is smooth and pulls away from the sides of the bowl. If the dough is wet and sticky, add more spelt flour, 1 tablespoon at a time, until the dough is smooth yet soft to the touch. If the dough is not soft to the touch but is very firm, add 1 tablespoon of water at a time, and process until the dough is smooth yet soft to the touch. Mix in the raisins. Cover the work bowl, and let the dough rise until doubled, about 1 hour. Or remove the dough to a lightly greased bowl, cover, and let rise until doubled, about 1 hour.

TO MIX THE DOUGH IN THE BREAD MACHINE

Pour the water (at room temperature) into the pan. Add the remaining ingredients, except the raisins, in the order listed. Make an indentation in the dry ingredients and add the yeast. Select *Dough,* and press *Start.* If the dough is wet and sticky, add more spelt flour, 1 tablespoon at a time, until the dough is smooth yet soft to the touch. If the dough is not soft to the touch but is very firm, add 1 teaspoon of water at a time, until the dough is smooth yet soft to the touch. Add the raisins when the machine signals it's time to add ingredients or when the cycle ends. The machine will stop when the dough is ready to shape and bake.

TO MIX AND BAKE THE BREAD IN THE BREAD MACHINE

Pour the water (at room temperature) into the pan. Add the remaining ingredients, except the raisins, in the order listed. Make an indentation in the dry ingredients and add the yeast. Select the *Whole Wheat* cycle, set the crust on *Medium,* and press *Start.* During the mixing cycle, if the dough is wet and sticky, add more spelt flour, 1 tablespoon at a time, until the dough is smooth yet soft to the touch. If the dough is not soft to the touch but is very firm, add 1 teaspoon of water at a time, until the dough is smooth yet soft to the touch. Add the raisins when the machine signals it's time to add ingredients.

TO SHAPE AND BAKE IN THE OVEN

Lightly grease an 8 × 4 1/2-inch or 9 × 5-inch loaf pan. Turn the dough out onto a lightly spelt-floured board or lightly oiled surface. Punch the dough down, and shape it into an oblong loaf. Place the loaf, with the smooth side up, into the pan. Cover, and let rise in a warm place until almost doubled, 45 minutes. Preheat the oven to 375°F. Bake 30 to 45 minutes, until the loaf is golden and a wooden skewer inserted into the loaf comes out clean and dry. Remove from the pan and cool on a wire rack.

KAMUT BREAD

Kamut flour performs well as a bread flour. Kamut contains a unique type of gluten, which many people who are allergic to regular wheat gluten can digest. Lemon juice in the mixture helps the gluten development. This is a close-textured, moist, grainy flavored bread.

Sampler Loaf

2/3 cup water

1 tablespoon freshly squeezed
    lemon juice

3 tablespoons honey

3 tablespoons canola oil

1 teaspoon salt

2 cups kamut flour

2 teaspoons active dry yeast

Regular Loaf

1 cup water

1 1/2 tablespoons freshly squeezed
    lemon juice

1/4 cup honey

1/4 cup canola oil

1 1/2 teaspoons salt

3 cups kamut flour

3 teaspoons active dry yeast

Large Loaf

1 1/3 cups water

2 tablespoons freshly squeezed
    lemon juice

1/3 cup honey

1/3 cup canola oil

2 teaspoons salt

4 cups kamut flour

4 teaspoons active dry yeast

TO MIX THE DOUGH BY HAND Heat the water until warm, between 105° and 115°F; pour it into a large, warmed bowl, and add the yeast. Let stand 5 minutes, until the yeast begins to bubble. Stir in the lemon juice, honey, oil, slat, and half of the kamut flour. Beat vigorously until very smooth (you may want to use a hand mixer). Cover, and let stand 15 minutes. Mix in most of the remaining kamut flour. Turn the dough out onto a very lightly kamut-floured board, and knead, adding the remaining kamut flour if necessary, until smooth; the dough will be sticky. Wash the bowl and grease it; place the dough back in the bowl, and turn it over to grease the top. Cover, and let rise until doubled, about 1 hour.

TO MIX THE DOUGH WITH A HEAVY-DUTY MIXER Heat the water until warm, between 105° and 115°F; pour it into the warmed mixing bowl, and add the yeast. Let stand 5 minutes, until the yeast begins to bubble. Add the lemon juice, honey, oil, salt, and half of the kamut flour. Beat on high speed for minutes, until the mixture is very smooth. Cover, and let stand 15 minutes. Mix in most of the remaining kamut flour. Knead the dough in the mixer with the dough hook, on medium to high speed, adding the remaining kamut flour as necessary, until the dough pulls away from the sides of the bowl and is smooth. Remove the dough hook, cover the bowl, and let the dough rise until doubled, about 1 hour.

TO MIX THE DOUGH IN THE FOOD PROCESSOR
Place the plastic dough blade into the work bowl.
Heat the water until very warm, between 120°
and 130°F; set aside. Place the remaining ingredients into the work bowl. Turn the processor on,
and slowly pour the water through the feed tube,
processing until the dough is smooth and pulls
away from the sides of the bowl. If the dough is
wet and sticky, add more flour, 1 tablespoon at a
time, until the dough is smooth yet soft to the
touch. If the dough is not soft to the touch but is
very firm, add 1 tablespoon of water at a time,
and process until the dough is smooth yet soft to
the touch. Cover the work bowl, and let the
dough rise until doubled, about 1 hour. Or
remove the dough to a lightly greased bowl, cover,
and let rise until doubled, about 1 hour.

**TO MIX THE DOUGH IN THE BREAD
MACHINE** Pour the water (at room temperature) into the pan. Add the remaining ingredients, in the order listed. Make an indentation in
the dry ingredients and add the yeast. Select
Dough, and press *Start.* If the dough is wet and
sticky, add more flour, 1 tablespoon at a time,
until the dough is smooth yet soft to the touch. If
the dough is not soft to the touch but is very
firm, add 1 teaspoon of water at a time, until the
dough is smooth yet soft to the touch. The
machine will stop when the dough is ready to
shape and bake.

**TO MIX AND BAKE THE BREAD IN THE
BREAD MACHINE** Pour the water (at room
temperature) into the pan. Add the remaining
ingredients, in the order listed. Make an indentation in the dry ingredients and add the yeast.
Select the *Whole Wheat* cycle, set the crust on

Medium, and press *Start.* During the mixing cycle,
if the dough is wet and sticky, add more flour, 1
tablespoon at a time, until the dough is smooth
yet soft to the touch. If the dough is not soft to
the touch but is very firm, add 1 teaspoon of
water at a time, until the dough is smooth yet soft
to the touch.

TO SHAPE AND BAKE IN THE OVEN Lightly
grease an 8 × 4¹/2-inch or 9 × 5-inch loaf pan.
Turn the dough out onto a lightly kamut-floured
board or lightly oiled surface. Punch the dough
down, and shape it into an oblong loaf. Place the
loaf, with the smooth side up, into the pan. Cover
and let rise in a warm place until almost doubled,
1 hour. Preheat the oven to 375°F. Bake 30 to 45
minutes, or until the loaf is golden and a wooden
skewer inserted into the loaf comes out clean and
dry. Remove from the pan and cool on a wire
rack.

OATMEAL SPELT BREAD

Even though spelt flour has a fair amount of gluten, a bit of tapioca flour and vegetable gum will help. The bread needs the extra kneading and the extra rising time of the *Whole Wheat* cycle on the bread machine. I have had better luck using active dry yeast than the rapid-rising yeast. Expect any nonwheat bread to be close textured. When you serve it, slice it thinly.

Sampler Loaf

2/3 cup water

1/3 cup quick-cooking rolled oats

3 tablespoons frozen apple juice concentrate, thawed

1 tablespoon extra-virgin olive or canola oil

3/4 teaspoon salt

2 cups spelt flour

1 tablespoon tapioca flour

1 tablespoon xanthan gum

2 teaspoons active dry yeast

1/4 cup raisins (optional)

Regular Loaf

1 cup water

1/2 cup quick-cooking rolled oats

1/4 cup frozen apple juice concentrate, thawed

1 1/2 tablespoons extra-virgin olive or canola oil

1 teaspoon salt

3 cups spelt flour

1 1/2 tablespoons tapioca flour

1 1/2 tablespoons xanthan gum

1 tablespoon active dry yeast

1/2 cup raisins (optional)

Large Loaf

1 1/3 cups water

2/3 cup quick-cooking rolled oats

1/3 cup frozen apple juice concentrate, thawed

2 tablespoons olive or canola oil

1 1/2 teaspoons salt

4 cups spelt flour

2 tablespoons tapioca flour

2 tablespoons xanthan gum

1 1/2 tablespoons active dry yeast

3/4 cup raisins (optional)

TO MIX THE DOUGH BY HAND Heat the water until warm, between 105° and 115°F; pour it into a large, warmed bowl, and add the yeast and rolled oats. Let stand 5 minutes, until the yeast begins to bubble. Stir in the apple juice concentrate, oil, salt, spelt flour, tapioca flour, and xanthan gum. Beat until smooth. Cover, and let stand 15 minutes. Turn the dough out onto a very lightly spelt-floured board, and knead, adding spelt flour if necessary, until smooth and springy, about 5 minutes. Knead in the raisins.

Wash the bowl and grease it; place the dough back in the bowl, and turn it over to grease the top. Cover, and let rise until doubled, about 1 hour.

TO MIX THE DOUGH WITH A HEAVY-DUTY MIXER Heat the water until warm, between 105° and 115°F; pour it into the warmed mixing bowl, and add the yeast and rolled oats. Let stand 5 minutes, until the yeast begins to bubble. Add the apple juice concentrate, oil, salt, spelt flour, tapioca flour, and xanthan gum. Beat until smooth. Cover, and let stand 15 minutes. Knead the dough in the mixer with the dough hook, on medium to high speed, adding spelt flour as necessary, until the dough pulls away from the sides of the bowl and is smooth and springy but still soft to the touch. Knead in the raisins. Remove the dough hook, cover the bowl, and let the dough rise until doubled, about 1 hour.

TO MIX THE DOUGH IN THE FOOD PROCESSOR
Place the plastic dough blade into the work bowl. Heat the water until very warm, between 120° and 130°F, and pour into the work owl. Add the rolled oats; and process until mixed. Place the remaining ingredients, except the raisins, into the work bowl. Process until the dough is smooth and pulls away from the sides of the bowl. If the dough is wet and sticky, add more flour, 1 tablespoon at a time, until the dough is smooth yet soft to the touch. If the dough is not soft to the touch but is very firm, add 1 tablespoon of water at a time, and process until the dough is smooth yet soft to the touch. Mix in the raisins. Cover the work bowl, and let the dough rise until doubled, about 1 hour. Or remove the dough to a lightly greased bowl, cover, and let rise until doubled, about 1 hour.

TO MIX THE DOUGH IN THE BREAD MACHINE Pour the water (at room temperature) into the pan. Add the remaining ingredients, except the raisins, in the order listed. Make an indentation in the dry ingredients and add the yeast. Select *Dough,* and press *Start.* If the dough is wet and sticky, add more flour, 1 tablespoon at a time, until the dough is smooth yet soft to the touch. If the dough is not soft to the touch but is

very firm, add 1 teaspoon of water at a time, until the dough is smooth yet soft to the touch. Add the raisins when the machine signals it's time to add ingredients or when the cycle ends. The machine will stop when the dough is ready to shape and bake.

TO MIX AND BAKE THE BREAD IN THE BREAD MACHINE Pour the water (at room temperature) into the pan. Add the remaining ingredients, except the raisins, in the order listed. Make an indentation in the dry ingredients and add the yeast. Select the *Basic* or *Whole Wheat* cycle, set the crust on *Medium,* and press *Start.* During the mixing cycle, if the dough is wet and sticky, add more flour, 1 tablespoon at a time, until the dough is smooth yet soft to the touch. If the dough is not soft to the touch but is very firm, add 1 teaspoon of water at a time, until the dough is smooth yet soft to the touch. Add the raisins when the machine signals it's time to add ingredients.

TO SHAPE AND BAKE IN THE OVEN Lightly grease an 8 × 4 1/2-inch or 9 × 5-inch loaf pan. Turn the dough out onto a lightly spelt-floured board or lightly oiled surface. Punch the dough down, and shape it into an oblong loaf. Place the loaf, with the smooth side up, into the pan. Cover and let rise in a warm place until almost doubled, 45 minutes. Preheat the oven to 375°F. Bake 30 to 45 minutes, until the loaf is golden and a wooden skewer inserted into the loaf comes out clean and dry. Remove from the pan and cool on a wire rack.

BUCKWHEAT YEAST WAFFLES

These are waffles that I developed for our grandson who is allergic to dairy products, eggs, wheat, corn, rye, and a number of other foods. I use 100% pure maple syrup to sweeten the waffles. The nice thing about a yeast-raised waffle batter is that it doesn't go flat if it has to wait for latecomers to breakfast!

4 LARGE WAFFLES

1 cup warm water, 105° to 115°F
1 package rapid-rising or active dry yeast
1/2 teaspoon salt
1 tablespoon 100% pure maple syrup

1 cup buckwheat flour
1/2 cup spelt flour
1 tablespoon canola oil

Pour the water into a large mixing bowl. Add the yeast, salt, and syrup. Let stand until the yeast begins to bubble. Stir in the flours and oil. Let rise until the batter seems fluffy. Preheat the waffle iron to medium. Coat the waffle iron with canola oil or vegetable spray and bake until lightly browned.

MAIL-ORDER SOURCES

WHOLE GRAINS AND FLOURS

Arrowhead Mills
110 South Lawton
Hereford, TX 79045
(806) 364-0730

Bob's Red Mill
5209 S.E. International Way
Milwaukie, OR 97222
(503) 654-3215
www.bobsredmill.com

Hodgson Mills
1203 Niccum Avenue
Effingham, IL 62401
(800) 525-0177
www.hodgsonmill.com

Homestead Mills
P.O. Box 1115
Cook, MN 55723
(800) 652-5233;
(218) 666-5233
www.homesteadmills.com

King Arthur Flour
P.O. Box 876
Norwich, VT 05055
(800) 827-6836
www.kingarthurflour.com

SCANDINAVIAN INGREDIENTS AND TOOLS

Sweet Celebrations Inc.
P.O. Box 39426
Edina, MN 55439-0426
(800) 328-6722
www.sweetc.com

INDEX